THE USE AND ABUSE OF POWER

THE USE AND ABUSE OF POWER

Multiple Perspectives on the Causes of Corruption

edited by

Annette Y. Lee-Chai
John A. Bargh

New York University

USA	Publishing Office:	PSYCHOLOGY PRESS
		A member of the Taylor & Francis Group
		325 Chestnut Street
		Philadelphia, PA 19106
		Tel: (215) 625-8900
		Fax: (215) 625-2940
	Distribution Center:	PSYCHOLOGY PRESS
		A member of the Taylor & Francis Group
		7625 Empire Drive
		Florence, KY 41042
		Tel: 1 (800) 634-7064
		Fax: 1 (800) 248-4724
UK		PSYCHOLOGY PRESS
		A member of the Taylor & Francis Group
		27 Church Road
		Hove
		E. Sussex, BN3 2FA
		Tel.: +44 (0) 1273 207411
		Fax: +44 (0) 1273 205612

THE USE AND ABUSE OF POWER: Multiple Perspectives on the Causes of Corruption

1 2 3 4 5 6 7 8 9 0

Printed by Sheridan Books, Ann Arbor, MI, 2001.
Cover design by Claire O'Neill.

A CIP catalog record for this book is available from the British Library.
∞ The paper in this publication meets the requirements of the ANSI Standard Z39.48-1984 (Permanence of Paper).

Library of Congress Cataloging-in-Publication Data
The use and abuse of power : multiple perspectives on the causes of corruption / edited by Annette Y. Lee-Chai and John A. Bargh.
    p. cm.
    Includes bibliographical references and index.
    ISBN 1-84169-022-8 (case : alk. paper — ISBN 1-84169-023-6 (pbk. : alk. paper)
    1. Control (Psychology).   2. Influence (Psychology).   I. Lee-Chai, Annette Y.
II. Bargh, John A.

BF611.U84 2001
303.3—dc21   00-062631

ISBN 1-84169-022-8 (case)
ISBN 1-84169-023-6 (paper)

for David Kipnis

Contents

About the Editors

Annette Y. Lee-Chai graduated cum laude from Cornell University in 1990. After receiving a B.A. in psychology, she worked at a large advertising agency for several years before pursuing a doctorate at New York University. At NYU, she worked closely with Dr. Bargh, researching the automatic activation of cognitions and behaviors, with particular focus on automatic goals within relationship orientations and situations of power. She received her Ph.D. from NYU in 2000 and is currently employed at a major Internet consulting firm.

John A. Bargh is Professor of Psychology and Director of the Graduate Program in Social-Personality at New York University. He graduated summa cum laude from the University of Illinois in 1977 and received his Ph.D. from the University of Michigan in 1981. His dissertation that year on automatic components of social perception won the "best of year" award from the Society for Experimental Social Psychology, and his continuation of that line of research resulted in an "Early Career" award for contributions to psychology from the American Psychological Association in 1989. His research interests focus on the automatic or nonconscious psychological processes—perceptual, evaluative, motivational, and behavioral—that are directly put into motion by environmental events without a need for an intervening conscious choice or act of will.

x

Contributors

Jeannette Alvarez
New York University
New York, NY, USA

Bruce Barry
Vanderbilt University
Nashville, TN, USA

Bonka S. Boneva
University of Pittsburgh
Pittsburgh, PA, USA

Daphne Blunt Bugental
University of California, Santa Barbara
Santa Barbara, CA, USA

Tanya L. Chartrand
Ohio State University
Columbus, OH, USA

Emmeline S. Chen
New York University
New York, NY, USA

Serena Chen
University of Michigan
Ann Arbor, MI, USA

Susan T. Fiske
Princeton University
Princeton, NJ, USA

Irene H. Frieze
University of Pittsburgh
Pittsburgh, PA, USA

Wendi L. Gardner
Northwestern University
Evanston, IL, USA

Michael A. Hogg
University of Queensland
Brisbane, Australia

Nihal Jayawickrama
Transparency International
Berlin, Germany

David Kipnis
Temple University
Philadelphia, PA, USA

Marc T. Kiviniemi
University of Minnesota
Minneapolis, MN,USA

Meni Koslowsky
Bar-Ilan University
Ramat Gan, Israel

Joseph Schwarzwald
Bar-Ilan Univresity
Ramat Gan, Israel

Eta K. Lin
University of California, Santa Barbara
Santa Barbara, CA, USA

Elizabeth A. Seeley
Northwestern University
Evanston, IL, USA

Felicia Pratto
University of Connecticut
Storrs, CT, USA

Mark Snyder
University of Minnesota
Minneapolis, MN, USA

Bertram H. Raven
University of California, Los Angeles
Los Angeles, CA, USA

Tom R. Tyler
New York University
New York, NY, USA

Scott A. Reid
University of Queensland
Brisbane, Australia

Angela Walker
University of Connecticut
Storrs, CT, USA

Preface

*I*t may have started as far back as the days of Adam and Eve and that infamous tree of knowledge. A command was given by a powerful figure, a direct order was violated, and insubordinates were duly punished. So began the human struggle with power. We hunger for it, fear it, revel in it, and abuse it. We learn the subtle dance done by two people occupying different levels of it. Power pervades our thoughts, our ambitions, our social interactions, and our society. Indeed, power pervades our lives.

With the enormity of its impact, however, it is curious how little we know about it. Though there have been philosophical discussions, there haven't been many scientific studies directly devoted to power. How does it color our thoughts and perceptions? How does it sway our emotions and actions? How does it change the dynamics of interactions between individuals and between groups? How do people use it, and what can we do to curb the abuse of it? These are the questions that at long last deserve attention.

In the past several years, our aim has been to bring power to the forefront, to make it a household name, at least in the social science circles. In 1998, we organized a symposium on power and corruption at the annual conference of the Society for the Psychological Study of Social Issues at Ann Arbor, Michigan. A number of excellent talks were given by prominent speakers, most of who have also contributed to this book. The interest we received from the symposium, both in attendance and positive feedback, inspired us to compile in one volume the works of individuals who are striving to understand the mechanisms of power and its abuse.

The people we invited to contribute to this volume are well respected in their areas of interest and bring with them a gentle mixture of both time-honored and cutting edge thinking. With topics ranging from stereotyping to child abuse to leadership to cultural interdependence, their chapters work to unmask the mystery of this enigmatic force from different angles, piece by piece. Hopefully, as the pieces of the puzzle gradually come together, we will be better able to use the power we have and slow the endless waves of corruption.

In our attempt to bring organization to the diverse collection of chapters, we loosely grouped them into four basic approaches. Of course, many of the chapters could have easily been categorized into more than one approach, and the choice was sometimes difficult to make. The first group of chapters investigates the intrapersonal effects of power—how it affects cognition and motivation. The second group looks at the effects of power within interactions between individuals, while the third group focuses on power within groups and organizations. The last group of chapters broadens the approach even more by looking at the use of power within societies. No matter what the approach, however, each chapter discusses how the use of power may lead to corruption and possible ways to keep the abuse in check.

In closing, we sincerely thank all the contributors to this volume. Their expertise, enthusiasm, and dedication to this project were unsurpassed, and we hope we never abused our own power as editors in bringing this book to fruition. Special thanks must go to David Kipnis, a legendary figure in power research, who sadly passed away shortly after completing his chapter. We are forever indebted to Carolyn Kipnis and Carole Wells for putting the finishing touches on his work. Finally, we would like to thank Psychology Press for believing in this project, and especially our editor, Alison Mudditt, for her confidence, cheery support, and patience.

ANNETTE Y. LEE-CHAI
JOHN A. BARGH

PART I

POWER WITHIN THE MIND

1

Using Power
Newton's Second Law

DAVID KIPNIS

The Hobbesian (1968) assumption that we are programmed by our desires, and by our dependence on other people to satisfy these desires,
provides an important perspective for understanding the use of power.
At times, our desires override our obligations to help others, to be decent, to be
charitable, and to be what society considers civil. We want things from others
from the moment of birth until death. We want affection, material goods, services, information, to be loved, to dominate, the chance to do better than others, to be treated fairly, and to be left alone, to name but a few of the many
desires that impel us to influence others. There is no end to our dependence on
others, because there is no end to the things we want. The dismal observation
of Hobbes that people's motivations consist simply of endless streams of appe-
tites appears as true today as when he wrote *Leviathan* (1968) in the 17th century.

If we accept these assumptions, then it follows that everyone must exercise
influence and power on a day-to-day basis. Thus, the critical question is not
whether people exercise power, but how they exercise power. That is, what are
the tactics people use to influence others and what happens next? This chapter
is about what happens next; that is, the consequences of exercising influence.

Some of these consequences have been examined by social psychologists,
in particular, how people respond to being influenced. Studies of attitude change,
leadership, conformity, reducing prejudice, affectionate relations, and more,
are basically concerned with understanding how target persons respond to influence acts designed to change their behavior. Far less attention is given, however, to the person who is trying to change the target person's behavior, called
here the powerholder.

3

BEHAVIOR TECHNOLOGIES

Technology can be defined as the use of systematic procedures to produce intended effects. Thus technology is not synonymous with engineering hardware, but includes techniques found in the social sciences and in everyday culture (Ellul, 1964). The goal of all technologies is to produce outcomes with less effort, and that are more uniform and predictable, than can be achieved by unassisted human effort. The use of technology, then, reduces the amount of uncertainty in attempts to solve practical problems. Reducing uncertainty means increasing the probability that events will occur as wanted.

Just as there are technologies to transform physical materials, there are technologies to transform behaviors (Kipnis, 1987, 1990). The goal of behavior technologies is to produce behaviors that are predictable and controllable from the point of view of an influencing agent (e.g., advertiser, psychotherapist, leader). One way of increasing control is to devise technologies that increase a target person's understanding of their activities (e.g, Langer, 1983; Schofield, Evans-Rhodes, & Huber, 1990). More typically, however, control is increased by devising technologies that reduce the amount of thinking and free choice available to the target of influence.

Thinking and free choice are limited by such techniques as reducing the amount of information available to the target person (one-sided arguments, media control; e.g., Herman & Chomsky, 1988), telling people what to think and how to behave (behavior therapy techniques), distorting people's self-appraisals (dissonance, foot-in-the-door, door-in-the-face techniques), substituting pleasure or pain for thinking (principles of reinforcement, ingratiation, coercion), controlling information (e.g., putting a spin on the news), using group processes such as democratic leadership to induce compliance, and developing jury selection techniques that identify biased jurors.

In short, many of the behavior technologies developed in social psychology use flimflam, deception, or coercion—what Petty and Cacioppo (1981) aptly labeled as peripheral techniques. From the perspective of the influencing agent, the use of logic and reason to persuade—that is, central techniques of influence—are inefficient. This is because the use of reason increases the uncertainty of desired outcomes, takes too much time, and gives too much control to the person being influenced.

METAMORPHIC EFFECTS OF POWER

In earlier writings Kipnis (1976, 1984), presented evidence that the act of influence can change not only the behavior of persons who are the targets of influence, but also the values and attitudes of persons doing the influencing. These changes in agents are called the metamorphic effects of power.

Metamorphic effects involve two sets of independent variables: 1) the strength of the influence tactics that are used to persuade the target person to comply; and 2) the subsequent attributions of the influencing agent concerning who controls the target person's behavior—the target person or external forces including the influencing agent.

When influencing agents successfully use strong and controlling tactics of influence ("I demand," "I tell them what I want done"), they believe, not surprisingly, that the person being influenced no longer controls his or her own behavior, but is controlled by the influencing agent's tactics. Stated in terms of attribution theory (Weiner, 1985), the successful use of strong tactics produces the belief that the person being influenced is externally controlled.

Further, when we believe that people are not in charge of their own behavior, we evaluate them unfavorably. An explanation for these less favorable evaluations is that the behavior of the person being influenced, no matter how excellent, is seen as guided by outside forces rather than by the person's abilities and motivations. Hence, he or she is not given full credit for anything that is accomplished.

Social relations also suffer under these circumstances. This is because we seldom treat as equals or actively seek the company of persons who are not in control of their own behavior. Finally, moral values that affirm the intrinsic worth of each person are seen as not applicable to the less powerful. These opinions about the target person set the stage for subsequent exploitation and abuse by the powerholder.

It should be noted that when rational tactics ("I explain my reasons," "I suggest") or weak tactics ("I beg," "I act more loving") are used successfully to persuade, the user attributes compliance to the decisions of the target person. Thus the exercise of influence, per se, is not problematic for social relations. Rather problems arise when strong and controlling tactics are used to get one's way.

ROUTINIZATION AND THE METAMORPHIC MODEL

Within the context of this view, it can be suggested that behavior technology provides influencing agents with strong tactics of influence. To the extent that these procedures are successful, it is reasonable to believe that the technology will be seen as the cause of the target person's behavior. Hence the target person will be given little credit for what he or she does.

Support for this view was initially found in several field studies that examined how the routinization of work affected manager's evaluations of their employees (Kipnis, 1984). Routinization is defined as the transfer of the skill and control components of work to machines and machine systems. The benefits to management of routinization are many, including increased control of the work flow, decreased reliance on employee skills, and consequently reduced labor costs. There is considerable evidence that work routinization reduces employee's feeling of competence and job satisfaction (Blauner, 1964; Gutek & Winter, 1990; Shaiken, 1985).

The findings of these field studies (Kipnis, 1984) were consistent with the metamorphic model. In these field studies, it was found that as a unit's work increased in routinization, managers increasingly attributed unsatisfactory work to the employee's lack of motivation, rather than to the employee's lack of ability. Further, managers' evaluations of their employees were directly related to technological changes in the work of their units. In all samples, employees who worked in routinized units were devalued by their managers. These employees were described as avoiding responsibility, requiring close supervision, and taking little pride in their work.

While these findings are consistent with the metamorphic model, it is clear that they can also be viewed as simply reflecting actual differences in attitudes and motivations of employees hired to do skilled and unskilled labor. The next section of this chapter describes more recent experimental studies of the ways in which behavior technologies change the attitudes of their users.

ATTITUDE CHANGING TECHNOLOGIES

For over six decades, social psychology has studied the interrelated questions of how attitudes are formed and maintained and how they mediate social behavior. In addition, considerable attention has been devoted to the development of systematic techniques for changing people's attitudes. Such techniques as door-in-the-face, democratic leadership, one- or two-sided arguments, communicator credibility, dissonance arousal, and more, have been shown to change attitudes in the direction chosen by an influence source.

Research about attitude changing technologies has focused, almost exclusively, on the question of validity, that is, whether these technologies actually change attitudes. Little consideration has been given to the possibility that these attitude change techniques might also change their users' attitudes and values. The metamorphic model suggests, however, that those who use peripheral attitude change techniques may believe that target persons have no choice but to change, and hence will disparage them.

To examine the issue, two experimental studies were conducted. In the first, Edgar O'Neal, Kelli Craig, and this author (1994) conducted an experimental study in which students were taught how to use one of three attitude change techniques. These were the door-in-the-face, the foot-in-the-door, or a technique based on the use of rational influence.

The door-in-the-face technique requires that influencing agents first ask for a very large favor. After this request is refused, the agent makes a lesser request and asks for what he or she really wants. The foot-in-the-door technique requires influencing agents to first ask for a small favor that is difficult to refuse. After this small favor is granted, the agent then asks for what he or she really wants. The rational influence technique, a central route technique, requires the agent to develop logical reasons why the target person should change and then asks the target person to think over these reasons.

Participants were told that we were developing exercises to demonstrate attitude change theory in introductory psychology courses. The goal of each persuader was to convince a target person to join a group advocating curriculum changes, using one of the influence techniques described in the preceding paragraph. These changes were initially opposed by the target person, but favored by the persuader. In all instances, the use of the assigned persuasion technique was programmed to be successful. That is, the target person responded to the technique by agreeing to do what the persuader wanted.

It had been expected that users of the door-in-the-face or foot-in-the-door techniques would perceive persons they influenced as submissive and lacking in the ability to exercise influence. An unexpected finding in the first study was that participants who used the door-in-the-face or the foot-in-the-door techniques described targets as more, rather than less, dominant when compared with participants who used rational influence. O'Neal, Kipnis, and Craig's (1994) explanation for this unexpected finding was based on research by Stahelski (1992). Stahelski reported that users of the door-in-the-face and foot-in-the-door techniques were consistently described by outside observers as less powerful than their targets of influence.

Taken together, the findings of O'Neal, Kipnis, and Craig, and of Stahelski indicate that the door-in-the-face and the foot-in-the-door techniques are seen as techniques used by people with little power to persuade the more powerful. Presumably, when the balance of power favors the target person, people assume that personal powers of persuasion, such as the use of reason, or even threats, are not likely to gain compliance. Rather more deceptive and indirect tactics are preferred.

To further explore this possibility, a second experimental study was conducted by Bruce Rind and David Kipnis (1999). This study added another persuasion technique, labeled authority technique, in which users simply demanded that participants comply. The second study retained the use of rational influence and the door-in-the-face technique, but dropped the foot-in-the-door technique. This was because the use of the door-in-the-face and the foot-in-the-door techniques yielded practically identical results in the first study.

In the second study, we also tested the idea that the use of rational influence would change the user's self-evaluations for the better; while the use of the door-in-the-face would change these self-evaluations for the worse. To our knowledge, the question of the relation between the use of these technologies and self-appraisals has not been examined.

Results

Attributions of Control.   Persons using rational influence described both themselves and the target as the origins of the target's compliance. That is, in both studies, users of rational influence attributed the target's compliance to the logic of the reasons that they offered and to the target thinking over these reasons ($p < .01$). Users of the authority technique described themselves as the origin of the target's compliance. They attributed target compliance to "my demands"

($p < .01$). Users of the door-in-the-face technique, however, did not describe themselves, nor the target, as the origin of the target's compliance. In both studies, they attributed target compliance to the automatic workings of the persuasion technique.

Evaluations of the Target. Our second prediction was that subjects using peripheral route techniques would evaluate the target person as less intelligent than subjects using central route techniques. Ratings of the following bipolar items were combined into an index of target intelligence: intelligent/not intelligent; thoughtful/not thoughtful; competent/incompetent. In both studies, we found that persons using rational influence evaluated target persons as more intelligent than subjects who employed either the foot-in-the-door technique or the authority technique ($p < .01$).

We also found in the second study that users of the authority techniques, who simply demanded compliance, described their targets as least powerful ($p < .02$). Power was measured by combining two bipolar scales: dominant/submissive and leader/follower.

User's Self-Evaluations. The persuasion techniques also influenced users' opinions of themselves. Those who used rational influence described themselves as more intelligent than users of either door-in-the-face or the authority technique ($p < .05$). Users of rational influence also described themselves as more friendly than users of the authority technique ($p < .05$). Not surprisingly, users of the authority technique described themselves as more powerful than users of the door-in-the-face technique ($p < .05$).

Of interest was the finding that users of the door-in-the-face technique had nothing positive to say about themselves. That is, they ranked their performance lowest in cognitive competence and in power, and second lowest in friendliness. An examination of users' explanations of the success of their influence technique offers one reason for these low self-evaluations. Users of the door-in-the-face technique made only an external explanation for target compliance—the technique they used. Both users of rational arguments and of authoritarian techniques, to the contrary, made internal attributions—"my reasons" or "my demands."

Finally, in both studies, users of rational influence said that they enjoyed using this persuasion technique more than users of the other techniques ($p < .05$). This finding is discussed in more detail later.

Comment. In the present studies, agents who used peripheral attitude change techniques devalued themselves and the people they successfully influenced. They described themselves as not very intelligent and not friendly. They also did not enjoy using their assigned technique. They believed that those they influenced were not responsible for the decision they made, nor were the targests competent enough to think through issues and decide for themselves.

Critical readers may say these results are obvious—probably an artifact of the instructions that were used. That is, both user and target persons in the rational influence condition were asked to think over the issues, and those in the peripheral route conditions were not. What else could be expected to happen?

One answer is that in the vast literature that describes attitude change techniques, with few exceptions (e.g., Zimbardo, 1969), there have been very few attempts to examine what influencing agents think about target persons, or about themselves. Experimental conditions in this study parallel the real life use of peripheral attitude change techniques. When agents cause people to change their attitudes without thinking about the issues involved, what else can agents believe but the obvious? That is, that those they influence are not too bright.

PSYCHOTHERAPY AND BEHAVIOR TECHNOLOGY

Recent developments have provided psychotherapists with a wide range of technologies for correcting patients' thoughts, feelings, and behavior. Such techniques as flooding, desensitization, hypnosis, homework, and cognitive restructuring are but a few of the many behavioral technologies that have been developed to change client behavior and feelings. It is fair to say that these techniques do not rely on patient insights about the cognitive-affective causes of their neurotic behavior. Rather, behavior is assumed to change as a consequence of the patient following the prescriptions of the therapist (London, 1976; Sweet, 1984).

In contrast, the task of humanistic and psychodynamic therapists is to provide patients with an understanding of the sources of stress and distress in their lives (Rogers, Gendlin, Keisler, & Truax, 1967). Insight is achieved through such techniques as reflective listening, encouraging the patient to connect what is happening within the therapy session to his or her life's stress, occasionally providing explanations about the patient's behavior that differ from the patients own explanation, and sometimes even frustrating the patient, so that he or she learns about how they cope with their frustrations and hostility. It is generally agreed that dynamic therapy is a long and uncertain process, whose success depends upon the ability of the patient to understand and eventually change his or her own behavior (London, 1976).

Stages in Technology

The evolutionary stages of technology. That is, most technologies follow a uniform path of development from human control to machine or system control. The industrial sociologist, William Faunce (1981), described this evolution as proceeding from craft production, in which management's dependence on the skills of labor is almost complete, to mechanized production in which dependence on labor is reduced by transferring the skilled components of work to machines and machine systems, and then to automated production in which machines do all of the work, and labor becomes responsible for monitoring and controlling the machines' performance. Each stage increases the efficiency of productive activity, reduces the costs of salaries, and at the same time changes the relation between workers and machines.

There are several ways in which psychodynamic therapy resembles the first stage in the development of technology, aside from the obvious fact that it was the first workable form of therapy. For one, psychodynamic techniques are labor intensive, that is, they depend on both the skills of the therapist and the capacity of the patient for insight. It is no accident that psychoanalysts write books about the art of therapy and the ability to listen with a third ear. Therapeutic outcomes appear to depend upon only partially understood therapists' skills. As a consequence, there is a fair amount of uncertainty in predicting the outcomes of psychoanalytic therapy. Another resemblance to the early stages of industrial technological development is in terms of costs. Psychoanalytic forms of therapy require two or three years to effect patient change. As a result, the costs of treatment are high in terms of money and in terms of therapist and patient time.

In contrast, cognitive behavior therapies represent the beginnings of the second stage in the development of a technology or psychotherapy. We hear less about the art of therapy and more about techniques when cognitive behavior therapies are discussed. There is a presumption that if the therapist uses the methods of this approach in therapy, there is a high probability that patient stress will be reduced. Thus, the art of psychodynamic therapy has been transferred to the techniques of cognitive behavior therapy. A benefit of this process of de-skilling the therapist's work is that the techniques themselves can be taught in a relatively short period of time. Needless to say, like the Luddites of the early 19th century, traditional psychoanalysts have bitterly attacked what they perceive as simplified approaches to therapy.

Some Predictions

In terms of social influence, the techniques used by cognitive behavior therapists to relieve client distress are more controlling and directive than the techniques used by psychodynamic therapists. Using the metamorphic model as a guide, it follows that cognitive behavior therapists should be less likely than psychodynamic therapists to attribute gains in therapy to their client's own efforts and motivations. The metamorphic model also assumes that people who are perceived as not responsible for their own behavior will be evaluated unfavorably. So we can predict that patients who are described as not responsible for their own therapeutic gains will be evaluated less favorably by their therapists, than patients who are described as responsible for their own therapeutic gains.

To test these ideas, Finy Hansen, April Fallon, and David Kipnis (1989) sent a questionnaire to 600 practicing clinical psychologists. The questionnaire asked each therapist to describe a recent episode in which an adult patient in individual psychotherapy, who was not institutionalized, psychotic, organically impaired, or retarded, showed progress in therapy. This represents an instance in which the use of therapeutic techniques achieved their intended effects of patient progress.

One hundred and thirteen therapists replied. These respondents all had doctoral degrees and had been in practice for an average of 14 years. After describing the nature of their client's progress, the therapist described the interventions they used that were most helpful in bringing about progress in therapy. The frequency with which therapists used either cognitive behavioral techniques (e.g., desensitization, homework) or psychodynamic techniques (e.g., interpretation and clarification) were coded into separate indices.

We next asked the therapists to rate the importance of several explanations for their client's progress. The following two explanations were included to measure the extent to which therapists perceived their client as responsible for progress: 1) The client's inner strength and drive toward health; 2) The client's capacity for insight. These two items were combined to form an Index of Client Responsibility (split-half reliability = .61), with high scores meaning that patients were seen as responsible for their gains in therapy.

We also asked therapists to rate their impression of their clients, following progress, on each of nine patient attributes, using a 7-point scale ranging from poor (1) to outstanding (7). The patient attributes were Flexibility, Intelligence, Capacity for insight, Ability to Experience Empathy, Competence, Interpersonal Skills, Ability to Function Autonomously, Ability to Maintain Therapeutic Gains, and Overall Functioning. These nine items were summed to provide a Patient Evaluation Scale (alpha = .81).

Techniques of Therapy and Attribution of Control

The first hypothesis predicted that therapists who use cognitive behavior techniques would be less likely than therapists who use dynamic techniques to attribute gains in therapy to their client's own efforts. This prediction was supported. The use of cognitive behavioral techniques was negatively related ($r = -.36, p < .01$), and the use of dynamic techniques was positively related ($r = .30, p < .01$) to the Index of Patient Responsibility.

Since the severity of client symptoms could affect therapists' attributions, client's were classified as presenting mild or severe symptoms. This classification was based upon two bits of information: the *Diagnositc and Statistical Manual of Mental Disorders*, third edition, revised (DSM-III-R; American Psychiatric Association [APA], 1987) and a profile of each client as provided by the therapist and/or whether the client had been previously hospitalized for psychiatric reasons. A total of 73 clients were classified as presenting mild symptoms. The analysis of these 73 cases found that the predicted relations were slightly stronger when patients with severe symptoms were excluded from the analysis (i.e., correlations with the Index of Patient Responsibility rose from $-.36$ to $-.41$ for cognitive behavior techniques, and from .30 to .34 for dynamic techniques).

Attributions and Evaluation

As mentioned previously, autonomy and evaluations are closely related. Thus, we can expect that clients who were described as responsible for their own therapeutic gains should be evaluated favorably by their therapists. In support of this expectation, the Index of Patient Responsibility correlated .46 ($p < .01$) with the Patient Evaluation Scale. The more patients were described as responsible for the gains that were made in their therapy, the more favorable were therapists' evaluations of them.

These results, within a therapeutic relation, confirm what has been reported in other settings. That is, as the strength of influence tactics increases, the perception that people are autonomous lessens, and evaluations of them become less favorable.

Failed Therapy

The findings of the above study dealt only with cases in which therapists reported improvements in patients. An interesting question to consider is what predictions can be made about therapists' evaluations of patients whom they see as therapy failures. Would cognitive behavior therapists evaluate their failed patients more unfavorably than dynamic therapists? Based on research concerning judgment of inadequate performance in industry (Kipnis, 1976; Mitchell, Larson, & Green, 1977), the answer is that it depends on the therapist's explanation for the failed therapy.

More particularly, if the therapist attributes failure to factors under the patient's control (e.g., lack of motivation, resistance), we suggest that the patient would be judged more harshly than if the therapist attributes failure to factors that were not under the patient's control (e.g., inadequate techniques). Since dynamic therapy assumes that the patient is responsible for outcomes, our first prediction is that dynamic therapists would be more likely than cognitive behavior therapists to say that patients were responsible for failing to make progress in therapy. A second prediction is that patients who were seen as responsible for the failed therapy would be judged more harshly than patients who were not seen as responsible.

To test these ideas, Kendall, Kipnis, and Otto-Salaj (1992) asked 1,000 practicing psychotherapists to describe an incident where a patient in private practice failed to progress in therapy. Three hundred and fifteen therapists described such incidents. Sixty-four percent of these patients were classified as presenting severe problems, using the same criteria described in the preceding study. It may be recalled that the earlier study of progress in therapy classified 35% of the patients as presenting severe problems. Apparently a major correlate of client progress, or failure to progress, is the severity of their mental illness.

We asked therapists to explain the lack of progress by rating the importance of two internal causes of failure: 1) client lacks ability to benefit from therapy, and 2) client lacks motivation for therapy. We also asked therapists to evaluate their patients' functioning using the items that comprised the Patient Evaluation Scale, described earlier.

As predicted, we found that dynamic therapists were more likely to attribute lack of progress to the clients inability to benefit from therapy than were cognitive behavior therapists ($p < .01$). Further, therapists who blamed their patients for lack of progress described them unfavorably. That is, the more therapists attributed their patients lack of progress to the patient's inability to benefit from therapy, or to the patient's lack of motivation for therapy, the less favorably patients were evaluated on the Patient Evaluation Scale ($p < .01$).

We also found that the severity of the patient's presenting problems (using an index based on the patient's *DSM-III-R* (APA, 1987) and prior psychiatric hospitalization) failed to correlate with therapists' explanations of lack of patient progress or therapists' evaluation of their patients. This index also failed to correlate with either the therapist's attributions or evaluations in the preceding study of patient progress. Thus, in both studies, therapists ignored relatively objective information about their patients' mental illness, when evaluating them.

In general, the results of both studies are consistent with the metamorphic model. Variations in the technology of therapy changed therapists' evaluations of their clients. The more controlling the therapy used, the less clients were judged as responsible for changes in their behavior. These judgments, in turn, guided therapists' subsequent evaluations of their clients.

Therapists' Satisfactions

Earlier in this chapter, the effects of attitude change technologies on users' satisfactions was reported. It may be recalled that those who used rational influence techniques enjoyed their experiences more than users of either the routinized door-in-the-face or the foot-in-the-door techniques. This result is consistent with the general finding that feelings of competence and satisfaction are associated with skilled activities (Blauner, 1964; Gutek and Winter, 1990; Shaiken, 1985). Presented below is evidence that variations in the skill requirements of psychotherapy also affect therapists' job satisfactions. The hypothesis is that the more the therapists' treatment techniques have been routinized, the less satisfied they will be with their work.

Dixon Bramblett and this author (Bramblett & Kipnis, 1996) examined this issue among a sample of psychotherapists. As suggested earlier, dynamic therapies resemble the craft stage and cognitive behavior therapies the beginnings of a mechanized or routinized stage of technology.

The procedure involved mailing every tenth member of the APA's Division 42, Psychologists in Independent Practice ($n = 516$) a Therapist Satisfaction Survey. A total of 249 therapists responded. This yielded a return rate of 57% after discounting 76 letters for such reasons as incorrect address or not a practicing therapist. The respondents closely matched the age and gender of the full membership of Division 42.

Since many cognitive behavior therapists do not belong to APA, but to the American Association of Behavior Therapists (AABT), a random sample of AABT members were also sent our survey. Sixty-seven cognitive behavior therapists from this association responded, representing a response rate of 66%.

The Therapist Satisfaction Survey consisted of items taken from several job satisfaction and job involvement scales (e.g., Hackman & Oldham, 1980). The items used measured therapists' overall job satisfaction, job involvement, and opportunity to express competence.[1] Items were answered on 7-point Likert scales. Table 1.1 presents the average satisfaction scores of cognitive behavior and psychodynamic therapists.

It can be seen that the findings are consistent with the industrial experiences of clerical and blue collar employees. That is, dynamic therapists expressed more satisfaction with their work on the measures of job satisfaction ($p < .01$), work involvement ($p < .01$), and the opportunity to express competence ($p < .01$) than cognitive behavior therapists. Once again, then, we find that the use of behavior technology changes users as well as targets of influence. In this instance, techniques that reduce dependence on the skills of the therapist, while having positive effects for clients, have negative effects on therapists' esprit.

CONCLUDING COMMENTS - THE ABUSE OF POWER

An implicit assumption in social psychological research is that behavior technologies change the behavior of targets of influence, but have no consequence for persons who control and use the technology. The findings presented in this chapter indicate that this assumption is incorrect. Both the field and laboratory research found that the use of behavior technologies changed influencing agents as well as their targets.

Technologies based on the use of reason encouraged the belief that the target person shared responsibility with the user for any outcomes that were achieved. The use of peripheral technologies, such as door-in-the-face, or cognitive behavior therapy, to the contrary, encouraged the belief that the target person was not responsible for outcomes that were achieved. Rather, these outcomes were believed to be controlled by the technology. One consequence is that users devalued the abilities of target persons.

---

1. Sample items: *Overall Job Satisfaction* (alpha = .63): If you had it to do over again, how likely would you be to choose psychotherapy? Overall, how satisfied are you with your therapy work? *Job Involvement* (alpha = .52): To what degree do you "eat, sleep, and breathe" your work? How often do you feel at the end of the day that you've accomplished something worthwhile as a result of doing therapy? *Opportunity to Express Competence* (alpha = .50): How creative do you feel you can be in therapy? To what degree is the performance of psychotherapy a good test of your skills and abilities?

TABLE 1.1. Mean Responses to Survey Indices:
Contrast Analyses Between Dynamic and
Cognitive Behavior Therapists

Index	Dynamic	Cognit. Behav.		F-ratio
		APA	AABT	
Satisfaction	5.73	5.33	5.28	7.95°
Involvement	4.83	4.50	4.40	7.52°
Competence	5.53	5.13	5.08	14.43°

°$p < .01$

A second consequence was that users of peripheral technologies devalued themselves. Users in the experimental studies described themselves as less friendly and less intelligent. In both the experimental and field study, they expressed less intrinsic enjoyment in their activities. Presumably, similar findings would be found for other behavior technologies that are designed to cause behavior in others.

The implication of these findings need to be worked out with some care. What is called to mind is Newton's second law, which states that for every action, there is an equal and opposite reaction. We can not change others without also changing ourselves. There are no free lunches when it comes to the use of power.

The findings also suggest that ethical issues may be involved in the use of peripheral behavior technologies. Ethical issues may be involved because these techniques cause users to develop contempt for themselves and for those they are influencing. Perhaps, like the warnings on prescription medicines, social psychological textbooks should be required to warn readers that constant attempts to use peripheral techniques can harm the user.

In books, the press, and in our daily lives, we continually encounter accounts of unethical behavior, mismanagement, exploitation, and cruelty. Terrence Mitchell and his colleagues recently wrote that the abuse of power by organizations and governments is of central concern around the world (Mitchell, Hopper, Daniels, Falvy, & Ferris, 1998). A question of particular interest to the present writer is why decent people are so frequently involved in foul acts?

One answer arises from the tactics we use to get our way. The metamorphic model states that the use of controlling forms of power leads to the devaluation of others. However, this model does not tell us when negative appraisals of others will lead to corrupt behavior, or when these opinions will lead to violations of others' rights. For that, we need to be able to classify the contextual events that encourage or restrain the abuse of power (Kipnis, 1997).

Clearly, an analysis of these events is beyond the scope of this chapter. No simple taxonomy can describe the many circumstances that encourage the abuse of power. Such a taxonomy would need to test the importance of the powerholder's moral values, personality (Lee-Chai & Bargh, 1999; Winters,

1973), greed, and self-interest, as well as many organizational and environmental factors that encourage abuse, for example, access to resources and absence of surveillance (Brief et al., 1996; Mitchell et al., 1998; Zimbardo, 1970). Above all, it would be necessary to describe how the control of unchallenged power erodes traditional moral restraints and replaces them with a new morality, designed to protect and extend the powerholder's resources.

REFERENCES

American Psychiatric Association. (1987). *Diagnostic and statistical manual of mental disorders* (3rd. ed., rev.). Washington, DC: Author.

Blauner, R. (1964). *Alienation and freedom.* Chicago: University of Chicago Press.

Bramblett, D., & Kipnis, D. (1996). *The routinization of professional work.* Unpublished manuscript.

Brief, A. P., Dukerich, J. M., Brown, P. R., & Brett, J. F. (1996). What's wrong with the Treadway commission report? Experimental analyses of the effects of personal values and codes of conduct on fraudulent reporting. *Journal of Business Ethics, 15,* 183–198.

Ellul, J. (1964). *The technological society.* New York: Knopf.

Faunce, W. (1981). *Problems of an industrial society.* New York: McGraw Hill.

Gutek, B., & Winter, S. J. (1990). Computer use and job satisfaction. In S. Oskamp & S. Spacapan (Eds.), *People's reactions to technology* (pp. 121–144). Newbury Park, CA: Sage.

Hackman, J. R., & Oldham, G. R. (1980). *Work redesign.* Reading, MA: Addison-Wesley.

Herman, E., & Chomsky, N. (1988). *Manufacturing consent.* New York: Pantheon.

Hobbes, T. (1968). *Leviathan.* England: Penguin Books.

Kendell, P., Kipnis, D. & Otto-Salaj, L. (1992). When clients don't progress: Influences on and explanations for lack of progress. *Cognitive Therapy and Research, 16,* 269–281.

Kipnis, D. (1976). *The powerholders.* Chicago: University of Chicago Press.

Kipnis, D. (1984). Technology, power, and control. In S. B. Bacharach & E. Lawler (Eds.), *Sociology of organizations.* Greenwich, CT: JAI Press.

Kipnis, D. (1987). Psychology and technology. *American Psychologist, 42,* 30–36.

Kipnis, D. (1990). *Technology and power.* New York: Springer-Verlag.

Kipnis, D. (1997). Ghosts, taxonomies, and social psychology. *American Psychologist, 52,* 205–211.

Kipnis, D., Hansen, F., & Fallon, A. (1989). Therapy and control: The metamorphic effects of power. Unpublished manuscript.

Langer, E. (1983). *The Psychology of Control.* Beverly Hills, CA: Sage.

Lee-Chai, A., & Bargh, J. A. (1999). *Letting power get to your head: Long term effects of social power on interpersonal orientation.* Manuscript submitted for publication.

London, P. (1976). *Behavior control.* New York: Harper & Row.

Mitchell, T., Hopper, H., Daniels, D., Falvy, J. G., & Ferris, G. R. (1998). Power, accountability, and inappropriate actions. *Applied Psychology: An International Review, 47,* 497–517.

Mitchell, T., Larson, J., & Green, D. (1977). Leader behavior, situational moderators, and group performance. *Organizational Behavior and Human Performance, 18,* 254–268.

O'Neal, E. C., Kipnis, D., & Craig, K. M. (1994). Effects of the persuader of employing a coercive influence technique. *Basic and Applied Social Psychology, 15,* 225–238.

Petty, R. E., & Cacioppo, J. T. (1981). *Attitudes & persuasion.* Dubuque, IA: Brown.

Rind, B., & Kipnis, D. (1999). Changes in self-perceptions as a result of successfully persuading others. *Journal of Social Issues, 55,* 141–156.

Rogers, C. R., Gendlin, E. T., Kiesler, D. J., & Truax, C. R. (1967). *The therapeutic relation and its impact.* Madison, WI: University of Wisconsin Press.

Schofield, J. W., Evan-Rhodes, D., & Huber, B. (1990). Artificial intelligence in the classroom: The impact of a computer-based tutor on teachers and students. *Social Science Computer Review*. Duke University Press.

Shaiken, H. (1985). *Work transformed: Automation and labor in the computer age*. New York: Holt Rhinehart & Winston.

Stahelski, A. (1992) The effects of the agent's choice of influence strategy upon the perception of power. Annual Meetings of the Western Psychological Association, Portland, Oregon.

Sweet, A. A. (1984). The therapeutic relation in behavior therapy. *Clinical Psychology Review, 4*, 253–272.

Weiner, B. (1985). *Judgements of responsibility*. New York: Guilford Press.

Winters, D. G. (1973). *The power motive*. New York: The Free Press.

Zimbardo, P. G. (1970). The human choice: Individuation, reason and order versus deindividuation, impulse and chaos. In W. J. Arnold & D. Levine (Eds.), *Nebraska symposium on motivation* (pp. 237–307). Lincoln, NE: University of Nebraska Press.

2

Influence in Organizations from a Social Expectancy Perspective

BRUCE BARRY

As participants in social systems characterized by political behavior and the use and abuse of power, people in organizations initiate and respond to frequent interpersonal influence attempts involving strategic choices that may convey benevolent, neutral, or malevolent intentions. The aim of this chapter is to advance the study of dyadic workplace influence through an analysis grounded in the social psychology of interpersonal expectations and attributions. A substantial body of empirical research has examined the determinants of the tactical choices organizational actors make when they seek influence, but mostly by looking at structural determinants of tactical behavior, such as organizational position or functional specialty. The literature has been largely silent on the question of how tactics are perceived in relation to social cognitive aspects of the context within which they are deployed. Yet is is likely that social perceptions determine the positive or negative interpersonal consequences of tactical choices, as well as the ultimate success or failure of an overall influence strategy. This chapter is focused on social interaction models that explain behavior in terms of the confirmation and violation of social expectancies (e.g., Burgoon, 1993; Darley & Fazio, 1980; Jones, 1990) as a way to understand dyadic influence processes. An expectancy-focused analysis suggests new ways to conceptualize the repertoire of influence tactics available to influencers and to theorize about tactical choices and effects.

The organization of the chapter is as follows. First, an abbreviated literature review summarizes dyadic influence research across disciplines, clarifies the need for theory, and speaks to the merits of an expectancy perspective. A transactional, dyad-level model of the structure of an organizationally-based influence episode is then proposed. The model treats expectancy confirmation and violation processes as the basis for understanding the linkages between tactical choices and situational contexts. Within the model, a taxonomy of influence tactics defines behavioral options in terms of underlying structural dimensions that reflect an expectancy analysis. The chapter concludes with a discussion of the model's implications for the use and abuse of power in organizations.

THE DYADIC INFLUENCE LITERATURE

A comprehensive synthesis of the dyadic influence literature exceeds the scope of this chapter (for comprehensive reviews see Barry & Watson, 1996; Kellermann & Cole, 1994; Miller et al., 1987; Seibold, Cantrill, & Meyers, 1985, 1994). The discussion below provides a synopsis of conceptual and empirical developments that inform the expectancy perspective under development here.

Influence Defined

Social influence, in broad terms, describes processes by which individuals modify their cognitions, attitudes, and behaviors in response to socially constructed contexts. Dyadic social influence refers more narrowly to the interpersonal case: The processes involved when an individual (an influence agent) actively seeks to elicit attitudinal or behavioral compliance from a single, target other. Previous definitions (e.g., Kelman &Hamilton, 1989; Seibold, Cantrill, & Meyers, 1994) have highlighted 1) the willful, goal-directed nature of influence attempts, 2) the use by influence seekers of both verbal and nonverbal strategies, and 3) a presumption of resistance: Influence attempts call on targets to do something they would not otherwise do independently. In line with these conditions and following Barry and Watson (1996), dyadic social influence can be defined as the use of deliberate verbal and symbolic actions by an individual (the influence agent) directed at another individual (the target) with the expectation that those actions will bring about a desired change in the cognitions or behaviors of the target that would not have otherwise occurred.

Dyadic Influence Research

Conceptual Models. Models of interpersonal influence share a common objective of trying to identify stages or sequences of forces and events that define an influence seeking episode. Some models vary by the choice of focal actor within the agent–target dyad. Kipnis (1974) and Marwell and Schmitt (1967a) discussed the stages of gaining compliance from the perspective of the agent, or powerholder. In contrast, Kelman's model of the structure of social influence situations (Kelman, 1974; Kelman & Hamilton, 1989) works from the perspective of the influence target: Targets comply when they anticipate that adoption of the influence request will facilitate goal achievement. Combined perspectives addressing both agent and target behavior are found in the work of Tedeschi and his colleagues (Tedeschi, Bonoma, & Schlenker, 1972; Tedeschi, Schlenker, & Linkskold, 1972) and in Raven's (1992) power/interaction framework analyzing the role of costs and benefits for both parties. Compared with prior models, Raven's approach incorporates a substantially more developed view of perceptual antecedents and motivational conditions that set the stage for an influence transaction. A few influence process frameworks have focused on the particular context of organizations, including Schein's (1977) resource model, an upward political influence model proposed by Porter, Allen, and Angle (1981), Cobb's (1984) power episode theory, and Barry and Watson's (1996) transactional stage model.

Collectively, influence models embody a variety of individual, dyadic, and contextual determinants of agents' tactical choices and targets' responses. Different models emphasize different stages and actors within the process of gaining compliance. There is greater attention in some models to psychological mechanisms of rationality and cognition than in others. Most at least hint at feedback processes that characterize influence episodes as reciprocal and iterative in nature, with perceptions defined dynamically in the course of an influence attempt. However, although some theorists have considered descriptively the kinds of tactics agents may engage (e.g., Marwell & Schmitt, 1967a; Porter, Allen, & Angle, 1981), no existing model explicitly integrates tactical behavior with a process view of the influence episode.

Empirical Studies.   A large volume of empirical research has been aimed at developing inventories of tactical behaviors, examining the conditions under which such behaviors are deployed, and exploring the effects of tactical choices on pertinent outcomes. An analysis of researchers' various attempts to propose inventories or typologies of tactical behavior reveals an ongoing tension between deductive and inductive methods. Initially, the focus was on deductive approaches whereby scholars worked from prior theoretical and empirical formulations to create tactical inventories (Marwell & Schmitt, 1967b; Mowday, 1978). Seeking to identify a wider variety of influence seeking behaviors, Kipnis, Schmidt, and Wilkinson (1980) employed data driven methods to explore tactics used by people at work to influence their superiors, coworkers, and subordinates. The approach taken by Kipnis and his colleagues, along with modifications proposed by Yukl and his colleague (Yukl & Falbe, 1990), formed the basis, directly or indirectly, for much of the ensuing research on influence tactics in organizations (see Barry & Watson, 1996, for a review).

Many published studies have explored the role of tactical behavior by examining predictors and consequences of tactical choice. Communication theorists have focused on the predictive power of situational perceptions (e.g., Cody et al., 1986; Dillard & Burgoon, 1985) and individual differences (e.g., Boster & Stiff, 1984; O'Hair & Cody, 1987). Organizational researchers have considered such topics as the characteristics of successful influence attempts (Schilit

& Locke, 1982), the association between organizational climate and tactical choices (Cheng, 1983), the role of pay and performance appraisal (Kipnis & Schmidt, 1988), and sex differences in tactical choice (Benson & Hornsby, 1988). The emphasis during the 1990s was on consequences of tactical choice (Falbe & Yukl, 1992; Yukl & Tracey, 1992) and the use of combinations of tactics within single influence attempts (e.g., Barry & Shapiro, 1992; Howard, 1995; Yukl, Falbe, & Youn, 1993).

The Need for Theory

Although voluminous and wide-ranging, empirical research on tactics is infrequently grounded in theory, and few connections have been made between conceptual models of influence and empirical investigations of influence seeking behavior. Thirteen years ago Miller et al. (1987) observed, "Rarely has theory been used to guide the choice of factors that may affect strategy selection and to derive predictions about the strategies selected, nor have findings been interpreted within accepted theoretical perspectives" (p. 108). Since then the volume of dyadic influence research has been sustained, but theoretical grounding has continued to be uncommon. Moreover, questions continue to be raised about the conceptual and empirical value of inventories and taxonomies used to classify influence tactics (Barry & Watson, 1996; Kellermann & Cole, 1994; Seibold, Cantrill, & Meyers, 1994).

Issues of both explanation and operationalization underlie the need for theory driven research on dyadic influence. With respect to explanation, empirical findings regarding contextual and individual difference antecedents have been scattered and inconsistent (for a recent review, see Barry & Watson, 1996), revealing little about the psychological processes that lead individuals to select certain tactics over others in a given situation. Inductive taxonomic research has shed light on the variety of tactics used within influence attempts, but shortchanges midrange theory development that would link contextual and tactical features of an influence episode within a common explanatory framework. Furthermore, existing research underplays the reciprocal and interactional nature of dyadic influence episodes, as some writers have observed (Barry & Watson, 1996; Yukl & Falbe, 1990). Methodological limitations are partly to blame: Many empirical studies of influence have relied on either self-reports of the frequency of tactical choice to influence a referent target (e.g., Kipnis et al., 1980; Yukl & Falbe, 1990) or on hypothetical stimulus-incident methods (e.g., Cody et al., 1986) as a way to focus on individual episodes. Both approaches are limited in their ability to provide rich context cues and elicit nuanced tactical responses.

A larger issue is a restrictive set of assumptions that guides research on dyadic influence. Most research has assumed that participants in an influence episode are rational, self-aware, and competent (Seibold et al., 1985), choosing and responding to tactics that possess consistent, objective meaning. In reality, a message can be intended and received in a number of different ways, depending on how it is said (Staley & Cohen, 1988) and the context within which it is given meaning, or framed (Mitchell & Beach, 1990). Expectancy approaches to social interaction assume that "the actions of another person do not automatically convey meanings, but are given meanings by the perceiver" (Darley & Fazio, 1980, p. 868). As such, an expectancy perspective on social influence stimulates an emphasis on the interpretive aspects of interpersonal behavior. This is the basis for the model presented next.

A SOCIAL EXPECTANCY APPROACH
TO DYADIC INFLUENCE

The social expectancy model of dyadic influence in Figure 2.1 depicts relationships among major classes of variables that comprise an influence episode. Following Porter et al. (1981), the model treats an influence episode as an ordered series of perceptions, cognitions, and decisions enacted in the pursuit of a specific and known influence goal. The model aggregates social cognitive elements into comprehensive groupings similar to those specified in the influence episode framework proposed by Barry and Watson (1996). Figure 2.1 expands their organizing framework into a process model by incorporating expectancy judgments at the points where agent and target come together. Below the role of each of the parties (agent and target) is briefly discussed, and the role of expectancies is analyzed.

Role of the Agent

Within influence episodes, the conditions under which agents make tactical choices become important given the widely accepted proposition that agents of influence select behaviors because they conform to constraints operating in a situation (Cody et al., 1986). Joining process perspectives on social influence (Cobb, 1984; Porter et al., 1981; Tedeschi, Bonoma, & Schlenker, 1972) with communication research on the situational elements of gaining compliance (e.g., Cody et al., 1986; Dillard & Burgoon, 1985; O'Hair, Cody, & O'Hair, 1991), Figure 2.1 indicates that variables antecedent to the actual implementation of an influence strategy fall in two categories: 1) perceptions by the influence agent regarding the participants in and nature of the episode, and 2) individual difference variables that describe characteristics of the influence agent.

With respect to the former, the model draws on the approach that dominates the communication theory literature (e.g., Cody et al., 1986; deTurck, 1985), where contextual elements relevant to influence strategy selection are described as perceptions held by the influence agent. Three perceptual categories are relevant: judgments about the personal characteristics of the selected influence target; perceptions regarding the relationship between agent and target, such as relative levels of power (Yukl & Falbe, 1990) and interpersonal intimacy (Dillard & Burgoon, 1985; Miller & Steinberg, 1975); and perceptions regarding the particular influence seeking situation the agent confronts, including

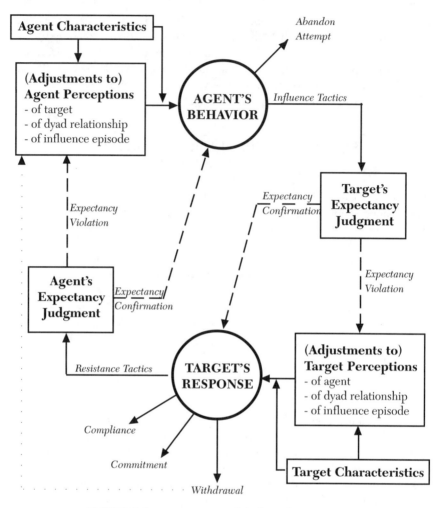

FIGURE 2.1. Expectancy Model of Dyadic Influence

goals (Yukl, Guinan, & Sottolano, 1995), anticipated levels of target resistance (Cody et al., 1986), and resource constraints such as time or channel availability (Porter, Allen, & Angle, 1981; Schein, 1977).

With respect to individual characteristics, personality traits may predispose individuals to decide to influence as well as to prefer certain influence methods. Machiavellianism, dogmatism, and locus of control are personality variables that have most frequently been associated with influence strategy choice (e.g., Boster & Stiff, 1984; O'Hair & Cody, 1987). Beyond traits, there is some empirical evidence, albeit limited and somewhat inconsistent, that sex is associated with tactical choice in dyadic influence (deTurck, 1985; Harper & Hirokawa, 1988).

Note that agent characteristics in the framework in Figure 2.1 exhibit both direct and indirect effects. Individual difference variables have been found to exert main effects on influence strategy choice as well as interact with situational perceptions (e.g., deTurck, 1985; O'Hair & Cody, 1987). But situational perceptions may also vary with individual differences; for example, perceptions of relative power between dyad members will conceivably reflect a perceiver's locus of control. Thus, individual differences are presented in the figure as directly influencing situational perceptions, as well as moderating the association between those perceptions and strategic behaviors.

Role of the Target

The framework in Figure 2.1 depicts the role of perceptions and individual differences from the perspective of the target as structurally similar to that of the agent, with the two sets of variables working both independently and interactively to determine the target's choice of response to the influence attempt. Tactical behaviors presented by the influence seeker are perceived and interpreted by the target in light of prior expectancies and social perceptions. As Reis and Shaver (1988) put it, one's interpertations of an interaction partner's actions are filtered through a cognitive mesh of dispositions, expectations, and schemas. Indeed, influence agents and targets do not always see influence seeking behavior as comprised of the same sets of tactics (Yukl & Falbe, 1990).

Target responses to the influence attempt are represented in the framework as possible outcomes that reflect variations in the effectiveness of the attempt (cf, Yukl, Kim, & Falbe, 1996). Four such outcomes are included. First, a target may yield to an influence request behaviorally but without underlying attitudinal adjustment, which is labeled "compliance" (Kelman, 1958). Secondly, a target may yield to the influence request with attitudinal "commitment." Third, a target may reject both the influence attempt and the possibility of future engagement over the issue, which effectively amounts to "withdrawal" from the episode. Withdrawal presumably means the influence attempt has failed, which may lead the influence seeker to adjust perceptions of the target (e.g., susceptibility to particular influence strategies). Thus, Figure 2.1 includes a (dotted line) feedback link between withdrawal and agent perceptions. Finally, a target may reject the attempt assertively through the use of "resistance" tactics of his or her own (e.g., O'Hair, Cody, & O'Hair, 1991). The last of these—resistance—perpetuates the influence seeking episode by providing the agent with additional opportunities to direct tactics at the target. A recent study by Yukl, Kim, and Chavez (1999) provided evidence that target perceptions mediate between tactical variations on the part of the agent and the likelihood of target commitment to an agent's request.

The Role of Expectancies

As defined by attribution theorists, expectancies are prior judgments, hunches, and predictions about the behavior of other individuals and the structure of social contexts within which interaction occurs (Jones, 1990; Kelley, 1971). Expectancies are presumably shaped by both individual characteristics and prior experiences (Darley & Fazio, 1980). An extensive social psychological literature on expectancy effects reveals that expectations regarding the personal characteristics and behaviors of interaction partners are related to social perceptions (Snyder, Tanke, & Berscheid, 1977), causal attributions (Weisz & Jones, 1993), an actor's self-concept (Swann & Reade, 1981), interaction goals (Andersen & Bem, 1981), negotiation strategies (Skrypnek & Snyder, 1982), communication patterns (Farina, Allen, & Saul, 1968), task performance (Eden & Shani, 1982), and the favorability of communication outcomes (Burgoon & Hale, 1988).

Analyses of expectancies in social psychology initially focused on self-fulfilling prophecies that arise in social interaction (e.g., Rosenthal & Rubin, 1978). In its simplest form, a perceiver carries prior judgments and expectations regarding the attributes or performance capabilities of a target into their interaction. As a result, the perceiver interprets actions by the target in ways that are consistent with prior expectancies (yielding perceptual confirmation), or behaves toward the target in ways that elicit new behaviors from the target that actually confirm the expectancy (behavioral confirmation) (see Darley & Oleson, 1993, for a more detailed explanation and review). These two forms of expectancy confirmation are orthogonal in the sense that you can have one without the other—perceptions may be confirmed even in the absence of confirming behavior if the individual perceiver sees that behavior as consistent with expectations (Miller & Turnbull, 1986).

Communication researchers have studied social expectancies from a slightly different perspective. Burgoon (1993) defined an expectancy as "an enduring pattern of anticipated behavior" (p. 31). Her theory of expectancy violations in communication (EV theory) identifies consequences of expectancy confirmations and violations in interpersonal interaction. Where the traditional social psychological approach examines how a perceiver's expectancies influence the perceiver's own judgments about and behaviors toward a target, EV theory considers how the perceiver responds to communication from another person that confirms or violates perceiver expectancies. Thus, the communication approach to expectancies focuses on how actual communication (verbal and nonverbal) matches or violates a message recipient/perceiver's preconceived notions about behavior that is "typical and appropriate" in a given situation (Burgoon, 1993, p. 31).

According to EV theory, when expectancy violations occur, the perceiver evaluates the violation as either positive or negative. Violations are positively valenced by the perceiver when behavior conforms more closely than anticipated to expectations (Burgoon & Miller, 1985) or otherwise elicits unexpected positive or favorable arousal (Burgoon, 1993). Violations are evaluated as negative when behavior is contrary to normative expectations or otherwise produces unexpectedly negative reactions. These valenced evaluations, in turn, influence subsequent interaction outcomes in ways that strict conformity to expectations does not (Burgoon & LePoire, 1993).

In EV theory and other approaches to communication expectancies, expectations about behavior are treated as fundamental forces that determine patterns of interaction. As Burgoon (1993) observed, "People plan and adapt their own communication according to the kind of encounter and communication style they anticipate from another actor. At the same time, expectancies serve as perceptual filters, significantly influencing how social information is processed" (p. 32). There is evidence that expectations about linguistic behaviors influence the reception and acceptance or rejection of verbal persuasive messages (see Burgoon & Miller, 1985, for a review), but the psychology of expectancies has not heretofore been applied to the study of influence seeking behavior in organizations.

In Figure 2.1, individual expectancy reactions mediate between one party's overt behavior and the other party's reception and response to that behavior. For the influence target, these processes are initiated in response to the agent's influence seeking tactics. The target evaluates the agent's tactical behavior in relation to the target's a priori expectancies about the other person, the dyadic relationship, and the influence situation. When expectations are violated—that is, when the agent's actions are viewed by the target as other than typical and appropriate—the target under some conditions is induced to alter his or her perceptions of some aspect of the episode or relationship. When expectations are confirmed, on the other hand, the target is presumed to formulate a response without significant adjustment of situationally relevant perceptions. For the influence agent, the target's resistance strategy initiates a judgment about whether the presence and nature of that resistance is consistent or inconsistent with the agent's prior expectations. Violated expectancies may elicit changes in the agent's perceptions of target, relationship, or situation that, in turn, influence subsequent influence seeking behaviors. Confirmed expectancies may still elicit further tactical behavior, but without underlying perceptual adjustment.

Linking Tactics and Expectancies

A basic premise of the model in Figure 2.1 is that the agent's choice of influence tactics triggers an expectancy-related judgment by the target. The particular tactics deployed within a given episode will either confirm or violate expectations held by the target regarding appropriate behavior within this dyad and this situation. To develop this linkage between tactics and expectancies, it is helpful to define the types of influence relevant expectancies that may be characteristic of organizational dyads, and onto which influence tactics can be mapped. A useful taxonomy of expectancies should meet two criteria. First, it should incorporate underlying dimensions that comport with psychological processes presumed to be important within an influence attempt. Second, a conceptually sound taxonomy of expectancies should be able to account for the range of tactical behaviors that previous studies of influence have identified and examined.

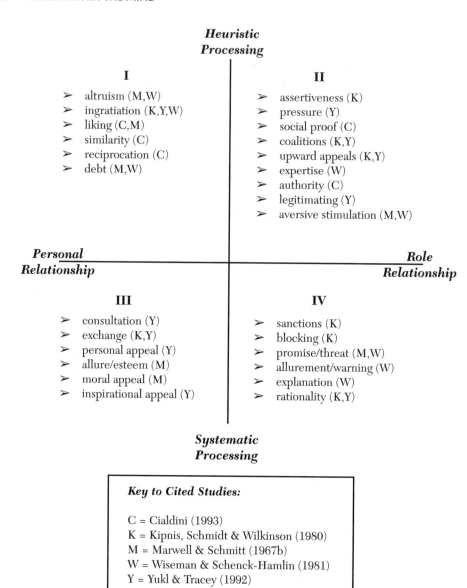

Heuristic
Processing

I

➢ altruism (M,W)
➢ ingratiation (K,Y,W)
➢ liking (C,M)
➢ similarity (C)
➢ reciprocation (C)
➢ debt (M,W)

II

➢ assertiveness (K)
➢ pressure (Y)
➢ social proof (C)
➢ coalitions (K,Y)
➢ upward appeals (K,Y)
➢ expertise (W)
➢ authority (C)
➢ legitimating (Y)
➢ aversive stimulation (M,W)

Personal
Relationship

Role
Relationship

III

➢ consultation (Y)
➢ exchange (K,Y)
➢ personal appeal (Y)
➢ allure/esteem (M)
➢ moral appeal (M)
➢ inspirational appeal (Y)

IV

➢ sanctions (K)
➢ blocking (K)
➢ promise/threat (M,W)
➢ allurement/warning (W)
➢ explanation (W)
➢ rationality (K,Y)

Systematic
Processing

Key to Cited Studies:

C = Cialdini (1993)
K = Kipnis, Schmidt & Wilkinson (1980)
M = Marwell & Schmitt (1967b)
W = Wiseman & Schenck-Hamlin (1981)
Y = Yukl & Tracey (1992)

FIGURE 2.2. Influence Tactics Classified in a 2 × 2 Taxonomy of Expectancies

In Figure 2.2, a four-fold taxonomy of influence related expectancies reflects variation along two conceptual dimensions. Each of the taxonomy's four quadrants represents a type of expectancy defined by a unique combination of the two dimensions. Entries within each quadrant in the figure are influence tactics sorted according to the judgment each tactic would be expected to elicit. The tactics included are drawn from influential conceptual and empirical research on influence seeking behavior published in the literatures of sociology (Marwell & Schmitt, 1967b), communication (Wiseman & Schenck-Hamlin, 1981), organizational behavior (Kipnis et al., 1980; Yukl & Tracey, 1992), and social psychology (Cialdini, 1993).

Relationship Dimension.   The horizontal dimension of Figure 2.2 addresses the nature of the dyadic affiliation between agent and target that is initiated or reinforced by tactical behavior. This dimension is grounded in the assumption from theories of relational communication (e.g., Montgomery, 1992) that inter-action patterns and dyadic relationships are reciprocally linked. Individuals make communication choices that reflect relational dynamics; they also make infer-ences about relationship dynamics on the basis of message characteristics (Fairhurst, Rogers, & Sarr, 1987). The relevance of these dynamics in organiza-tional settings is highlighted within research on role relationships (Katz & Kahn, 1978), authority models (Kahn & Kram, 1994), and leader–member exchange (e.g., Dansereau, Graen, & Haga, 1975). In organizations, interacting dyad members may harbor expectations and make behavioral choices based on as-sumptions that their relationship revolves around organizational roles on the one hand, or around personal ties on the other.

Accordingly, it is proposed that the basis for affiliation between agent and target is a distinguishing characteristic of influence related expectancies and, by extension, influence tactics. Role relationship expectancies reflect assump-tions that relationships and communication strategies are based largely on is-sues of status and hierarchy in the organization, with social distance preserved and minimal attention to personal thoughts and feelings (Kahn & Kram, 1994). Also included in this category are perceptions and tactics that de-emphasize status and authority, but remain focused on organizational roles—that is, de-fined by the functional requirements of the organization (Katz & Kahn, 1978). In contrast, personal relationship expectancies highlight the personal, rather than organization-based, relationship between agent and target. Based on as-sumptions of reduced social distance between agent and target, these expect-ancies stem from mutual liking, admiration, and respect (Katz & Kahn, 1978), as well as from detailed knowledge about one another's patterns of behavior (Miller & Steinberg, 1975). The contrast between role and personal relation-ship expectancies can be viewed as an organization relevant extension of the distinction in social psychology (e.g., Weisz & Jones, 1993) between category-based expectancies (based on knowledge about a target person's social affilia-tions) and target-based expectancies (derived from knowledge about the par-ticular target individual).

Information Processing Dimension.   The vertical dimension in Figure 2.2 addresses the extent of information processing that parties to an influence at-tempt may expect to encounter, and that tactics may be expected to evoke. This dimension is an outgrowth of theories of attitude change that distinguish be-tween systematic, effortful processing of the content of influence seeking messages and less controlled heuristic mechanisms for reacting to such messages. The best known of these theories are the elaboration likelihood model (Petty & Cacioppo, 1986) and the heuristic systematic model (Chaiken, 1987). These two models make some overlapping predictions but are not redundant; see Eagly and Chaiken (1993) for a review of their supporting research and discussion of their similarities and differences.

It is proposed in Figure 2.2 that influence relevant expectancies can be distinguished as either heuristic or systematic. Heuristic processing expectancies are present when the influence target believes that typical or appropriate influence seeking behavior by the agent will not ask the target to engage in effortful, systematic information processing of the agent's request. In the argot of the elaboration likelihood model (Petty & Cacioppo, 1986), the target anticipates only that peripheral cues will be used by the agent to elicit influence. For example, if Max, an influence target, assumes based on past experience that Susan, an influence agent, will typically seek influence by making forceful demands (assertiveness) or by invoking past favors Susan performed for Max (reciprocation, debt), then Max brings a heuristic expectancy to the exchange. As message recipient, Max in this example does not anticipate being called upon to think carefully about the influence request, only to invoke simple decision rules or heuristics (Chaiken, 1987).

In contrast, systematic processing expectancies are present when the influence target anticipates that an influence seeker will prefer tactics that tend to involve the target in mindful information processing. Put another way, the target believes it to be typical or appropriate for the influencer to choose tactics that call upon the target to engage in systematic or elaborated thinking about the influence request. For instance, if our influence target Max believes that the influence seeker Susan will choose logical or argumentative tactics that present evidence for Max to weigh in deciding whether to comply, then Max is anticipating that Susan wants her target to think effortfully about her request—he carries a systematic processing expectancy into the interaction. The likelihood that a particular target person will harbor this sort of expectation may vary with such factors as social norms, past experience with a given agent, situational constraints, or personal characteristics of the individuals involved.

Four Expectancy Types. The two dimensions just discussed combine in Figure 2.2 to define four modal types of influence related expectancies. In quadrant I, an influence target expects that an agent will seek influence by playing on the personal relationship in a way that does not require systematic thought by the target. In quadrant II, a target anticipates that an agent will use tactics that emphasize their organizational affiliation in terms of role, status, hierarchy, and so forth, and do so in a way that does not demand systematic processing. In quadrant III, a target expects tactics that are personal in nature but that do invite some effortful consideration of the request being made. In quadrant IV, a target anticipates appeals based on organization-based roles or ties that invite elaborated thinking about the request. The use of an influence tactic within a given quadrant presumably would confirm the expectancy defined by that quadrant. (However, the approriate classification of some tactics may depend in a particular influence situation on how the tactic is formulated and delivered. For example, a promise or threat tactic could be placed on either side of the relationship dimension depending on whether the promised or threatened outcome is personal in nature or organizationally relevant.)

Consequences of Expectancy Violations

The model in Figure 2.1 holds that expectancy violations elicit adjustments of dyad and situation relevant perceptions—for targets when tactics put forth by the agent violate expectancies, and for agents when responses by the target violate expectancies. However, it has been demonstrated (e.g., Burgoon & LePoire, 1993) that not all expectancy violations produce identical outcomes; the consequence of a given violation may depend on the nature of the initial expectancy and on the nature of the violation in relation to that expectancy. In this section the variable effects of expectancy violations in organization-based influence seeking are analyzed.

Relationship Expectancies. A straightforward prediction of the model presented thus far is that violations of relationship oriented expectancies will lead to adjustments of the perceiver's peceptions regarding the dyadic relationship. For instance, consider the situation where a target, Bob, views his relationship with the influence seeker, Jerry, as low in social proximity and focused primarily around organizational roles and structures. Jerry's use of tactics that signal a personal relationship, such as liking, similarity, or reciprocation, violates expectancies in a way that may induce Bob to reassess the strength of their personal ties. Conversely, in a situation where Bob views the relationship as high in social proximity, Jerry's unexpected use of role-focused tactics, such as assertiveness, expertise, coalitions, or legitimation, would stimulate a reassessment by Bob of the closeness of the personal relationship.

Roles in the organization's status hierarchy occupied by agent and target may buffer the likelihood and impact of these adjustments to relationship perceptions. Organization members have greater opportunities to derive instrumental benefits (status, power) from social proximity with powerful others than with less powerful others. Accordingly, influence episode participants are inclined to view unexpectedly personal tactics as a positive expectancy violation when the agent is a relatively powerful other, but view such tactics as a negative expectancy violation when the source is a less powerful other. In simpler terms, one welcomes personal attention from those in power, but shuns such attention from the powerless.

The use of unexpectedly nonpersonal tactics—that is, expectancy violations that signal an emphasis on the parties' organizational role relationship over their personal relationship—would be viewed as a negative violation in situations where the presence of a personal relationship was desirable to the party experiencing the violation. Again, the impact is predicted to be particularly acute when interacting with a powerful other: Tactics that signal an attenuation of one's personal relationship with a high status individual may threaten the perceiver's own organizational status and power. A lessening of personal ties with a less powerful other does not project the same implications for organizational status, but would still be perceived negatively to the extent that the perceiver is motivated to maintain and develop friendship ties with others.

Information Processing Expectancies. As discussed above, tactical behavior varies in the extent to which it encourages the other party to engage in effortful, elaborated analysis of the message conveyed (systematic processing), or, alternatively, to respond via abbreviated decision rules without careful thought (heuristic processing). Influence episodes in workplace settings involve a variety of task objectives and interpersonal status dynamics (Kipnis et al., 1980; Yukl, Guinan, & Sottolano, 1995). For individuals occupying positions that afford many opportunities to initiate or respond to influence attempts, it is likely that demands for systematic versus heuristic processing of other parties' tactics will be variable. An expectancy violation pertaining to information processing occurs when tactical behavior provokes systemetic processing contrary to perceiver expectations that typical or appropriate behavior (from this other person or in this type of situation) would call for a simpler, heuristic reaction. Consider, for example, a boss who typically negotiates disagreements with a subordinate by making an assertive request or invoking authority without entertaining discussion; this behavior may violate a systematic processing assumption on the part of the influence target. Conversely, a violation occurs when behavior unexpectedly encourages the individual who anticipates heuristic inducing tactics to engage in effortful message processing.

Social cognitive models of attitude change (e.g., Petty & Cacciopo, 1986) make clear that motives to process information are critical determinants of whether or not effortful thinking takes place in a given situation. In the framework developed here, these same motives may influence the likelihood that an unexpected influence tactic will actually be experience by the target as a meaningful expectancy violation, as well as the valence (positive or negative) of that experience. Accordingly, there are three motivational factors that may act to moderate the effects of information processing expectancy violations.

First, involvement, defined as the importance of the episode to the message recipient, is a factor that encourages elaborated thinking about persuasive messages (Maheswaran & Chaiken, 1991). Under conditions of high recipient involvement, an unexpectedly heuristic tactic would therefore be expected to trigger a negative perception of the expectancy violation, and an unexpectedly systemetic tactic would be expected to trigger a positive evaluation of the violation. Under conditions of low recipient involvement, the reverse should occur.

Second, the degree to which violations are consequential may vary with the relative organizational position, in terms of power or hierarchy, that agent and target occupy. There is ample research evidence that influence agents adopt different strategies depending on whether the hierarchical direction of an influence attempt is upward, downward, or lateral (e.g., Barry & Bateman, 1992; Kipnis et al., 1980). Moreover, as Fiske (1993) has argued, individuals are more motivated to pay careful attention to the actions and messages of powerful others, but more likely to rely instead on heuristics and stereotypes in perceiving the actions of less powerful others. This suggests that for the case of downward influence, a target (in a lower power position, relative to the influence seeker) may be more inclined to engage in systematic processing of tactics even when they weren't intended in that manner, and also more likely to detect expectancy violations. In contrast, targets of upward influence would be biased toward heuristic processing, and less likely to react when influence seeking behavior violates expectancies.

Third, the effects of violations pertaining to information processing may depend on the nature of the personal relationship (i.e., social distance) between the parties. In terms of the typology in Figure 2.2, this moderating effect can be described as an interaction between the typology's two dimensions. When parties maintain a personal relationship, influence related actions by one that violate the information processing expectancies of the other should not consistently elicit a positive or negative evaluation of the violation. There is no basis to expect that message recipients, in the context of a personal relationship, prefer either heuristic or systematic processing. On the other hand, when the relationship between the parties is focused on organizational roles, individuals are expected to attend more to issues of personal control over their outcomes. Tactics that elicit systematic processing may convey an opportunity to participate in the situation, and hence would be received more favorably as contributing to perceptions of control (e.g., Langer, 1983). Thus, given low social proximity between dyad members, expectancy violations that involve the use of unexpectedly heuristic tactics are hypothesized to elicit negative judgments, and violations that involve unexpectedly systematic tactics are predicted to elicit positive judgments.

Effects of Positive and Negative Violations on Influence Outcomes

What effects do positive and negative expectancy violations have on the message recipient's response to the other party's tactical behavior? Irrespective of valence, arousal of the type generated by nontrivial expectancy violations can be expected to heighten attention to the source and content of the arousal (Burgoon & Hale, 1988). In a marketing context, Sujan (1985) demonstrated that consumers who encounter information that is discrepant from prior knowledge generate more substantive thoughts and arrive at judgments more deliberately. For an influence target, arousal induced by expectancy violations would be expected to direct the perceiver's attention to the influence agent and to the substance of the influence seeking appeal. Positively valenced violations presumably dispose the perceiver more favorably toward the agent and the influence objective, and negative violations presumably do the opposite; both, however, may lead to greater scrutiny and analysis of the request. Thus, simple compliance (behavioral conformity without attitude change) is hypothesized as less likely when influence tactics violate target expectancies, especially when the violation is negatively valenced.

This line of reasoning suggests that an influence target is most likely to respond with commitment (conformity accompanied by attitude change) under two conditions. First, as the elaboration likelihood model of persuasion (Petty & Cacioppo, 1986) suggests, internalized commitment is more likely when effortful processing of a persuasion seeking message takes place. Thus, given influence seeking behavior that confirms expectancies, commitment is more likely when the agent chooses tactics that encourage systematic processing of the request than when the agent chooses tactics that encourage a heuristic response. Second, given influence seeking behavior that violates expectancies, the prospects for commitment are enhanced when the violation is in the direction of systematic information processing (i.e., unexpectedly inducing targets to engage in effortful processing of the influence request) *and* when that violation is positively valenced by the target. In such cases, attention to the influence request is highest and the affective conditions guiding the target's response to the request are positively oriented.

An important complication left unaddressed by this analysis to this point concerns situations where expectancy violations lead to situations that combine positive and negative evaluations of tactics and violations within a single episode. How should the expectancy framework account for different combinations of valence that different influence participants may perceive? Consider, for example, the situation where an influence target's expectation that the influence seeker will behave in a positively perceived way (e.g., by seeking the target's consultation on the request) is met instead with something perceived as distinctively negative (e.g., a barked order to comply). Now consider a second situation, where the target views the same expectation as negative (e.g., the target doesn't want to be involved in negotiating the request), and the violation as positive (he or she welcomes the barked order as a decisive way to settle the matter without the fuss of consultation). Are these two situations structurally identical? Does the arrangement of positively and negatively valenced judgments within the influence affect how expectancy violations are perceived, and ultimately determinative of influence outcomes? This issue goes beyond the scope of the initial formulation of an expectancy framework in this chapter, but clearly needs to be addressed if an expectancy approach is to account for the full compexity and nuance of influence episodes.

IMPLICATIONS FOR POWER USE AND ABUSE

The expectancy-focused framework allows for an analysis of the subtleties of dyadic influence in a way that can illuminate how power is used and potentially misused in workplace settings. With its emphasis on judgments of expectancy confirmation and violation as the social cognitive nexus between one party's tactical behavior and the other's response, the model suggests explanations for why similar tactics deployed in different situations may or may not elicit desired outcomes. The expectancy approach, for example, offers a path to understanding why impression management behaviors sometimes fail to alter impressions; why threats don't always threaten; why obligations don't necessarily obligate; and why pressure doesn't always coerce. An example related to potentially unethical workplace behavior will help to illustrate the model's implications for the use and possible abuse of power.

A Workplace Ethics Example

An organization member, Alice (the influence agent), is aware that another member having roughly equal status and power, Tom (the influence target), intends to hire an acquaintance to fill an open position without following standard procedures regarding public posting of job opportunities. Assume that Alice's outcome objective is to change Tom's intended behavior so that the circumvention of accepted practice does not occur; however, Alice may or may not be concerned with whether or not Tom changes his attitudes about the hiring policy or the appropriateness of the intended behavior.

It is conceivable that from Alice's perspective, internalized commitment is desirable but not necessary; simple compliance is acceptable and feasible as the outcome of the episode. Given equal power and status between the parties and the acceptibility of either compliance or commitment as outcome, many different tactics represent conceivable paths to successful influence depending on expectancies. Quadrant I tactics may be appropriate if their use confirms information processing expectancies and either confirms relationship expectancies or violates them in a positively valenced manner. If successful, however, the result is likely to be compliance rather than internalized commitment. Quadrant II tactics may succeed if their use confirms both forms of expectancies, but are not likely to be successful if Alice's use of tactics that signal a role oriented relationship is unexpected by Tom. Again, compliance rather than commitment would be the outcome.

Alternatively, to achieve commitment (conformity with attitude change), the model suggests a role for expectancy violations associated with the use of tactics in quadrants III and IV; the efficacy of these tactics may depend on such factors as Tom's level of personal involvement in this particular issue and the nature of the preexisting relationship between Alice and Tom. Specifically, Tom may be receptive to tactics that encourage systematic processing to the extent that Tom attaches personal importance to the issues involved in the influence request. Also, in the absence of a personal relationship between Alice and Tom, tactics that violate Tom's expectancies by unexpectedly encouraging systematic processing may be more likely to be well received than heuristic tactics.

In this sort of hypothetical situation, according to the expectancy model, successful influence depends on the agent's ability to sense the information processing requirements and conformity needs of the influence request, and to arrive at appropriate assessments of the agent–target relationship and of the target's information processing expectations. Based on these perceptions, the effective influencer makes tactical choices that either confirm expectancies or violate them in ways that are positively valenced by the influence target. The expectancy model demonstrates that achieving successful influence requires substantially more than simple congruence between influence objectives and influence tactics, as existing influence research tends to imply.

Abuse of power may be said to occur when an influence seeker manipulates the power episode in ways that rely on deception or blatant misrepresentation in order to achieve influence objectives. The expectancy model suggests a couple of tactical avenues through which this might happen. First, along the relationship dimension of the tactics taxonomy, a duplicitous agent might feign an affiliation of one type in order to capitalize on expectancy effects by invoking tactics that elicit contrary relational perceptions. Similarly, with respect to information processing expectancies, an agent could seek to exaggerate a target's perception of the severity of an expectancy violation (e.g., unexpectly inviting systematic processing) by engaging in prior interactions that manipulate expectancy perceptions in the other direction (toward expectations of heuristically oriented requests). Certainly these machinations on the part of an influence seeker are complex and depend on participation in expectancy-generating interactions over time and across influence goals. The extent to which such actions, if successfully implemented, rise to the level of an abuse of power that challenges ethical norms is unclear and beyond the scope of this chapter (see Anton, 1990, for an examination of perceptions of the relative ethicality of different forms of misrepresentation in social interaction). Less elusive is the prospect that an expectancy model of interpersonal influence can help shed light on the linkages among context, motives, tactics, and perceptions that are interwoven into the fabric of an influence episode.

CONCLUSION

The model introduced in this chapter adds value to to research on organizational-based influence by integrating the structure of influence seeking behavior with the process through which influence is achieved within a common framework. Social expectancies are the basis both for distinguishing among tactics and for theorizing about the conditions under which particular tactics will general influence outcomes. In contrast to prior models that adopt the perspective of one party to an influence episode, the approach taken here considers both influencer and influence target as separate but interdependent parties to a transactional process, each of whom brings with them independent relational and situational perceptions. Through the mechanisms of expectancy confirmation and violation, these perceptions are dynamically redefined within the boundaries of an ongoing influence episode. Understanding influence attempts in this way sheds light on specific conditions under which the imaginary line between power use and power abuse may blur.

REFERENCES

Andersen, S. M., & Bem, S. L. (1981). Sex typing and androgyny in dyadic interaction: Individual differences in responsiveness to physical attractiveness. *Journal of Personality and Social Psychology, 41,* 74–86.

Anton, R. J. (1990). Drawing the line: An exploratory test of ethical behavior in negotiation. *International Journal of Conflict Management, 1,* 265–280.

Barry, B., & Bateman, T. S. (1992). Perceptions of influence in managerial dyads: The role of hierarchy, media, and tactics. *Human Relations, 65,* 555–574.

Barry, B., & Shapiro, D. L. (1992). Influence tactics in combinations: The interactive effects of soft versus hard tactics and rational exchange. *Journal of Applied Social Psychology, 22,* 1429–1441.

Barry, B., & Watson, M. R. (1996). Communication aspects of dyadic social influence in organizations: A review and integration of conceptual and empirical developments. In B. R. Burleson (Ed.), *Communication yearbook 19* (pp. 269–317). Thousand Oaks, CA: Sage.

Benson, P. G., & Hornsby, J. S. (1988). The politics of pay: Use of influence tactics in job evaluation committees. *Group & Organization Studies, 13,* 208–224.

Boster, F. J., & Stiff, J. B. (1984). Compliance-gaining message selection behavior. *Human Communication Research, 10,* 539–556.

Burgoon, J. K. (1993). Interpersonal expectations, expectancy violations, and emotional communication. *Journal of Language and Social Psychology, 12,* 30-48.

Burgoon, J. K., & Hale, J. L. (1988). Nonverbal expectancy violations: Model elaboration and application to immediacy behaviors. *Communication Monographs, 55,* 58–79.

Burgoon, J. K., & LePoire, B. A. (1993). Effects of communication expectancies, actual communication, and expectancy disconfirmation on evaluations of communicators and their communication behavior. *Human Communication Research, 20,* 67–96.

Burgoon, M., & Miller, G. R. (1985). An expectancy interpretation of language and persuasion. In H. Giles & R. N. St. Clair (Eds.), *Recent advances in language, communication, and social psychology* (pp. 199–229). London: Erlbaum.

Chaiken, S. (1987). The heuristic model of persuasion. In M. P. Zanna, J. M. Olson, & C. P. Herman (Eds.), *Social influence: The Ontario Symposium* (Vol. 5, pp. 3–39). Hillsdale, NJ: Erlbaum.

Cheng, J. L. C. (1983). Organizational context and upward influence: An experimental study of the use of power tactics. *Group & Organizational Studies, 8,* 337–355.

Cialdini, R. B. (1993). *Influence: Science and practice* (3rd ed.). New York: HarperCollins.

Cobb, A. T. (1984). An episodic model of power: Toward an integration of theory and research. *Academy of Management Review, 9,* 382–393.

Cody, M. J., Greene, J. O., Marston, P. J., O'Hair, H. D., Baaske, K. T., & Schneider, M. J. (1986). Situation perception and message strategy selection. In M. L. McLaughlin (Ed.), *Communication yearbook 9* (pp. 390–420). Beverly Hills: Sage.

Dansereau, F. Jr., Graen, G., & Haga, W. J. (1975). A vertical dyad linkage approach to leadership within formal organizations: A longitudinal investigation of the role making process. *Organizational Behavior and Human Performance, 13,* 46–78.

Darley, J. M., & Fazio, R. H. (1980). Expectancy confirmation processes arising in the social interaction sequence. *American Psychologist, 35,* 867–881.

Darley, J. M., & Oleson, K. C. (1993). Introduction to research on interpersonal expectations. In P. D. Blanck (Ed.), *Interpersonal expectations: Theory research, and applications* (pp. 45–63). Cambridge: Cambridge University Press.

deTurck, M. A. (1985). A transactional analysis of compliance-gaining behavior: Effects of noncompliance, relational contexts, and actors' gender. *Human Communication Research, 12,* 54–78.

Dillard, J. P., & Burgoon, M. (1985). Situational influences on the selection of compliance-gaining messages: Two tests of the predictive utility of the Cody-McLaughlin typology. *Communication Monographs, 52,* 289–304.

Eagly, A. H., & Chaiken, S. (1993). *The psychology of attitudes.* Fort Worth, TX: Harcourt Brace.

Eden, D., & Shani, A. B. (1982). Pygmalion

goes to boot camp: expectancy, leadership and trainee performance. *Journal of Applied Psychology, 67,* 194–199.

Fairhurst, G. T., Rogers, L. E., & Sarr, R. A. (1987). Manager-subordinate control patterns and judgments about the relationship. In M. L. McLaughlin (Ed.), *Communication yearbook 10* (pp. 395–415). Beverly Hills: Sage.

Falbe, T., & Yukl, G. (1992). Consequences for managers of using single influence tactics and combinations of tactics. *Academy of Management Journal, 35,* 638–652.

Farina, A., Allen, J. G., & Saul, B. B. (1968). The role of the stigmatized person in affecting social relationships. *Journal of Personality, 36,* 169–182.

Fiske, S. T. (1993). Controlling other people: The impact of power on stereotyping. *American Psychologist, 48,* 621–628.

Harper, N. L., & Hirokawa, R. Y. (1988). A comparison of persuasive strategies used by female and male managers I: An examination of downward influence. *Communication Quarterly, 36,* 157–168.

Howard, D. J. (1995). "Chaining" the use of influence strategies for producing compliance behavior. *Journal of Social Behavior and Personality, 10,* 169–185.

Jones, E. E. (1990). *Interpersonal perception.* New York: W.H. Freeman.

Kahn, W. A., & Kram, K. E. (1994). Authority at work: Internal models and their organizational consequences. *Academy of Management Review, 19,* 17–50.

Katz, D., & Kahn, R. L. (1978). *The social psychology of organizations* (2nd ed.). New York: Wiley.

Kellermann, K., & Cole, T. (1994). Classifying compliance-gaining messages: Taxonomic disorder and strategic confusion. *Communication Theory, 4,* 3–60.

Kelley, H.H. (1971). Attribution in social interaction. In E. E. Jones, D. Kanouse, H. H. Kelley, R. E. Nesbitt, S. Valins, & B. Weiner (Eds.), *Attribution: Perceiving the causes of behavior* (pp. 1–26). Morristown, NJ: General Learning Press.

Kelman, H. C. (1958). Compliance, identification, and internalization: Three processes of attitude change. *Journal of Conflict Resolution, 2,* 51–60.

Kelman, H. C. (1974). Further thoughts on the processes of compliance, identification, and internalization. In J. T. Tedeschi (Ed.), *Perspectives on Social Power* (pp. 125–171). Chicago: Aldine.

Kelman, H. C., & Hamilton, V. L. (1989). *Crimes of obedience: Toward a social psychology of authority and responsibility.* New Haven: Yale University Press.

Kipnis, D. (1974). The powerholder. In J. T. Tedeschi (Ed.), *Perspectives on social power* (pp. 82–122). Chicago: Aldine.

Kipnis, D., & Schmidt, S. M. (1988). Upward-influence styles: Relationship with performance evaluations, salary, and stress. *Administrative Science Quarterly, 33,* 528–542.

Kipnis, D., Schmidt, S. M., & Wilkinson, I. (1980). Intraorganizational influence tactics: Explorations in getting one's way. *Journal of Applied Psychology, 65,* 440–452.

Langer, E. J. (1983). *The psychology of control.* Beverly Hills, CA: Sage.

Maheswaran, D., & Chaiken, S. (1991). Promoting systematic processing in low motivation settings: Effect of incongruent information on processing and judgment. *Journal of Personality and Social Psychology, 61,* 13–25.

Marwell, G., & Schmitt, D. R. (1967a). Compliance-gaining behavior: A synthesis and model. *The Sociological Quarterly, 8,* 317–328.

Marwell, G., & Schmitt, D. R. (1967b). Dimensions of compliance-gaining behaviors. *Sociometry, 30,* 350–364.

Miller, G. R., Boster, F. J., Roloff, M. E., & Seibold, D. R. (1987). MBRS rekindled: Some thoughts on compliance gaining in interpersonal settings. In M. E. Roloff & G. R. Miller (Eds.), *Interpersonal processes: New directions in communication research* (pp. 89–116). Newbury Park, CA: Sage.

Miller, G. R., & Steinberg, M. (1975). *Between people: A new analysis of interpersonal communication.* Chicago: Science Research.

Miller, D. T., & Turnbull, W. (1986). Expectancies and interpersonal processes. *Annual Review of Psychology, 37,* 233–256.

Mitchell, T. R., & Beach, L. R. (1990). "Do I love thee? Let me count..." Toward an understanding of intuitive and automatic decision making. *Organizational Behavior and Human Decision Processes, 47,* 1–20.

Montgomery, B. M. (1992). Communication as the interface between couples and culture. In S. A. Deetz (Ed.), *Communication yearbook 15* (pp. 475–507). Newbury Park, CA: Sage.

Mowday, R. T. (1978). The exercise of upward influence in organizations. *Administrative Science Quarterly, 23,* 137–156.

O'Hair, D., & Cody, M. J. (1987). Machiavellian beliefs and social influence. *The Western Journal of Speech Communication, 51,* 279–303.

O'Hair, M. J., Cody, M. J., & O'Hair, D. (1991). The impact of situational dimensions on compliance-resistance strategies: A comparison of methods. *Communication Quarterly, 39,* 226–240.

Petty, R. E., & Cacioppo, J. T. (1986). The elaboration likelihood model of persuasion. *Advances in Experimental Social Psychology, 19,* 123–205.

Porter, L. W., Allen, R. W., & Angle, H. L. (1981). The politics of upward influence in organizations. In B. M. Staw & L. L. Cummings (Eds.), *Research in organizational behavior* (pp. 109–149). Greenwich, CT: JAI Press.

Raven, B. H. (1992). A power/interaction model of interpersonal influence: French and Raven thirty years later. *Journal of Social Behavior and Personality, 7,* 217–244.

Reis, H. T., & Shaver, P. (1988). Intimacy as an interpersonal process. In S. W. Duck (Ed.), *Handbook of personal relationships* (pp. 367–389). New York: Wiley.

Rosenthal, R., & Rubin, D. B. (1978). Interpersonal expectancy effects: The first 345 studies. *The Behavioral and Brain Sciences, 3,* 377–386.

Schein, V. (1977). Individual power and political behaviors in organizations: An inadequately explored reality. *Academy of Management Review, 2,* 64–72.

Schilit, W. K., & Locke, E. A. (1982). A study of upward influence in organizations. *Administrative Science Quarterly, 27,* 304–316.

Seibold, D. R., Cantrill, J. G., & Meyers, R. A. (1985). Communication and interpersonal influence. In M. L. Knapp & G. R. Miller (Eds.), *Handbook of interpersonal communication* (pp. 551–611). Newbury Park, CA: Sage.

Seibold, D. R., Cantrill, J. G., & Meyers, R. A. (1994). Communication and interpersonal influence. In M. L. Knapp & G. R. Miller (Eds.), *Handbook of interpersonal communication* (2nd ed., pp. 542–588). Newbury Park, CA: Sage.

Skrypnek, B. J., & Snyder, M. (1982). On the self-perpetuating nature of stereotypes about men and women," *Journal of Experimental Social Psychology, 18,* 277–291.

Snyder, M., Tanke, E. D., & Berscheid, E. (1977). Social perception and interpersonal behavior: On the self-fulfilling nature of social stereotypes. *Journal of Personality and Social Psychology, 35,* 656–666.

Staley, C. C., & Cohen, J. L. (1988). Communicator style and social style: Similarities and differences between the sexes. *Communication Quarterly, 36,* 192–202.

Sujan, M. (1985). Consumer knowledge: Effects on evaluation strategies mediating consumer judgments. *Journal of Consumer Research, 12,* 31–46.

Swann, W. B. Jr., & Reade, S. J. (1981). Self-verification processes: How we sustain our self-conceptions. *Journal of Experimental Social Psychology, 17,* 351-372.

Tedeschi, J. T., Bonoma, T. V., & Schlenker, B. R. (1972). Influence, decision, and compliance. In J. T. Tedeschi (Ed.), *The social influence processes* (pp. 346–418). Chicago: Aldine.

Tedeschi, J. T., Schlenker, B. R., & Linkskold, S. (1972). The exercise of power and influence: The source of influence. In J. T. Tedeschi (Ed.), *The social influence processes* (pp. 287–345). Chicago: Aldine.

Weisz, C., & Jones, E. E. (1993). Expectancy disconfirmation and dispositional inference: Latent strength of target-based and category-based expectancies. *Personality and Social Psychology Bulletin, 19,* 563–573.

Wiseman, R. L., & Schenck-Hamlin, W. (1981). A multidimensional scaling validation of an inductively-derived set of compliance gaining strategies. *Communication Monographs, 48,* 251–270.

Yukl, G., & Falbe, C. M. (1990). Influence tactics and objectives in upward, downward, and lateral influence attempts. *Journal of Applied Psychology, 75,* 132–140.

Yukl, G., Falbe, C. M., & Youn, J. Y. (1993). Patterns of influence behavior for managers. *Group & Organization Management, 18,* 5–28.

Yukl, G., Guinan, P. J., & Sottolano, D. (1995). Influence tactics used for different objectives with subordinates, peers, and superiors. *Group & Organization Management, 20,* 272–296.

Yukl, G., Kim, H., & Chavez, C. (1999). Task importance, feasibility, and agent influence as determinants of target commitment. *Journal of Applied Psychology, 84,* 137–143.

Yukl, G., Kim, H., & Falbe, C. M. (1996). Antecedents of influence outcomes. *Journal of Applied Psychology, 81,* 309–317.

Yukl, G., & Tracey, J. B. (1992). Consequences of influence tactics used with subordinates, peers, and the boss. *Journal of Applied Psychology, 77,* 525–535.

3

The Road to Hell

Good Intentions in the Face of Nonconscious Tendencies to Misuse Power

JOHN A. BARGH
JEANNETTE ALVAREZ

My most intimate fear is corruption. If our reforms are accompanied by corruption, democracy itself will be threatened.

—Petar Stoyanov, President of Bulgaria
June 17, 2000

D epressingly, reports of corruption and the misuse of power are so frequent and regular that they appear to be the norm—and because of that all the more in need of explanation. Within organizations in which some people are given official power over the important outcomes of others who have no reciprocal control of their own (i.e., social power; French & Raven, 1959; Thibaut & Kelley, 1959) abuse of this power occurs, and at all levels of the power hierarchy. From national governments to university academic departments, large corporations to local employee unions, individual powerholders often use their officially sanctioned, legitimate power over others in illegitimate ways for personal and selfish gain.

In the past year alone, the commissioners of the European Union resigned in the midst of charges of widespread nepotism and fraud ("What's wrong,"

Preparation of this chapter was supported in part by Grant R01-MH60767 from the Public Health Service.

41

2000). France's finance minister was forced out of office because of an investigation into illegal payments he allegedly accepted. The discovery of corrupt practices in campaign financing blackened the formerly near-iconic reputation of former Chancellor Helmut Kohl of Germany ("Is Europe corrupt?", 2000). The corruption of the current Russian government apparatus is so widely known it has earned public admonishment by the U.S. Secretary of State. In recent years it was government corruption that caused the fall, through massive public demonstrations and popular uprisings, of dictators Marcos of the Philippines and Suharto of Indonesia; and it was widespread governmental corruption, not the desire for democratic government, that was the true impetus for the Tiananmen Square uprising in China in 1989.

But corruption is not limited to governmental or political organizations. The recent revelation (through leaking of internal documents) of widespread misappropriation of 5 million dollars of funds for private gain by dozens of officials of the second largest union in the United States (AFSCME) prompted a spokesman for the union to offer the defense that corruption in their union was no worse than in many others—a position, in fact, that was endorsed as well by labor experts outside of the union (Greenhouse, 2000).

THE HIGH COSTS OF POWER ABUSE

According to the chief executive officer of Transparency International—an organization founded specifically to fight corruption in business and government—such corruption at the level of government contracts and customs duties is a major obstacle to the operation of free markets and the ability of all members, not just a few, of a given society to prosper economically (Jayawickrama, this volume). In our view as well, not to mention that of leaders of fledgling democracies such as President Stoyanov, abuse of official power at the individual level is the major obstacle to the emergence of truly democratic institutions and government worldwide. Because most government systems are democratic and republican in constitutional form—that is, on paper—it is the subversion of the constitutional system by corrupt individuals, not the lack of a democratic system in the first place, that is the real obstacle to the spread of democracy (see "A world full of phony democracies," 2000).

But just as damaging to the lives and aspirations of the average person are the abuses of power occurring at the more mundane, lower levels of the societal and organizational hierarchies. In the case of sexual harassment, for example, it is estimated, based on the incidence data as well as on large-scale surveys of federal employees and employees of trade union shops and universities, that one out of every two women will be harassed at some point in their careers (Fitzgerald, 1993a, 1993b; Gutek, 1985). This harassment can be as blatant as a quid pro quo proposal of exchanging sex for a raise or promotion, or just to be allowed to keep one's job. It can take less intrusive forms as well, such as objectifying the victim in terms of her sex through suggestive sexualized remarks, thus creating a hostile work environment. Indeed, treating subordinates as a member of their social category is a way of devaluing their worth (by denying their individuality or special attributes and abilities), thus serving to perpetuate the supervisor's position of relatively higher worth (see Fiske, 1993). This relative valuation in turn has the consequence that the supervisor's own goals, needs, ideas, and so forth also become more important than those of the subordinate (see Kipnis, 1976).

The subversion of official organizational power for individual gain has substantial costs not only to those whose ability to pursue their life goals is hindered by the subjective and inequitable treatment, but also for the aims and purposes of the organization itself, be it society, government, business, or academia. A conflict thus exists between individual's need for power and the organization's need to have that power used to serve the organization's, not the individual's, agenda. Hierarchically structured organizations can be likened to electrical systems, substituting the flow of power for the flow of electricity through the system. The organization has some overarching purpose and goal; it is created and structured in order to attain this goal. The people who fill the various roles and slots within the organization have legitimate and official power over decisions within a certain restricted domain of that organization. The personal needs and goals of the individuals who happen to occupy these positions are irrelevant to the overarching purposes of the organization. The use of officially licensed organizational power for personal needs and goals is thus an inefficiency of power use from the point of view of the organization as a whole; it is similar to poor insulation or a faulty connection in an electrical system. Thus, to the extent that the powerholder is using his or her official power for his or her own personal goals, this necessarily decreases the amount of power that the organization has (i.e., its ability) to attain its goals.

It should be apparent that the use of official power for unofficial reasons damages the ability of the organization to reach its stated purpose. At the level of representative democracies, no matter how democratic the governmental system is on paper, it is not so in practice if the elected representatives follow the wishes of those who donate most to their campaigns instead of the people they were elected to represent. To the extent that well qualified people do not get promoted, or a place in one of the better universities or professional schools, because of the prejudices of the people making such decisions, or because of legacies and other preferential treatment of the sons and daughters of those already in power (see Chen & Tyler, this volume), the society as a whole suffers from the lack of the talented services of these individuals and the absence of their future contributions. But the costs to society are diffused and unnoticed for the most part. That is not the case at the individual level, by those whose advancement is frustrated or hindered by the power-holding gatekeeper who rewards instead his or her friends and family, or those who provide bribes or other kickbacks.

But there is an even greater potential cost to the organization or to society. Consider that the abuse of power can lead to resistance and conflict from subordinate members, which, in turn, further thwarts the organization's goals. We note here that in assessing the impact of power, the primary focus has been on the downward impact of power—that is, the powerholder's impact on his or her subordinates. An important omission, then, is the assessment of the opposing force that is a direct consequence of the exertion of power—how the subordinate attempts to resist or subvert the power play. And make these attempts, they will—people have a very basic need to be treated fairly, and are strongly motivated to react against a system or treatment by individual members of that system when they perceive they are not being treated fairly (Tyler et al., 1997). As originally discussed by Lewin (1951) the power of A over B is not only a function of the maximum force exerted by A, but of the maximum resistance exerted by B on A as well (see also Cartwright, 1959). In some cases, this resistance force might appear to be minimal because the subordinate might not have any overt means with which to directly express their opposition (i.e., lack of a power base) or the situational context (e.g., cultural norms) might lead to the stifling of explicit resistance (see Coleman, 2000). However, even under these conditions resistance does occur; for example, it can take the form of an Islamic woman wearing Western clothing underneath the traditional veil (hijab) or the deliberate taking on of stereotypical roles (e.g., "the dumb Indian") to achieve one's own ends (Karp & Yoels, 1986, pp. 161–186).

Thus, when the powerholder uses his or her power in an unfair manner, to attain his or her own selfish goals, the relationship between the powerful and the powerless is no longer perceived as just, and so given the right opportunity the subordinates will attempt to engage in overt or covert resistance. On a societal level, this can lead to the establishment of popular movements and rebel organizations (e.g., the PLO and IRA; see Deutsch, 1973), and ultimately to revolution, where the powerholders are overthrown, often in a violent manner (as in the American, French, and Russian Revolutions, and in the more recent past the Philippines, Indonesia, and Eastern Europe).

WHO WILL ABUSE POWER?

But because power is, at essence, the ability to attain one's desired outcomes (Russell, 1938), at some level the goal of all members of an organization is the attainment of power. Thus, conflict between those with power and those without power is a direct consequence of the basic human motivation to achieve control over one's own outcomes (see Winter, 1973). There is evidence, in fact, that having power within a hierarchy and using that power are pleasurable at a physiological level in humans as well as other primates (Tiger, 1992, Ch. 7). Moreover, as argued by philosophers and psychologists such as Hobbes, Nietzsche, and Adler, one's sense of self-worth and self-esteem is intimately connected to the ability to achieve power (see Barge & Raymond, 1995). Adler (1928), for example, argued that "our guiding ideal is concretized as power over others, and this problem is too much in the foreground for everybody, overshadows all other problems, and directs all movements of our psychological life into its path" (p. 168).

The determining factor of whether an individual will abuse power is therefore not whether that person has a drive to gain and acquire power, because it would appear we all do, but rather the nature of the individual powerholder's important, self-defining goals (see Wicklund & Gollwitzer, 1982)—in other words, what the individual will want to *do* with that power. This depends on what the individual's important goals are. These can be selfish and attained only at the expense of others, but they can also be prosocial and overlap with the goals of the organization or society. Such individual differences in important goals are key components of our research into power abuse, described below.

CONSCIOUS AND NONCONSCIOUS CAUSES OF POWER ABUSE

In our analysis, the form the solution to the problem of corruption and power abuse takes depends on whether or not the misuse of power is an intentional, strategic, and knowing act on the part of the abuser. Certainly much power abuse for personal gain is deliberate, motivated by greed or desire for more power and dominance, and so on. It is therefore understandable that individuals want to have and to use power. Thus, power abuse is often a calculated risk on the part of the powerholder, a strategic attempt to get what one wants, with full realization of the impropriety of such activity and with full appreciation of the harm and costs to others.

For power abuse that happens with such impunity, with the individual knowingly pursuing self-centered goals at the expense of others, we have few remedies to offer. We direct the reader instead to the several chapters in this volume that have the underlying assumption that power abuse is driven by these intentional and strategic activities, so that legal and political solutions are recommended in order to thwart these individuals (e.g., Chen & Tyler, Jayawickrama, and Pratto & Walker, this volume). We deal here with a different form, one that we believe is actually far more insidious and prevalent—namely, the misuse of power by those who do not realize they are doing so, who at a conscious level believe that they are acting in an objective and fair minded manner and in the best interests of their subordinates.

In support of this assertion about relative prevalence, we cite the conclusion drawn by Fitzgerald (1993a) from her detailed analysis of the sexual harassment case literature, that three out of four "simply don't understand that they are harassers" (p. 22), don't perceive that they caused the victim any distress, and instead ascribe their behavior, which they acknowledge, to some more acceptable motive. We assert that this conclusion applies more generally about the relative prevalence of the two sources of power abuse.

In what follows we first make the case for the existence of nonconscious influences on one's judgments and behavior, and then focus more specifically on the nonconscious pursuit of one's important goals—evidence that it happens as well as research on the mechanism by which it occurs. We conclude by considering the different sources and determinants of power abuse, investigated at different levels of analysis, and the remedies that these different analyses suggest.

WHY GOOD INTENTIONS ARE NOT ENOUGH

We begin by pointing to literature indicating a disconnect or discontinuity between one's self-attributed motives and those that manifest themselves in implicit ways, such as on projective tests (McClelland, Koestner, & Weinberger, 1989). The correlation between these two methods of measuring motivations is essentially zero. For present purposes, this fact highlights the fact that people are often unaware of the motivations underlying their actions—not a new idea by any means (e.g., Freud, 1933) but one that has been strongly substantiated in recent research. Wilson and Brekke (1994), for example, concluded from their review of the relevant research that people are often if not usually not aware of the true reasons for their decisions and behaviors, relying instead on their theories of what should have caused them to respond the way they did. And research on stereotyping and prejudice commonly finds that implicit measures of racism and prejudice do not correlate well with self-report measures (e.g., Fazio et al., 1995; Greenwald & Banaji, 1995; Wittenbrink, Judd, & Park, 1997).

Thus there is reason to believe that individuals are not fully in touch with the reasons for their judgments and actions. What then is the basis for them, if not conscious choice and strategic, deliberate guidance? Several nonconscious sources of decisions and action control have been identified over the past decade or so (for reviews, see Bargh, 1997; Bargh & Chartrand, 1999; Bargh & Ferguson, 2000). Of these, two are of most relevance to the possibility of nonconscious abuse of power: those instigated by immediate, automatic evaluative and affective reactions to the people and events in one's current situation, and those driven by nonconsciously activated goals that have become linked to that situation over time.

Automatic Negative Evaluations of Subordinates

First, evaluations of social objects, including individual people, as either good or bad (liked or disliked) have been found to occur unintentionally and within a split second (e.g., Bargh et al., 1996; Fazio et al., 1986). Stereotyping of individuals has also been found to occur in this automatic fashion (see review in Bargh, 1999) and stereotypes are known to contain within them affective reactions or evaluations of the group (see Fiske, 1982; Fiske & Neuberg, 1990). For these two reasons, then, affective reactions to people on the basis of their social group can become active immediately and thus be a potential influence on how one decides to judge and behave towards them.

Indeed, Fazio et al. (1995) found these immediate evaluative reactions to African-American related stimuli to be the best predictor of actual subsequent behavior towards an African-American experimenter. However, because people are not aware of the automatic affective reaction, they misattribute it to other sources that are seen as plausible and reasonable (see Schwarz, 1990; Wilson & Brekke, 1994). In this way, powerholders can be nonconsciously biased in their evaluations and decision making regarding underlings for whom they have negative affective reactions, either because of their personal feelings for the individual (and vice versa) or their feelings towards the social group of which the subordinate is a member—yet they will tend to misattribute the negative feelings to some aspect of the person that would be a reasonable basis for them, such as job performance, their attitude, motivation level, and so on.

Automatic Activation and Operation of Goals

Power can also be misused because the mental concept of "having power" is associated strongly with one's own important goals. Power as a situational feature is likely to be linked to one's important strivings and goal pursuits because these situations are by definition the ones in which a person is able to get what he or she wants. Thus by the basic principle of mental association, namely the coactivation of mental representations (in this case the representation of the situation in which one has power and those for the goals one wants to pursue; see Bargh, 1990), strong and even automatic associations will form between those situations and those goals. The net result is that, over time, being in that situation of power is sufficient in itself to activate the goal, and put it into operation.

Following this logic, there are now several studies demonstrating the automatic activation and operation of goals (Bargh et al., 2000; Bargh et al., 1995; Chartrand, 2000; Chartrand & Bargh, 1996; Chen, Lee-Chai, & Bargh, 2001; Moskowitz et al., 1999). In two experiments, Chartrand and Bargh (1996) nonconsciously activated the information processing goal of forming an impression of someone for some but not other participants, through presenting participants with goal-relevant or control stimuli (e.g., judge, evaluate carrot, walk) in a first study ostensibly on language ability. Next, all participants were given the same explicit instructions to read each of a series of social behaviors because questions would be asked about them later. There was nothing in these instructions about forming an impression of the person, yet in both experiments those for whom the goal of impression formation had been primed showed signs of having done so, while those in the control condition did not. Moreover, participants showed no awareness of having pursued the nonconsciously activated goal.

Bargh et al. (2000) primed the goal to perform well for some participants, and not others in a control group, in four experiments. Not only did the experimental group outperform the other on the assigned verbal tasks, they also showed the classic signs of being motivated to attain high performance on the task (e.g., Lewin, 1935)—they were more likely to resume the task following a disruption, more likely to persist on it when obstacles were put in their way, and so on. Thus, behavioral as well as information processing goals can be activated and then operate in a nonconscious fashion, producing not only the same outcomes as do consciously pursued goals, but also the same motivational-state qualities.

Chartrand (2000) pushed the operational parallels between nonconscious and conscious goals still further, by showing that nonconscious goal pursuit also has the same self-evaluative consequences as does conscious goal pursuit following the attempt to attain the goal. Traditional research on conscious and intentional goal pursuit (e.g., Bandura, 1990, 1997; Heckhausen, 1991) has shown that succeeding versus failing to attain the desired goal has consequences for one's subsequent mood, as well as for one's degree of motivation to try for the goal again. Through similar goal priming manipulations as described above, Chartrand (2000) in three experiments found that people were in a better mood when they had succeeded at a goal they didn't even know they had, and a worse mood when they had failed, while the moods of participants in a control group who also succeeded rather than failed were unaffected. Moreover, goal primed participants subsequently worked on a similar task harder (and did better) following success than if they had previously failed, while subsequent task performance of nonprimed participants was no different whether they had previously succeeded or failed. Thus even to the point of the self-evaluative consequences of goal pursuit, nonconscious goals operate identically to consciously chosen and pursued goals.

Situational Power as the Automatic Trigger of One's Goals

These studies show that goals can become activated by relevant environmental features and then operate in the same way as they would have if consciously chosen, except that the individual is unaware of their operation and effect on their behavior. But what does this have to do with power use and abuse? A great deal. In a study of sexual harassment tendencies, Bargh, Raymond, et al. (1995) hypothesized that the concept of having power would have become automatically associated with the goal of sexuality for those participants with sexual harassment tendencies, and not for others. In other words, when in a situation where they have some form of power and control over an attractive woman, it was assumed that these men had frequently thought about and perhaps also pursued the goal of sexually attracting the woman—either through flirting, smiling, friendliness, or more overt means. The repeated pairing of situational power with pursuit of this goal would cause that goal to become, eventually, activated and pursued automatically, without conscious choice when the individual was in a position of power (see Bargh, 1990; Bargh & Chartrand, 1999).

In the first experiment, a sequential priming manipulation was used to demonstrate the automaticity of the power-sex association for men high in sexual harassment tendencies (as determined by the Attractiveness of Sexual Aggression (ASA) scale; Malamuth, 1989). For these men, but not for those scoring low on the ASA scale, the presentation of words related to power immediately and automatically activated the concept of sex (i.e., response times to sex related words were facilitated, even though there were not sufficient time to strategically prepare a response to them; see Bargh & Chartrand, 2000; Neely, 1977). The consequences of this automatic association between power and sex was further tested in the next experiment, in which the concept of power was surreptiously primed for some participants but not for others, after which all of them interacted with an attractive female confederate who was posing as a fellow participant. Men high in sexual harassment tendencies considered the woman to be more attractive and had a stronger desire to get to know her better if the concept of power had been primed versus not primed, whereas for men low in sexual harassment tendencies, the priming of the concept of power made no difference in their level of attraction to the female confederate.

These findings are in line with our model of nonconscious power abuse. Situational power features automatically activate those goals one has thought about and pursued in the past in situations where one is in a position of power. Over time, the connection between the mental representation of powerful situations and those goals becomes so strong that those goals become active and operate without the person consciously selecting those goals. In this way, one can pursue selfish and personal goals when one has relative power over another person, without knowing or realizing one is doing so.

The Bargh, Raymond, et al. (1995) studies afford one other important conclusion—that there are individual differences as to the automatic tendency to abuse power, because there are individual differences as to which goals are automatically associated with the concept of power. Those men low in sexual harassment tendencies showed no evidence of an automatic association between power and sex, and so their attraction towards a female confederate was unaffected by covert activation of the concept of power. While it is certainly possible that these men had personal or selfish goals other than sex automatically associated with the concept of power (e.g., greed, nepotism), it is also possible that power is not a universally corrupting situational feature, as some have argued (e.g., Kipnis, 1976). Rather, some people may take advantage of relative power to pursue their personal and selfish goals, while other people may not—indeed, they may instead become concerned with the responsible and scrupulous use of their official power.

Individual Differences in the Automatic Effects of Power

What type of person might be more likely than others to seek to use social power in a responsible and concerned manner? Chen, Lee-Chai, and Bargh (2001) reasoned that those with a communal relationship orientation (Clark & Mills, 1979) would be likely candidates, because communal, as opposed to exchange oriented relationships, are characterized by a selfless concern for the welfare of the other person (e.g., a parent towards his or her children). We hypothesized, therefore, that communally oriented individuals would have prosocial goals automatically associated with power, so that when the concept of power was nonconsciously activated, these people would become more, not less concerned with the welfare of others, and less, not more self-centered in their behavior. Exchange oriented participants, it was presumed, would react to power in the opposite manner.

In four experiments, it was indeed found that priming the concept of power caused communally oriented individuals to behave less selfishly and more generously towards others—such as by expressing more socially acceptable attitudes (e.g., egalitarianism) on questionnaires, and by taking the greater share of the assigned task workload from another participant—compared to the no priming condition. Exchange oriented participants, on the other hand, expressed more socially unacceptable attitudes (e.g., racism) and left the greater share of the task workload for the other participant to do, after the concept of power had been primed compared to not primed. These priming effects were observed not only with semantic (verbal) priming of the power concept but with naturalistic priming as well—as when one participant was assigned in an offhanded manner to sit at a professor's desk while completing the experimental tasks, while the other sat in the student's chair in front of that desk.

In sum, goals can be activated without conscious choice and awareness by the features of those situations in which the goals had been pursued often in the past. Once activated, goals guide behavior and information processing in the same way as if they had been consciously chosen. Power is a situational feature likely to be associated with goals because having power means having the ability to attain desired goals. Thus, as the research has shown, relative power within a situation causes the automatic activation of one's important goals and the individual's behavior is then guided towards those goals, often if not usually without the person being aware of this influence on his or her behavior. Importantly, however, there are individual differences as to whether one's important goals are selfish or prosocial. Power does not automatically produce its misuse; those who are communally oriented, for example, show even greater prosocial and nonselfish tendencies when in power than when not.

REMEDIES

The present volume is replete with different causes of power misuse, at several levels of analysis. The remedies suggested are a function, naturally, of the cause identified. At the level of international trade and commerce, Transparency International (Jayawickrama, this volume) takes the tendency of individuals towards corruption as a given and proposes legal remedies and solutions to make it more difficult to occur. At the level of society, Chen and Tyler (this volume) propose similar structural changes in U. S. society's double standard of criticizing and seeking to eliminate as unfair and nonegalitarian affirmative action policies that help minority groups and the relatively powerless, while at the same time not seeing much wrong with "affirmative action for the rich" in the form of, for example, "legacy" admissions to elite universities and movie roles for fledgling actors who happen to be the sons or daughters of famous actors and directors. Clearly the remedy here is a political one, to push for elimination of such inequitable advantages.

Again, these very valuable approaches take for granted the tendency for many people to misuse their position of greater power, as human nature if you will, and seek ways to constrain, inhibit, or prevent these tendencies from reaching fruition. Potential remedies for those of us analyzing corruption at the level of the individual powerholder are necessarily different in quality; unlike the systemic analyses, our remedies must be psychological or educational. Thus, at the individual level, Bugental (this volume) describes how erroneous beliefs about relative power within a relationship (e.g., parent-child, husband-wife) can serve as the faulty basis for ostensibly reasonable behavioral choices (e.g., use of one's superior physical size and strength). The research described above (see also Lee-Chai, Chen, & Chartrand, this volume) focuses on the intrapsychic link between having power within a situation, and one's personal and selfish goals. What kind of remedies are available here?

Certainly in the case of child or spouse abuse, to the extent it is identified and made known to the relevant societal organizations (i.e., police, social services), there is some potential for the perpetrator to receive counseling and therapeutic treatment that will focus, it is hoped given Bugental's substantial program of research, on changing the irrational and erroneous belief system regarding relative power within the relationship, and the inappropriateness in any event of physical force as a problem-solving option. The potential also exists with sexual harassers when they go too far and are exposed (as in the well known case of Senator Packwood) or decision makers when their conflict of interest is so obvious as to exceed the usually kept-to boundaries of plausible deniability (see Bargh & Raymond, 1995, pp. 86–87 for examples). But the percentage of those caught, especially in the latter cases, is very small, and after the fact solutions do not do much to decrease the prevalence of the problem.

For individuals who accept the fact of nonconscious goal pursuit and bias and who are motivated to do something about these possible tendencies, remedies based on the available research are certainly possible. One such remedy is to consider oneself strongly accountable for decisions affecting those over whom one has power (e.g., Tetlock & Kim, 1987), in that one should be able to explain to another person the reasons for one's decisions and behavior. This puts the conscious focus on the objective situation and on the causes and effects of one's own behavior. In the same vein, even a cursory examination of who stands to gain, and what exactly is the nature of the gain, for a course of action decided upon for a subordinate, can quickly alert one to situations where that course seems to be more in one's own best interests than the subordinate's.

But people are generally unwilling to accept the fact that one is not the sole captain of one's ship insofar as decision-making is concerned, and to combine this with an egalitarian orientation so strong as to motivate effortful vigilance over one's daily interactions with subordinates further restricts the likely scope of such a remedy (see Bargh, 1999). It is fine on a case by case basis but not likely to achieve large-scale amelioration of power abuse. Therefore, educational or "consciousness-raising" within organizations, and at the popular press and mass media level, would thus appear to be the best approach to substantial and large-scale change at the individual level. The idea is to make people aware, in a way similar to the consciousness-raising efforts in the 1960s and 1970s by civil rights and women's groups, of the possibility that they can tend to pursue their own personal goals when they have power over someone else. More than any program of psychological research demonstrating the nonconscious basis of much prejudicial bias,[1] the consciousness raising efforts of the liberation movements of the 1960s and 70s caused many people to understand that they could be biased without knowing of it.

But the liberation movements were successful in persuading large numbers of people about this possibility mainly because they could point to the actuarial facts: the very low numbers of African-Americans or women in law and medical schools, the very few in corporate management positions, and so on. The facts of discrimination were there, and faced with those along with their conscious beliefs of their own fairness and good intentions, there were few options for the decision makers responsible for the situation but to accept the possibility of nonconscious bias (i.e., given this situation of cognitive dissonance, this was the path of least resistance to resolving the discrepancy between word and deed).

Thus, research efforts to understand the psychological bases for power use and misuse must work in conjunction with those at the societal level (see Chen & Tyler, and Pratto & Walker, this volume; Sidanius & Pratto, 1999) in attempting to provide remedies for power misuse within organizations. The data those analyses provide at the societal level constitute the facts that powerholders must confront, and then attempt to reconcile with their presumed beliefs about their own egalitarian and objective values and intentions. The societal level analyses uncover the fact of the bias—that it occurs—and the psychological analysis provides further evidence of its mechanisms within the individual—how it occurs. The two approaches need each other to eventually make the necessarily persuasive pitch and raise the consciousness of the lay public to the fact that good intentions are not enough when it comes to being a perfect conduit of power.

---

1. The efforts of Anthony Greenwald, Mahzarin Banaji, and Brian Nosek to make their Implicit Association Test measure of nonconscious affective bias (e.g., Greenwald, McGhee, & Schwartz, 1998) widely known, through the website *www.yale.edu/implicit* as well as national network television news coverage, is a recent candidate for an exception to this rule.

CONCLUSIONS

Corruption and the misuse of power are widespread phenomena. They are one of the major, if not the major, threats to democratic government and the rule of law. But at the lower ends of the power hierarchies as well, in society as well as organizations, the abuse of power is a major obstacle in the way of many people's pursuit of happiness. Moreover, the diversion of official organizational power for the selfish ends of the powerholder is necessarily detrimental to the aims and goals of the organization or society.

This chapter's analysis of the psychological bases of power abuse began by noting the apparently universal need for power in one's life, so that need for power itself cannot explain why some people do, while others do not, abuse their power over others. Rather, this chapter highlighted the fact that individuals differ in their important and self-defining goals—with some having self-centered and others more prosocial goals. Finally, it was argued that these goals can become automated over time, so that they are pursued whenever the individual is in a position of relative power over someone, without that person being aware of choosing or pursuing that goal in that situation. Thus, the misuse of power cannot be prevented by a person's examination of his or her own purposes, and finding there only positive, good intentions towards others. As they say, the road to hell is paved with those.

REFERENCES

Adler, A. (1928). The psychology of power. In F. Kobler (Ed. and Trans.), *Gewalt und Gewaltlosigkeit: Handbuch des aktiven Pazifimus* (Violence and nonviolence: Handbook of active pacifism). Zurich: Rotapfel-Verlag.

A world full of phoney democracies (2000, June 24). *The Economist*, cover, pp. 17–18.

Bandura, A. (1990). Self-regulation of motivation through anticipatory and self-reactive mechanisms. In R. A. Dienstbier (Ed.), *Perspectives on motivation: Nebraska symposium on motivation* (Vol. 38, pp. 69–164). Lincoln, NE: University of Nebraska Press.

Bandura, A. (1997). *Self-efficacy.* New York: Freeman Press.

Bargh, J. A. (1990). Auto-motives: Preconscious determinants of thought and behavior. In E. T. Higgins & R. M. Sorrentino (Eds.), *Handbook of motivation and cognition* (Vol. 2, pp. 93–130). New York: Guilford Press.

Bargh, J. A. (1997). The automaticity of everyday life. In R. S. Wyer, Jr. (Ed.), *The automaticity of everyday life: Advances in social cognition* (Vol. 10, pp. 1–61). Mahwah, NJ: Erlbaum.

Bargh, J. A. (1999). The cognitive monster: The case against controllability of automatic stereotype effects. In S. Chaiken & Y. Trope (Eds.), *Dual process theories in social psychology* (pp. 361–382). New York: Guilford

Bargh, J. A., Chaiken, S., Raymond, P., & Hymes, C. (1996). The automatic evaluation effect: Unconditionally automatic attitude activation with a pronunciation task. *Journal of Experimental Social Psychology, 32,* 185–210.

Bargh, J. A., & Chartrand, T. L. (1999). The unbearable automaticity of being. *American Psychologist, 54,* 462–479.

Bargh, J. A., & Chartrand, T. L. (2000). The mind in the middle: A practical guide to priming and automaticity research. In H. Reis & C. Judd (Eds.), *Research methods for the social sciences* (pp. 253–285). New York: Cambridge University Press.

Bargh, J. A., & Ferguson, M. J. (2000). Beyond behaviorism: On the automaticity of higher mental processes. *Psychological Bulletin, 126.*

Bargh, J. A., Gollwitzer, P. M, Lee-Chai, A. Y., & Barndollar, K. (2000). *Bypassing the will: Nonconscious activation and operation of behavioral goals.* Unpublished manuscript, New York University.

Bargh, J. A., & Raymond, P. (1995). The naive misuse of power: Nonconscious sources of sexual harassment. *Journal of Social Issues, 26,* 168–185.

Bargh, J. A., Raymond, P., Pryor, J., & Strack, F. (1995). Attractiveness of the underling: An automatic power → sex association and its consequences for sexual harassment and aggression. *Journal of Personality and Social Psychology, 68,* 768–781.

Cartwright, D. (1959). A field theoretical conception of power. In D. Cartwright (Ed.), *Studies in social power.* Ann Arbor, MI: Institute for Social Research.

Chartrand, T. L. (2000). *Mystery moods and perplexing performance: Consequences of succeeding or failing at a nonconscious goal.* Unpublished manuscript, Ohio State University.

Chartrand, T. L., & Bargh, J. A. (1996). Automatic activation of impression formation and memorization goals: Nonconscious goal priming reproduces effects of explicit task instructions. *Journal of Personality and Social Psychology, 71,* 464–478.

Chen, S., Lee-Chai, A. Y., & Bargh, J. A. (in press). Relationship orientation as a moderator of the effects of social power. *Journal of Personality and Social Psychology, 80.*

Clark, M. S., & Mills, J. (1979). Interpersonal attraction in exchange and communal relationships. *Journal of Personality and Social Psychology, 37,* 12–24.

Coleman, P. T. (2000). Power and conflict. In M. Deutsch & P. T. Coleman (Eds.), *The handbook of conflict resolution: Theory and practice* (pp. 108–130). San Francisco, CA: Jossey-Bass.

Deutsch, M. (1973). *The resolution of conflict: Constructive and destructive processes.* New Haven, CT: Yale University Press.

Fazio, R. H., Jackson, J. R., Dunton, B. C., & Williams, C. J. (1995). Variability in automatic activation as an unobtrusive measure of racial attitudes: A bona fide pipeline? *Journal of Personality and Social Psychology, 69,* 1013–1027.

Fazio, R. H., Sanbonmatsu, D. M., Powell, M. C., & Kardes, F. R. (1986). On the automatic activation of attitudes. *Journal of Personality and Social Psychology, 50,* 229–238.

Fiske, S. T. (1982). Schema-triggered affect: Applications to social perception. In M. S. Clark & S. T. Fiske (Eds.), *Affect and cognition: The 17th annual Carnegie symposium on cognition* (pp. 55–78). Hillsdale, NJ: Erlbaum.

Fiske, S. T. (1993). Controlling other people: The impact of power on stereotyping. *American Psychologist, 48,* 621–628.

Fiske, S. T., & Neuberg, S. L. (1990). A continuum of impression formation, from category-based to individuating processing: Influences of information and motivation on attention and interpretation. In M. P. Zanna (Ed.), *Advances in experimental social psychology* (Vol. 23, pp. 1–74). New York: Academic Press.

Fitzgerald, L. F. (1993a). *The last great open secret: The sexual harassment of women in the workplace and academia.* Edited transcript of a Science and Public Policy Seminar presented by the Federation of Behavioral, Psychological, and Cognitive Sciences, Washington, D.C.

Fitzgerald, L. F. (1993b). Sexual harassment: Violence against women in the workplace. *American Psychologist, 48,* 1070–1076.

French, J. R. P. Jr., & Raven, B. (1959). The bases of social power. In D. Cartwright (Ed.), *Studies in social power* (pp. 150–167). Ann Arbor, MI: Institute for Social Research.

Freud, S. (1933). *New introductory lectures on psychoanalysis* (W. J. H. Sprott, Trans.). New York: Norton.

Greenhouse, S. (2000, January 21). Report details corruption within government union. *New York Times,* p. A1.

Greenwald, A. G., & Banaji, M. R. (1995). Implicit social cognition: Attitudes, self-esteem, and stereotypes. *Psychological Review, 102,* 4–27.

Greenwald, A. G., McGhee, D. E., & Schwartz, J. L. K. (1998). Measuring individual differences in implicit cognition: The Implicit Association Test. *Journal of Personality and Social Psychology, 74,* 1464–1480.

Gutek, B. (1985). *Sex and the workplace.* San Francisco: Jossey-Bass.

Heckhausen, H. (1991). *Motivation and action.* Berlin: Springer.

Is Europe corrupt? (2000, January 29). *The Economist*, pp. 57–59.

Karp, D. A. & Yoels, W. C. (1986). Power and stratification in everyday life: The politics of interaction. In D. A. Karp & W. C. Yoels (Eds.), *Sociology and everyday life* (pp. 161–186). Itasca, IL: F. E. Peacock.

Kipnis, D. (1976). *The powerholders*. Chicago: University of Chicago Press.

Lewin, K. (1935). *A dynamic theory of personality*. New York: McGraw-Hill.

Lewin, K. (1951). *Field theory in social science*. New York: Harper.

Malamuth, N. M. (1989). The attraction to sexual aggression scale: Part one. *Journal of Sex Research, 26*, 26–49.

McClelland, D. C., Koestner, R., & Weinberger, J. (1989). How do self-attributed and implicit motives differ? *Psychological Review, 96*, 690–702.

Moskowitz, G. B., Gollwitzer, P. M., Wasel, W., & Schaal, B. (1999). Preconscious control of stereotype activation through chronic egalitarian goals. *Journal of Personality and Social Psychology, 77*, 167–184.

Neely, J. H. (1977). Semantic priming and retrieval from lexical memory: Roles of inhibitionless spreading activation and limited-capacity attention. *Journal of Experimental Psychology: General, 106*, 226–254.

Petar Stoyanov, Bulgaria's gladiatorial president (2000, June 17). *The Economist*, p. 38.

Russell, B. (1938). *Power: A new social analysis*. New York: Norton.

Schwarz, N. (1990). Feelings as information: Informational and motivational functions of affective states. In E. T. Higgins & R. M. Sorrentino (Eds.), *Handbook of motivation and cognition* (Vol. 2, pp. 527–561). New York: Guilford Press.

Sidanius, J., & Pratto, F. (1999). *Social dominance: An intergroup theory of social hierarchy and oppression*. New York: Cambridge University Press.

Tetlock, P. E., & Kim, J. I. (1987). Accountability and judgment processes in a personality prediction task. *Journal of Personality and Social Psychology, 52*, 700–709.

Thibaut, J. W., & Kelley, H. H. (1959). *The social psychology of groups*. New York: Wiley.

Tiger, L. (1992). *The pursuit of pleasure*. New York: Little Brown.

Tyler, T. R., Boeckmann, R., Smith, H. J., & Huo, Y. J. (1997). *Social justice in a diverse society*. Boulder, CO: Westview.

What's wrong with nepotism, anyway? (1999, March 20). *The Economist*, p. 54.

Wicklund, R. A., & Gollwitzer, P. M. (1982). *Symbolic self-completion*. Hillsdale, NJ: Erlbaum.

Wilson, T. D., & Brekke, N. (1994). Mental contamination and mental correction: Unwanted influences on judgments and evaluations. *Psychological Bulletin, 116*, 117–142.

Winter, D. G. (1973). *The power motive*. New York: The Free Press.

Wittenbrink, B., Judd, C. M., & Park, B. (1997). Evidence for racial prejudice at the implicit level and its relationship with questionnaire measures. *Journal of Personality and Social Psychology, 72*, 262–274.

4

From Moses to Marcos

Individual Differences in the Use and Abuse of Power

ANNETTE Y. LEE-CHAI
SERENA CHEN
TANYA L. CHARTRAND

P ower is, perhaps, the ultimate Rorschach test—how one uses it often reflects one's personal values and beliefs. Thus, at one extreme might be
individuals who view power as an opportunity to better the lives of others
and improve society. And, at the other extreme might be individuals who view it
as a license to pursue selfish goals. We need only look at leaders throughout
history to see the diversity with which power has been used. For example, while
Moses used his power to lead the Hebrews from Egyptian slavery, Ferdinand
Marcos used his power in the Philippines to impose martial law and create a
government filled with corruption. While Abraham Lincoln labored to unite a
country torn by war and emancipate Blacks from slavery, Adolph Hitler com-
manded the invasion of countries and death to millions of gypsies and Jews.
And, while Nelson Mandela brought an end to Apartheid and is currently raising the living standards of Blacks in South Africa, Josef Mengela used his ranking to conduct unthinkable medical experiments on concentration camp in-
mates at Auschwitz.

It is evident, therefore, that power affects individuals in a variety of ways.
Contrary to the popular notion that power acts as a corrupting influence, for
some it is a cue for heightened social responsibility. But what are the factors
that are associated with socially benevolent, as opposed to self-serving, tendencies among individuals with power? Are certain individuals more prone to behave one way rather than the other? And is it possible to predict how an indi-

vidual will be affected by power? In this chapter, recent insights into individual differences in the effects of power are reviewed, and a new scale measuring the likelihood to misuse power is introduced.

POWER: A DANCE WITH THE DEVIL?

For centuries, philosophers, scientists, and laypersons alike have speculated about the corrupting influence of power. People in high places, they surmised, could not and should not be trusted. In 1887, Lord Acton declared his belief that "power corrupts, and absolute power corrupts absolutely." And today, surrounded by seemingly rampant reports of crooked government leaders, police brutality, and child abuse, people are quick to attribute destructive or selfish behavior by elite members of society to their powerful status.

It is this sentiment that echoed through early psychological research on social power and which was epitomized by Kipnis's (1976) work on the Metamorphic Effect. This effect refers to what he initially argued was the general and pervasive way that power changes people, inducing them to pursue selfish ends (see also Kipnis, 1972; Kipnis et al., 1976; Kipnis et al., 1981). Kipnis and colleagues theorized that because powerholders are typically in control of desired resources, they are likely to find their ideas and views readily agreed with by subordinates. Because of actor-observer differences in person perception (Jones & Nisbett, 1972), powerholders may be insensitive to the role that their power plays in producing such yea-saying, and may instead attribute it to the quality and value of their input. Consequently, they come to believe that their ideas and views are superior, implying that they are somehow special as compared to their subordinates, and thus perhaps deserving of the resources, privileges, and so forth that typically come with power. In this way, Kipnis and colleagues argued, powerholders may come to devalue the worth of their subordinates and perceive them as mere objects for manipulation in the service of the powerholders' own (more important) goals. Moreover, they may adjust their code of ethical behavior in order to rationalize such manipulation. Thus, over time, even the most well-intentioned individual has the potential to be corrupted by power.

Kipnis was not alone in his early view of power. Whether in the form of a personality variable (e.g., McClelland, 1975; Winter, 1973) or a situational variable, power has been linked to such vices as stereotyping (Fiske, 1993), sexual harassment (Brewer, 1982; Pryor, LaVite, & Stoller, 1993), sexual aggression (Groth, 1979), child abuse (Bugental et al., 1997), and self-destructive behavior (McClelland, 1987).

Contrary to its reputation, however, power is not a universally corruptive force, and to gain a position of power is not an automatic engagement to dance with the devil. After all, we often aspire to rise in the ranks, and when colleagues or friends are tapped for more powerful positions, they are often congratulated, not shunned. Therefore, at some level, though still wary of the metamorphosis some individuals seem to undergo, we must recognize that power has the potential to lead to positive, even socially beneficial, consequences. So, while power may lead to selfishness and moral deterioration in some, it may also lead to benevolence and moral fortification in others. The range of effects that power may have is wide, and scientific appreciation and interest in such individual differences are only recently emerging.

THE TRUTH ABOUT POWER REVEALED

The idea that individual differences might exist in the effects of power emerged early on in research on leadership behavior. In an effort to identify the behaviors that constitute effective leadership, Shartle (1961; see also Bales & Strodbeck, 1951; Cattell, 1951; Fiedler & Garcia, 1987; Likert, 1961) uncovered two basic types of leadership behavior. One behavior cluster, labeled "considerate behavior," included attending to the opinions of other group members and showing concern for the welfare of others. The second behavior cluster, labeled "initiation of structure in interaction," included assigning tasks and requiring that certain task standards be met. These two behavior sets, or interaction styles, were later linked to certain personality types. Specifically, through the development of the Least Preferred Coworker (LPC) scale, Fiedler and his colleagues (e.g., Fiedler & Chemers, 1984; Fiedler & Garcia, 1987) were able to identify and differentiate between leaders scoring high and low on the scale. Whereas individuals with low LPC scores are said to be focused on finishing a given task (high task motivation), those with high LPC scores are described as more concerned with relating to other group members (high relationship motivation).

In recent years, further empirical evidence regarding individual differences has accrued in various power-related domains. One such area is that of stereotyping, which Fiske and her colleagues (Fiske, 1993; Fiske & Dépret, 1996; Fiske & Morling, 1996; Goodwin et al., 2000; Goodwin, Operario, & Fiske, 1998) conceive of as one possible manifestation of power. According to their model, powerholders stereotype at times by default or passive means. That is, because powerholders' outcomes do not depend so much on the actions of subordinates (while the outcomes of subordinates depend heavily on the decisions of powerholders), powerholders are not likely motivated to devote much attention or effort to processing individuating information about their underlings. Powerholders may also simply be unable to carefully attend to individuating information about individual subordinates because of the sheer number of subordinates they must supervise. The model argues as well that powerholders may at times stereotype by design (Fiske & Dépret, 1996; Goodwin et al., in press; Goodwin et al., 1998). That is, they may use effortful and intentional strategies to perceive and interpret subordinates in stereotype-consistent ways. By doing so, they constrain the behavior of subordinates in ways that confirm and maintain their preconceived perceptions of others. Stereotyping by design essentially reflects the powerholder's motivation to confirm expectations and justify the use of power.

Research conducted in support of the model suggests that being other-oriented may play a role in individual differences in the effects of power. In particular, Goodwin, Gubin, et al. (2000) suggest that one's own sense of responsibility toward others may be a factor that moderates the power-stereotyping effect. Under the pretense that they were to review job applications, participants were placed either in a relatively powerful position (i.e., their inputs counted toward 30% of the final decision) or a powerless position (i.e., their inputs did not affect the final decision). Some participants also had their concept of responsibility preactivated or primed through completing the Humanitarian-Egalitarian Values Scale (Katz & Hass, 1988) prior to the application review task. As predicted, participants who were primed with responsibility related items, compared to those who were not, subsequently paid more attention to individuating applicant information, reflecting a decrease in their tendency to stereotype. Furthermore, trends in the data suggested that of the participants primed with responsibility, the majority of those who increased their attention to individuating information were in the high power condition. Thus, stereotyping need not be an inevitable result of power. Individuals who have developed feelings of responsibility towards others may possess a natural immunity to this aspect, at least, of power's effects.

More blatant forms of domination and power abuse are sexual aggression and sexual harassment, and research suggests that power and sex are indeed related (Bargh et al., 1995; Pryor & Stoller, 1994). Dominance motives, for instance, are present in men who are likely to sexually aggress. In both an incarcerated population of convicted rapists (Groth, 1979) and a nonincarcerated population (Lisak & Roth, 1988; Malamuth, 1986), tendencies toward sexual aggression have been found to be associated with power motives. Similarly, Pryor and his colleagues (Pryor, 1987; Pryor, LaVite, & Stoller, 1993; Pryor & Stoller, 1994) have demonstrated a cognitive association between the concepts of power and sex but, notably, only for individuals who are likely to sexually harass. More specifically, using a paired-associates memory task, Pryor and Stoller (1994) found that men with sexual harassment tendencies perceived an illusory correlation between power-related and sex-related words, yet this correlation was not exhibited by men without such tendencies. Other studies have demonstrated individual differences in behavior as well. For instance, when placed in situations in which they held power over a female subordinate (a confederate) by virtue of their role (e.g., golf instructor), men with sexual harassment tendencies touched the subordinate more often and expressed more sexualized comments than men without such tendencies (Pryor, 1987; Pryor et al., 1993).

Individual differences in the power-sex association are also apparent at the nonconscious level (see Bargh & Alvarez, this volume). Bargh et al. (1995) subliminally primed participants, who were first pretested on their tendencies to sexually harass and sexually aggress, with power-related words in a pronunciation task. They found that participants who were likely to sexually harass or sexually aggress were faster than participants without such tendencies to pronounce sex-related words immediately after being primed with power-related words. In other words, for these participants, activation of the power concept led to the automatic activation of the sex concept, enabling them to pronounce the sex-related words more quickly. A second study demonstrated that participants with tendencies toward sexual aggression were more likely to rate a female confederate as attractive after being primed with power-related words than with neutral words. There was no such effect on perception, however, for participants without sexual aggression tendencies. The concepts of power and sex were thus shown to be automatically associated, and therefore vulnerable to nonconscious activation, but only for individuals possessing sexual harassment or sexual aggression tendencies. Together with the findings of Pryor and his colleagues, these studies reveal one mechanism by which power can lead individuals to exhibit behaviors that are in line with sexual harassment and sexual aggression. They also reveal individual differences in power's effects on cognition, perception, and behavior.

Dean and Malamuth (1997) propose that individual differences in the proclivity to sexually aggress may be moderated by factors related to being other-oriented. Specifically, they argue that among males who are at a high risk of sexually aggressing, those who can be categorized as nurturant are less likely to actually sexually aggress, whereas those who are more self-centered are more likely to sexually aggress. Additionally, when their levels of empathy are low, men who tend to become aroused by witnessing sexual aggression are more likely to sexually aggress themselves. In contrast, when their levels of empathy are high, the link between arousal from witnessing sexual aggression and sexually aggressive behavior is diminished (Malamuth, Heavey, & Linz, 1993).

Together, these pieces of evidence from independent and diverse topics of study hint at the same conclusion: whereas some individuals in power may behave rather unscrupulously, without regard to the needs and feelings of those beneath them, others appear to behave in the opposite manner, with greater felt responsibility and consideration for their subordinates. Thus, some powerholders can end up stereotyping underlings—a selfish act, since it saves the powerholder the time and energy of processing another person's individuating information, while at the same time bolstering their own preconceived notions about the other. Powerholders with heightened feelings of responsibility, however, may take the necessary time to form individual, more accurate impressions. Similarly, some powerholders may sexually harass or coerce their underlings, reflecting the selfish pursuit of needs and desires without consideration of the impact such behavior will have on the victims. Yet those who possess feelings of nurturance and empathy may be less likely to take advantage of their elevated position to satisfy sexual goals. In summary, power seemingly promotes self-serving behavior for some and other-oriented behavior in others, and it is this difference that may eventually lead to the abuse or responsible use of power, respectively.

INDIVIDUAL DIFFERENCES IN RELATIONSHIP ORIENTATION AS A MODERATOR OF THE USE OF POWER

Although there is a relative wealth of research on the negative effects of power, studies that focus directly on positive effects are few, and only recently have efforts been made to study individual differences in power's use and abuse (see Dépret & Fiske, 1993, for a review). In their search for moderators, Chen, Lee-Chai, and Bargh (in press) investigated the role of individual differences in relationship orientation in understanding the effects of power. They reasoned that powerholders' behavior toward subordinates may extend logically from the ways they tend to relate to others in general. Chen and her colleagues chose to examine communal and exchange relationship orientations, first proposed by Clark and Mills (1979).

According to Clark and her colleagues (Clark & Mills, 1979; Clark, Mills, & Powell, 1986; Clark et al., 1987; Mills & Clark, 1982), individuals differ in their communal and exchange orientations to varying degrees. Individuals with a strong communal orientation are generally concerned with other people's welfare; benefits are given in response to others' needs without any specific expectation of benefits in return. Individuals with a strong exchange orientation, on the other hand, are typically unconcerned with others' welfare per se; rather, the focus is on the fair exchange of benefits, which are given with the specific expectation of receiving something comparable in return or as payment for a benefit previously received.

Considerable research supports the distinction between communal and exchange orientations. Individuals with communal orientations, for example, have been shown to lend help to others more than individuals with exchange orientations (Clark, Ovellette, et al., 1987). Even when actual helping is not possible, communal individuals keep track of the needs of the other more often than exchange individuals (Clark, Mills, et al., 1986). Moreover, communal individuals report feeling better if they have helped another than if they had not (Williamson & Clark, 1989, 1992). Communal individuals, therefore, appear to have a chronic goal to respond to others' needs or to be socially responsible. Accordingly, their personal goals and interests may often be in accord with the goals and interests of others (see also Triandis, 1995).

Individuals with exchange orientations, on the other hand, display a more favorable reaction than communal individuals to being given immediate compensation for a benefit given (Clark & Mills, 1979). And if not repaid, these individuals tend to feel that they have been exploited (Clark & Waddell, 1985). Additionally, when working on a joint task that will lead to a reward, exchange individuals are more likely to keep track of each person's input (Clark, 1984). Together, these studies show that exchange individuals tend to be more focused on making sure they are being treated fairly than on helping others and responding to their needs. They wish neither to be owed a personal favor, nor to owe a favor to another individual. Exchangers, therefore, appear to have a chronic goal to pursue more self-oriented goals, and this focus on the self may not, at times, coincide with the interests of others.

Regardless of their different relational pursuits, power may serve to heighten the goals and interests of communals and exchangers by making the resources necessary to attain one's goals more readily available. Furthermore, for communals, being in a position of power may imply that those without power have a greater need for benefits than the self. As a result, communal powerholders may feel a desire to respond to the needs of those who are dependent on them (Berkowitz & Daniels, 1963). In contrast, for exchangers, being in a position of power may imply that they have more to offer, and are thus more deserving of benefits, in relationship exchanges. They may therefore perceive it is as fair and appropriate to focus primarily on benefits for the self.

TESTING THE RELATIONSHIP ORIENTATION—POWER INTERACTION

Chen and her colleagues (in press) theorized that individuals who are primarily communal tend to be more socially responsible than individuals who are primarily exchange oriented, and that this difference would be amplified when these individuals are placed in a position of power. In their depiction of the socially responsible personality, Berkowitz and Lutterman (1968) argued that socially responsible people are highly involved in their society and adhere to cultural norms. In one study, therefore, Chen and her colleagues reasoned that communals, compared to exchangers, would be more likely to present themselves as followers of social norms, particularly when in power (Chen et al., in press, Study 2). They may desire to be, as it were, ideal citizens or role models for others. In the study, pairs of participants who were primarily communal or exchange were brought to a professor's office. One participant in each pair was casually guided to sit behind the professor's desk while the other was guided to sit in the guest chair directly across from the desk. With this seating arrangement, participants were contextually primed with either power (professor's desk) or powerlessness (guest chair) (see Bargh, 1989, 1992, 1994). Participants completed two scales that either directly or indirectly measured social responsibility. One scale was the Marlowe Crowne Social Desirability scale (Crowne & Marlowe, 1964), and the other was the Modern Racism Scale (McConahay, 1986). The first scale measures respondents' concerns with social approval and acceptance directly, whereas the latter does so indirectly (endorsing racist beliefs on the Modern Racism Scale is likely to be perceived as inviting social disapproval). As predicted, communally oriented individuals exhibited a greater concern with social responsibility when primed with power than with a relative lack of power. That is, they had higher Social Desirability scale scores and expressed less racist (i.e., more socially acceptable) opinions on the Modern Racism Scale when sitting in the power chair. Exchange oriented individuals, meanwhile, had a tendency to exhibit less concern with social responsibility when primed with power than with powerlessness. They tended to exhibit less direct concern with social desirability and to express more racist attitudes.

In subsequent study, Chen and her colleagues examined the effect of power on the behavior of communally versus exchange oriented individuals (Chen et al., in press, Study 3). Once again, communal and exchange participants were primed with the concepts of power and powerlessness via their seating arrangement in a professor's office. This time, only one participant was brought to the office at a time. However, each participant was led to believe that a second participant was also scheduled for the session but was running late. While waiting, the experimenter explained that ten exercises from a list would be divided between the two participants for each to complete. Then, after waiting several minutes for the fictitious other participant to arrive, the experimenter asked the participant to peruse the list of exercises and select five, adding that whichever ones he or she did not choose would be left for the other participant to complete. The list of exercises, which was made to appear as if it were originally intended for only the experimenter's reference, contained information about each exercise, including the length of time required to complete it. Participants were told that they were free to leave once they completed the five exercises they chose for themselves. The amount of time participants committed to via their five exercise choices was taken as a measure of socially responsible versus self-serving behavior. That is, opting to complete the longer exercises meant sacrificing one's own time and benefiting the other participant, whereas choosing the shorter exercises meant being able to leave the experiment earlier, but at the other participant's expense. As predicted, communal and exchange participants were influenced by the power cues to make their choices in opposing ways. While communal participants chose more of the longer exercises for themselves when primed with the concept of power versus powerlessness, exchange participants chose more of the shorter exercises when primed with the concept of power versus powerlessness.

Lee-Chai and Bargh (2000) demonstrated that these findings are not merely brief, initial effects but differences that persist over time. Additionally, whereas the Chen et al. (in press) studies used subtle contextual cues to nonconsciously prime power and powerlessness, Lee-Chai and Bargh (2000) showed that these effects hold even when participants are fully aware of their power over others. For their study, communal and exchange participants were recruited through job advertisements in the university paper. They were hired to serve as supervisors in a data collection project that spanned ten weeks. Each participant supervised the work of two subordinates, who in actuality were fictitious, and communicated with them through electronic messages. While one subordinate was cheerful, thorough, and prompt, the other tended to be curt, sloppy, and tardy. Periodically throughout the 10 weeks, participants agreed to complete various scales to help the principal investigator with a purported ancillary project. These scales included several power-related measures: the Social Dominance Orientation scale (Pratto et al., 1994), Machiavellianism IV scale (Christie & Geis, 1970), and Misuse of Power scale (see below for a more full description). Participants also completed biweekly evaluations of their subordinates, monitored the work of their subordinates, and made decisions regarding payment to subordinates.

Consistently throughout the 10-week period, communal supervisors were less likely than exchange supervisors to view power as an opportunity to dominate and pursue selfish goals, as evidenced by lower scores on the Social Dominance Orientation, Machiavellianism IV, and Misuse of Power scales. Moreover, trends in the data suggested that these differences between communal and exchange supervisors became more pronounced over time, rather than dwindling as some may have speculated. In terms of supervisory behaviors and judgments, communal supervisors monitored their subordinates more thoroughly than exchange supervisors, checking their work more often for errors and logging onto their e-mail accounts more frequently to check for correspondences from them. Such greater attention to subordinates by communal supervisors was also reflected by their evaluations of them. Communal supervisors differentiated their two subordinates to a greater degree than exchange supervisors. Thus, the good subordinate received a much more positive evaluation than the poor subordinate. Finally, when asked to divide bonus money among group members, communal supervisors tended to keep less of the cash award for themselves than did exchange supervisors. In general, communal supervisors were more responsible in their role than exchange supervisors.

These studies show that whether individuals use their power for social good or selfish gain may depend, in part, on their chronic relationship orientations. Individuals who are primarily communal are chronically motivated to respond to the needs of others. Power may simply better enable them to fulfill this need. Individuals who are primarily exchangers, meanwhile, are chronically motivated to protect their own interests. They may view power as an opportunity to pursue self-interests more fully when resources are more available.

Though recent studies suggest that relationship orientation may be one way to predict the nature of power's effects over a particular individual, there may be more direct methods of assessment. Relationship orientation, after all, is concerned with rules of interaction more generally and does not specifically speak to power dynamics. Moreover, although an adherence to exchange rules might make one more inclined to pursue self-oriented goals when in power, it is not intended to be synonymous with exploitation and corruption. To be sure, self-oriented goals are not the only goals pursued by exchangers, and not all self-oriented goals conflict with the goals of others. Additionally, when power differences are minimal in an interpersonal relationship, exchange oriented individuals tend to be primarily concerned with equity and fairness. Thus, we created a new measure in an effort to better predict individual differences in the likelihood to misuse power. Moreover, because fewer measures of power exploitation exist than measures of social responsibility, and because of the greater urgency revolving around the detection of potential abusers, this measure focuses on the attitudes, beliefs, and behaviors that we believe abusive powerholders are likely to hold.

THE MISUSE OF POWER SCALE

Tendencies to misuse power, by definition, are behaviors that emerge only under circumstances in which the individual holds power, whether it be in the form of behavioral control or fate control (Thibaut & Kelley, 1959), or based on factors such as expertise, reward capability, coercion, legitimacy, or reference (French & Raven, 1959). The misuse of power also requires that the individual hold certain beliefs about entitlement and dominance and have somewhat cavalier attitudes toward propriety. Thus, it is distinct from conceptually similar variables, such as Machiavellianism (Christie & Geis, 1970), which addresses one's beliefs that others may be manipulated for self-gain and which may manifest itself regardless of the individual's power status. The misuse of power is also distinct from Social Dominance Orientation (Pratto et al., 1994), which focuses on beliefs in the inequality of social groups, and that one's own group is superior to outgroups. It is, more or less, a hybrid of these variables within a power context, and one that speaks directly to interpersonal situations in which one individual has the ability to influence the behavior or control the outcomes of the other. It is this essence that Lee-Chai and Chartrand (2000) attempted to capture with the Misuse of Power scale.

Construction of the Misuse of Power Scale

Many of the items on the Misuse of Power scale (MOP) were intended to measure general attitudes toward the misuse of power (e.g., Darwin's "survival of the fittest" not only applies to biological evolution, but also to society; if people did not break the rules every now and then, society would remain stagnant). Some items, however, addressed a variety of specific goals that may be associated with power. For instance, an individual may misuse power in order to gain monetary or material gains (e.g., It is acceptable for people in high positions to take liberties with their company's fringe benefits as a form of extra compensation), to gain status or prestige (e.g., Sometimes it is better to hire a less qualified applicant to protect one's level of superiority), to exact revenge or alleviate personal distress (e.g., Under the constant pressures of a high-powered job, it is understandable if one occasionally takes out a bad mood on one's employees), or to influence another individual's attitudes or behavior (e.g., It's good to have at least one friend who can be easily manipulated and coaxed into doing just about anything). Many of the items reflected a blatant disregard for ethical rules of conduct and the consequences of one's behavior on others. Items for the initial version of the MOP were generated independently by three researchers and were based in part on words associated with power that were solicited from undergraduates in a pretest. The initial version of the MOP consisted of 49 critical Likert items and 11 fillers. Respondents were asked to rate their agreement with each statement on a scale from 1 (disagree strongly) to 9 (agree strongly).

Once all potential items had been amassed, they were administered to 133 undergraduates (49 males, 84 females) at New York University who were enrolled in an introductory psychology course and who received credit toward a course requirement. Participants were told that the purpose of the study was to pretest various measures for several different researchers in the psychology department. One of these measures was the MOP.

As previously noted, the misuse of power is likely to be related to beliefs in the social dominance of certain groups over others, the inherent goodness or evil in human nature, and the morality of manipulating others for personal benefit. In addition, one's general likelihood to misuse power should be reflected in one's tendencies to misuse power in specific situations, such as in cases of sexual harassment or sexual aggression. Several scales, therefore, were administered with the MOP in order to assess convergent validity: Social Dominance Orientation scale (SDO), Philosophies of Human Nature scale (PHN, Wrightsman, 1964), which includes the subscales of cynicism and trust; Machiavellianism IV scale (Mach); and Right Wing Authoritarianism scale (RWA, Altemeyer, 1981), which measures one's attitudes toward authority and obedience. In addition, measures involving specific situations of the misuse of power were included: Likelihood to Sexually Harass scale (LSH, Pryor, 1987), which includes items assessing the likelihood that respondents would engage in blatant, quid pro quo sexual harassment, as well as more subtle forms of sexual harassment such as using one's power to secure a date with another individual, and Attractiveness of Sexual Aggression (ASA, Malamuth, 1989a, 1989b) scale, which measures one's likelihood to rape or sexually force another individual.

The researchers also measured the likelihood that participants would commit exploitative or self-serving behaviors by administering a measure containing 16 scenarios. These scenarios were used to assess predictive validity for the MOP scale. Each scenario asked participants to imagine themselves in a position in which they held power. The form of power varied from reward power to coercive power to legitimate power (see French & Raven, 1959). In each situation, participants could use their power to attain selfish gains or take certain liberties. Participants were asked to assume that no matter what the behavior, nothing bad would be likely to happen as a result of their action. A sample scenario reads as follows:

> Imagine you have been elected as student body president. As president, it is up to you to decide which campus organizations get to hold certain activities. One day, a fraternity asks for your authorization to hold a social activity. However, their agenda goes against a few school policies, and you tell them your concerns. In response, the fraternity offers you $500 to overlook the policy infractions and authorize their application. How likely are you to do the following: a) accept their offer and authorize their activity; b) ignore their offer and reject their application for the activity; c) report the proposed bribe to the University Judiciary Board?

Participants rated the likelihood of each behavior on a 5-point Likert scale (1 = not at all likely, 5 = very likely).

Participants completed the MOP and other power-related scales over two sessions. In the first session, participants were given the SDO, PHN, Mach, and RWA scales, interspersed with three filler scales unrelated to power. Half of all participants received the measures in the above order, while the other half received them in reverse order. One week later, participants returned for the second session, during which they completed the MOP, scenarios, LSH, and ASA scales. The items on the MOP were administered both in a forward and reverse order. Whereas the MOP and the scenarios alternated for which was presented first, the LSH and ASA scales were always administered last due to their graphic nature.

After adjusting for reversed items, responses were averaged across the 49 critical items on the MOP. The mean score was 2.92, with a standard deviation of .85. The MOP was first subjected to an analysis of variance to test for the effects of sex and order. Because gender effects are generally found on other power-related scales such as the SDO, RWA, LSH, and ASA, we expected to find a gender effect on the MOP as well. As predicted, the analysis of variance revealed a significant main effect of sex, $F(1, 129) = 19.81$, $p < .001$, with males ($M = 3.18$) exhibiting higher scores than females ($M = 2.76$). The order of items was not significant, nor was there an interaction between sex and order.

For all 49 items, the reliability coefficient reached .89. In order to create a shortened, more manageable version of the scale, items that had item total correlations of at least .40 were culled. These 18 items, which are listed in Table 4.1, have a coefficient alpha of .87. The mean score on the 18-item version was 2.76, with a standard deviation of .44.

A factor analysis was then conducted on the 18 items of the shortened MOP. A principal components analysis with varimax rotation satisfactorily yielded one main factor that accounted for 32.4% of the variance. The eigenvalue for this factor was 5.84 with the next largest factor carrying an eigenvalue of 1.58 and only 8.8% of the variance. Item loadings on the main factor ranged from .25–.68. These results confirm that the 18 items of the shortened MOP measure a single variable with adequate reliability.

Convergent and Predictive Validity

Participants' responses on the SDO, PHN, Mach, RWA, LSH, and ASA scales were used to assess convergent validity for the MP scale. The 18-item version was used for all analyses. Furthermore, the PHN was broken down into its Cynicism and Trust subscales, since past research has revealed only a moderately negative correlation between these two subscales (Wrightsman, 1964). Additionally, the items on the Trust subscale were reversed and will hereafter be referred to as the Distrust scale.

A correlation matrix was generated for all power-related measures (see Table 4.2). The MOP correlated positively with all other power-related scales at

TABLE 4.1. Items on the Misuse of Power Scale

1. People who have spent their lives working their way up the corporate ladder have earned the right to bend the rules here and there once they finally get to the top.
2. There is nothing wrong with occasionally taking credit for one of your subordinates' ideas, since they will be doing the same to their subordinates in due time.
3. It is not acceptable for people in high positions to take liberties with their company's fringe benefits as a form of extra compensation.
4. One should always take advantage of any opportunity that comes one's way, regardless of the consequences for others.
5. It is unacceptable to shift the blame for a bad idea onto a subordinate, even though his or her career would not be jeopardized by the mistake like yours would.
6. Greed is beneficial, since it helps to increase one's productivity.
7. Given enough opportunities, everyone can be corrupted.
8. It is wrong for people to try to take advantage of each other.
9. If I had the opportunity to sue another individual, I would sue for all the money he or she was worth.
10. It is not right for physically stronger people to try to intimidate weaker people for personal gains.
11. Rules are not meant to be broken, even if no one finds out, and no one is directly hurt.
12. It is never acceptable to deceive one's subordinates, even when the truth will tarnish one's reputation as a leader.
13. Those who allow others to walk all over them deserve what they get.
14. It is unacceptable to push your opinions on others, even if those people never seem to form coherent opinions of their own.
15. The best method of getting your way with someone is to make him or her feel guilty.
16. People in high positions have not earned the right to receive special treatment.
17. One should take care not to step on people on the way to the top.
18. It's good to have at least one friend who can be easily manipulated and coaxed into doing just about anything.

a significant level ($ps \leq .001$), except for Distrust ($r = -.11$, ns). Correlation coefficients ranged from $+.30$ with RWA to $+.63$ with SDO. The MOP, therefore, conceptually resembles other measures related to power without being completely redundant. Surprisingly, Distrust correlated only slightly or not at all with the other power-related measures, suggesting that dominating or taking

TABLE 4.2. Correlations Coefficients for the MOP
and Power-Related Measures

	MOP	SDO	Distrust	Cynicism	Mach	RWA	LSH	ASA
MOP	1.00							
SDO	.63°°	1.00						
Distrust	−.11	−.05	1.00					
Cynicism	.37°°	.17°	.12	1.00				
Mach	.60°°	.47°°	.18°	.47°°	1.00			
RWA	.30°°	.38°°	−.14	.28°°	.20°	1.00		
LSH	.39°°	.40°°	−.01	.31°°	.38°°	.22°	1.00	
ASA	.32°°	.42°°	.06	.27°°	.34°°	.13	.55°°	1.00

°$p < .05$
°°$p < .01$

advantage of less powerful others requires an element of trust, perhaps that the other will not rebel or betray their subordinate position. At the same time, however, cynicism does positively correlate with other power-related measures. Thus, while not wholly distrustful of others, individuals who are likely to misuse power tend to be cynical about human nature.

In a second analysis, the researchers correlated the MOP with an indirect measure of the use of power, the Communal and Exchange Orientation scales. Communal and exchange scores were obtained for 113 of the participants. At the beginning of the semester, students in the introductory psychology course had completed a battery of scales, including the Communal and Exchange Orientation scales, for preselection purposes. The MOP correlated negatively with the Communal Orientation scale, $r = -.40$, $p < .001$, and positively with the Exchange Orientation scale, $r = +.23$, $p = .015$. Furthermore, an analysis of variance comparing participants who were primarily communal to those who were primarily exchange confirmed that communal participants had significantly lower MOP scores ($M = 2.21$) than exchange participants ($M = 3.09$), $F(1, 66) = 24.85$, $p < .001$. Thus, mirroring the results of Chen and her colleagues (in press) and Lee-Chai and Bargh (2000), communal individuals had a lower likelihood of misusing power than exchange individuals.

Scores on the scenarios were next summed to assess predictive validity for the MOP. For each scenario, only the behavior that reflected a misuse of power was included in the calculations. Scores for the scenarios correlated strongly with scores on the MOP, $r = +.53$, $p < .001$. However, compared to the MOP, the scenarios had a weaker negative correlation with communal scores ($r = -20$, $p = .04$) and did not correlate with exchange scores ($r = .09$, ns), suggesting that communal and exchange orientations may not predict scores on the power-related scenarios as well as scores on the MOP. Because correlations between the MOP and RWA, SDO and Mach were strong, we conducted an analysis to confirm that the MOP holds predictive value above and beyond these other power-related measures. Scores on the MOP were regressed onto scores from the scenarios after first entering scores on the RWA, SDO, and Mach in the analysis. The three power-related measures, combined, accounted for 31.25% of the variance, with the MOP accounting for an additional 4.51% of the variance, $p = .03$ ($b = .20$, $t(113) = 2.82$, $p < .01$). Thus, it appears that the MOP provides a contribution to the prediction of power abuse tendencies separate from the RWA, SDO, and Mach scales.

Together, these analyses demonstrate preliminary evidence for the usefulness of the Misuse of Power scale in predicting selfish, inappropriate behavior by powerful individuals. This evidence is bolstered even more by the effectiveness of the MOP in reflecting differences between communal and exchange powerholders in the longitudinal study of power, described earlier (Lee-Chai & Bargh, 2000). Further testing of the Misuse of Power scale, however, is needed in both laboratory and field settings to better evaluate the predictive value of the new measure. In these early studies, administration of the MOP and scenarios in close succession may have led participants to be concerned with consistency in their responses, thus enhancing the effectiveness of the MOP to predict abusive tendencies in the scenarios. Additionally, though the scenarios were of common, plausible situations to which undergraduates could easily relate, responses may not have fully reflected actual behavior. Future testing of the MOP begs for a study in which participants actually have the opportunity to misuse their powerful status for selfish gain.

CONCLUSION

Just as there is more than one way to skin a cat, there is more than one way to detect individual differences in the use and misuse of power. Goodwin et al. (2000) found that feelings of responsibility moderated the power-related behavior of stereotyping. Dean and Malamuth (1997) argue that individuals with more self-centered personalities are more likely to sexually aggress, whereas those who are more nurturant are less likely to sexually aggress. The Chen et al. (in press) and Lee-Chai and Bargh (2000) studies suggest that communal and exchange orientations may moderate the effects of power, leading to either prosocial, responsible gestures or more self-oriented aims. And the creation of the Misuse of Power scale, which reflects the pursuit of selfish goals and disregard for the welfare of others, potentially provides a more direct method of detecting individual differences in the use of power.

Despite their diversity, these varying methods of detection share two common factors. First, it should be noted that much of the research reviewed in this chapter has approached the question of power from a Person × Situation angle. In other words, the researchers have proposed that the effect of the situation is likely to differ depending on various individual differences. The presence of power cues in the environment interacts with personality variables, such as nurturance or relationship orientation, to produce effects, whether they be positive or negative.

Second, each research points to the direction of one's primary focus, whether it be toward selfish interests or the interests of others, as a moderator for power's effects. When an individual's own needs and interests receive primary attention, chances increase that the needs and interests of others, both physical and emotional, become overlooked or blatantly disregarded. On the other hand, when the needs and interests of others receive primary attention, it becomes less likely that others will suffer negative consequences as a result of an individual's actions. It does not necessarily follow, however, that if the needs and interests of others receive primary attention, one's own needs and interests become neglected. Just as Clark and Mills (1993) argued in their depiction of the communal orientation, meeting the needs of others may simultaneously meet one's own needs as well as the needs of others. In other words, since the goal to benefit others is also a personal goal, meeting one automatically meets the other.

Of course, investigating self-focus versus other-focus may not be the only route to predicting the use or misuse power. Other possibilities include perceptions of ingroup versus outgroup, perceptions of the self as distinctive versus nondistinctive, or collective versus individualistic tendencies (see also Gardner & Seeley, this volume). Further research is needed to broaden our understanding of factors that promote and prevent the misuse of power.

Possession of such knowledge may prove useful in the fight against corruption, with applications possible in virtually any realm involving hierarchical structures. Political offices, government employees, militaries, police academies, and businesses are only a few areas that might benefit from the information. Care must be taken, however, to ensure that knowledge of an individual's proclivities in situations of power is not itself misused. After all, predictive measures are never entirely accurate, and tendencies toward the abuse of power do not guarantee eventual behavior. Rather than adopting an attitude of prevention, it may be wiser to adopt an attitude of promotion. That is, rather than testing individuals and convicting them before any crime is committed, it would be more ethical and prudent to establish programs that train individuals in becoming more other-focused. Such programs are already underway in the form of sensitivity training in major corporations for individuals who exhibit abusive behavior toward others. Regardless of the form of training, there is no doubt that efforts to curb the misuse of power must be made worldwide.

REFERENCES

Altemeyer, B. (1981). *Right-wing authoritarianism.* Winnipeg: University of Manitoba Press.

Bales, R. F., & Strodbeck, F. L. (1951). Phases in group problem solving. *Journal of Abnormal Social Psychology, 46,* 485–495.

Bargh, J. A. (1989). Conditional automaticity: Varieties of automatic influence in social perception and cognition. In J. S. Uleman & J. A. Bargh (Eds.), *Unintended thought* (pp. 3–51). New York: Guilford Press.

Bargh, J. A. (1992). Being unaware of the stimulus versus unaware of its effect: Does subliminality per se matter to social psychology? In R. Bornstein & T. Pittman (Eds.), *Perception without awareness* (pp. 236–258). New York: Guilford Press.

Bargh, J. A. (1994). The Four Horsemen of automaticity: Intention, efficiency, awareness, and control as separate issues in social cognition. In R. S. Wyer & T. K Srull (Eds.), *Handbook of social cognition* (2nd ed., Vol. 1, pp. 1–40). Hillsdale, NJ: Erlbaum.

Bargh, J. A., Raymond, P., Pryor, J., & Strack, F. (1995). Attractiveness of the underling: An automatic power ←→ sex association and its consequences for sexual harassment and aggression. *Journal of Personality and Social Psychology, 68,* 768–781.

Berkowitz, L., & Daniels, L. R. (1963). Responsibility and dependency. *Journal of Abnormal and Social Psychology, 66,* 429–436.

Berkowitz, L., & Lutterman, K. (1968). The traditionally socially responsible personality. *Public Opinion Quarterly, 32,* 169–185.

Brewer, M. B. (1982). Further beyond nine to five: An integration and future directions. *Journal of Social Issues, 38,* 149–158.

Bugental, D. B., Lyon, J. E., Krantz, J., & Cortez, V. (1997). Who's the boss? Differential accessibility of dominance ideation in parent-child relationships. *Journal of Personality and Social Psychology, 72,* 1297–1309.

Cattell, R. B. (1951). New concepts for measuring leadership in terms of group syntality. *Human Relations, 4,* 161–184.

Chen, S., Lee-Chai, A., & Bargh, J. A. (in press). Relationship orientation as a moderator of the effects of social power. *Journal of Personality and Social Psychology.*

Christie, R. & Geis, F. (1970). *Studies in*

Machievallianism. New York: Academic Press.

Clark, M. S. (1984). Record keeping in two types of relationships. *Journal of Personality and Social Psychology, 47,* 549–557.

Clark, M. S., & Mills, J. (1979). Interpersonal attraction in exchange and communal relationships. *Journal of Personality and Social Psychology, 37,* 12–24.

Clark, M. S. & Mills, J. (1993). The difference between communal and exchange relationships: What it is and what is not. *Personality and Social Psychology Bulletin, 19,* 684–691.

Clark, M. S., Mills, J., & Powell, M. (1986). Keeping track of needs in communal and exchange relationships. *Journal of Personality and Social Psychology, 51,* 333–338.

Clark, M. S., Ouellette, R., Powell, M., & Milberg, S. (1987). Recipients' mood, relationship type, and helping. *Journal of Personality and Social Psychology, 53,* 94–103.

Clark. M. S., & Waddell, B. (1985). Perception of exploitation in communal and exchange relationships. *Journal of Social and Personal Relationships, 2,* 403–413.

Crowne, D. P. & Marlowe, D. (1964). A new scale of social desirability independent of psychopathology. *Journal of Consulting Psychology, 24,* 349–401.

Dean, K. E., & Malamuth, N. M. (1997). Characteristics of men who aggress sexually and of men who imagine aggressing: Risk and moderating variables. *Journal of Personality and Social Psychology, 72,* 449–455.

Dépret, E., & Fiske, S. T. (1993). Social cognition and power: Some cognitive consequences of social structure as a source of control deprivation. In G. Weary, F. Gleicher, & K. L. Marsh (Eds.), *Control motivation and social cognition* (pp. 176–202). New York: Springer-Verlag.

Fiedler, F. E., & Chemers, M. M. (1984). *Improving leadership effectiveness: The leader match concept* (2nd ed.). New York: Wiley.

Fiedler, F. E., & Garcia, J. E. (1987). *New approaches to effective leadership: Cognitive resources and organizational performance.* New York: Wiley.

Fiske, S. T. (1993). Controlling other people: The impact of power on stereotyping. *American Psychologist, 48,* 621–628.

Fiske, S. T., & Dépret, E. (1996). Control, interdependence and power: Understanding social cognition in its social context. In W. Stroebe & M. Hewstone (Eds.), *European Review of Social Psychology* (Vol. 7, pp. 31–61). Chichester: Wiley.

Fiske, S. T., & Morling, B. (1996). Stereotyping as a function of personal control motives and capacity constraints: The odd couple of power and anxiety. In R. M. Sorrentino & E. T. Higgins (Eds.), *Handbook of motivation and cognition* (Vol. 3, pp. 322–246). New York: Guilford Press.

French, J. R. P. Jr. & Raven, B. (1959). The bases of power. In D. Cartwright (Ed.), *Studies of social power.* Ann Arbor, MI: Institute for Social Research.

Goodwin, S. A., Gubin, A., Fiske, S. T., & Yzerbyt, V. (2000). Power can bias impression formation: Stereotyping subordinates by default and by design. *Group Processes and Intergroup Relations, 3,* 227–256.

Goodwin, S. A., Operario, D., & Fiske, S. T. (1998). Situational power and interpersonal dominance facilitate bias and inequality. *Journal of Social Issues, 54,* 677–698.

Groth, A. N. (1979). *Men who rape: The psychology of the offender.* New York: Plenum Press.

Jones, E. E., & Nisbett, R. E. (1972). The actor and the observer: Divergent perceptions of causality. In E. E. Jones, D. E. Kanouse, H. H. Kelley, R. E. Nisbett, S. Valins, & B. Weiner (Eds.), *Attribution: Perceiving the causes of behavior* (pp. 79–94). Morristown, NJ: General Learning Press.

Katz, I., & Hass, R. G. (1988). Racial ambivalence and American value conflict: Correlational and priming studies of dual cognitive structures. *Journal of Personality and Social Psychology, 55,* 893–905.

Kipnis, D. (1972). Does power corrupt? *Journal of Personality and Social Psychology, 24,* 33-41.

Kipnis, D. (1976). *The powerholders.* Chicago: University of Chicago Press.

Kipnis, D., Castell, P. J., Gergen, M., & Mauch, D. (1976). Metamorphic effects of power. *Journal of Applied Psychology, 61,* 127–135.

Kipnis, D., Schmidt, S., Price, K., & Stitt, C. (1981). Why do I like thee: Is it your performance or my orders? *Journal of Applied Psychology, 66,* 324–328.

Lee-Chai, A. Y., & Bargh, J. A. (2000). *Letting power go to your head: Behavioral effects of long-term social power depend on interpersonal orientation.* Manuscript submitted for publication.

Lee-Chai, A. Y., & Chartrand, T. L. (2000). MOP: The Misuse of Power scale. Technical Report 2000A, Research Center for Human Relations, New York University.

Lisak, D., & Roth, S. (1988). Motivational factors in nonincarcerated sexually aggressive men. *Journal of Personality and Social Psychology, 55,* 795–802.

Malamuth, N. M. (1986). Predictors of naturalistic sexual aggression. *Journal of Personality and Social Psychology, 50,* 953–962.

Malamuth, N. M. (1989a). The attraction to sexual aggression scale: Part One. *Journal of Sex Research, 26,* 26–49.

Malamuth, N. M. (1989b). The attraction to sexual aggression scale: Part Two. *Journal of Sex Research, 26,* 324–354.

Malamuth, N. M., Heavey, C., & Linz, D. (1993). Predicting men's antisocial behavior against women: The "interaction model" of sexual aggression. In G. N. Hall, R. Hirschmann, J. R. Graham, & M. S. Zaragoza (Eds.), *Sexual aggression: Issues in etiology and assessment and treatment* (pp. 63–97). New York: Hemisphere.

McClelland, D. C. (1975). *Power: The inner experience.* New York: Irvington.

McClelland, D. C. (1987). *Human motivation.* New York: Cambridge. (Original work published 1985)

McConahay, J. G. (1986). Modern racism, ambivalence, and the modern racism scale. In J.F. Dovidio & S.L. Gaertner (Eds.), *Prejudice, discrimination, and racism* (pp. 91–125). New York: Academic Press.

Mills, J., & Clark, M. S. (1982). Communal and exchange relationships. In L. Wheeler (Ed.), *Review of personality and social psychology.* Beverly Hills, CA: Sage.

Pratto, F., Sidanius, J., Stallworth, L. M., & Malle, B. F. (1994). Social dominance orientation: A personality variable predicting social and political attitudes. *Journal of Personality and Social Psychology, 67,* 741–763.

Pryor, J. B. (1987). Sexual harassment proclivities in men. *Sex Roles, 17*(5–6), 269–290.

Pryor, J. B., LaVite, C. M., & Stoller, L. M. (1993). A social psychological model for predicting sexual harassment. *Journal of Vocational Behavior, 42,* 68–83.

Pryor, J. B., & Stoller, L. M. (1994). Sexual cognition processes in men high in the likelihood to sexually harass. *Personality and Social Psychology Bulletin, 20,* 163–169.

Shartle, C. L. (1961). Leadership and organizational behavior. In L. Petrullo & B. M. Bass (Eds.), *Leadership and interpersonal behavior.* New York: Holt, Rinehart & Winston.

Thibaut, J. W., & Kelley, H. H. (1959). Power and dependence. In J. W. Thibaut & H. H. Kelley (Eds.), *The social psychology of groups* (pp. 100–125). New York: Wiley.

Triandis, H. C. (1995). Attributes of individualism and collectivism. In H. C. Triandis (Ed.), *Individualism and collectivism* (pp. 43–80). Boulder, CO: Westview Press.

Williamson, G. M., & Clark, M. S. (1989). Providing help and desired relationship type as determinants of changes in moods and self-evaluations. *Journal of Personality and Social Psychology, 56,* 722–734.

Williamson, G. M., & Clark, M. S. (1992). Impact of desired relationship type on affective reactions to choosing and being required to help. *Personality and Social Psychology Bulletin, 18,* 10–18.

Winter, D. G. (1973). The need for power. In D. C. McClelland & R. S. Steele (Eds.). *Human motivation. A book of readings* (pp. 279–286). Morristown, New Jersey: General Learning Press.

Wrightsman, L. S. (1964). Measurement of philosophies of human nature. *Psychological Reports, 14,* 743–751.

5

Power Motivation and Motivation to Help Others

IRENE H. FRIEZE
BONKA S. BONEVA

A s we examine expressions of power, it is important to consider what role personality factors play in why people might or might not be interested in having power over others. A large body of research has suggested that people have relatively stable patterns of underlying nonconscious motives. Such motives are among the factors that determine how people make choices and what goals they seek. Motives are believed to develop in childhood and are an aspect of one's personality throughout ones life.

One of these motives is power motivation. This chapter examines some of the research and theory related to the expression of power motivation. As will be discussed, power motivation is related to a number of diverse behaviors, including overt aggressiveness and desires to help others. First the approach of motivation theory is briefly outlined and then research specifically on power motivation and its correlates is reviewed. The chapter then illustrates how helping behavior may be motivated by power motivation. Finally, we turn to a discussion of how to measure power motivation generally, and helping power motivation in particular is presented.

SOCIAL MOTIVES

One of the major theorists examining human social motives is David McClelland (e.g., McClelland, 1987). McClelland (1987) argues that most social behavior can be understood in terms of an interaction between underlying motives and features of the environment. He suggests that there are three basic motives:

achievement, affiliation, and power. Achievement motivation is believed to predict one's approach to doing concrete tasks. Those high in achievement motivation strive to do things better and to perform at a high level. The person high in achievement motivation is motivated to work harder after failure and has a high belief in his or her own ability. Being high in achievement motivation does not necessarily mean one is always successful, but it is associated with expecting success and responding positively to experiences of nonsuccess in performing a task.

Affiliation motivation predicts ones desire to have friends and to be with other people. Those high in affiliation motivation make strong efforts to meet others, make friends, and maintain friendships. Having this affiliative goal of having lots of friends does not imply that those high in affiliation motivation are always more popular or successful in making friends.

Power motivation is somewhat more complex. In McClelland's (1987) basic framework, it was seen as predicting desires to control or influence others. The power motive has been defined as the inner need or disposition to seek power or a concern for having a strong impact on others (McClelland, 1975; Veroff, 1957; Winter, 1973b; 1993). As with achievement and affiliation motivation, power motivation is not necessarily associated with having power or being successful in exerting power, but rather in the desire to have power. There could be a number of reasons for people to actually have power, but these questions are addressed in other chapters in this book.

EXPRESSIONS OF POWER MOTIVATION

There are many ways in which power motivation can be expressed. As McClelland (1987) and others (McAdams, 1988; Winter, 1993) have shown, power motivation is not a simple formation. There are many outlets for this motive. Power motivated expressions include attempting to control others through overt aggression. One can also express power goals or power motivation through gaining influence or reputation. Being known to others enhances ones bases of power (Bruins, 1999; Raven, 1999). Other behaviors associated with high power motivation include trying to effect the emotions of others, or providing (often unsolicited) advice or help. This association of helping behavior with other, more aggressive or assertive behavior does not seem intuitively obvious, but these diverse behaviors are tied together since they have all been found to be ways of exerting power over others.

One reason that power motivation can be displayed in so many different ways may relate to the fact that having or expressing desires for power typically has a negative connotation in our society. Most people feel that power motivation is not a socially desirable motive, and they may seek indirect ways of expressing this motive (cf. McClelland, 1987). When we think of power, we often think about aggression and hurting others. It is true that such behavior is associated with desires for power. People high in power motivation may get into physical fights or verbal arguments with others (Dutton & Strachan, 1987). Those high in power motivation are sometimes described as having chronic anger (McClelland, 1987). Those who do express their power needs as overt aggression may also have high fears of being seen as powerless or weak (Veroff, 1992; Veroff & Veroff, 1971). Thus, the image of this form of power motivation expression is quite negative.

Desires for power or impact over others can also be expressed in less physically aggressive ways. Power motivation can be manifested as a direct expression of influence or leadership in group situations. Such leadership may still be a form of aggression, but it is less direct than overt violence or anger. Those high in power motivation may exploit others and are not above manipulating others to get what they want (McClelland, 1987; Winter, 1996). However, overt desires for power are not considered to be socially acceptable. Thus, self-centered leadership may not be acknowledged as an expression of the desire for power over others. Within the United States, it is rare for a leader to say his or her actions are motivated by power. A more likely statement would be that they are motivated by "service" or "duty" (Winter, 1992).

Other forms of power motivated behavior are even less obviously related to desires for power over others. High levels of alcohol consumption have been associated with higher power motivation. Being somewhat drunk makes one feel strong and powerful (McClelland et al., 1972). Being interested in sexual seduction, another form of attempting to gain control over another, has also been found empirically to characterize some men high in power motivation (McClelland, 1987).

In outlining the strategies used by power motivated individuals to obtain power, Winter (1996) sees them as following some of the tactics outlined many centuries ago in the writings of Machiavelli (1513). One of these power tactics is becoming visible and well known to others. This can be done today, for example, by college students taking public risks that bring attention, writing letters to a campus newspaper, or wearing something highly unusual at graduation (Winter, 1996). Having prestige possessions that are admired by others in one's group is another method of being visible (Winter, 1996). Visibility can also be gained by acting out in college or driving fast (McClelland, 1987). High power motivation was also shown to predict having more creative solutions to an engineering problem, but only when such solutions were rewarded with feedback about the positive impact of such solutions (Fodor, 1990).

All of the expressions of power motivation discussed so far are related to having power over others for one's own benefit. But, according to McClelland's theories, there is another form of power motivation expression. McClelland (1973b) argues that there are two "faces" of power—power thoughts centered on personal dominance, which is a socially unacceptable expression of the power motive, and power thoughts centered on having impact for the sake of others, which is a socially acceptable, even desirable, form of expressing the power motive. On this basis, McClelland (1972; 1975; 1987) and Winter (1973b) proposed dividing power motivation into "personalized power" (pPower) and "socialized power" (sPower). pPower is thought of as a relatively direct desire for control and power. Individuals high in pPower see life as a "zero-sum game" and have a "me-against-the-world" outlook (McClelland, 1975).

Socialized power has been associated with holding offices, joining organizations and being more apt to become officer in these organizations (McClelland, 1973b; 1987; Winter, 1973b). Within the organization, the leader motivated by sPower is influential by strengthening and inspiring the subordinates. The leader arouses confidence in his or her followers. With a leader motivated by sPower, the followers feel better able to accomplish whatever goals the leader and they share (McClelland, 1973b). Socialized power is meant to strengthen and uplift, to make people feel like origins, not pawns of the sociopolitical system (de Charms, 1968). Individuals high in socialized power have an one-with-the-world outlook (McClelland, 1987).

As outlined, leadership behavior can be motivated either by pPower or sPower. It is also quite possible that leaders are motivated by both forms of power. In real life, McClelland (1973b) argues that actual leaders constantly balance between expressing personal dominance and exercising the "more socialized type of leadership" (p. 311). Empirical support for this idea can be found in work by Chusmir (1986) who finds business managers to be relatively high in both pPower and sPower.

We have thus far argued that people who have high levels of desires for power may express such desires in many different ways. The particular forms of expression of power motivation are affected by cultural values and specific socialization experiences. Power expressions depend on social class (Winter, 1996), and on one's sense of social responsibility (McClelland, 1987).

An important factor in determining forms of expression of power motivation is gender role socialization (McClelland, 1975; Stewart & Chester, 1982; Winter, 1988). More aggressive forms of power motivation expression, and pPower generally, may be more associated with masculinity than femininity. For example, gender appears to relate to the expression of violence in close relationships. Mason and Blankenship (1987) found that college men higher in power motivation were more likely to be violent toward their female partners, but there was no effect of power motivation on violence for women. Other data also indicate that determinants of violence in close relationships may be different for women and men (Ryan, Frieze, & Sinclair, 1999). Violent men do tend to use other forms of power in marriages, as well as violence, when compared to nonviolent men (Frieze & McHugh, 1992).

Gender differences in the expression of power motivation have been shown in other studies. Peterson and Stewart (1974) studied a group of former University of Michigan students, sampled at about the age of 28. For this group, power motivation was associated with having children and parental involvement for women. Having children was also predicted by affiliation motivation for women, but involvement with their children was highest for women high in power motivation. Thus, women appeared to be expressing underlying power motivation (sPower) in a traditionally female form of maternal behavior.

Peterson and Stewart's (1993) findings for men's expressions of power motivation were more complex. Men's power motivation was correlated with a set of items associated with "doing something important," but not with having children. Once they had children, men who were more involved parents were higher in achievement motivation and affiliation motivation, but not in power. This association of power-related concerns and personal achievements for men has also been cited by others. Baumeister and Sommer (1997) argue that men achieve social status in their social group through their achievements, and that this achieved status gives them power and influence.

Since leadership and aggressive power expressions, both of which are associated with male role behavior, are the most commonly known forms of power motivation, this motive is often described as higher in men than women. However, in empirical studies, it is not the case that men consistently score higher on power motivation than women (e.g. Peterson & Stewart, 1993). This may be due to power being expressed as sPower, in forms that are acceptable for women. Studies of college students in the U.S. and other countries often show women as high, if not higher, than men in overall power motivation levels (e.g., Boneva, et al., 1997; 1998).

POWER MOTIVATED HELPING

Since an open expression of the desire for power over others can often be socially unacceptable, those high in power motivation may express this motive in a variety of more socially acceptable forms of having control, and influencing or having impact over others or the world. The expression of power through giving unsolicited help to others has been identified as one of these acceptable forms of power (e.g., Winter, 1993).

Helping Behaviors as Expressions of Power Motivation

Although the activity of providing unsolicited help to others is considered part of sPower, there has been little, if any, specific discussion of helping, in the theoretical literature. Not all helping behaviors are necessarily expressions of power motivation. However, certain types of helping do appear to fit well within the framework of power motivated behavior.

One form of indirect evidence for helping as a form of power motivation can be seen in studies of the patterns of friendship often seen in those with high power motivation. McAdams (1988) reports that in his work on motivation, people high in power motivation tend to display "agentic" behavior in their relationships with close friends. "Examples included taking charge of a situation, assuming responsibility, making a point in a debate or argument, *helping another, giving advice*, making plans, organizing activities, and attempting to persuade others" (italics added, p. 88). McAdams goes further to describe helping a friend as an active assertion of the self, attempting to effect change in another. The helper is dominant, and helping behavior creates a hierarchical relationship, at least temporarily. The role of helper can, and probably does, change within the relationship of two people who are both high in power motivation (McAdams, 1988).

There is other evidence that points to an association of power motivation and social or occupational-role-related helping behavior. Winter (1988) reports that college students who served as dormitory counselors tended to be high in power motivation. Another less obvious form of helping power can be seen in one of the power tactics identified by Winter (1996)—building alliances with lower status individuals, who will assist one in feeling more powerful, but will not threaten one's leadership. An example of such an interpersonal style is mentoring. Mentors build an alliance in order to counsel, guide, or help someone with a lower status. Successful mentoring could increase one's feeling of impact, of being powerful. Data reported by Schmidt (1997), investigating mentoring behavior in business settings, tested these ideas, and showed empirically that power motivation is a predictor of engaging in mentoring activity. Results also indicated that the higher the power motivation of the mentors, the more likely they were to see their mentoring behavior as resulting in increased reputation for themselves or as building a power base, presumably through developing an alliance with the less powerful individuals mentored. These data once again point to multiple expressions of power motivation, with components of both pPower and sPower in mentoring behavior.

Although not directly analyzing power motivation, Baumeister and Sommer (1997) argue that helping others can be motivated by a desire to look good to others as a way of enhancing ones status within a group. Helping strangers in the presence of others may be especially representative of this underlying motive. This appears to be a type of helping behavior that is more associated with men than women (Baumeister & Sommer, 1997).

Generativity is another concept that appears to be related to helping power motivation. As discussed by Erikson (1963), generativity refers to the adult's concern for and commitment to the well-being of the next generation, as manifested in parenting, teaching, mentoring, and other behaviors aimed at establishing a positive legacy for the person involved. McAdams and de St. Aubin (1992) define generativity as a desire for symbolic immortality and a desire to be needed by others. In many ways, this might be interpreted as a form of power motivation, leaving out its aggressive, exploitative aspects. The Loyola Generativity Scale was developed by McAdams and de St. Aubin (1992) to measure their conception of generativity. Based on this scale, generativity scores were found to correlate with helping someone else, doing something that others considered unique or important, making a decision that influenced many people, and producing a plan for some group outside the family. All of these behaviors can easily be seen as indicators of power motivation, and several relate directly to helping power.

In another study of generativity, the Peterson and Stewart (1993) study of Michigan graduates discussed earlier included a measure of societal concerns that included items such as "contributing to my community" and "helping others," along with having influence and being a part of a community. This was correlated with power motivation for men, but not for women.

A possibly related line of research, Clary and his colleagues have been looking at the motivations of volunteers (Clary et al., 1998). Volunteerism is defined as "voluntary, sustained, and ongoing helpfulness" (p. 1517). They proposed that volunteerism had multiple functions, including humanitarian concerns for others, finding new learning experiences, developing relationships with other people, helping one prepare for a (new) career, reducing guilt feelings about those who are less fortunate than the self, and building self-esteem. An item pool to measure these functions was developed and administered to a sample of volunteers, with an average age of 41. An oblique rotation of item scores indicated a slightly different pattern in the empirical data, with factors (represented by their highest loadings) of volunteering being a good escape, feeling compassion toward people in need, networking, other people feeling it is important, exploring ones personal strengths, and making one feel better about oneself, as motivations for volunteering. These data do not speak directly to the issue of dispositional motives, although the function of feeling compassion could be interpreted as a form of helping power. The idea of volunteering because others see it as important could be seen as a form of enhancing one's social status, another aspect of power motivation. These data do suggest, though, that there are many reasons for helping others, and that power motivation, if related at all, is only one of many underlying motivations for volunteering to help others in a structured setting.

It is also interesting to note that one of the predictors of adult power motivation is taking care of younger siblings as one was growing up (Winter, 1988). This would provide early socialization of being powerful by helping those with less power. And, indeed, research suggests that the eldest (or only) sons have higher power motivation as compared to their siblings (Winter, 1973a).

Thus, evidence from various sources supports the idea that at least some forms of helping behavior can be seen as a form of power motivation. Although helping power can include components of pPower, it is generally not done for the purpose of personal enhancement, without consideration for the person being helped. It has been argued that when one helps a friend who asks for assistance or advice, this is more properly seen as a form of intimacy motivation, a type of motivation related to affiliation motivation (McAdams, 1980). Further empirical research is needed to more clearly separate intimacy and power motivated helping.

Desires to help others can also be affected by factors in the immediate environment. According to McClelland's motivational theories, each of the major social motives tends to be more often expressed in some environments than in others. For example, arousing fears of social rejection tends to raise levels of affiliation desires and affiliative motivated behavior. In a set of studies manipulating levels of injustice experienced by others, Foster and Rusbult (1999) found that when students experienced more injustice, they displayed a number of power seeking desires and behaviors. Could it be that perhaps perceptions of injustice increase desires for helping?

Helping Power Motivation in Job Choice

By helping someone else, one is able to influence that person and have some degree of control over that person's future behavior. Thus, it is not surprising that people high in power motivation have been found to be strongly represented in many of the professions known as "helping professions" (Winter, 1973b; Winter, 1996).

The helping professions involve influencing other people, presumably for their own good. Based on empirical research, Winter (1973b) identifies the professions of teacher, clergy, and psychologist (either clinicians or research psychologists) as being especially attractive to those high in power motivation. Such positions give the occupant high levels of autonomy as well as the opportunity to influence others (Winter, 1996). For example, the process of therapy can be described as a power relationship where the therapist attempts to influence the client (McCarthy & Frieze, 1999).

All of the helping profession jobs appear to involve what can be labeled as desires for helping power. Of course, power motivation can also be expressed through a career as a business manager or some other occupation that gives one power over others or in high visibility jobs such as research scientist or journalist (McClelland, 1987). The particular choice of occupation is probably dependent on one's levels of pPower and sPower, and one's assessment of how likely he or she is to be able to successfully influence or have control over others in different occupations.

In a test of some of these ideas about the role of motivation in career choice and career satisfaction, Jenkins (1994) analyzed careers of a sample of college women tested first in 1967 and again in 1981. As college seniors, those with higher power motivation scores were more likely to plan careers as teachers or psychotherapists. Those high in power motivation were also more likely to select a career as a business executive or journalist. These latter two jobs would reflect more of the nonhelping components of power motivation. Thus, Jenkin's (1994) findings, again based on overall power motivation scores rather than on pPower and sPower scores, were consistent with Winter's (1973b) earlier data and with the theory outlined here.

Frustrated Needs for Power and Helping Power

As is true generally of motivations, their expressions may not be successful in achieving the desired goal. Wanting to help others in order to influence their lives may not result in satisfaction of the power motive. For example, others may not appreciate one's helping efforts (Newsom, 1999). This lack of appreciation may contribute to burnout. Burnout is defined as a state involving emotional exhaustion, depersonalization of one's clients, and reduced feelings of personal accomplishment (Maslach & Jackson, 1981). Burnout can be seen as a response to frustrated helping power motives. Studies of nurses and social workers—both helping professionals—have shown them to report high levels of burnout and desires to change careers. Given that those in such professions may be motivated by helping power, it may be clearer why those in the helping professions are especially prone to burnout when they don't feel appreciated and influential with their clients.

Some of this type of frustrated power motivation can also be seen in individuals working in other "helping professions." Jenkins' (1994) longitudinal study of college women found that those who initially planned to be teachers, and were high in power motivation, were especially likely to leave this career, presumably in order to find a field that allowed them more opportunity to express power motivation (Jenkins, 1994). If someone enters the teaching profession, for example, primarily to influence students, and those students do not respond as the person wanted, this would be especially frustrating. Veroff (1992) reports on an unpublished doctoral dissertation by Mueller (1975) of career path music students. In this study, it was found that those high in power motivation were least satisfied as teachers, and found doing musical performances much more satisfying. Perhaps these students were better able to express their needs for power by influencing others through performance of their music than as teachers?

In another study providing indirect support for the proposal that burnout is especially likely in those high in power motivation, Brondolo and colleagues (1998) found that New York city traffic enforcement agents with higher levels of anger were more likely to experience burnout. As mentioned earlier, power motivation has been associated with chronic anger and hostility (McClelland, 1987). McCarthy and Frieze (1999) found that burned out therapists were more likely to display coercive power, involving a number of aggressive behaviors often associated with power motivation. Such observations indicate that those with high power motivation who are unable to effectively influence others would be especially likely to display burnout and might seek other outlets for their power motivation.

Helping Power Motivation and Gender

As suggested earlier, more aggressive forms of power may be less socially acceptable for women than men (Cox, Stabb, & Hulgus, 2000). Just as gender relates generally to the expression of power motivation, it may also predict helping power motivation expression. For example, women are more likely than men to express power through working as teachers or other traditional feminine helping profession (McClelland, 1975). In *Power: The Inner Experience*, McClelland (1975) argues that women are socialized to be more interdependent and people-oriented than men, as part of their gender-role socialization. As a consequence, women may tend to express power motivation more often than men in the form of helping power. On the other hand, McClelland (1975) also found that certain behaviors that might be associated with helping behavior were not found to be correlated with power motivation in women. For example, being inspired by others, belonging to organizations, and loaning things to others were found to be associated with high power motivation in men, but not in women (McClelland, 1975). Meanwhile, dieting, trying to take care of the body, and donating one's organs to science were most associated with power motivation for women. McClelland (1975) interpreted these data as indicating, first, that women had fewer outlets for the expression of power motivation than men did since the stereotypic male assertiveness was not seen as feminine. He also characterized women's power motivation expression as building resources that could then be used by others (or that might allow them to be more effective helpers). However, these results were based on data collected from a relatively small sample of mostly well-educated adults, many years ago. Women were less likely to have careers at that time, and thus, may have had few outlets for expression of power motives other than motherhood. The role of gender in predicting expressions of power motivation generally, and helping power in particular, needs to be replicated today.

Winter (1988) has further developed the argument about the role of gender-role socialization in the expression of power motivation in a review of previously published and new data. Citing extensive research showing that girls are given more responsibility training than boys, Winter (1988) argues that females are relatively more likely to display power motivation as "responsible nurturance" while males are relatively more likely to display "egoistic dominance." This gender difference is at least partially explained by the fact that girls are more likely to be asked to take care of younger siblings, and that this early training is associated with the development of power motivation in both sexes. Thus, Winter's work would lead to the prediction that women are more likely than men to express power motivation in the form of helping behavior and to be motivated by desires to help others.

Measuring Helping Power Motivation

Most research on power motivation generally, and therefore, of pPower and sPower, relies on the Thematic Apperception Test (TAT). The TAT involves showing people a picture or describing a scenario to them. They are asked to write a story outlining what is going on, who the people are, and what will happen. Such stories are then coded for power-oriented imagery, using an established coding system (see Smith, 1992). This type of projective testing suffers from both reliability and validity problems. As an alternative to this type of testing, we have been developing a measure of power motivation that involves asking people if they have any of the characteristics found to be empirically associated with high and low power motivation. More recently, we have been developing a measure of helping power motivation.

Toward a Helping Power Scale

Based on theory and empirical research findings from TAT measurement, Schmidt and Frieze (1997) developed a scale to assess general levels of power motivation. Some of these items are shown in Table 1. The scale shown in Table 1 has been used in several studies and consistently yields an overall alpha of .80 or better (see e.g., Boneva et al., 1997, 1998). As can be seen, this general power motivation scale includes items measuring various aspects of power motivation, including helping power.

In a later study of the power motivation of potential migrants, Boneva and colleagues (Boneva et al., 1997) identified three subscales within this power motivation scale: leadership, prominence, and helping power. The subscales are identified in Table 5.1. These results showed that, as expected, the power motivation is not a unitary formation, and helping power is an essential component of the power motive.

These findings strengthened our conviction that there is a necessity to develop a fuller measure of helping power motivation. Also, based on theory and empirical research findings, there were certain indications that helping power was not itself a unitary structure. Within helping power there might be a differentiation between helping friends or others, and helping strangers. Also, we expected that doing something good for the society in general, which is often connected with a desire to have an impact on future generations or humanity in general (generativity), might not be part of this same framework. In order to

TABLE 5.1. Items to Assess Power Motivation

1. If given the chance, I would make a good leader of people. (L)
2. I enjoy planning things and deciding what other people should do. (L)
3. R-I dislike being the center of attention at large gatherings. (P)
4. I would like doing something important where people looked up to me. (P)
5. R-It isn't necessary to hold important positions in life. (P)
6. I like to have people come to me for advice. (P)
7. I find satisfaction in having influence over others. (P)
8. I enjoy debating with others in order to get them to see things my way. (P)
9. I like to have a lot of control over the events around me. (L)
10. I would like for my ideas to help people. (H)
11. I hope to one day make an impact on others or the world. (H)
12. I think I would enjoy having authority over other people. (L)
13. I like to give orders and get things going. (L)
14. I want to be a prominent person in my community. (P)
15. I often worry that the next generation will live in a worse world than the one I live in. (H)
16. I like to be admired for my achievements. (P)
17. I think I am usually a leader in my group. (L)
18. I am very concerned over the welfare of others. (H)
19. When people I know are trying to solve a problem, my gut instinct is to offer them helpful suggestions. (H)
20. It would be very satisfying to be able to have impact on the quality of others' lives. (H)

Note: L = Leadership; P = Prominence; H = Helping; R = Reversed item.

explore further the complexity of the motive, a fuller measure of helping power motivation is being developed.

A pool of items was designed to measure the above three different types of helping activities. Factor analysis of these items suggested only two factors. Items measuring helping friends or other individual people who we often know formed a separate factor from items asking about helping people in general or doing something good for the society. The two sets of items—helping people we know and helping people in general—are shown in Table 5.2. The first set of items included, for example, "When people I know are trying to solve a problem, my gut instinct is to offer them helpful suggestions"; "I often give advice to friends"; "Friends know they can count on me when they are in trouble"; "I dislike when others bother me with their troubles" (reversed); and "I loan money to friends when they need it." The second set of items included items such as, "I like to give money to charities"; "Doing volunteer work is very satisfying"; "The best thing about being a nurse would be to make a difference in people's lives"; "I hope to one day make an impact on others or the world"; and "I would like for my ideas to help people." Based on a sample of 222 college students, Cronbach's alpha for the Helping individual people subscale was .85; for the helping people in general subscale the alpha was .84.

TABLE 5.2. Items to Assess Helping Power Motivation

Helping friends (Alpha = .85)

1. When people I know are trying to solve a problem, my gut instinct is to offer them helpful suggestions.
2. I often give advice to friends.
3. Friends often ask me for advice.
4. When I see someone who needs help, I take the initiative to do something for them.
5. I feel good when I can give useful advice to someone.
6. I loan money to friends when they need it.
7. Friends know they can count on me when they are in trouble.
8. I dislike it when others bother me with their troubles. (R)

Helping people in general (Alpha = .84)

1. Doing volunteer work is very satisfying.
2. It is important to give money to charities.
3. Making other people feel comfortable is important to me.
4. When strangers ask for directions, I try to help them out.
5. I would enjoy being a therapist.
6. The best thing about being a nurse would be to make a difference in people's lives.
7. I would love to be a teacher who inspires students.
8. I would like to make a difference in someone's life.
9. I would like for my ideas to help people.
10. I hope to one day make an impact on others or the world.
11. I often worry that the next generation will live in a worse world than the one I live in.
12. I am very concerned over the welfare of others.
13. It would be very satisfying to be able to have impact on the quality of others' lives.

Note: R = Reversed item.

Both of these subscales were found to correlate with desiring a job that would allow one to help others. Also, as expected, helping people in general correlated strongly with a desire to hold a job that helps others ($r = .55; p < .01$), while desiring to help people we know correlated less strongly with wanting a helping job, although the correlation was still significant ($r = .38; p < .01$). As mentioned earlier, it was expected that desires to help those we know personally should be more correlated with intimacy motivation than desires to help strangers or society in general. When one helps someone with whom one has a relationship, this can be motivated by helping power or by desires to maintain and enhance the relationship (the concern of those high in intimacy motivation) or a combination of the two. Thus, both theoretically and empirically, helping power is also associated with intimacy motivation as well as with power motivation. We are continuing to explore this question of the relationship of intimacy, helping motivation and power motivation.

FUTURE DIRECTIONS FOR RESEARCH

Based on this review of previous research, as well as our own data, it does appear that one of the most socially acceptable behaviors—helping—can in fact satisfy one's power motivation. In addition, it appears that within the helping power motivation, at least two aspects of helping can be differentiated: helping individual people, and helping others in general, or caring about humanity.

Helping behavior, no doubt, is not always driven by power motivation. Helping others and society can be a result of a number of personality and environmental factors. However, helping behavior can also indicate high power motivation. Helping someone, or others in general, means having influence, or impact over other people's lives—the core of socialized power motivation. It is logical to assume that the need to control or influence others, or to have an impact over the world can be expressed, for example, in charitable activity, volunteering, or mentoring.

The fact is that power, by and large, has a negative connotation in our culture. As McClelland (1973b) emphasized, "it is a fine thing to be concerned about doing things well (Achievement motivation) or making friends (Affiliation motivation), but it is often considered reprehensible to be concerned about having influence over others (Power motivation)" (p. 302). This makes any discussion of helping power difficult, since people may not readily admit, or even be aware, that their need for power is an underlying explanation of helping others. Thus, helping behavior remains the most neglected expression of power motivation (cf. McClelland, 1973a; 1987). As other chapters in this book suggest, there is a growing need to emphasize "the positive face of power" (cf. McClelland, 1973b). This positive face is easily seen as helping power.

REFERENCES

Baumeister, R. F., & Sommer, K. L. (1997). What do men want? Gender differences and two spheres of belongingness: Comment on Cross and Madson (1997). *Psychological Bulletin, 122*, 38–44.

Boneva, B. S., Frieze, I. H., Ferligoi, A., Jarasova, E., Pauknerova, D., & Orgocka, A. (1997). East-West European migration and the role of motivation in emigration desires. *Migracijske teme, 13*(4), 335–362.

Boneva, B. S., Frieze, I. H., Ferligoj, A., Jarasova, E., Pauknerova, D., & Orgocka, A. (1998). Achievement, mpower and affiliation motives as clues to (e)migration desires: A four-countries comparison. *European Psychologist, 3*, 247–254.

Brondolo, E., Masheb, R., Stores, J., Stockhammer, T., Tunick, W., Melhado, E., Karlin, W. A., Schwartz, J., Harburg, E., & Contrada, R. J. (1998). Anger-related traits and response to interpersonal conflict among New York City traffic agents. *Journal of Applied Social Psychology, 28*, 2089–2118.

Bruins, J. (1999). Social power and influence tactics: A theoretical introduction. *Journal of Social Issues, 55*, 7–14.

Chusmir, L. H. (1986). Personalized vs. socialized power needs among working men and women. *Human Relations, 39*, 149–159.

Clary, E. G., Ridge, R. D., Stukas, A. A., Snyder, M., Copeland, J., Haugen, J., & Miene, P. (1998). Understanding and assessing the motivations of volunteers: A functional approach. *Journal of Personality and Social Psychology, 74*, 1516–1530.

Cox, D. L., Stabb, S. D., & Hulgus, J. F. (2000). Anger and depression in girls and boys. *Psychology of Women Quarterly, 24*, 110–112.

de Charms, R. (1968). *Personal causation*. New York: Academic Press.

Dutton, D. G., & Strachan, C. E. (1987). Motivational needs for power and spouse-specific assertiveness in assaultive and non-assaultive men. *Violence and Victims, 2*, 145–156.

Erikson, E. H. (1963). *Childhood and Society*. (2nd Ed.). New York: Norton.

Fodor, E. M. (1990). The power motive and creativity of solutions to an engineering problem. *Journal of Research in Personality, 24*, 338–354.

Foster, C. A., & Rusbult, C. E. (1999). Injus-

tice and powerseeking. *Personality and Social Psychology Bulletin, 25*, 834–849.

Frieze, I. H., & McHugh, M. C. (1992). Power and influence strategies in violent and nonviolent marriages. *Psychology of Women Quarterly, 16*, 449–465.

Jenkins, S. R. (1994). Need for power and women's careers over 14 years: Structural power, job satisfaction, and motive change. *Journal of Personality and Social Psychology, 66*, 155–165.

Ladd, E. C. (1999). *The Ladd report*. New York: The Free Press.

Maslach, C., & Jackson, S. E. (1981). The measurement of experienced burnout. *Journal of Occupational Behaviour, 2*, 99–113.

Machiavelli, N. (1513). *The prince*, W. K. Mariott translations. In R. M. Hutchins (Ed.), *Great books of the western world* (Vol. 23, pp. 1–37). Chicago: Encyclopedia Brittanica, 1953.

Mason, A., & Blankenship, V. (1987). Power and affiliation motivation, stress, and abuse in intimate relationships. *Journal of Personality and Social Psychology, 52*, 203–210.

McAdams, D. P. (1980). A thematic coding system for the intimacy motive. *Journal of Research in Personality, 14*, 413–432.

McAdams, D. P. (1988). *Power, intimacy, and the life story: Personological inquiries into identity*. New York: Guilford Press.

McAdams, D. P., & de St. Aubin, E. (1992). A theory of generativity and its assessment through self-report, behavioral acts, and narrative themes in autobiography. *Journal of Personality and Social Psychology, 62*, 1003–1015.

McCarthy, W. C., & Frieze, I. H. (1999). Negative aspects of therapy: Client perceptions of therapists' social influence, burnout, and quality of care. *Journal of Social Issues, 55*, 33–50.

McClelland, D. C. (1972). What is the effect of achievement motivation in schools? *Teachers College Record, 74*, 129–145.

McClelland, D. C. (1973b). The two faces of power. In D. C. McClelland & R. S. Steele (Eds.), *Human motivation. A book of readings* (pp. 300–316). Morristown, NJ: General Learning Press.

McClelland, D. C. (1975). *Power: The inner experience*. New York: Wiley.

McClelland, D. C. (1987). *Human motivation.* New York: Cambridge.

McClelland, D. C., Davis, W. N., Kalin, R., & Wanner, E. (1972). *The drinking man.* New York: The Free Press.

Mueller, S. (1975). *Motivation and reactions to the work role among female performers and music teachers.* Unpublished doctoral dissertation, University of Michigan, Ann Arbor.

Newsom, J. T. (1999). Another side to caregiving: Negative reactions to being helped. *Current Directions in Psychological Science, 8,* 183–187.

Peterson, B. E., & Stewart, A. J. (1993). Generativity and social motives in young adults. *Journal of Personality and Social Psychology, 65,* 186–198.

Raven, B. (1999). Influence, power, religion, and the mechanisms of social control. *Journal of Social Issues, 55,* 159–186.

Ryan, K. M., Frieze, I. H., & Sinclair, H. C. (1999). Physical violence in dating relationships. In M. A. Paludi (Ed.), *The psychology of sexual victimization: A handbook* (pp. 33–54). Westport, CT: Greenwood Press.

Schmidt, L. C. (1997). *A motivational approach to the prediction of mentoring relationship satisfaction and future intention to mentor.* Unpublished doctoral dissertation, University of Pittsburgh.

Schmidt, L. C., & Frieze, I. H. (1997). A mediational model of power, affiliation and achievement motives and product involvement. *Journal of Business and Psychology, 4,* 425–446.

Smith, C. P. (Ed.). (1992). *Motivation and personality: Handbook of thematic content analysis.* New York: Cambridge University Press.

Stewart, A. J., & Chester, N. L. (1982). Sex differences in human social motives: Achievement, affiliation, and power. In A. J. Stewart (Ed.), *Motivation and society* (pp. 172–218) San Francisco: Jossey-Bass.

Veroff, J. (1957). Development and validation of a projective measure of power motivation. *Journal of Abnormal and Social Psychology, 54,* 1–8.

Veroff, J. (1992). Power motivation. In C. P. Smith (Ed.), *Motivation and personality: Handbook of thematic content analysis* (pp. 100–109). New York: Cambridge University Press.

Veroff, J., & Veroff, J. B. (1971). Theoretical notes on power motivation. *Merrill-Palmer Quarterly of Behavior and Development, 17*(1), 59–69.

Winter, D. G. (1973a). The need for power. In D. C. McClelland & R. S. Steele (Eds.), *Human motivation. A book of readings* (pp. 279–286). Morristown, NJ: General Learning Press.

Winter, D. G. (1973b). *The power motive.* New York: Macmillan.

Winter, D. G. (1988). The power motive in women—and men. *Journal of Personality and Social Psychology, 54,* 510–519.

Winter, D. G. (1992). Power motivation revisited In C. P. Smith (Ed.), *Motivation and personality: Handbook of thematic content analysis* (pp. 301–310). New York: Cambridge University Press.

Winter, D. G. (1993). The Power motive revisited. In C. P. Smith (Ed.), *Motivation and personality: Handbook of thematic content analysis* (pp. 301–310). Cambridge: Cambridge University Press.

Winter, D. G. (1996). *Personality: Analysis and interpretation of lives.* New York: McGraw Hill.

PART II

POWER BETWEEN INDIVIDUALS

6

Dominance in Disguise
Power, Beneficence, and Exploitation in Personal Relationships

FELICIA PRATTO
ANGELA WALKER

"*I*t's for your own good." "This hurts me more than it hurts you." These phrases invoke a relationship in which a stronger, more capable, more knowledge-able member claims responsibility for another's well-being and exerts control to meet that responsibility. Such relationships are commonly called pater-nalistic (Keinig, 1983) due to the historical European legal mandate that fathers both control and care for their sons, although similar relationships, such as those between middle class women and their maids or welfare clients have been called maternalistic (e.g., Gordon, 1994; Rollins, 1993). These parental metaphors characterize not only many parent-child relationships but also relationships between teacher and student, mentor and mentee, doctor and patient, master and slave, and institutions (e.g., colleges, social service agencies) and their wards. According to the parental ideal, subordinates are succored. However, abuse of children and other subordinates within such relations is not uncommon, and that fact demands that one consider whether control actually benefits subordinates or only ostensibly benefits subordinates. In this chapter, we consider how power is used and abused within parentalistic relationships.[1]

To examine how power operates in parentalistic relationships, we find it necessary to examine 1) the benefits and costs of the relationship to each mem-

---

1. Parentalistic relationships blend a quality more associated with male gender, namely power, with another quality more associated with female gender, namely caretaking. Yet clearly both men and women can wield power and nurture, so we use the more gender-inclusive term *parentalistic* to describe these relationships generally.

ber, 2) the relationship's ostensible purpose and nature, 3) the freedom and desire that each member has to remain in, change, or exit the relationship, and 4) the justifications made for power and actions. As we will see, power in parentalistic relationships cannot be described without situating the relationship in its larger social-structural and ideological context. Our analysis therefore draws not only upon theories of interpersonal relationships, but also on theories of intergroup relations and ideology, reviewed below. Two prevalent examples of parentalistic relationships to draw out the theoretical questions to be asked are presented below; then, a new theory of parentalistic relationships is described.

PARENTALISTIC RACISM

The history of racism in the U.S. shows that oppressive relations can be either antagonist or parentalistic, and that both are aided by ideologies that justify unequal power and resource distribution. During Britain's colonial expansion prior to 1650, American British colonists' believed Blacks to be bestial, uncivilized, and evil (Gossett, 1963). People often describe groups they seek to dominate as inferior and contemptible (e.g., Keen, 1986; Sherif & Sherif, 1966), but this does not mandate holding them in contempt, nor eliminating them as competitors. During the antebellum period, Southern Whites' belief that Blacks were savage and childlike led them to justify slavery as a benevolent institution for both slaves and their masters (Turner & Singleton, 1978). Indeed, proslavery tracts referred to the mutual interests of master and slave, likened their relation to friendship, and suggested that dissolving this friendship was detrimental to both parties, all hallmarks of communal relations:

> Slavery identifies the interests of rich and poor, master and slave, and begets domestic affection on one side, and loyalty and respect on the other. . . . The Southerner is the negro's friend, his only friend. Let no intermeddling abolitionist, no refined philosophy, dissolve this friendship.
> Fitzhugh (1854, p. 43, 95), quoted by Jackman (1994, p. 71)

Clearly, intergroup dominance is not always characterized by overt intergroup hostility, physical segregation, or by an admission of a zero-sum game between competing groups. Indeed, the periods of U.S. and Brazilian history in which racism was parentalistic rather than hostile were those in which the races lived in close proximity (in the same neighborhoods or households) and shared work "cooperatively" (as in share-cropping or plantation agriculture; van den Berghe, 1967).

American slavery illustrates features of parentalistic relationships that are addressed in our analysis. First, it shows that power differentials, oppression, and abuse can be justified by the guise of care. Second, it shows that the stated intentions of the dominant can be scrutinized by discerning whether the dominant or the subordinate benefits differentially from the relationship. Third, it shows that interpersonal relationships, such as those between slave and master, cannot be understood without reference to their social-structural context. Fourth, it shows that exploitative intergroup relations, such as those between colonizers and colonized, may be predicated on interpersonal relationships.

PARENTALISTIC SEXISM

Women's access to power and resources is often restricted in the name of benevolence. For example, a number of U.S. chemical companies barred women from jobs that would expose them to certain chemicals. This ostensibly caring stance can be scrutinized by the costs it had for women employees and the benefits it had for the companies. Faludi (1991, pp. 440–453) documents that the jobs from which women were barred paid much higher than female-dominated jobs. To meet their families' financial needs, some women underwent surgical sterilization against their personal wishes to "qualify" themselves for higher-paying jobs. The chemical companies' ostensible concern for women did not extend to reducing employees' exposure to chemicals by retooling the plants, or to raising the pay of female-dominated jobs, or even to systematic research into which chemicals actually posed risks. The companies, however, benefited by limiting their liabilities and capital expenditures for plant safety improvements, and their practices were upheld in court. Widespread acceptance of parentalism allows institutions to collude in "protecting" women by limiting their access to education, political power, health care, legal standing, and economic resources. Helping oneself to another's resources while declaring that one is helping the other is a mechanism for exploitation.

A related mechanism can be enacted in face-to-face relationships through a particular institution, namely marriage. Married men and women often share a household, children, financial assets, and love, and the mutuality of this union is celebrated and indeed romanticized. But marriage is also the most common site for the division of labor between men and women. In an astounding variety of cultures, marriage limits women's power more than men's while obliging women to contribute more to the family, such as in childcare, food preparation, and housework (e.g., Collier, 1988; Okin, 1989; Sacks, 1974).

Like parentalistic racism, parentalistic sexism shows that exploitation can be disguised as care and false mutuality. Sexism also shows the impossibility of understanding power as solely an interpersonal or an intergroup phenomenon. After all, gender-role prescriptions transcend family and workplace and society. For example, men are often expected to play protective roles: in families they protect family honor and women's "virtue," at work they guard valuables, and in society they serve as police officers and in the military. As described above, constraints on women's power in their families limits their power with their employers and vice versa. Just as the private/public border is key to understanding the durability of inequality (Jackman, 1994; Pratto, 1996; Sanday, 1981;

Tilly, 1998), an analysis of the dynamic intersection of interpersonal and inter-group relations is critical to understanding parentalism.

For this reason, reviewing theories of intergroup relations and theories of interpersonal relations are reviewed next in this chapter. Theories of intergroup relations are helpful for understanding parentalism because they address power, ideology, and the larger social context of interpersonal relationships. Most do not, however, address the interpersonal aspects of power or of intergroup rela-tionships directly. Theories of intimate relationships are helpful for understand-ing parentalism because they describe interpersonal communal relationships, and the roles, power, and norms of close relationships. But interpersonal theo-ries have paid less attention to power and ideology than have intergroup theo-ries, and where they have done so, they have largely ignored how power and ideology within an interpersonal relationship are contingent on the larger social context. The current review of both kinds of theories will highlight concepts that dynamically link interpersonal and intergroup relations, notably power, dependency, boundaries, and ideology.

THEORIES OF INTERGROUP RELATIONS

Group Conflict Theories

With some important exceptions noted below, most theories of intergroup rela-tions assume that intergroup conflict stems from competition over real (mate-rial) goods (cf. Blumer, 1960; Campbell, 1965). This assumption portrays inter-group relations as hostile, segregated, and in zero-sum competition (Jackman, 1994, p. 24). From this standpoint, power is a tool for controlling resources, and exploitation is the forced extraction of resources from another.

Marxism

Conceived by Karl Marx and Frederich Engels, Marxism also champions eco-nomic analysis as the key to intergroup exploitation. According to Marx (1904), when one group controls the means of production of economic value (e.g., natural resources, factories), that group can exploit those who can gain access to value only through their relationship. In broader terms, Marxism suggests that con-trol over other people results from controlling things people value or need, an idea the reader will see echoed in interpersonal theories. People who cannot gain access to resources elsewhere are compelled to enter and remain in a rela-tionship, and can therefore be exploited by those who have choice. Okin (1989), for example, argues that to the extent that women have more to lose and less to gain through marital exit, marriage exploits women. Thus, the dynamic of power within a relationship has to do with its borders to the outside. Following Engels (1884/1902), Marxism has examined how the intersecting borders of different kinds of social categories (e.g., race, class, gender, cf. Davis, 1981) afford exploitation. Engels (1884/1902) argued that shifting production out of the family and allowing men more entry into the external workforce than women enabled the exploitation of women and of working-class men (see Sacks, 1974). Hence, interpersonal and intergroup relationships jointly structure exploitation.

Besides materialism, Marx and Engels (1846/1970) identified ideology as a tool for power and exploitation. They argued that dominants also controlled the production of social discourse, which, being based on the dominants' worldview, justified their use of power. The ideological hegemony of the ruling class can lead subordinates to find practices that exploit themselves acceptable. Not only do such ideologies privilege dominants, they lead subordinates to participate in their own oppression (Jackman, 1994; Johnson, 1994; Sidanius & Pratto, 1999; Turner & Singleton, 1978). For example, women's romance with chivalric ideals contributes to gender inequality (Glick & Fiske, 1996; Jackman, 1994; Millet, 1970, p. 73).

THEORIES OF INTERPERSONAL RELATIONSHIPS

Like theories of intergroup relations, theories of interpersonal relations have emphasized economic analyses to examine power, but have considered how individuals value not just capital but also respect, affection, and harmony. Interdependence theory (Kelley, 1979; Kelley & Thibaut, 1978; Thibaut & Kelley, 1959; see Rusbult & van Lange, 1998 for a review) defines power as one's ability to influence the quality of outcomes for the other (Thibaut & Kelley, 1959, p. 101), and considers high mutual power a sign of cohesiveness (Thibaut & Kelley, 1959, p. 114). Interdependence theory identifies two types of power: determining the other's outcomes no matter what the other does, and influencing the other's behavior by providing rewards for desired behaviors (Thibaut & Kelley, 1959, pp. 101–103). Satisfaction with the relationship is defined as how well one's outcomes compare with what one thinks one deserves, but one's valuation of alternatives to the relationship could lead one to desire exit and thus limits the power the other has. Thus, although Thibaut and Kelley (1959, p. 117) argue that there is no necessary relationship between a person's power and his or her outcomes, they generally expect that the person who has the most to offer or the most to withdraw from a relationship will obtain the outcomes he or she desires more often. Like Marxism, interdependence theory implies that power in a relationship can be derived from controlling more resources, controlling critical resources, or from having the least need.

Interdependence theory allows that relationships may be mutually beneficial even when not strictly equal (when members have different inputs and outcomes), and suggests that cohesiveness can lead members to value one another and being together. Yet all of the strategies for increasing power in the theory assume a zero-sum game in which more power for one means less power for the other (Thibaut & Kelley, 1959, pp. 120–122). On the other hand, interdependence theory states that relationships in which each member obtains maximum rewards when the other's outcomes are poor will be unstable (Thibaut & Kelley, 1959, p. 108), so both persistent conflict and long-term exploitation are unlikely unless one member has no alternatives. This analysis initially made domestic violence and other forms of power asymmetries in marriage seem more unlikely than subsequent research proved them to be. However, consistent with the interdependence theory's predictions about control of resources and ability to exit, victims of domestic violence have been found to have lower income backgrounds than their abusers (see Marshall & Vitanza, 1994, for a review).

Interdependence theory also identifies a position for norms and roles. A consensually shared behavioral rule (a norm, or if linked to a social position, a role) decreases the necessity of deploying power moment-to-moment in the relationships (Thibaut & Kelley, 1959, pp. 126–127). For example, the shared expectation that husbands cook removes the need for either spouse to induce the other to cook and bypasses potential conflict over who should. The more interdependent the relationship, the more necessary norms are (Thibaut & Kelley, 1959, p. 133). Furthermore, norms and roles learned in one relationship might be transferred to another relationship, re-creating roles and norms (Thibaut & Kelley, 1959, p. 145; see also Tilly, 1998). These ideas are compatible with our analysis of how ideologies structure power relationships (e.g., Pratto et al., 2000; Sidanius & Pratto, 1999).

Another economic approach, exchange or equity theory, assumes that because people are self-interested, they are motivated to avoid both giving beneficence and being exploited. Equity theory specifically posits that people will seek equity, or equivalent ratios of inputs and outputs of each member, in relationships (Homans, 1961). Although developed by Homans (1961) to describe impersonal economic relationships such as those between employer and employee, Walster, Bersheid, and Walster (1973) presumed that equity theory could describe even close, marital relationships.

However, Clark and Mills (1979) questioned whether people believe all their relationships are about economics. They distinguished between exchange relationships, which are typical among acquaintances or business associates, and communal relationships, such as those between friends, lovers, and between parents and children. The purpose of exchange relationships is to exchange benefits, and so in them favors incur debts, and their duration is fixed. In experimentally-induced exchange relationships, people keep track of what they have received from and given to the other (Clark & Mills, 1979; Clark & Waddell, 1985). Communal relationships exist to care for another's welfare and to please the other member. People in communal relationships attend more to other's needs than to inputs and outputs (Clark, 1984; Clark, Mills, & Powell, 1986; Clark & Waddell, 1985). The mutual concern for each other's well-being leads to interdependence, the expectation of a long-term relationship, emotional expression, and emotional closeness.

Mills and Clark (1986) postulated that exploitation can be perceived when people in exchange or communal relationships either misrepresent the type of relationship they have, misrepresent their received benefits, or misrepresent their abilities to fulfill the obligations of the relationship. Their postulates about exploitation are useful to understanding parentalism for two reasons. First, they imply that exploitation can occur within communal relations, which are often idealized as egalitarian. Second, they indicate that people refer to generally held norms in judging whether people in interpersonal relationships are behaving ethically. In our view, this indicates that ideologies are as useful to understanding interpersonal relationships as they are to understanding intergroup relationships.

But Mills and Clark's (1986) analysis of exploitation includes no explicit analysis of power, for they describe both members as equally capable of deception. Yet we have seen in both Marxism and interdependence theory that there are many bases of power (see French & Raven, 1959 for a taxonomy), including expertise, control of resources or their distribution, lack of need, referent power, and freedom to enter or to exit the relationship, and these also enable exploitation.

In fact, the most predominant form of communal relationship, that between parent and child, cannot be characterized without delineating the many forms of power differences between parents and children and indeed between adults and children. Children are legally, emotionally, and physically less able to exit or to do without the parent-child relationship than their parents are, and many of their needs are more critical because of their developmental status. Parents can also have more power than children due to greater expertise, legal recognition, control of financial resources, physical strength and agility, social standing, and authority invested from their social roles. Most of these power differences are contingent on others recognizing that parents have certain rights over and obligations toward their children. As with parentalistic racism and sexism, then, parent-child relationships are contingent on the shared beliefs that structure social relations.

IDEOLOGY

People within a culture share understandings about how people ought to behave and use those understandings to justify or to disapprove of people's actions and social practices. We call such shared understandings "ideologies" (e.g., Pratto et al., 2000; Pratto, Tatar, & Conway-Lanz, 1999). We now describe how ideologies help to create power differences and enable exploitation.

We saw that people have different moral standards and behavioral expectations for communal and exchange relationships. In our terms this means that each relationship type has its own ideology. But consideration of communal and exchange norms is not sufficient.

Thibaut and Kelley (1959) expected cohesive relationships to establish or import norms and roles, and substantial research shows that ideologies such as gender-role norms and race stereotypes easily come to mind and prescribe power (see Fiske, 1998; Pratto, 1999 for reviews). As such, there is reason to be suspicious that people use pure communal and exchange norms. Ideologies like sexism and capitalism hold certain people to higher standards for meeting needs or being self-interested, so such ideologies can change people's obligations to uphold communal or exchange norms. Indeed, gender roles prescribe that women should act as if they are in communal relationships (e.g., family-oriented, nurturing) and that men should act as if they are in exchange relationships (e.g., business-oriented, rational). Marriages and other particular relationships that are predicated on these complementary gender roles cannot be described as purely communal or purely exchange. Ideologies, like capitalism, sexism, and gender-role prescriptions, can also determine what resources each member brings to a relationship and the freedom to exit the relationship, thereby determining the power distribution (Thibaut & Kelley, 1959). Moreover, when an ideology differentially benefits one member, exploitation is not accomplished through deception in reference to an ideology (Mills & Clark, 1986), but by enacting an ideology.

Ideologies like dominative racism and chauvinism can subordinate people by demeaning them. Two recent analyses posit that ideological control can be exercised through benevolent attitudes. Jackman (1994) argues that using hostility and force to maintain dominance can be counterproductive, especially in intimate relationships. Instead, she argues that paternalistic ideologies that disguise the iron fist in a velvet glove are more effective. As sexual reproduction requires intimacy, gender relations will not typically be segregated, competitive, and hostile, but rather intimate and affectionate albeit controlling. In U.S. national opinion data, Jackman (1994) finds that paternalism is the predominant form of intergroup attitudes with respect to class, race, and gender, with race relations being the most conflictual and gender relations the most paternalistic. Fully 60% of the men sampled oppose equal job opportunities and equal legal treatment for men and women while feeling positive toward women (Jackman, 1994, p. 288). Jackman (1994) argues that dominants' positive feelings toward subordinates make it easier for them to wield control and to justify exploitation while avoiding accusations of immorality. On the subordinates' side, complementary attitudes help maintain exploitative interdependency. Jackman (1994, p. 284) finds that women's most prevalent attitude pattern complemented men's paternalism in that about 45% of women also opposed equal job opportunities and equal legal treatment while feeling more positive about their own gender, a stance Jackman labels "deferent."

Glick and Fiske (1996) also argue that the domestic structure of heterosexual relationships leads sexism to be benevolent, albeit controlling, more often than it is hostile. Using factor analysis, they find that benevolent and hostile sexism toward women are distinct attitudes, and that scales measuring each predict different reactions to women with power (career women) versus women who serve (housewives; see also Glick et al., 1997). Moreover, across countries, the degree of individuals' benevolent sexism correlates with the country's level of gender inequality (Glick et al., 2000). Benevolent sexist beliefs may then help to create or to justify limits on women's power. Both Jackman's (1994) and

Glick and Fiske's (1996) analyses are compatible with interdependence theory because it postulated that affection, praise, and expressions of shared outcomes become part of the value of relationships and mitigate conflict.

From the perspective of interdependence theory or these analyses of paternalistic sexism, it is unsurprising to find dominance without hostility. Yet in the racial attitudes literature, the absence of overtly hostile racial attitudes among Whites in the face of their persistent opposition to ameliorative racial policies has presented an enormous intellectual puzzle (see also Jackman, 1994). Some theorists (cf. McConahay, 1986) stressed that opposition to ameliorative racial policies is no longer justified by old-fashioned hostile racism, but by a new modern kind of racism. Others (Katz & Hass, 1988; Sears, 1988) theorized that people justified their racist policy attitudes without seeming racist by referring to ostensibly nonracial principles like the Protestant Work Ethic. Still others deny that opposing ameliorative policies is racist at all, but rather, argue that such policy positions are justified by principles of conservative ideology (cf. Sniderman et al., 1991).

Regarding parentalism, this body of work illustrates two important ideas. First, as historical studies of racism have shown, racist attitudes do not have to have a hostile face. The one research team that denies that opposition to government aid for Blacks is racist base their claim on the fact that in an experimental survey, more conservatives rather than liberals felt that a Black (versus White) man should receive government aid when his difficulties were not self-caused (Sniderman et al., 1991). Sniderman et al. (1991) also found that more liberals rather than conservatives felt that a woman (versus a man) should receive more government aid when her difficulties were not self-caused. While we agree that granting aid does not sound like hostile prejudice, these findings could be described as evidence of parentalistic sexism among liberals and paternalistic racism among conservatives, rather than, as indicating that political ideology is unrelated to group bias.

Second, this body of research shows that racial policy attitudes can be justified and perhaps disguised by a variety of general ideologies such as antiradicalism, meritocracy, and conservatism that are not overtly about race. In fact, some general ideologies both justify group discrimination and are endorsed most by people who support group dominance (e.g., Pratto, Stallworth, & Conway-Lanz, 1998; Sidanius, Pratto, & Bobo, 1996). One may well ask how ideologies that are ostensibly general and not group-prejudiced can justify group dominance. The answer lies in the use of universal rhetoric, which disguises the reality that many ideologies are linked to group position. Universalizing helps enable the powerful to convince others and themselves that ideologies that come from and privilege their vantage points are general and even natural (Sampson, 1993). For example, many Americans consider freedom to be universally desired and a universal human right. Yet one attempt to universalize this right and others favored by individualistic nations, the U. N. Declaration of Human Rights, is resisted on political grounds by China and other communal nations for whom duty to others is more valued than freedom from obligation to others (see

Moghaddam Slocum et al., 2000, for a related discussion). In fact, interdependence theory implies that freedom from obligation is a form of power. Thus, universal liberalism is not politically neutral. More generally, declaring that ideologies that serve the powerful best are right for everyone is another way to mask dominance in ideology. As a consequence, one can exploit by prescribing ideologies as general under the pretense that interests are in common when they actually diverge.

Ideology can also be used to exploit by portraying people as having different amounts of power than they actually have. bell hooks (1984) provides a perverse example, equating milder discrimination with overt oppression under the guise of group unity, which she argued Betty Friedan (1974) did in declaring that all women, regardless of class, race, or education level, are equally oppressed. Bugental and her colleagues have found that parents who perceive themselves to have low power compared with their children think more often about dominance (Bugental et al., 1997), use more coercion and negative affect in interacting with their children, and are more likely to abuse children (Bugental, Blue, & Cruzcosa, 1989). In both cases, portraying the relatively powerful party as low in power, and the relatively powerless party as high in power, fomented or justified exploitation or abuse.

Several ways ideologies can be used to create or justify an imbalance of power and to enable exploitation have been outlined. First, certain ideologies establish power as being only appropriately exercised by some, to the disadvantage of others. Such ideologies are usually overtly linked to groups, but do not necessarily demean the group whose power they limit or elevate the group whose power they increase. Second, ideologies give more power to those whose needs are prioritized, who are declared unable to meet needs, and give less power to those declared able to meet needs. Note again that this has nothing to do with the surface positivity or negativity of these prescriptions. The laundry detergent commercials that portray men as so inept at doing laundry that they need women's help do nothing for the cause of gender equality, nor does the belief that women are superior childcare givers, because such stereotypes bind women to doing laundry and childcare while freeing men from such obligations. Third, when an ideology of communion is used to mask differences in interests and needs, this deception can result in exploitation. Fourth, when ideologies that serve the powerful are said to be general principles that apply equally to everyone, less powerful people are disadvantaged. Fifth, when dominants use ideologies to define subordinates needs and desires in ways that serve dominants, they not only prescribe exploitation but justify it as what subordinates' want (cf. Sampson, 1993). Sixth, ideologies that describe people as having more or less power than they actually have can enable an exploitative arrangement to appear equitable or even make an exploiter seem exploited. Finally, ideologies that disguise control in affectionate and benevolent attitudes toward those they subordinate enable exploitation to go uncontested.

Only the first ideological means of establishing power described can be overt. All the other ways that ideology can aid exploitation disguise inequalities in power, needs, or resources in the masks of equality, equal treatment, communalism, benevolence, and affection. Our analysis of ideology, then, also calls for scrutinizing when communal relationships are beneficent or exploitative.

BENEFICENCE AND EXPLOITATION IN COMMUNAL RELATIONSHIPS

Unequal communal relationships can be beneficent when power is used to meet the less powerful member's needs, but can be exploitative when power is used to prioritize the more powerful members' needs. Both of these communal relationships are usefully contrasted with each other and with egalitarian exchange.

In egalitarian exchange, members have equal power because they are equally free to enter into, exit, and negotiate the terms of exchange. Satisfaction is based on their need for exchange and on equity. Equality in exchange is predicated on equal access to valued goods and equal access to exchange relationships. As neither condition is present in stratified societies, egalitarian exchange between members of different strata is assuredly rare. Exploitation within an exchange relationship is facilitated by external conditions that lower the value of one member's "goods" or their exchangeability. For example, an employer can underpay people who are discriminated against by other potential employers or who live where there are few other labor prospects. While such conditions do not require an employer to exploit workers, it follows from the exchange model that whenever one member is advantaged the other is exploited.

In communal relationships in which one member has more power, that power might go unused, or it can be used to differentially benefit the subordinate or the dominant. In contrast to exchange relationships, in communal relationships differentially benefiting the subordinate does not necessarily exploit the dominant. In fact, some communal relationships are understood to have an unequal obligation to meet the members' needs, for example, the relations between newborns and their parents or between undergraduates and their professors. Here, dominants are understood to be responsible for subordinates' needs, subordinates fill dominants' needs mainly by their existence, and dominants are understood to have their other needs fulfilled elsewhere. Such beneficence represents one form of extreme asymmetry in communal relationships; in less extreme asymmetries, subordinates fulfill some of dominants' needs and require less of dominants. Even if a dominant's obligations to care for the subordinate's needs demands so much of the dominant that the dominant's own needs are not being met, the dominant cannot be exploited by the subordinate, who by definition does not have the power to coerce the dominant.[2] In this situation, the dominant might be being exploited by another person or by an

---

2. Although the subordinate might attempt to manipulate or exert influence over the dominant.

institutional practice that forces the dominant to provide resources to the subordinate without adequate replenishment. Such situations have been brought to light by the abandonment of special-needs children in hospitals by parents who were overwhelmed by their parental obligations and who could obtain no medical or financial help for their children otherwise. Conversely, when a subordinate is obliged to fulfill the dominant's needs, but the dominant prioritizes his or her own needs at the expense of the subordinate's, the dominant exploits the subordinate.

Power in communal relationships, then, can be used for beneficence or exploitation, its use and abuse. Both beneficent and exploitative parentalism exist for the ostensible purpose of meeting their members' needs, and have one more powerful and one less powerful member. The difference between beneficent and exploitative parentalism hinges on the priorities for meeting the dominant's and subordinate's needs.

Beneficent parentalistic relationships will be warm and committed. Subordinates will not desire exit unless that meets the dominants' needs, the dominant cannot meet their needs, or they have outgrown their dependency. Dominants will allow subordinates to leave the relationships if the subordinates' needs can be met elsewhere. Beneficent parentalism characterizes some people's moral ideals for relationships between parents and small children, teachers and students, and mentors and mentees. Indeed, cultural ideologies like nurturing role prescriptions and maturation scripts are foremost among the external conditions that facilitate these relationships.

Exploitative parentalism is more complex, for it binds communion and competition, hiding contradictions. The relationship exists ostensibly for the meeting of the members' needs, and has some warmth. But when the subordinate's needs are repeatedly defined by the dominant as nonneeds, trivialized, put off, and ignored, the subordinate will experience resource depletion (e.g., fatigue, stress, lack of time, money, or independent accomplishment). A subordinate with some sense of self-respect is likely to then feel confused, frustrated, insulted, and angry. If the subordinate expresses negative feelings, the dominant may become angry or confused at the "ingratitude" of the subordinate, but may attend to the subordinate's needs and feelings. If so, the subordinate will be obliged to repair the union. If the dominant reverts to putting the other's needs last, the subordinate will again experience negative feelings. This relationship, then, is an emotional rollercoaster. With repeated episodes, the subordinate may learn to expect less and to ignore his or her feelings and lose the sense of self, especially when cultural ideologies aid that process ("What do you know? You're just a kid!" "I don't know how to help you. Men can't understand women.") Even this kind of learning is not guaranteed to smooth out the emotional rollercoaster. Borderline personality disorder is thought to develop as a response to having one's needs and emotions repeatedly ignored and denied, but people with this disorder are emotionally volatile and extraordinarily unstable in their interpersonal relationships (e.g., Linehan, 1993).

Given some sense of entitlement, when subordinates experience resource shortages or negative emotions, and perhaps realize that they are being exploited, they will feel like changing or leaving the relationship. But if subordinates consider the power differential, they will recognize that exiting, expressing dissatisfaction, and changing the needs priorities of the relationship carry risks, such as the loss of shared joint work, expertise, credibility (referent power), access to resources the dominant controls, acquiring a spoiled reputation (e.g., ungrateful, trouble-maker), and the dominants' neglect or wrath. Subordinates in exploitative parentalistic relationships are at risk if they do leave and at risk if they don't. In addition, because the dominant does benefit in these relationships, dominants will use power, express concern, and invoke the subordinate's obligation to the relationship to prevent exit or to make it less attractive. In such ways the dominant can coerce the subordinate into staying in the relationship, into caring for the dominant's needs, and even into putting the subordinates' own needs last. The conflicting goals within and between the members make these relationships rocky. Subordinates may also stay in the relationship to try to recoup their investments, and because being exploited has depleted them too much to find alternatives. If, however, there are available cultural ideologies that prescribe the dominants' priorities (e.g., sexism, apprenticeship), people may perceive the relationship as moral rather than as exploitative. And when subordinates have learned to deny self-entitlement, these same ideologies can lead to self-blame and prevent dissatisfaction with the relationship.

The external social conditions that facilitate exploitative parentalism are a monstrous reflection of those that facilitate beneficent parentalism. Social ideologies prescribing caretaking in beneficent parentalism hide the abuse of power of exploitative parentalism. For example, assuming that parents take care of their children might lead one to overlook neglect or abuse. Where greater authoritative power, expert power, referent power, and reward power can be used to benefit the subordinate in beneficent parentalism, this power also enables a dominant to take credit for the subordinate's contributions and to coerce those contributions. Such exploitation may be tolerated by all if it seems temporary, as the "casting couch" may appear to young actresses hoping to land roles. It may even seem a necessary and legitimate path to a goal, as when medical students "get pimped," being humiliated by doctors in rounds. But history cautions us to be suspicious of temporary exploitative arrangements: Chattel slavery and apartheid were derived from indentured servitude (see Frederickson, 1981; Jordon, 1974).

Dominants can get away with exploitation because their superior social standing or expert power (French & Raven, 1959) leads people to accept the dominant's stated (good) intentions at face-value, and because the subordinate's expression of own needs and of being exploited may be dismissed as inappropriate or naive. When ideologies such as racism or sexism diminish the personhood of subordinates, others may pay little attention to how their needs are being defined and whether their needs are actually being met (Sampson, 1993).

Our theory suggests that both beneficent and exploitative parentalism will be perceived as communal rather than as exchange relationships. Further, the apparent communality of exploitative parentalism will make it difficult to perceive its danger to subordinates. These hypotheses were tested by assessing people's responses to vignettes about dyadic relationships (Walker & Pratto, 2000). Because the theoretical definitions of these relationships can pertain to both personal (e.g., familial) relationships and impersonal (e.g., work) relationships, there was one set of vignettes about relationships between parent and child, and another about relationships between a boss and an intern. Although we suspect that individuals' external social standing (e.g., due to class, race, gender, expertise) can influence their power in interpersonal relationships, we also believe that the theoretical depictions of the three relationship types transcend these. Thus, our family vignette was about a father and his teenage son, and the work vignette concerned two women. Each relationship was depicted in one of three vignettes as egalitarian exchange, exploitative parentalism, or beneficent parentalism. Each of the three family vignettes had the same basic plot; likewise for the three work vignettes. In the exchange relationships, there was less emotional sharing and more bargaining than in the other two relationships. In both parentalistic relationships, the dominant asked for the assistance of the subordinate, but in the beneficent relationship, this help was acknowledged publicly and the dominant also attended to the subordinate's needs, whereas in the exploitative relationship, the subordinate's help was not publicly acknowledged and the subordinate's emotional state and other needs got little attention from the dominant. For example, in the father-son exchange relationship, the father and son agreed on a rate for paying the son to do household chores. Though the son intended to earn the money for a date, he never communicated that to his father, and he sought the advice of a friend rather than that of his father in planning his date. In the beneficent parentalistic relationship, the son did household chores because he saw they needed to be done and to distract himself from concerns about his date, sought and received his father's advice and personal stories about dating, and received money and other help from his father to plan his date. When the son helped the father with some computer presentations for work, the father acknowledged the help he'd received to his colleagues. In the exploitative parentalistic relationship, the father largely ignored his son's hints about dating concerns, but asked his son not only for help with household chores but for extraordinary help with a project at work. The father thanked the son for his help, but when his father's performance was praised at work, he took his wife out to dinner to celebrate, leaving the son to babysit a younger sibling.

In the work exchange vignette, the relationship was polite but unemotional. The boss monitored the intern's performance weekly and they agreed on how to divide their work. In the communal work relationships, the boss used more emotional expression and attended to her intern's emotional states. In the beneficent relationship, the boss asked about the intern's future career plans and helped her plan her next professional steps to achieve the intern's goals. When the team landed a big contract and the boss was publicly praised for her work, she insisted that her intern's contributions to the project were acknowledged and she asked that her intern work on the new high-prestige project. In the exploitative relationship, the boss demanded substantial extra work from the intern and praised her for it privately, but in public, took all the credit for landing the big contract herself, and then suggested it would be in the intern's best interests to work in another department rather than on the high-prestige project.

Despite the differences in the actor's genders, settings, and plot of the work and family vignettes, the results were similar for both sets of vignettes. As we expected, participants rated both parentalistic relationships as more communal than the exchange relationships up until the dominant's failure to properly recognize the subordinate's help and to respond to the subordinate's needs was revealed. Participants felt that the dominants' coercive power was higher in the exchange and the exploitative relationships than in the beneficent relationships, in which they felt that the dominants' reward power was higher than in the other two. Participants rated the beneficent relationship as the least rocky.

When asked whether the subordinates should stay in the relationship, only a few participants thought the subordinate should leave the work or family beneficent relationship. In contrast, for both the work and family vignettes, participants were completely divided as to whether the subordinate should leave the exploitative relationship. Those who believed the subordinate should stay in the relationship still rated the relationship as highly communal, whereas those who thought the subordinate should leave rated the relationship low in communality. These results reflect the ambivalent position of the subordinate's situation in an exploitative parentalistic relationship; there are risks to both leaving and staying. Further, these results show that the belief that the relationship is communal can lead people to fail to see the harm done to subordinates in these relationships. People's general expectations that communal relationships are caring and egalitarian help disguise the abuse of power that sometimes occurs in them.

These experimental studies reflect the pseudo-trust and ambivalence over what people in real subordinate positions feel when exploited. Graduate students do not trust faculty who coerce them, and intend to end the professional relationship as soon as they can, but also comply with coercive faculty if the faculty have legitimate power over them (Aguinis et al., 1996). Black domestic workers who are confided in but not respected by their employers will lie to their employers when asked about personal details of their own or other Black people's lives, but will affect obsequious mannerisms to keep their jobs (Rollins, 1993). Subordinates' behavior may then communicate that they have a positive, intimate relationship with a superior because their low power gives them little choice, even when they privately feel that their superior's coercion and disrespect are inappropriate. Such behavior holds the dominant's mask of beneficence in place.

STRUCTURAL AND INTERPERSONAL CONDITIONS FOR EXPLOITATIVE PARENTALISM

The apparent contradictions between community and unequal power and between communion and exploitation make their co-occurrence seem unlikely. This may be why parentalism has received little research attention. Yet the examples described indicate that many communal relationships have unequal power, and there are both social-structural and psychological reasons to expect exploitation to occur in some of them.

Structural Conditions

Scarcity of human resources may lead to the desire to extract benefit from others continually, rather than depleting and discarding those sources. This may lead people to control, exploit, and care for those other human resources at the same time. For example, mediaeval European feudal landowners were dependent on peasant labor, and with few other means of support, peasants could be coerced by landowners. Yet landowners held the chivalric ideal that they cared for and served their peasants (Swabey, 1999; Tuchman, 1978). In China women have been most oppressed within families when female infanticide made them most rare (Cardarelli, 1996).

Second, when establishing the relationship is costly, it becomes more desirable to form a stable, extractive relationship that subordinates the other. For example, in societies in which prospective grooms offer a bride-price of gifts to the bride's family, women have less power and prestige than in societies in which dowries are given from the prospective bride's family to the groom's (Goody, 1973). The expense of the bride-price may disenable men from earning other wives, and so motivate them not only to keep the wife they have, but also to extract as much as they can from her. A bride-price also gives a woman's birth family an interest in severing their ties to her, whereas a dowry, which usually stays with the woman, does not sever that tie.

Third, when preparing the other to be a resource is costly but such investment pays, continuing extractive relationships is desirable. It is well-known that adults who expect their children to contribute to the family income (e.g., through manual agriculture) produce more children than adults who do not reap the rewards of their children's labor. Many faculty advisors have joked that they should not allow their best students to graduate, but we know some who actually have done this to extract more ideas and intellectual labor from their students.

Interpersonal Conditions

Continual extractive relationships between members of different groups are often intimate as well as exploitative. For example, parentalism is common in heterosexual relations, parent-child relations, domestic labor, and sharecropping (Glick & Fiske, 1996; Jackman, 1994; Kleinig, 1983; Rollins, 1993; van den

Berghe, 1967). Intimacy affords methods of influence such as emotional contagion and induction, conversation, physical contact, and using intimate knowledge that more distal relationships do not. But intimacy also restrains influence tactics because subordinates can easily harm dominants by lying, poisoning, humiliating, destroying property, and neglect. These restraints necessitate some level of trust between dominants and subordinates that may temper both the severity of coercion and the emotional tone of interactions. For these reasons, more intimate relations between members of hierarchical groups may have a more benevolent quality than impersonal intergroup relations.

The smooth functioning of people in complementary oppressive relationships is greatly facilitated by shared ideologies (Sidanius & Pratto, 1999), and given the necessity of trust, it is not surprising that benevolent and other apparently nonprejudicial ideologies are prevalent in such relationships. These ideologies are also effective because they can disguise control, unequal outcomes, and noncommon interests while preventing the resentfulness and rebellion that forceful dominance can bring. Dominants may prefer to emphasize affectionate and communal ideologies rather than their own power not only for the political advantages, but because parentalistic ideologies provide positive (beneficent, nonprejudiced) self-images, because they believe in their own authority and have attended little to the situations of subordinates, and because such ideologies seem more egalitarian than overtly dominative ones. Subordinates may treasure affectionate and communal ideologies and relationships with dominants because these appear an oasis of acceptance and equality in the desert of hostility and subordination. If they worry that their inputs to a relationship are not as valuable and they are therefore cheating as an equity analysis suggests, subordinates may value communal ideologies for providing an alternative to that conclusion.

So long as the judgments and worldviews of dominants are bolstered by power and appear right, both dominants and subordinates may be persuaded by dominants' expressions of beneficence, regardless of whether subordinates are being exploited and whether their needs are being met. When dominants fail to attend to the actual conditions and needs of subordinates, especially when they stifle or ignore the voices of subordinates, their prescriptions of what is good for subordinates can easily extract value from subordinates without replenishment.

Our emphasis on the potential for exploitation in parentalistic relationships is only intended as an antidote against its many disguises, not a conclusion that no beneficence exists. Indeed, much human development, from infant maturation to musical genius, requires that more fully developed persons share their expertise and care with less fully developed persons. Beneficent parentalism would appear essential to bringing about greater equality; as group-based hierarchy is ubiquitous (Sidanius & Pratto, 1999), and rebellions by subordinates are usually crushed, it is difficult to imagine how more equality can be brought about without using power to empower subordinate people. For these reasons, it is critical to understand how to ensure that attempts at beneficent parentalism do not instead become exploitative, and that exploitative parentalism not be allowed to masquerade as beneficent.

METHODS OF PREVENTING EXPLOITATIVE PARENTALISM

The critical difference between beneficent and exploitative parentalism is whether the dominant's power is used to prioritize the dominant's or the subordinant's needs. The most obvious way of preventing exploitative parentalism, then, is to be very strict in not allowing dominants to put their needs ahead of subordinates'. For example, exploitation and abuse should not be allowed on the grounds that they are temporary. To assess their needs accurately, subordinates' voices must be heard even if this causes discomfort. Given the pull of dominants' motivations and the limits of subordinates' power, those outside the relationship in question can help prevent exploitation by institutionalizing priorities and by spreading ideologies that disapprove of the abuse of power. In addition, dominants and subordinates can communicate, their expectations and needs to explicate the terms of their relationship so that its obligations and benefits are clear.

The second way to prevent exploitation is to limit dominants' power over subordinates. Subordinates can do so by taking care that they are attractive relationship partners to others outside the relationship. Institutionalizing and normalizing ways that more than one person can meet someone's needs can limit power imbalances within a dyad by limiting the degree of dependency a person has on the other and by limiting caregivers' inability to exit or to use their resources for themselves. It may be helpful to remember that the goal of a communal relationship is not to enact a particular ideology (e.g., being the perfect mother), but to meet needs. Finding others to meet needs can prevent a dominant from refusing to recognize a subordinate's need because the dominant does not feel capable of meeting it or does not want to meet that need herself. It can also ensure that a dominant does not force a subordinate to meet a need inappropriately or force a dominant to go without simply because the subordinate can't or shouldn't meet the dominant's need.

In addition, dominants' power can be limited by institutionalizing subordinates' exit from parentalistic relationships, and by ritual recognition of subordinates' development (and lesser dependency). Power imbalances can also be tempered by providing information about the boundaries of dominants' rights and of what subordinates' rights are. Institutions can do this by publicizing guidelines for dominants' behavior (e.g., what demands are legitimate to make on secretaries or children and what are not) and subordinates' rights, by supporting networking among subordinates while allowing them privacy, by publicly acknowledging the wrongness of exploitation when it occurs, and by punishing dominants who exploit. Dominants' ideological power can be reduced by calling them on it when dominants use ideologies that reduce the value and power of the other, such as sexist remarks. To prevent prejudicial ideologies from influencing people's outcomes, institutions should make the criteria for judging meritorious performance explicit, should standardize how these judgments are made, and evaluate whether the criteria and process of evaluation disadvantage certain groups. Finally, subordinates must not accept affection as a substitute for respect. Respect can earn one power, resources, and prestige, but love is not exchangeable and neither is feigned affection.

The third way of preventing exploitative parentalism is to change the structural situations that drive people into them. In low technology agricultural societies, unequal private land ownership promotes feudalism, whereas common stewardship of land promotes greater equality. In technological societies, institutions can reward good mentorship and teams of people, rather than rewarding individuals for work that is accomplished by teams. Institutions can also have effective mentors teach other people how to mentor, and reward that teaching. Opportunity structures for excluded groups must be opened up to lessen the possibility that their members can be exploited by any given dominant.

Much of this chapter described how dominance and exploitation could be disguised in communal norms, positive stereotypes, and beneficent attitudes. The fourth way to prevent exploitative parentalism, then, is to scrutinize: Compare the subordinate's actual well-being and needs against the dominant's actions. To scrutinize, one must first allow that different people even in intimate communal relationships might have different goals and needs, so that dominants cannot equate subordinates' needs with their own. To assess subordinates' needs separately from dominants' pronouncements, subordinates must be allowed voice and given attention by others, must learn to articulate their own needs, and must use their own voices. Developing this articulation should be made part of the developmental goals of parentalistic relationships. Institutions and dominants can structure regular times to hear from subordinates, and must take care not to punish answers other than those they expect or find comfortable.

The process of scrutiny can also be aided by mental models of what exploitative parentalism is, and how it is both different than and similar to beneficent parentalism. As most people play dominant and subordinate roles, everyone needs to understand exploitative parentalism. Naming exploitative parentalism and explaining how it works was the purpose of this work. There is a need for cultural narratives to give a face and a name to exploitative parentalism so that it can be recognized and referenced in discourse. If people can learn to be suspicious that their financial needs will be met by a loan shark who says, "I'm gonna take care of you real good," then they can learn when to be suspicious and when to trust bosses, teachers, family members, collaborators, and mentors, who say the same thing.

REFERENCES

Aguinis, H., Nesler, M. S., Quigley, B. M., Lee-Suk-Jae, & Tedeschi, J. T. (1996). Power bases of faculty supervisors and educational outcomes for graduate students. *Journal of Higher Education, 67,* 267–293.

Blumer, H. (1960). Race prejudice as a sense of group position. *Pacific Sociological Review, 1,* 3–5.

Bugental, D. B., Blue, J., & Cruzcosa, M. (1989). Perceived control over caregiving outcomes: Implications for child abuse. *Developmental Psychology, 25,* 532–539.

Bugental, D. B., Lyon, J. I., Cortez, V., & Krantz, J. (1997). Who's the boss? Accessibility of dominance ideation among individuals with low perceptions of interpersonal power. *Journal of Personality and Social Psychology, 72,* 1297–1309.

Campbell, D. T. (1965). Ethnocentric and other altruistic motives. In D. Levine (Ed.), *Nebraska symposium on motivation* (pp. 283–311). Lincoln, NE: University of Nebraska Press.

Cardarelli, L. (1996). The lost girls. *Utne Reader, May-June.* pp. 13–14.

Clark, M. S. (1984). Record-keeping in two types of relationships. *Journal of Personality and Social Psychology, 47,* 549–557.

Clark, M. S., & Mills, J. (1979). Interpersonal attraction in exchange and communal relationships. *Journal of Personality and Social Psychology, 37,* 12–24.

Clark, M. S., Mills, J., & Powell, M. C. (1986). Keeping track of needs in communal and exchange relationships. *Journal of Personality and Social Psychology, 51,* 333–338.

Clark, M. S., & Waddell, B. (1985). Perceptions of exploitation in communal and exchange relations. *Journal of Social and Personal Relationships, 2,* 403–418.

Collier, J. (1988). *Marriage and inequality in classless societies.* Stanford, CA: Stanford University Press.

Davis, A. Y. (1981). *Women, race, and class.* New York: Vintage.

Engels, F. (1884/1902). *The origin of the family, private property, and the state.* (E. Untermann, Trans.) Chicago: E. H. Kerr. (Original work published 1884)

Faludi, S. (1991). *Backlash: The undeclared war against American women.* New York: Crown Publishers.

Fiske, S. T. (1998). Stereotyping, prejudice, and discrimination. In D. T. Gilbert, S. T. Fiske, & G. Lindzey (Eds.), *Handbook of social psychology, II* (pp. 357–411). New York: McGraw-Hill.

Fitzhugh, G. (1854). *Sociology for the South, or the Failure of Free Society.* New York: Burt Franklin.

Frederickson, G. M. (1981). *White supremacy: A comparative study of American and South African history.* New York: Oxford University Press.

French, J. R. P., & Raven, B. H. (1959). The bases of social power. In D. Cartwright (Ed.), *Studies in social power.* Ann Arbor, MI : Institute for Social Research. (pp. 150-167).

Friedan, B. (1974). *The feminine mystique.* New York: Norton.

Glick, P., Deibold, J., Bailey-Werner, B., & Zhu, L. (1997). The two faces of Adam: Ambivalent sexism and polarized attitudes toward women. *Personality and Social Psychology Bulletin, 23,* 1323–1334.

Glick, P., & Fiske, S. T. (1996). The ambivalent sexism inventory: Differentiating hostile and benevolent sexism. *Journal of Personality and Social Psychology, 70,* 491–512.

Glick, P., Fiske, S. T., Abrams, D., Masser, B., Brunner, A., Willemsen, T. M., Dardenne, B., Dijksterhuis, A., Wigboldus, D., Eckes, T., Six-Materna, I., Exposito, F., Moya, M., Foddy, M., Kim, H., Mladanic, A., Mucchi-Faina, A., Romani, M., Saiz, J. L., & SakallI, N. (2000). *An ambivalent and subtle, yet traditional and pervasive prejudice: Ambivalent sexism across cultures.* Unpublished manuscript, Lawrence University.

Goody, J. (1973). Bridewealth and dowry in Africa and Eurasia. In J. Goody & S. J. Tambiah (Eds.), *Bridewealth and dowry* (pp. 1–58). Cambridge, UK: Cambridge University Press.

Gordon, L. (1994). *Pitied but not entitled: Single mothers and the history of welfare.* New York: Free Press.

Gossett, T. F. (1963). *Race: The history of an idea in America.* Dallas: Southern Methodist University Press.

Homans, G. C. (1961). *Social behavior: Its elementary forms.* Burlingame, CA: Harcourt, Brace, and World.

hooks, b. (1984). *Black women: Shaping femi-*

nist theory. *Feminist theory: from margin to center* (pp. 1–15). Boston: South End Press.

Jackman, M. R. (1994). *The velvet glove: Paternalism and conflict in gender, class, and race relations*. Berkeley, CA: University of California Press.

Johnson, W. R. (1994). *Dismantling apartheid: A South African town in transition*. Ithaca: Cornell University Press.

Jordan, W. D. (1974). *The white man's burden: Historical origins of racism in the United States*. New York: Oxford University Press.

Katz, I., & Hass, R. G. (1988). Racial ambivalence and American value conflict: Correlational and priming studies of dual cognitive structures. *Journal of Personality and Social Psychology, 55*, 893–905.

Keen, S. (1986). *Faces of the enemy*. San Francisco: Harper and Row.

Keinig, J. (1983). *Paternalism*. Totowa, NJ: Rowman & Allanheld.

Kelley, H. H. (1979). *Personal relationships*. Hillsdale, NJ: Erlbaum.

Kelley, H. H., & Thibaut, J. W. (1978). *Interpersonal relationships*. New York: Wiley.

Linehan, M. M. (1993). *Cognitive-behavioral treatment of borderline personality disorder*. New York: Guilford.

Marshall, L. L., & Vitanza, S. A. (1994). Physical abuse in close relationships: Myths and realities. In A. L. Weber & J. H. Harvey (Eds.), *Perspectives on close relationships* (pp. 263–284). Boston: Allyn and Bacon.

Marx, K. (1904). *A contribution to a critique of political economy*. London: Charles Kerr.

Marx, K., & Engels, F. (1846/1970). *The German ideology*. New York: International Publishers.

McConahay, J. B. (1986). Modern racism, ambivalence, and the modern racism scale. In J. F. Dovidio & S. L. Gaertner (Eds.), *Prejudice, discrimination and racism* (pp. 91–125). New York: Academic Press.

Millet, K. (1970). *Sexual politics*. Garden City, NY: Doubleday.

Mills, J., & Clark, M. S. (1986). Communications that should lead to perceived exploitation in communal and exchange relations. *Journal of Social and Clinical Psychology, 4*, 225–234.

Moghaddam, F. M., Slocum, N. R., Finkel, N., Mor, T., & Harre, R. (2000). Toward a cultural theory of duties. *Culture and Psychology, 6*, 275–302.

Okin, S. M. (1989). *Justice, gender, and the family*. New York: Basic Books.

Pratto, F. (1996). Sexual politics: The gender gap in the bedroom, the cupboard, and the cabinet. In D. M. Buss & N. M. Malamuth (Eds.), *Sex, power, and conflict: Evolutionary and feminist perspectives* (pp. 179–230). New York: Oxford.

Pratto, F. (1999). The puzzle of continuing group inequality: Piecing together psychological, social, and cultural forces in social dominance theory. *Advances in Experimental Social Psychology, 31*, 191–263.

Pratto, F., Liu, J., Levin, S., Sidanius, J., Shih, M., Bachrach, H., & Hegarty, P. (2000). Social dominance orientation and the legitimization of inequality across cultures. *Journal of Cross-Cultural Psychology, 31*, 369–409.

Pratto, F., Stallworth, L. M., & Conway-Lanz, S. (1998). Social dominance orientation and the legitimization of policy. *Journal of Applied Social Psychology, 28*, 1853–1875.

Pratto, F., Tatar, D., & Conway-Lanz, S. (1999). Who gets what and why? Determinants of social allocations. *Political Psychology, 20*, 127–150.

Rollins, J. (1993). Deference and maternalism. In A. M. Jaggar & P. S. Rothenberg (Eds.), *Feminist frameworks: Alternative theoretical accounts of the relations between women and men* (pp. 335–345). New York: McGraw-Hill.

Rusbult, C. E. & van Lange, P. A. M. (1998). Interdependence processes. In A. Kruglanski & E. T. Higgins (Eds.), *Handbook of social psychology* (pp. 564–596). New York: Guilford Press.

Sacks, K. (1974). Engels revisited: Women, the organization of production, and private property. In M. Z. Rosaldo & L. Lamphere (Eds.), *Women, culture, and society* (pp. 207–222). Stanford, CA: Stanford University Press.

Sampson, E. E. (1993). *Celebrating the other*. Boulder, CO: Westview Press.

Sanday, P. R. (1981). *Female power and male dominance*. Cambridge, UK: Cambridge University Press.

Sears, D. O. (1988). Symbolic racism. In P. A. Katz, & D. A. Taylor (Eds.), *Eliminating racism* (pp. 53–84). NY: Plenum Press.

Sherif, M., & Sherif, C. W. (1966). *Groups in harmony and tension*. New York: Octagon Books.

Sidanius, J., & Pratto, F. (1999). *Social dominance*. New York: Cambridge University Press.

Sidanius, J., Pratto, F., & Bobo, L. (1996). Racism, conservatism, and affirmative action: A matter of principled conservatism or social dominance? *Journal of Personality and Social Psychology, 70*, 476–490.

Sniderman, P. M., Piazza, T., Tetlock, P. E., & Kendrick, A. (1991). The new racism. *American Journal of Political Science, 35*, 423–447.

Swabey, F. (1999). *Medieval gentlewoman: Life in a gentry household in the latter middle ages*. New York: Routledge.

Thibaut, J. W., & Kelley, H. H. (1959). *The social psychology of groups*. New York: Wiley.

Tilly, C. (1998). *Durable inequality*. Berkeley, CA: University of California Press.

Tuchman, B. W. (1978). *A distant mirror: The calamitous 14th century*. New York: Ballantine Books.

Turner, J. H., & Singleton, R. (1978). A theory of ethnic oppression: Toward a reintegration of cultural and structural concepts in ethnic relations theory. *Social Forces, 56*, 1001–1018.

Van den Berghe, P. (1967). *Race and racism A comparitive perspective*. New York: Wiley.

Walker, A., & Pratto, F. (2000). *Exploitation and beneficence in parentalistic relationships*. Unpublished manuscript, University of Connecticut.

Walster, E., Berscheid, E., & Walster, G. W. (1973). New directions in equity research. *Journal of Personality and Social Psychology, 25*, 151–176.

7

The Many Faces of Power
The Strange Case
of Dr. Jekyll and Mr. Hyde

DAPHNE BLUNT BUGENTAL
ETA K. LIN

*"Mr. Hyde . . . had a displeasing smile; he had borne
himself . . . with a sort of murderous mixture of timidity
and boldness . . . "*
— Robert Louis Stevenson (*Dr. Jekyll and Mr. Hyde*)

We are all familiar with the polar twins of Dr. Jekyll and Mr. Hyde. The basic characters reflect the opposed forces of reasoned, controlled, responsible thought and action (Dr. Jekyll) and impulsive, uncontrolled, self-serving thought and action (Mr. Hyde). The characters have commonly be invoked as an allegory for the inconsistency that is true of all of us. However, we also speak of someone as having a Jekyll and Hyde personality, and reveal both fear and fascination in response to such individuals. Here we picture the public figure who charms us all but then acts out a murderous rage or shows an unthinkable disregard for others. We may also picture the innocuous, seemingly submissive coworker who goes home to abuse a partner or children.

Nineteenth century literature, along with the emerging fields of psychology and psychiatry, shared a fascination with the duality of human nature. Consistent with the focus on moralism in this period, such dualism revolved around the polarities of good and evil—the human capacity to be the arrogant, hedo-

Funding for this chapter was provided by grants from NIMH (R01 MH3995) and NSF (BNS-9021221) to the first author.

115

nistic, uncaring monster at one time, and at other times the compassionate, upright, responsible member of society. Freud's (1938) notions of superego and id (as regulated by the ego) reflected this basic duality. A companion theme within much of this work was the focus on unconscious processes that play themselves out seemingly against one's will, and the reflective, socialized processes that serve to overcome or correct the more basic processes.

Although dualities are present in many features of human functioning, the management of power-based relationships easily yield examples of duplicity or inconsistency. Across different settings, we occupy changing positions of power and we respond in different ways within those contexts. Kipnis (1976) developed the notion of the transformational properties of power consistent with Lord Acton's (1887) well known admonition that "Power tends to corrupt, and absolute power corrupts absolutely." In this chapter, the nature of such transformations are explored as a means of explaining why there are such contradictions in the properties associated with power. That is, some findings suggest that those who have high power are particularly likely to be aggressive whereas—paradoxically—other findings suggest that it is those who lack power who are more likely to be aggressive. As another apparent contradiction, those who have high power are sometimes described as accurate readers of the intentions of others; however, other findings suggest that those who lack power are canny observers of others. One possible resolution of this paradox is that those who occupy a position of authority but are uncertain of their actual power may show both sets of responses on different occasions. In this chapter, contextual and individual differences that may foster the coexistence of the polar twins of appeasement and assertion/aggression are examined.

DEFINING POWER

Ways of Conceptualizing Power

Before we go on to consider the many faces of power, a few words of definition are in order. Social power has traditionally been defined on the basis of the demonstrated ability of one individual to exert influence over others and to defend against the power of others (e.g., Cartwright, 1959; Hollander, 1985; Weber, 1947). This ability rests with the resources or status held by the individual as a potential premise for influence. Other research has focused on the different bases of power and the ways in which such differences influence interactions (e.g., Kipnis, 1976; Raven, 1993). As a third theme, attention has been given to perceived power as a guide to affect, action, and cognition (e.g., Bugental, 1993; Ng, 1980; Sagrestano, Heavey, & Christianson, 1999).

Self-perceived Power

In this chapter, the focus is on the role of self-perceived power among those who occupy a formal position of authority. This chapter is concerned with the power they attribute to self versus the power they attribute to others, that is, the perceived balance of power within interdependent relationships. Consistent with the formulations of Fiske and her colleagues (e.g., Fiske, Morling, & Stevens, 1996), attention is directed to the relative control that individuals have (and believe that they have) over each other's fate (individual or joint outcomes). Within this approach, the emphasis is on mutual or interdependent influence (Kelley, 1979; Thibaut & Kelley, 1959).

Perceived Power as a Social Schema.   The perceived balance of power within relationships may be conceptualized as a social schema. Within both social and developmental psychology, there has been an increasing interest in cognitive representations of relationships as guides to expectancies, affect, and interaction (e.g., Andersen & Glassman, 1996; Baldwin, 1992; Bowlby, 1980). Bugental (e.g., Bugental et al., 1997) has been concerned with the ways in which adults represent their relationships with the young, that is, how individuals differ in the extent to which they define their relationships as involving hierarchical, asymmetrical power. Perceived power (as measured by the Parent Attribution Test; Bugental, Blue, & Cruzcosa, 1989) includes the orthogonal components of power/influence attributed to self, and power/influence attributed to children. Those who attribute high power to children and low power to self are described as having a low perceived balance of power within the relationship (see Figure 7.1).

Chronic Accessibility of Power Schemas.   Power schemas, like other well learned knowledge structures, eventually become chronically accessible. For example, parents with a low perceived balance of power have been found to easily access social dominance ideation. In a recent study (Bugental, Lyon, Cortez, & Krantz, 1997), parents were asked to carry out a judgment task in which they compared themselves with their children on adjectives that reflected both affect and power. They made these judgments either under cognitive load (holding a number string in memory) or no load conditions. It was expected that low power parents would make dominance judgments (comparing self versus child on negative, high power words such as "bossy") just as quickly in the

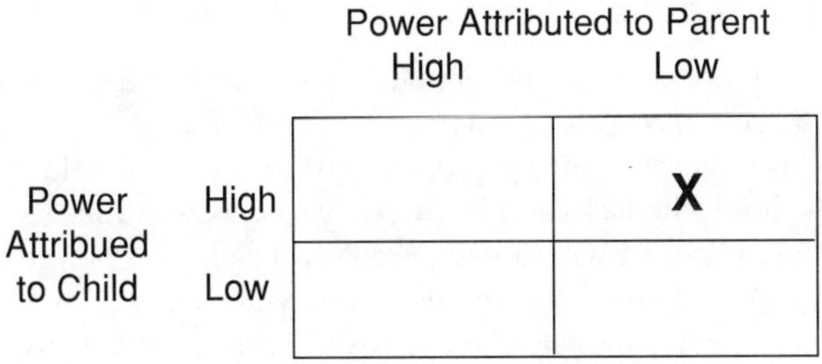

Power Attributed to Parent

		High	Low
Power Attribued to Child	High		**X**
	Low		

FIGURE 7.1. Perceived balance of power.

presence or absence of dual attentional demands—consistent with the notion that such ideation is chronically accessible for them. Confirming this prediction, low power parents were indeed found to make such judgments just as quickly in the presence or absence of a cognitive load. In contrast, other parents were slowed in making such judgments under cognitive load (reflecting the lower levels of accessibility of such ideation for these individuals). No equivalent differences were found for latencies in judging other adjectives (i.e., positive-strong, positive-weak, negative-weak, or neutral adjectives).

"Correction" of Automatic Processes.   Reflective or controlled cognitive processes have traditionally been viewed as placing attentional demands on the information processor (Shiffrin & Schneider, 1977). Thus, any effort to override or correct automatic cognitions can be more effectively executed when the individual has the requisite attentional resources, that is, when they are not cognitively busy (Gilbert, Pelham, & Krull, 1988). In the study described above, low power parents (consistent with their schematic representation of parent-child relationships) were more likely than other parents to rate children as more dominant than self—but only under conditions of cognitive load (Bugental et al., 1997). This same grouping of parents showed exactly the opposite pattern without this attentional constraint. That is, they described themselves as much more dominant than their children (a cognitive correction process).

Here we see initial evidence for the coexistence of power polarities. Judgments made under cognitive load may be interpreted as reflecting implicit cognitive processes. That is, the judgment of self as powerless is made relatively automatically. However, it also appears to directly activate power repair processes in which the self is seen as having exceptionally high power. Whereas we tend to think of corrective strategies as the rational "soldiers of awareness" that tame the "monster" of automaticity (Bargh, 1999, p. 361), they may also include more destructive processes. For example, power repair motivation may ultimately foster exaggerated power assertion as well as self-protective appeasement or avoidance.

POWER PARADOXES

Apparent Contradictions in the Effects of Power

The relationship between power (actual or perceived) and power relevant response patterns often reveals a high degree of variability. Indeed, the responses shown comprise something of a paradox by virtue of the polarities revealed—in particular by those who lack (or perceive they lack) power. Like the upstanding Dr. Jekyll, the individual with a low perceived balance of power seems to be easily transformed into his or her opposite, the tyrannical Mr. Hyde. Or alternatively, the cues to both roles can sometimes be seen simultaneously. The question is, which is the real person? Or could it be the case that the real person truly has the capability for both roles?

In my program of research, the current author has been specifically concerned with the relationship between perceived power and response inconsistency (e.g., Bugental & Shennum, 1984; Bugental et al., 1993; Bugental et al., 1997; Bugental & Johnston, 2000). The highly variable, seemingly inconsistent panoply of maneuvers that one individual may employ on different occasions emerges as a cohesive, organized pattern when attention is directed to that individual's view of his or her relationships with others. The apparent duplicity or polarities shown by those with low perceived power can be seen in both their processing of information, and their power assertion.

Polarities in Processing Accuracy. The first of these polarities can be found within information processing patterns. On the one hand, those in a position of lesser power have often been found to be exceptionally accurate in their processing of information about others. As put forward by Fiske et al. (1996), those with higher power have less need, less processing resources, and less motivation to accurately process those with lesser power. In contrast, those who lack control or who have been deprived of control regularly demonstrate a higher level of motivation for processing accuracy (e.g., Erber & Fiske, 1984; Pittman & D'Agostino, 1989). This same position has been supported by the research of Keltner and his colleague (e.g., Keltner & Robinson, 1996) showing that those with greater power are less accurate in processing information about others but are themselves more accurately perceived by others.

However, under some circumstances, those with lesser power have been found to be less accurate than are those with higher power. As suggested by Fiske et al. (1996), such deficits may occur when the individual lacks any reasonable possibility of regaining power (e.g., Ruscher & Fiske, 1990). In this case, accuracy deficits may result from anxiety. When anxiety exceeds some level, the resultant attentional demands serve as a cognitive load and serve to interfere with information processing capacity. Fiske and her colleague (e.g., Fiske & Emery, 1993) have proposed that highly control deprived individuals—due to associated anxiety and intrusive thoughts—show processing capacity deficits. Such deficits lead to increases in motivation for accuracy but decreased ability to do so. Under these circumstances, loss of control ultimately produces simplified, less accurate perceptions of others.

Polarities in Power Assertion. As another paradox, those who see themselves as lacking in power have been found not only to show higher levels of appeasement in their interactions with those of higher power (e.g., Keltner, Young, & Buswell, 1997), they have also been found on other occasions to be more aggressive or abusive than others (e.g., Bradley & Peters, 1991; Bugental, Blue, & Cruzcosa, 1989; Dutton & Strachan, 1987; Strachan & Dutton, 1992). Those who lack confidence in their power, even when occupying a formal position of authority, may temporarily show schema-consistent displays of deference or submission in response to the possibility of social challenge to their position. At other times, these same individuals become tyrants. For example,

Raven and Kruglanski (1970) demonstrated that those who lack confidence in their individual power are more likely to make use of coercive tactics when placed in a position of authority. Kipnis (1976) pointed out that coercive tactics can be used to shore up the individual's sense of worth or control.

Perceived Powerlessness as a Moderator of the Effects of Veridical Power

In light of the discrepant relationship found between social power and social response patterns, consideration needs to be given to the changing contexts of power. Ultimately, one must consider the interactive effects of externally defined power affordances and subjectively defined power perceptions.

Those who perceive themselves as powerless appear to be highly reactive to the contextual cues to potential challenge or threat. From this standpoint, self-perceived power (as a relationship schema) is best understood as a conditional variable (Mischel & Shoda, 1995). Power perceptions rarely produce main effects on the responses of parents to the young (Bugental & Johnston, 2000). Instead, they serve in a moderator role. For example, parents with low perceived power show very different kinds of responses in different settings. Their polarized responses reveal the "if–then" nature of their defensive reactions. If the environment affords good opportunities for gaining or regaining control, they may be assertive, exceptionally accurate processors. If, however, the environment affords few opportunities to regain control, they may respond with submissiveness and attentional disengagement as a means of regulating their distress (e.g., Cortez & Bugental, 1994). In ambiguous, potentially threatening settings, they may reveal both patterns. In sum, we can see a picture of a chameleon-like individual who changes with the colors of the context.

If, as suggested, power perceptions are viewed as conditional cognitions, we can potentially specify the circumstances under which disparate response patterns will be shown. As suggested above, adults with low perceived power as caregivers (or teachers) are particularly reactive to environmental cues to power affordances—either due to the characteristics of the context or the characteristics of the child. In representing the range of contextual variations, we can think in terms of settings that: 1) allow an unambiguous opportunity to gain or regain social control, 2) unambiguously prevent or constrain social control, or 3) pose an ambiguous threat to social control.

Consistent with their schematic representation of authority-based relationships, adults with low perceived power are more likely than other adults to be simultaneously prepared to deploy their attention broadly in caregiving or teaching settings if there is an opportunity for social control, or to limit their attention to sources of potential threat in settings that prevent this opportunity. In similar fashion, they may appear to be simultaneously prepared for power assertion or submission/appeasement. In situations that allow a clear opportunity for control, low power adults may appear to be self-assured and observant.

However, in situations that clearly prevent control, they may appear to be apprehensive or submissive, and narrowly focused in their observational abilities.

Possibly the most informative window on those with low perceived power emerges in response to ambiguous threat. Under these circumstances, individuals are particularly likely to rely on their cognitive representation of relationships as a means of attempting to disambiguate the social environment. If they access a low power schema, they can be expected to initially access thoughts of low power, followed by the triggering of power repair routines. Thus, they may initially reveal an appeasing/submissive manner, followed by a shift to power assertion—or even by the cooccurence of cues to low versus high dominance.

Perceived Power, Veridical Power, and Information Processing

What is the evidence? What changes in processing pattern may be anticipated as a function of the interaction between perceived power and veridical power? It may reasonably be anticipated that individuals with low perceived power—when confronted with loss of control—will show a reduced attentional capacity to process extraneous or peripheral information or to engage in cognitively demanding tasks. Cognitive interference effects may occur either as a function of intrusive thoughts, attentional avoidance, or associated emotions (Ellis & Ashbrook, 1988; Seibert & Ellis, 1991), or even by the direct effects of stress related hormones on relevant areas of the brain (e.g., Bremner & Narayan, 1998). In contrast, they may show attentional vigilance if the situation affords the opportunity for control or is ambiguous with respect to such opportunities.

Attentional Narrowing. An experimental investigation (Bugental et al., 1999), we explored the reactions of adults with relatively high or low perceived power to different levels of veridical power in a teaching interaction with children. Nonparental women were placed in a setting in which they believed they were interacting (via linked computers and closed-circuit TV) with an eight-year-old boy in another location. Women were either told that they would subsequently be evaluating children as trainees (a high power condition), that children would subsequently be evaluating them as teachers (a low power condition), or they were uninstructed with regard to future evaluations (an ambiguous condition). As all women were unrelated to children (and would not see them again), there was no basis for control over child outcomes beyond those suggested within the instructions they received. Thus, this study was important in providing a high level of control over the veridical power afforded to adults in their interactions with children.

As a means of determining participants' processing patterns, we gave them a memory task immediately following their interaction with child trainees (Bugental, 1999). That is, they were given a set of adjectives to check for spelling accuracy. Subsequently, they were asked for their free recall of those adjectives. In addition, participants were asked to recall details about the child trainee himself (as depicted in videotapes showing him interacting on a game task with the experimenter). The focus of interest was on the adult's memory for incidental, peripheral information of two types: 1) memory for neutral adjectives, and 2) memory for task-irrelevant comments made by the child (e.g., comments regarding summer activities). Additional measures were taken of memory for more central information: memory for evaluative adjectives, and memory for negative actions directed to the adult (on the videotape). Significant effects were found only for peripheral memory. For both peripheral memory measures, an interaction was found between perceived power and veridical power (as shown in Figures. 7.2 and 7.3). Participants with high perceived power showed no consistent differences in their response to power inductions. In contrast, low power participants reacted differentially to the inductions. Low power women showed peak levels of attentional narrowing (i.e., low recall of peripheral information) when they had low veridical power; in contrast, they showed broader attentional processing in high power or ambiguous power conditions. Such attentional narrowing may then provide the basis for the processing inaccuracies observed for those with low power (Ruscher & Fiske, 1990).

Reduced Cognitive Capacity.   Another study of social power and processing capacity was conducted with nonparental adults. In this investigation, we assessed the reactions of adults to their own past history in caring for children as a function of their perceived power within caregiving relationships (Bugental,

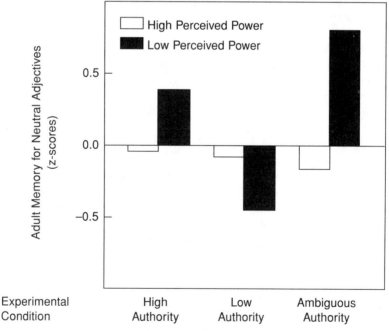

FIGURE 7.2. Recall of neutral adjectives by adults with high versus low perceived power following different power inductions.

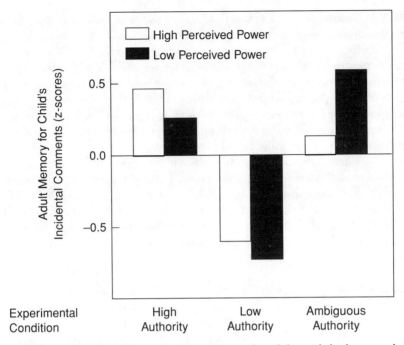

Figure 7.3. Recall of child's incidental comments by adults with high versus low perceived power following different power inductions.

Brown, & Reiss, 1996). The goal of the investigation was to determine whether adults with low perceived power show greater cognitive deficits in response to threat ideation (recalled loss of control) than did adults with higher levels of perceived power. We asked undergraduate women to recall their experiences taking care of an unrelated child, and to either think about a time when the interaction went very well or very badly. Women with low perceived power, in contrast with those with higher levels of perceived power, responded differentially to the two conditions. After thinking about a very difficult or unsuccessful interaction with a child, they showed subsequent interference in their ability to carry out a cognitively demanding task (a mental arithmetic task). No comparable differences were found following a success recollection (or a control condition). These findings support the notion that low power individuals—when primed for thoughts of lost control—show a reduced level of attentional resources. As a result, they are less able to perform well on an extraneous, cognitively demanding task.

Perceived Power, Veridical Power, and Power Assertion

In addition, power schemas serve to activate defensive social motives and behavioral routines. Just as shared social schemas (e.g., schematic representations of the elderly, minority groups, gender groupings) serve as automatic organizers of behavioral responses (Bargh, Chen, & Burrows, 1996), power schemas serve as organizers of relevant response routines.

Consistent with their conditional nature, power schemas differentially direct responses based upon the power affordances available within the immediate environment. When the setting allows the possibility of regaining control, those with low perceived power are likely to show high power assertion. These same individuals, however, are likely to show appeasement or submissiveness if the situation precludes any opportunity to regain control. Finally, those with low perceived power may be expected to show an inconsistent pattern of assertion if they are confronted with ambiguities in the opportunity to gain or regain control. In ambiguous settings, low power parents may reveal their motives through their more directly controllable responses (e.g., their verbal content, their control tactics) while leaking their fears within their less easily controlled behaviors (e.g., vocal intonation). They may also display inconsistent patterns within those channels that are only partially subject to deliberate regulation (e.g., facial actions).

Facial Actions. Facial actions provide a highly informative window on the mixed motives and affects experienced by those with low perceived power. The face has often been described as a deceptive channel of communication in which some expressive components reflect the communicator's intentions and other components reveal the communicator's underlying emotions (Ekman & Friesen, 1969). Alternatively, inconsistent facial actions have been described as reflecting the presence of mixed motives (Fridlund, 1994).

Adults with low perceived power, have indeed been found to open their interactions with children who potentially challenge their authority with appeasing smiles (Bugental, Blue, & Lewis, 1990). The patterning of their smiles is inconsistent with the patterning of smiles found to accompany true happiness or amusement ("Duchenne" smiles; Ekman, Davidson, & Friesen, 1990). Their brief, wan smiles are not accompanied by the eye involvement found to accompany true positive affect, and they may indeed be accompanied by facial indicators of affective distress (e.g., a worried brow) (Bugental, 1986; Bugental, Brown, & Reiss, 1996; Bugental, et al., 1990). These initial bursts of positive facial displays are relatively short in duration, and are soon replaced with facial actions judged to reflect disinterest (Bugental et al., 1990).

Vocal Prosody. In addition, the vocal prosody of adults with low perceived power—when confronted with different power affordances within the environment—is revealing of their underlying motives and affects. For example, their voices (at different times) have been found to be both louder and softer than those of others (Bugental & Lewis, 1998). When given a relatively high level of control over children (the opportunity to provide on-screen feedback to child trainees during interaction), they spoke with unusually loud voices during their subsequent interactions. If, however, they could only provide very brief feedback after the game was already over, they spoke with unusually soft voices during their subsequent interactions.

When confronted with ambiguous threat, those with low perceived power typically reveal a pattern of uncertainty in their vocal intonation. For example, low power adults attempting to teach a computer game to a somewhat unresponsive child were found to be more likely than other adults to punctuate their verbal instructions with brief pauses—a pattern that suggested hesitancy or uncertainty (Bugental & Lewis, 1999). In addition, this same grouping of parents was also more likely to show vocal qualities judged to be weak or as having the features of baby talk (Bugental & Shennum, 1984).

Verbal Content and Behavioral Control Tactics. In contrast to the above, low power parents directly reveal their power motives in their more controllable actions. In an experimental investigation, parents were primed for power ideation as a function of making social judgments in which they compared themselves with their children (Bugental & Happaney, in press). This task may be thought of as providing an ambiguous threat in that there was no objective information available regarding their true power or competence relative to their children. They were subsequently placed in an unstructured interaction with one of their children (and were given only a drawing made by the child as a stimulus). In this ambiguous setting, low power parents (in particular, fathers) showed increases in verbal derogation (e.g., making fun of drawings made by their children).

In community-based research, parents with low perceived power were found to be more likely to make use of coercive or abusive tactics with their own children (Bugental, Blue, & Cruzcosa, 1989). Mills (1998; in press) has observed that mothers with low perceived power are particularly likely to show high levels of power assertion in response to children who show a submissive temperament pattern. She suggests that the social cues provided by such children foster the opportunity for low power parents to demonstrate successful power assertion.

Ultimately, the use of verbal or physical aggression by subjectively powerless adults may be thought of as a temporary power repair strategy. That is, by demonstrating their power over the child (by belittling them or overpowering them physically), they temporarily establish their dominance within the relationship.

Perceived Power, Veridical Power, and Physiological Mobilization

Consideration has also been given to the interaction of perceived power and veridical power on physiological response patterns. That is, when confronted with the possibility of power threats, those with low perceived power are particularly likely to show a pattern of autonomic mobilization. They are set to either attack or flee. The perception that there is something out there that might pose a threat triggers a cascade of physiological responses in preparation for action. The sympathetic nervous system represents the first line of defense—

directing energy to muscle groups that are most likely to be needed in managing an emergency, and shutting down unnecessary systems.

The Jekyll-Hyde narrative includes an allegorical representation of such transformations:

> My devil had long been caged, he came out roaring. I was conscious, even when I took the draught, of a more unbridled, a more furious propensity to ill. It must have been this, I suppose, that stirred in my soul that tempest of impatience with which I listened to the unhappy civilities of my victim . . . I struck in no more reasonable fashion than that in which a sick child may break a plaything. (p. 141)

The significance of autonomic mobilization processes resides within their implications for both behavior and cognition. To the extent that higher levels of sympathetic activation are shown (resulting in redistribution of energy to skeletal muscles), the greater the force that is likely to be used in response to the young. As a result, autonomic activation may exacerbate the intensity of physical aggression. In addition, increases in autonomic mobilization have been shown to lead to increases in memory for emotionally upsetting events and deficits in memory for peripheral events (e.g., Easterbrook, 1959; Christianson, 1992). Thus, if those who perceive themselves as powerless show high levels of sympathetic activation in response to potential threat, they also may be more likely than others to recall the central features of those events rather than the surrounding contextual features or incidental aspects of the interaction.

In ambiguous settings, the physiological response patterns shown by lower power adults simultaneously prepare them for dominance/aggression or appeasement/withdrawal. When confronted with an ambiguous stimulus, they show a pattern of autonomic mobilization (increases in heart rate and electrodermal activity (Bugental & Cortez, 1988; Bugental et al., 1993; Bugental et al., 2000). They have also been found to show reduced skin temperature (Bugental & Cortez, 1988), a response that is consistent with fear. These responses are outside the individual's deliberate control and represent a very basic preparation for physical action.

Women with low perceived power, facing an ambiguous threat, also show an exceptionally high level of motoric activation (physical force exerted in operating computer controls)—in particular, when providing punishing responses to child trainees (Bugental et al., 1999). This response is consistent with the preferential shunting of blood to skeletal muscles in response to emergencies.

Although increases in heart rate were found to mediate increases in use of force, neither pattern (heart rate or motoric change) was found to mediate the memory deficits observed here. It is possible that such deficits are more powerfully influenced by other stress related physiological changes. In subsequent research, we found that power focused mothers were more likely than other mothers to show increases in cortisol production (a stress related hormone) during stressful interactions with their own children (Bugental & Kaufman,

1999). These women also demonstrated attentional narrowing in their memory for ongoing events. Cortisol increases were found to mediate such changes, supporting the notion that stress related physiological responses may ultimately have negative consequences for information-processing during challenging interactions.

PERCEIVED POWER AND SELF-FULFILLING PROPHECIES

Consistent with the operation of other social schemas or stereotypes, those who hold power biased views easily access schema-consistent affect (Fiske & Pavelchak, 1986) and schema-consistent behavioral routines (Bargh, Chen, & Burrows, 1996). Activation of power biased schemas (as with activation of other social stereotypes) generate response patterns that may ultimately operate in a self-fulfilling fashion. The response patterns shown by powerless individuals serve to frame their interactions with others as contests—in response to which, others are more likely to act in a competitive fashion. As pointed out by Bargh and his colleagues (Bargh, 1999; Chen & Bargh, 1997), the perceiver easily accesses schema-consistent response routines as a result of the express link between perception and action (in this case, the defensive coupling of the perceived possibility of power loss, and power-based response patterns). Others may respond in kind to the implicit power contest suggested by the power initiator's actions. Ultimately, then, the power biased individual receives confirmation of such relationships as power oriented.

The net effect of the inconsistent and changing interaction pattern is to create distress and confusion. For example, children who have received instructions from women with low perceived power subsequently show indications of avoidance or disengagement (Bugental, Kopeikin, & Lazowski, 1991; Bugental et al., 1999). In addition, they are subsequently less able than other children to perform a cognitively demanding task (Bugental et al., 1998).

Children's responses to the communication style of low power women act to confirm the adult's perceived powerlessness. Such individuals expect to be unable to influence children, and their style of interaction guarantees that they will be unable to do so. They may—in the short term—be able to stop the apparent power challenges from dependent others. In the long term, however, they will be less likely than others to have desired long-term effects on the young.

IMPLICATIONS FOR REMEDIATION

Power schemas, like stereotypes, can be expected to be resistant to change. As pointed out by Bargh (1999), efforts to deliberately control biased construals of relationships may easily produce ironic effects (Wegner, 1994). Rather than leading to reduction in power orientation, effortful attempts to overcome such ideation may actually backfire to increase the probability of such thoughts at a later time when effortful control is no longer active (e.g., Macrae et al., 1994). In particular, such ideation is likely to be activated in response to some immediate loss of self-perceived power or self-esteem (e.g., Spencer et al., 1998). Given the striking evidence concerning the resilience of stereotypes and their resistance to change (Bargh, 1999), one would have good reason to be pessimistic concerning the possibilities for change in power biased parents.

In our program of research, our attempts to produce positive changes in power biased parents have focused on prevention efforts (before a child is born) rather than remediation (after a well entrenched response style has developed). Within this program (Bugental, 1999), new parents repeatedly discuss caregiving problems, and provide their subjective appraisal of the causes of those problems. The approach focuses on encouraging an ever-broadening search for explanations and potential resolutions that are not rooted in power. Repeated exposure to such counterstereotypical search processes (in comparison with a social support-based intervention or a control condition) was found to lead to significantly lower levels of harsh or abusive parenting at the end of one year.

The basis for the success of these efforts may be explained in a number of different ways. For example, it may be based on repeated response substitution when schemas are activated (an explanation that is consistent with cognitively-based clinical remediations (e.g., Beck, 1976). Alternatively, it may be based upon an individuating process that occurs in response to a particular child.

Ultimately, the greatest long-term benefits may be anticipated as a function of the changes in the developing child. As described by Bargh (1999), attempting to change well entrenched stereotypes (or, in this case, power biased relationship schemas) in adults may be like "pulling dandelions" (p. 378). That is, the problems will re-appear in some other setting. If, however, parents successfully interrupt their automatically activated cognitions with a particular child, that child may experience permanent benefits. In this case, the seeds of a destructive cognitive bias will not be planted initially in the child's developing model of the social world.

CONCLUSIONS

Perceived power acts as an important moderator of the effects of the power affordances present in the environment. Individuals with a low perceived balance of power show exaggerated reactivity to potential power cues. They are relatively socially assertive and show broad attentional deployment in settings that reliably allow them control. In contrast, they are relatively unassertive and show attentional deficits in settings that unambiguously deprive them of control. In settings characterized by ambiguous threat (e.g., unclear authority, social comparison with their children, child unresponsiveness), they show the most striking pattern of polarity in their behavioral responses. They show a mixed picture of exaggerated appeasement and exaggerated aggression. In addition, they show a high level of attentional vigilance (possibly in the service of power appraisal processes). Finally, parents with low perceived power, under conditions of ambiguous threat, show peak levels of physiological activation—including sympathetic, and motoric mobilization.

Ultimately, the perception of power—considered in the light of the power affordances present in the real world—have profound consequences for authority-based relationships. Perceived powerlessness (and very possibly, an exaggerated or illusory sense of power) creates a high risk for violence within such relationships. The implications of this pattern at an applied level are quite apparent. At a theoretical level, these findings suggest the value of determining the role of perceived power as a moderator of more objective power parameters. Many of the anomalies in the relationships among power, processing and action may be resolved by consideration of the combined influence of perceived and true power. Like the Jekyll–Hyde character, those individuals who chronically focus on the balance of power in their relationships may be doomed to dualities. Their interaction can be expected to include a recurring vacillation between attentional vigilance and avoidance, and between appeasement and assertion—based upon the changing power parameters within their lives.

REFERENCES

Acton, Lord (John Emerich Dalberg). (1887). Letter to Bishop Mandell Creighton.

Andersen, S. M., & Glasman, N. S. (1996). Responding to significant others when they are not there: Effects on interpersonal inference, motivation, and affect. In R. M. Sorrentino & E. T. Higgins (Eds), *Handbook of motivation and cognition: The interpersonal context,* (Vol. 3, pp. 262–321). New York: Guilford Press.

Baldwin, M. W. (1992). Relational schemas and the processing of social information. *Psychological Bulletin, 112,* 461–484.

Bargh, J. A. (1999). The cognitive monster: The case against the controllability of automatic stereotype effects. In S. Chaiken & Y. Trope (Eds.), *Dual-process theories in social psychology* (pp. 361–382). New York: Guilford Press.

Bargh, J. A., Chen, M., & Burrows, L. (1996). Automaticity of social behavior: Direct effects of trait construct stereotype activation on action. *Journal of Personality and Social Psychology, 71,* 230–244.

Beck, A. T. (1976). *Cognitive therapy and the emotional disorders.* New York: International Universities Press.

Bowlby, J. (1980). *Attachment and loss: Vol. 3. Loss: Sadness and depression.* New York: Basic Books.

Bradley, E. J., & Peters, R. D. (1991). Physically abusive and nonabusive mothers' perceptions of parenting and child behavior. *American Journal of Orthopsychiatry, 61,* 455–460.

Bremner, J. D., & Narayan, M. (1998). The effects of stress on memory and the hippocampus throughout the life cycle: Implications for childhood development and aging. *Development and Psychopathology, 10,* 871–885.

Bugental, D. B. (1999, October). *Power-oriented cognitions as predictors of family violence.* Paper presented at the Meetings of the Society for Experimental Social Psychology, St. Louis, Missouri.

Bugental, D. B. (1993). Communication in abusive relationships: Cognitive constructions of interpersonal power. *American Behavioral Scientist. 36,* 288–308.

Bugental, D. B. (1986). Unmasking the "polite smile": Situational and personal Determinants of managed affect in adult-child interactions. *Personality and Social Psychology Bulletin, 12,* 7–16

Bugental, D. B., Blue, J., Cortez, V., Fleck, K., Kopeikin, H., Lewis, J., & Lyon, J. (1993). Social cognitions as organizers of autonomic and affective responses to social challenge. *Journal of Personality and Social Psychology. 64,* 94–103.

Bugental, D. B., Blue, J. B., & Cruzcosa, M. (1989). Perceived control over caregiving outcomes: Implications for child abuse. *Developmental Psychology, 25,* 532–539.

Bugental, D. B., Blue, J. & Lewis, J. (1990). Caregiver cognitions as moderators of affective reactions to "difficult" children. *Developmental Psychology, 26,* 631–638.

Bugental, D. B., Brown, M., & Reiss, C. (1996). Cognitive representations of power in caregiving relationships: Biasing effects on interpersonal interaction and information-processing. *Journal of Family Psychology, 10,* 397–407.

Bugental, D. B., & Cortez, V. L. (1988). Physiological reactivity to responsive and unresponsive children—as moderated by parental attributions. *Child Development, 59,* 686–693.

Bugental, D. B., & Happaney, K., (in press). Parent-child interaction as a power contest. *Journal of Applied Developmental Psychology.*

Bugental, D. B., & Johnston, C. (2000). Parental and child cognitions in the context of the family. *Annual Review of Psychology, 51,* 315–344.

Bugental, D. B., Johnston, C., New, M., & Silvester, J. (1998). Measuring parental attributions: Conceptual and methodological issues. *Journal of Family Psychology, 12,* 459–480.

Bugental, D. B. & Kaufman A. (1999). *Effects of stressful caregiving interactions on memory.* Unpublished manuscript. University of California, Santa Barbara.

Bugental, D. B., Kopeikin, H., & Lazowski, L. (1991). Children's responses to authentic versus polite smiles. In K. J. Rotenberg (Ed.), *Children's interpersonal trust* (pp. 58–79). New York: Springer-Verlag.

Bugental, D. B., & Lewis, J. C. (1999). The paradoxical misuse of power by those who see themselves as powerless: How does it happen? *Journal of Social Issues, 55,* 51–64.

Bugental, D. B., & Lewis, J. (1998). Interpersonal power repair in response to threats to control from dependent others. In M. Kofta, G. Weary, & G. Sedek (Eds.), *Personal control in action: Cognitive and motivational mechanisms* (pp. 341–362). New York: Plenum Press.

Bugental, D. B., Lewis, J. C., Lin, E., Lyon, J., & Kopeikin, H. (2000). In charge but not in control: The management of authority-based relationships by those with low perceived power. *Developmental Psychology, 35,* 1367–1378.

Bugental, D. B., Lyon, J. E., Cortez, V., & Krantz, J. (1997). Who's the boss? Accessibility of dominance ideation among individuals with low perceptions of interpersonal power. *Journal of Personality and Social Psychology, 72,* 1297–1309.

Bugental, D. B., Lyon, J. E., Lin, E., McGrath, E. G., & Bimbela, A. (1999). Children "tune out" in response to the ambiguous communication style of powerless adults. *Child Development, 70,* 214–230.

Bugental, D. B., & Shennum, W. A. (1984). "Difficult" children as elicitors and targets of adult communication patterns: an attributional-behavioral transactional analysis. *Monographs of the Society for Research in Child Development, 49,* 1–70.

Cartwright, D. (Ed.) (1959). *Studies in social power.* Ann Arbor, MI: Research Center for Group Dynamics. University of Michigan.

Chen, M., & Bargh, J. A. (1997). Nonconscious behavioral confirmation processes: The self-fulfilling consequences of automatic stereotype activation. *Journal of Experimental Social Psychology, 33,* 541–560.

Christianson, S. (1992). Emotional stress and eye witness memory: A critical review. *Psychological Bulletin, 112,* 284–309.

Cortez, V., & Bugental, D. B. (1994) Children's visual avoidance of threat: A strategy associated with low social control. *Merrill-Palmer Quarterly, 40,* 82–97.

Dutton, D. B., & Strachan, C. E. (1987). Motivational needs for power and spouse-specific assertiveness in assaultive and nonassaultive men. *Violence and Victims, 2,* 145–156.

Easterbrook, J. A. (1959). The effect of emotion on cue utilization and the organization of behavior. *Psychological Review, 66,* 183–201.

Ekman, P., Davidson, R. J., & Friesen, W. V. (1990). The Duchenne smile: Emotional expression and brain physiology: II. *Journal of Personality and Social Psychology, 58,* 342–353.

Ekman, P., & Friesen, W. V. (1969). Nonverbal leakage and clues to deception. *Psychiatry, 32,* 88–106.

Ellis, H. C., & Ashbrook, P. W. (1988). Resource allocation model of the effects of depressed mood states on memory. In K. Fiedler & J. Forgas (Eds.), *Affect, cognition and social behavior* (pp. 25–43). Toronto: Hogrefe.

Erber, R., & Fiske, S. T. (1984). Outcome dependency and attention to inconsistent information. *Journal of Personality and social Psychology, 47,* 709–726.

Fiske, S. T., & Emery, E. J. (1993). Lost mental control and exaggerated social control: Social cognitive and psychoanalytic speculations. In D. M. Wegner & J. S. Pennebaker (Eds.), *Handbook of mental control* (pp. 171–199). Englewood Cliffs, NJ: Prentice-Hall.

Fiske, S. T., Morling, B. & Stevens, L. E. (1996). Controlling self and others: A theory of anxiety, mental control, and social control. *Personality and Social Psychology Bulletin, 22,* 115–123.

Fiske, S. T., & Pavelchak, M. A.. (1986). Category-based versus piecemeal affective responses: Developments in schema-triggered affect. In R. M. Sorrentino & E. T. Higgins (Eds.), *Handbook of motivation and cognition: Foundations of social behavior* (Vol. 1, pp. 167–203). New York: Guilford Press.

Fridlund, A. J. (1994). *Human facial expression.* San Diego: Academic Press.

Gilbert, D. T., Pelham, B. W., & Krull, D. S. (1988). On cognitive busyness: When person perceivers meet persons perceived. *Journal of Personality and Social Psychology, 54,* 733–740.

Freud, S. (1938). The basic writings of Sigmund Freud; translated and edited, with illustrations by A. A. Brill. New York: The Modern Library.

Hollander, E. P. (1985). Leadership and power. In G. Lindzey & E. Aronson (Eds.), *Handbook of social psychology,* 3rd edition (pp. 485–537). New York: Random House.

Kelley, H. H. (1979). *Personal relationships.* Hillsdale, NJ: Erlbaum.

Keltner, D., Young, R. C., & Buswell, B., N. (1997). Appeasement in human emotion, social practice, and personality. *Aggressive Behavior, 23,* 359–374.

Kipnis, D. (1976). *The powerholders.* Chicago: University of Chicago Press.

Macrae, D. N., Bodenhausen, G. V., Milne, A. B., & Jetten, J. (1994). Out of mind but back in sight: Stereotypes on the rebound. *Journal of Personality and Social Psychology, 67,* 808–817.

Mills, R. S. (in press) Exploring the effects of low power schemas in mothers. In P. D. Hastings & C. C. Piotrowski (Eds.), *Maternal beliefs about child-rearing and children's misbehavior: The causes and effects of beliefs in conflict situations. new directions for child development.* San Francisco: Jossey-Bass.

Mills, R. S. (1998). Paradoxical relations between perceived power and maternal control. *Merrill-Palmer Quarterly, 44,* 523–537.

Mischel, W., & Shoda, Y. (1995). A cognitive-affective- system theory of personality: Reconceptualizing situations, dispositions, dynamics, and invariance in personality structure. *Psychological Review, 102,* 246–268.

Ng, S. H. (1980). *The social psychology of power.* New York: Academic Press.

Pittman, T. S. & D'Agostino, P. R. (1989) Motivation and cognition: Control deprivation and the nature of subsequent information-processing. *Journal of Experimental Social Psychology, 25,* 465–480.

Raven, B. H. (1993). The bases of power: Origins and recent developments. *Journal of Social Issues, 49,* 227–251.

Raven, B. H., & Kruglanski, A. W. (1970). Conflict and power. In P. Swingle (Ed.), *The structure of conflict* (pp. 69–110). San Diego, CA: Academic Press.

Ruscher,, J. B., & Fiske, S. T. (1990). Interpersonal competition can cause individuating processes. *Journal of Personality and Social Psychology, 58,* 832–843.

Sagrestano, L M., Heavey, D. L., & Christianson, A. (1999). Perceived power and physical violence in marital conflict. *Journal of Social Issues, 55,* 65–79.

Seibert, P. S., & Ellis, H. C. (1991). Irrelevant thoughts, emotional mood states, and cognitive task performance. *Memory and cognition, 19,* 507–513.

Shiffrin, R. M., Schneider, W. 1977. Controlled and automatic information process: II. Perceptual learning, automatic attending, and a general theory. *Psychological Review, 84,* 127–188.

Spencer, S. J., Fein, S., Wolfe, C. T., Fong, D., & Dunn, M. A. (1998). Automatic activation of stereotypes: The role of self-image threat. *Personality and Social Psychology Bulletin, 24,* 1139–1152.

Strachan, C. E., & Dutton, D. G. (1992). The role of power and gender in anger responses to sexual jealousy. *Journal of Applied Social Psychology, 22,* 1721–1740.

Thibaut, J. W., & Kelley, H. H. (1959). *The social psychology of groups.* New York: Wiley.

Wegner, D. M. (1994). Ironic processes of mental control. *Psychological Review, 101,* 34–52.

8

Getting What They Came For

How Power Influences the Dynamics and Outcomes of Interpersonal Interaction

MARK SNYDER
MARC T. KIVINIEMI

Many social interactions are indelibly tinged by issues of power and of power differences. Consider some common social interactions: First, imagine a job candidate going in for an interview with a potential employer. Next, consider a teacher meeting new students on the first day of class. Then, imagine two people meeting for a first date. Finally, imagine two college roommates meeting for the first time at the beginning of the semester. Each of these scenarios contains at least two common features, which together set the stage for the arguments that are offered in this chapter. First, each scenario involves a situation in which two people are meeting for the first time—the participants are getting acquainted with one another. Second, in each scenario, there are considerations of power that may influence the dynamics and the outcomes of the interactions that occur between the participants.

Few would argue with the assertion that, in the first two situations, the individuals involved are characterized by different amounts of social power—in classrooms, teachers typically have more power than students and, in an employment interview, the potential employer has a great deal of power over the outcomes of the potential employee. The role-based power differences in the first two examples are fairly obvious, for the roles of teacher and of employer explicitly confer power over students and employees. However, even these two situations may have power dynamics that are more complex than a surface-level analysis would suggest. And, examining the complexity of power differences

133

will make it clear that power differences may well be present even in the latter two scenarios, the first date and the roommate meeting. These scenarios, although not marked by obvious role related differences in social power, contain features such as differences in knowledge, expertise, or investment that may lead to power differences emerging.

The focus of this chapter is on an exploration of how power influences the dynamics of interpersonal interactions such as the ones in the examples, and how these power influenced dynamics determine the outcomes of interactions. First the nature and the complexities of the power differences present in these sorts of interactions are described, and then an exploration of the relation of power to the dynamics and outcomes of such interactions is presented.

THE COMPLEXITY OF POWER DIFFERENCES

An important preliminary to discussing the nature of these power complexities is to first delineate what is meant by power. For the purposes of this discussion, the widely accepted definition of power proposed by French and Raven (1959; see also Bannester, 1969; Huston, 1983) is used. This way of considering power has received widespread attention, and acceptance, in the research literature (see Podsakoff & Schriesheim, 1985, for a review). According to the French and Raven analysis of the bases of power, a person's social power is defined as the extent to which that person has the potential ability to influence another person in a given setting. This influence may take a number of forms. The most straightforward form of this influence occurs when a high power person influences the actual behaviors of a lower power person, but the potential for influence may also extend to creating changes in a person's thoughts and beliefs, or eliciting changes in the person's affective states (see also Raven, 1992).

Turning back to the initial examples of dyadic interaction, the form of power difference in the first two examples (the teacher and the new student, the employer and the prospective employee) is that of *legitimate power*, which French and Raven define as the ability to influence another because of a socially proscribed role giving legitimacy to one's influence. In our society, teachers are supposed to have influence over their students and employers are allowed to influence their employees. Two other fairly clearly defined forms of social power present in these first two dyads are those of *reward* and *coercive* (or punishment) power. Clearly teachers have the ability to give rewards (e.g., good grades, praise) and punishments to influence the behaviors of their students. Employers also have a variety of rewards and punishments (e.g., job positions, salaries, other benefits) to influence employee behavior. Although these types of power differences may also from time to time be present in the date and roommate situations, they are less likely to be a central feature of those sorts of interactions.

However, the power dynamics in even these first two situations are far more complex than this initial analysis would suggest. Delving deeper into each situation, it seems that three other bases of power posited by French and Raven

(1959, and further elaborated by Raven, 1992, 1993) are also present in the first two examples, and have every potential to be present in the latter two as well. Consider first *expert power*, the ability to influence because one is seen as an expert on a particular issue and therefore should be believed and obeyed. Clearly, in classroom settings, the teacher is viewed as the expert on a variety of issues and thus has power to influence the student. Similarly, in an employment interview, an applicant may submit to the influence of the interviewer because that person is seen as the expert on matters relating to one's employment in a particular position. In the first date scenario, one member of the dyad may be more likely to be seen as the expert dater by virtue of age, dating experience, general sociability, and so forth. Similarly, in the roommate situation, one person may be seen as an expert on a particular subject, such as information about social life, or may be generally viewed as the person to go to with questions, thus conferring expert power.

Reference power, or power conferred because one feels (or wants to feel) a sense of identity or oneness with the person, also plays a role in each of these situations. Teachers are powerful socialization agents, and the desire to be like the teacher may lead to the teacher having reference power over the student. In an employment setting, the interviewee is presumably there, in part, because she or he wants to become a part of the employer's in group—to join the company. Thus, in each of these situations, reference power may be present. In addition, in the dating and roommate scenarios, one person may have a stronger desire (perhaps because the other person is very attractive, very popular, or has other desirable qualities) to be friends or to develop a relationship. This desire gives the other person more reference power (e.g., Peplau, 1979; Waller & Hill, 1951).

Finally, consider *informational power*, the ability to influence based on the higher power person having information that the lower power person does not possess. Clearly, teachers and employers have, respectively, more academic and more workplace information than do students and potential employees. In the context of a first date, the person who initiated the date often has more information, since she or he presumably knows more about the planned activities to take place. If the date is to be to a play, concert, or movie, the member of the dyad who knows what movies are playing and what plays are showing may have more informational power. With roommates, one may have information that the other needs in order to interact smoothly with other residents or to participate in dorm activities.

A second important type of knowledge that may lead to informational power differences is information about the other person in the dyad. Typically, teachers have a variety of kinds of information about their students before they meet on the first day of class. They have the student's permanent record, have probably discussed the student's progress with other teachers, and may have heard about the student from other sources. Likewise, an employer often has a great deal of information about the employee—a résumé, references from former employers, and perhaps results from a battery of selection tests.

In the dating situation, one member of a dating dyad may well have more knowledge about the other, particularly if the two were set up by a mutual acquaintance. One roommate may have knowledge about the other as a result of campus gossip, information from other students, or other informal sources. These informational differences create a power differential such that the teacher, the employer, the date, and the roommate each have more power than the other member of the dyad.

OVERVIEW OF THE CHAPTER

In this chapter, we will consider the effects that differences in power have on dyadic interactions including, but not limited to, those discussed above. We will focus our discussion on understanding how power differences influence the behaviors that ensue during interactions between individuals marked by high and low power, as well as the influence of power on the outcomes of these interactions. First the sorts of influences power has on the dynamics of interactions is examined. Next, how and why power influences these interactions is discussed. Finally, some observations and speculations concerning the implications of this analysis for several phenomena in social and personality psychology are offered.

WHAT EFFECTS DOES POWER HAVE IN INTERPERSONAL INTERACTION?

Given the richness (and possibly even the pervasiveness) of power differences inherent in many interpersonal interactions, it is critical to understand the dynamic influence of power on the processes involved in, and the outcomes of, interactions. It is possible to consider the role of power dynamics at many points in the interpersonal interaction sequence. First, power may influence the initial choice of partners with whom to interact (Kerckhoff, 1974; Parks & Eggert, 1991). In a business setting, for example, a higher power person may simply choose not to interact with a subordinate because the subordinate has no control over the higher power person's outcomes. Conversely, the low power person may elect not to interact with the higher power person for fear of doing something to negatively impact the higher power person's control over outcomes.

Next, power can determine the first impressions formed about an interaction partner—power differences can influence the likelihood of using individuating information about a person versus relying on expectations and stereotypes (Fiske, 1993; Neuberg & Fiske, 1987). For example, the high power supervisor in a work setting may rely on information about the employee garnered from others or on ideas about what "that sort of employee" is like when forming an impression.

Finally, power can have implications for choosing to continue or discontinue an interaction. High power people may well have far more freedom to exit from interactions they do not enjoy or do not find productive, since their outcomes are not dependent on the lower power person (Gelles, 1976; Huston, 1983; Strube, 1988). A high power business person can choose to stop interacting with the lower power person without fear of losing his or her job, position, or salary, a freedom not accorded to the lower power person.

In this chapter, we will address the role of power in interaction by focusing in on one critically important stage of this interaction sequence, namely the initial interaction in which people get acquainted with one another. Two main issues are addressed: First, the effects of power on the dynamics of these initial interactions, and second, the question of how and why power influences interactions. The motivations that individuals with differing levels of social power might bring to such interactions and how those motivations might lead them to conduct themselves in ways that lead to particular interaction dynamics are discussed.

Why might these initial acquaintanceship settings be a particularly appropriate venue within which to study power dynamics? Obviously, interactions and relationships must have beginnings, and these beginnings importantly set the stage for any further interactions and relationship development to come (see Murstein, 1976). Thus, the importance of these initial interactions cannot be understated. The impressions formed in these initial interactions color the remainder of the relationship between the individuals, whether that relationship lasts for ten minutes or ten years (e.g., Asch, 1940; Hovland, Janis, & Kelley, 1953). Second, these initial interactions are situations in which the effects of power can be easily and productively observed and manipulated; since the interactions are not yet tinged by a history of relationship, it may well be easier to observe the dynamics and effects of power in these early interaction settings. Finally, a large body of work on interpersonal interaction has concerned this initial person perception and initial acquaintanceship process, making it a useful venue to relate analyses of power to other relevant research findings (e.g., Hays, 1985; Kerckhoff, 1974; Murstein, 1976; Snyder, Tanke, & Berscheid, 1977).

A STRATEGY FOR EXPLORING THE EFFECTS OF POWER

An initial question is this: How do power differences in a dyad influence the process of initial acquaintanceship and interpersonal interaction? To explore this question, consider a setting that has features common to interpersonal acquaintanceship and which also contains power differences. What features of acquaintanceship might be important here? Obviously, we need a setting in which two previously unacquainted individuals are meeting and interacting for the first time. But consider also that, when individuals interact for the first time, they frequently come to that initial meeting with a set of preexisting expectations about the other person. These expectations can develop from many sources. For example, stereotypes about a group to which the person belongs can be a source of beliefs about what the person will be like. Also, one may have received information about the person from a common acquaintance. In the examples above, factual information, such as résumés or school records, can provide a source for a mental picture of what the person will be like.

In addition to being a common feature of interpersonal acquaintanceship, these expectations have the potential to be a source of power differences in their own right. Recall the earlier discussion about informational power differences as a result of one person knowing more about the other. To the extent that expectations are unequally distributed across members of the dyad (as they will surely be when one party to the interaction approaches it with prior expectations and the other does not), the person with more expectations has more information (even if that information is not accurate) and thus has some informational power over the other member of the dyad.

Our strategy for addressing the influences of power on acquaintanceship is to delve into the dynamics of a well-studied process of interpersonal interaction, that of *behavioral confirmation* (Snyder, 1984, 1992). Behavioral confirmation scenarios have both of the features defined as important for this chapter's exploration of power. First, the scenario is set up for two previously unacquainted individuals to interact. Second, the very nature of the behavioral confirmation scenario is such that one person has been provided with an expectation about the other person which, as discussed above, leads to the person with the expectation having informational power.

What is Behavioral Confirmation?

As we have pointed out above, a common feature of acquaintanceship interactions is that the individuals frequently have expectations about each other. These expectations play an important guiding role in how we perceive the other person—both our perceptions of who they are (e.g., their personalities) and our perceptions of what they do (e.g., their behaviors). In this sense, what we see when we interact with the person is a function of what we expect to see—a phenomenon referred to as *perceptual confirmation* (Snyder, 1984).

Perceptual confirmation is an interesting phenomenon in its own right, for the purposes here, an even more intriguing effect of these preconceived expectations is the influence that they can have on behavior towards the target of those expectations, and ultimately on the actual behaviors of that target person. People may choose behaviors based on their expectations of what the other person will be like (e.g., we will be very talkative with the person we believe to be extraverted). Behavior based on those expectations, however, can have important consequences—the actions of the holder of the expectations can lead the target of those expectations to actually behave in ways that confirm those original beliefs. This process has been referred to by a number of names in the research literature (e.g., expectancy effects (Rosenthal, 1994) and self-fulfilling prophesies (Merton, 1948; Jussim, 1986). For our discussion, we will choose the term behavioral confirmation (Snyder, 1984), for it specifically refers to the defining aspects of the phenomenon—the person's behavior is such that it confirms our expectations about them.

A Prototypic Demonstration of Behavioral Confirmation

In an early demonstration of the behavioral confirmation effect, Snyder, Tanke, and Berscheid (1977) had previously unacquainted male-female dyads interact over an intercom system (so that they could talk to, but not see, one another). Prior to the conversation, the researchers manipulated the male member of the dyad's expectations about the female member. To do this, they gave each male participant (who we will refer to as the perceiver) a picture ostensibly of his female partner (who we will refer to as the target). In reality, the picture was not of the target, but rather was a picture that was randomly assigned to be of either a physically attractive or a physically unattractive woman.

Based on this manipulation, the male perceivers entered into the acquaintanceship conversation with an expectation about their partner—an expectation based on, depending on condition, stereotypes of attractive or unattractive women. These stereotypes include the idea that attractive women are more sociable, more outgoing, and more interpersonally warm than are unattractive women. The perceiver-target dyads then engaged in a 10 minute, unstructured conversation. Following the conversation, the male perceiver rated his impressions of the female target. The target's side of the conversation was then coded by independent raters for the amount of outgoingness, warmth, and sociability she displayed.

The results of the study showed that targets whose partners believed them to be physically attractive behaved during the interaction in ways that led them to be seen by independent raters as more sociable, warm, and outgoing than did targets whose perceivers believed them to be unattractive. The initial beliefs that the male perceivers held about their female targets turned into self-fulfilling prophesies in the course of their interactions—the targets behaved in ways that actually confirmed their perceivers beliefs.

Why is the Behavioral Confirmation Paradigm a Useful Way to Address Issues of Power?

Let us consider now the ways in which behavioral confirmation paradigms may address issues of power. The informational power differences that are a defining feature of the confirmation scenario were presented earlier. However, in addition to this informational power difference, examining the procedural paradigms used in behavioral confirmation studies through the lens of power suggests that there may be other aspects of power built into these paradigms. Informational power is discussed formally below, then some of these additional power differences are addressed.

Informational Power: Asymmetry of Knowledge. As discussed previously, the experimental paradigm for studying behavioral confirmation by its very nature creates situations in which the perceiver, by virtue of having an expectation, possesses greater informational power than does the target. The nature of the experimental manipulation is that the perceiver is given a piece of information—an expectation—about the target. Of course this informational manipulation is critical to the examination of confirmation as experimenters must give the perceiver an expectation in order to examine whether that expectation has been perceptually and behaviorally confirmed. An unintended side effect of this presentation of information, however, is that the perceiver has information and the target does not, which puts the perceiver in a position of having informational power (French & Raven, 1959) in that they are given a sense of what to expect of the target and, more generally, what to expect to occur in the situation.

Of course, having this knowledge also puts the perceiver in the position of having additional opportunities to act on the expectations given. This functionally puts the target in the position of responding to the perceiver's conversational guidance, providing information about themselves. This power to initiate and control the flow of information may be another important determinant of the confirmation effects observed. In many confirmation scenarios, this power creates a flow of influence from perceiver to target because the perceiver is eliciting information from the target (Mobilio & Snyder, 1996). This flow of information and control is, by itself, related to power differences (Mullen, Salas, & Driskell, 1989; Ng, Bell, & Brooke, 1993).

The same sort of analysis can highlight the inherently low power position of the target. The target operates from an initial position of information deficit. The experimental manipulation creates a situation in which the target doesn't know about the perceiver what the perceiver knows about the target. This deficit of information puts the target in the functional position of needing to act off of cues provided by the perceiver—giving them relatively little power to control, guide, and shape the conversation.

Legitimate Power: Role Differences. In addition to the informational power that is inherent in the behavioral confirmation interactional paradigm, additional power differences may exist. Although not originally intended to test the role of different types of power in interpersonal interactions, many classic demonstrations of behavioral confirmation effects have in effect included legitimate power as an implicit feature by nature of their experimental paradigm. Several studies have, either naturalistically or experimentally, used role relationships in which the perceiver has more power than the target. For example, Word, Zanna, and Cooper (1974) studied interactions between job interviewer perceivers and job applicant targets, Rosenthal and Jacobson (1968) examined teachers' perceptions of their students, and both Harris and Rosenthal (1986) and Snyder and Copeland (1995) studied interactions between perceiving counselors and client targets.

Summary: Power and Confirmation

Power differences, as we have seen, are imbedded into the functional roles of perceivers and targets in behavioral confirmation scenarios. The power statuses in the dyad covary with the roles they are assigned in the interaction. This state of affairs could be mere coincidence, but one might also hypothesize that perhaps perceptual, and particularly behavioral, confirmation are phenomena of power due, perhaps, to the high power position inherent in the perceiver role and the low power position that characterizes the target.

PUTTING TOGETHER THE PIECES: DO POWER DIFFERENCES ACCOUNT FOR BEHAVIORAL CONFIRMATION EFFECTS?

To begin to put the pieces of power and behavioral confirmation together one must look at the causal role of power in leading to behavioral confirmation effects. The literature on behavioral confirmation that has been reviewed thus far in this chapter tentatively suggests the possibility that behavioral confirmation may be one important effect of power differentials in dyadic interaction. That is, situations characterized by a relatively powerful perceiver (by virtue of either a given position or by virtue of informational power differences) and a relatively powerless target are situations in which confirmation effects are observed. In these situations, expectations held by the perceiver about the target lead to the target behaving in ways that confirm those expectations.

In addition, the nature of the expectations held by perceivers may enhance the role of power in leading to confirmation. Behavioral confirmation may be facilitated by expectations that are dispositional in nature, as such expectations may provide relatively simple and clear cut guidelines for interacting with the target in ways that may elicit confirmatory actions from them. Moreover, forming expectations that are relatively simple, clear cut, and dispositional in nature may be facilitated by paying relatively little attention to individuating information about the target and the influence of the context of the situation on the target's behavior in that situation. In fact, research has shown that high power people are less likely to pay attention to their interaction partners (e.g., Fiske, 1993), which may make them particularly likely to form simple, clear cut dispositional expectations of targets, which in turn may set the stage for confirmation to be particularly likely to occur.

Of course, to confidently conclude that the effects observed are in fact a result of the inherent power differentials between perceivers and targets, and that behavioral confirmation is in reality a phenomenon of power, the evidence of a study that directly tests this possibility by manipulating power differentials orthogonal to expectations is needed. Such a study was done by Copeland (1994). Copeland gave perceivers an expectation about the extraversion of their interaction partner—the partner was reported to be either rather introverted or rather extraverted. Orthogonal to that manipulation, Copeland manipulated the relative power of the participants such that either the perceiver or the target was the more powerful member of the dyad. This manipulation was done by giving the powerful member control over participation in a subsequent task in which rewards could be earned.

If behavioral confirmation results from the power inequities in the dyad, these effects should be exacerbated when the perceiver is the high power person (since the experimentally manipulated power adds on to their existing informational power in the interaction) and should be attenuated when the target is the high power person (since relative power is more equalized). By contrast, if the effects observed are due to something other than the power differential, experimentally manipulating power should not influence the extent of the behavioral confirmation effect.

Copeland's (1994) results support our assertion that power differentials in the dyad account for behavioral confirmation effects. When the target was the higher power member of the dyad, no behavioral confirmation was observed—targets were rated as equally extraverted for both expectations. By contrast, when the perceiver was the high power person, behavioral confirmation did occur. Targets whose high power perceivers thought them to be extraverted behaved significantly more extravertedly than did targets who were thought to be introverted.

Copeland's (1994) results confirm what the above discussion has suggested—the power differential between perceiver and target that is created by structural features of the behavioral confirmation scenario leads to behavioral confirmation effects. In situations where that power differential is equalized (by giving the target power over the perceiver) the confirmation effect disappears. When the power differential is made greater by giving the perceiver even more power over the target, confirmation continues to occur.

WHY DOES CONFIRMATION OCCUR?
THE ROLE OF MOTIVATIONS

Having established that behavioral confirmation results from situations in which, in addition to having an expectation about the target, the perceiver is in a position of high power relative to the target, we can now turn to addressing the question of how and why power exerts these effects on the interaction process. What is it about interpersonal interactions marked by power differentials that makes them venues in which behavioral confirmation can occur?

This section focuses on looking for these explanations in the motivations that people bring with them to these initial interactions. Why might motivation be a good place to search for the causes of power's influence on behavioral confirmation? First, motivations have long been held to be a determinant of the "perceptual concomitants" of social interaction (Jones & Thibaut, 1958, p. 159). The motivations that people bring with them to social interactions determine how they perceive those interactions and how they behave during them. Second, there is a well worked out set of motivations that people bring with them to social interactions—motivations that may relate to confirmation (see Snyder, 1992). Finally, there is existing literature on the role of motivations themselves on the behavioral confirmation phenomenon, literature which will provide us a base of knowledge from which to make inferences about power's potential role.

To make the argument that differences in interaction motivations are responsible for the effects of power on behavioral confirmation, one must, conceptually, argue for a mediational model showing, first, that the motivations of high and low power people differ in meaningful ways, and then showing that those different motivations are systematically related to behavioral confirmation. Thus motivations high and low power people might bring with them to interpersonal interactions are discussed first. Then, after discussing the nature of these motivations, how motivations held on the part of perceivers and targets might influence the process of behavioral confirmation are explored.

WHAT MOTIVATIONS DO PEOPLE HIGH AND LOW IN POWER BRING TO SOCIAL INTERACTIONS?

If motivations are to be implicated in the search for the causes of power difference effects in acquaintanceship interactions, we first need to show that people high and low in power are guided by different motivations in the course of these interactions. Copeland's (1994) study, described in detail earlier, provides evidence that interaction motivations differ for people with different levels of power. In the study, high power and low power perceivers and targets were asked to report the strategies they used when interacting with their partners. Copeland's (1994) analysis of those strategies revealed an important difference: high power individuals, whether perceiver or target, were particularly likely to report being guided by a desire to get to know the other person, whereas low power individuals, again regardless of role, were particularly likely to be guided by a motivation to get along with the other person. Other researchers have uncovered similar motivational differences underlying power differences in information processing in person perception (e.g., Fiske, 1993; Fiske & Depret, 1996; Neuberg & Fiske, 1987).

WHAT IS THE NATURE OF THESE INTERACTION MOTIVATIONS?

Copeland's (1994) analysis suggests that an additional feature of power in acquaintanceship interactions is that it leads individuals to have different motivations guiding them during the course of the interaction. Prior to discussing reasons why these motivational differences might exist, "getting to know" and "getting along" motivations must be delineated. What are people with each of these motivations trying to get from or accomplish through their initial interactions with others?

These two motivations have been identified as guiding many acquaintanceship processes, not just those concerned with power (see Snyder, 1992, for a more extensive review of this literature). First, people may have as a guiding motivation getting to know one another—developing a stable impression of the other person's traits, behaviors, feelings, and values. As another motivation, people may be particularly interested in *getting along* with one another—facilitating pleasant, smooth interactions. In more precise language, the getting to know motivation involves the "acquisition and use of social knowledge," whereas the getting along motive involves the "regulation and facilitation of social interaction" (Snyder & Haugen, 1994, p. 220).

Getting To Know as an Interaction Motivation

One of the well documented functions of acquaintanceship conversations is one of getting to know one's interaction partner. Getting to know a person with whom one is interacting has obvious benefits—it gives a stable impression of the other person's thoughts, emotions, behaviors, values, preferences, and so forth—a stable impression that can then be used as information to guide both further perception and action. Several theorists have posited that having such information about the interaction partner helps individuals maintain a sense of their worlds as ordered, stable, predictable places (e.g., Heider, 1958; Jones & Davis, 1965; Kelley, 1967).

In addition to acting to gain knowledge, people may use initial acquaintanceship conversations as an opportunity to "check out" expectations they have or preliminary information they have received about the person with whom they will be interacting. This process has clear implications for behavioral confirmation scenarios, which are by definition critically dependent on preconceived expectations. Having one's preconceived notions validated (e.g., believing that someone is an extravert and then, though behavioral confirmation, having them actually behave in an extraverted manner) increases one's belief in the stability and predictability of the social world.

This inclusion of checking out expectations in the getting to know motivation highlights an important point about the nature of the motive—the guiding force behind the motivation is not necessarily formation of an accurate impression, nor is the mental picture formed through this process guaranteed to be an accurate one. Rather, the guiding idea is that the goal is to form a stable image of the person that can then be readily used to guide further cognition and behavior. To the extent that this image is largely based on preexisting expectations, it may in fact be largely inaccurate. For further elaboration of this distinction between accuracy motivations and getting to know motivations, as well as their differing implications and consequences for behavioral confirmation scenarios, see Snyder (1992) and Snyder and Haugen (1994, 1995).

In terms of the behavioral confirmation scenario, perceivers who behave as though the expectations about others are true may be doing so in the service of confirming those expectations, which satisfies the getting to know goal of having a stable prediction of one's partner's behavior. This sense of stability is, if anything, further reinforced when, down the line, one's partner actually starts to behave in ways that confirm the expectations.

Getting Along as an Interaction Motivation

A second important motivation guiding people's social interactions involves getting along with the interaction partner—being motivated to ensure a smooth interaction by trying to fit in, be responsive, and be generally accommodating to one's partner. Behaviors such as saying the right thing, trying to make the other person feel comfortable, allowing the other person to be themselves, and so forth all flow from this motivation to get along with the partner. This motivation helps to ensure smooth, pleasant, flowing interactions (Goffman, 1959; Jones, 1990; Schlenker, 1980; Snyder, 1987).

How might this motivation relate to behavioral confirmation? One might treat an interaction partner in ways dictated by expectations because, if one truly believes that is what the partner is like, then treating them in that way allows him or her to "be themselves." Allowing the other person to be him- or herself is arguably an excellent strategy for ensuring a smooth, coordinated interaction. So, from the perspective of this motivation, facilitating smooth interactions and being responsive to the partner's needs and dispositions may be at the heart of the expectation confirming behaviors of behavioral confirmation.

WHY DO THESE MOTIVATIONS CHARACTERIZE HIGH AND LOW POWER PEOPLE?

Why might power positions relate to particular patterns of interaction motives? Consider first the position of the low power person. The low power person enters the interaction being dependent on the higher power person for outcomes—whether those outcomes be rewards, punishments, information, and so forth. This fundamental dependence, which is at the heart of power differences, makes getting along with the partner particularly important for the low power person. This leads to the getting along motivation being a central feature of the low power person's actions.

In addition, the low power person is also strongly influenced by impression management concerns (Jones & Pittman, 1982). Leaving a good impression with the higher power person can help to ensure that the low power individuals get the desirable outcomes they desire. Going along and getting along with the high power person is one strategy for leaving that desirable impression. In fact, the low power person may not be able to "afford" conflict with the high power person, both because of the outcome dependency and because of the negative impression that such conflict may create (see Sexton & Perlman, 1989).

What of the motivations guiding the high power person? The high power person is in a position of being able to exert influence over the low power person. This desire to exert influence may manifest itself in control over the dynamics of the conversation. Motivation to control the conversation may involve taking active control of the conversation and of the topics covered (Kollock, Blumstein, & Schwartz, 1985; Zimmerman & West, 1975), allowing the perceiver to push the agenda of forming an impression of the target.

One critical need for an ability to exert such influence is to be able to predict the actions and reactions of the lower power person (Copeland, 1994). So, the formation of a stable, predictable impression that is at the heart of the getting to know motivation may be particularly important to the high power person. In addition, the high power person has no need to accurately know the low power person (Glazer-Malbin, 1975; Miller, 1976), making reliance on expectations more likely.

HOW DO THESE MOTIVATIONS RELATE TO BEHAVIORAL CONFIRMATION?

Having established that these two motivations, getting to know and getting along, relate to the relative power held by individuals in an interaction, the important question of whether these motivations influence the process of behavioral confirmation is addressed, thus adding the last link in this mediational chain. Does interacting in the service of one or the other of these agendas make a perceiver more or less likely to elicit behavioral confirmation? Is a target acting under one or the other of these agendas more likely to fall victim to behavioral confirmation?

Snyder and Haugen (1994, 1995) conducted a series of studies to address these questions. In both studies, Snyder and Haugen set up a behavioral confirmation scenario in which the motivations of the perceivers (Snyder & Haugen, 1994) or of the targets (Snyder & Haugen, 1995) were experimentally manipulated to be either getting to know or getting along motivations. In the getting to know condition, individuals were told to use the conversation as an opportunity to "check out your first impressions of your partner. Find out what [the partner] is like, what [the partner's] personality traits are, and find out what someone with [the partner's] personality can be expected to say and do." Individuals in the getting along condition were told to use strategies that "will allow you to get along with the type of person that [the partner] might be, making sure that the two of you have a smooth and pleasant conversation . . . " (Snyder & Haugen, 1994, p. 228).

What did Snyder and Haugen (1994, 1995) discover about motivations and behavioral confirmation? They found that, when the perceiver had a motivation to get to know the target, to form a stable impression of the targets traits and behaviors, both perceptual and behavioral confirmation occurred. Perceivers with getting along functions and control perceivers did not report perceptual confirmation and did not elicit behavioral confirmation. Similar results were found when Copeland and Snyder (1995) gave students playing the role of counselors instructions to diagnose their clients versus instructions to establish rapport with their clients. Also consistent with this finding, perceivers who are concerned with getting their interaction partners to like them do not report perceptual confirmation (Neuberg et al, 1993).

For perceivers, a getting to know motivation seems to elicit behavioral confirmation whereas getting along does not. What about the motivations that targets bring to an interaction? Here, the getting to know condition did not elicit perceptual and behavioral confirmation. Instead, for target motivations, being motivated to get along led to behavioral confirmation (see also Smith et al., 1997).

What are we to conclude from these two studies? When describing the motivational conditions that elicit behavioral confirmation, situations in which the perceiver is guided by a getting to know motive and the target is guided by a getting along motive seem to elicit confirmation. By contrast, confirmation is attenuated and even eliminated in situations in which the target has a get to know motive and the perceiver has a getting along motive.

PUTTING TOGETHER THE PIECES: POWER, MOTIVATION, AND CONFIRMATION

Again, let us pause to tie together the various threads that have characterized our discussion of power, motivation, and behavioral confirmation. First, we have seen that high and low power people typically enter interactions with different motivations—high power people are guided by a desire to get to know the other person whereas low power people are guided by a motivation to get along with the person. These motivations may be a result of the differences in outcome dependency that characterize high and low power people.

Next, we have seen that these motivations relate differentially to behavioral confirmation. When the perceiver is guided by a getting to know motivation and the target is guided by a getting along motivation, confirmation is particularly likely to occur. Conversely, when the target is guided by getting to know and the perceiver by getting along, confirmation does not occur.

We now begin to see the full range of possible linkages between confirmation and power. Power differences may set up situations in which the high power person is particularly likely to be the perceiver, both because of role related power differences and differences in power due to information. High power perceivers are particularly likely to induce confirmation. In addition, high power people are particularly likely to be guided by getting to know motivations—a motivation that, in its own right, also leads to confirmation. Thus, the dynamics of interactions marked by power differences may work synergistically to lead to confirmation—position, power, and motivation are all guiding the interaction in ways that lead to expectations being confirmed.

The direct and definitive test of these relationships, of course, would be an exploration of the extent to which the relationship between power and confirmation is actually mediated by motivational differences. To our knowledge, however, no study has fully explored this relationship. Such a study would be a useful step in furthering research on behavioral confirmation and power. Either orthogonally manipulating power, expectation, and motivation in the same design, in order to explore their interacting effects, or doing a mediational analysis of the role of motivation in linking power and confirmation would provide a critical piece of knowledge about the role that motivation plays in determining power's influence on behavioral confirmation.

BROADENING THE PERSPECTIVE: IMPLICATIONS FOR PERSONALITY AND SOCIAL PSYCHOLOGY

This chapter has so far established that power differences fundamentally shape the dynamics of interpersonal interactions by the influence they have on the form and consequences of initial acquaintanceship conversations and has further explored some of the reasons for these differences by examining the differences in motivations that high and low power individuals bring with them to interactions. These analyses are now built upon to offer some observations and speculations about the implications that the analysis may have for a fuller understanding of the nature and consequences of interpersonal interaction and power. We seek to broaden the scope of the analysis first by extending the understanding of power differences and interpersonal interaction from situationally based power differences to dispositional differences in power and then by exploring the implications and consequences of the interpersonal dynamic of interaction to the group level, looking at the consequences of interpersonal power for stereotyping and intergroup processes.

FROM SITUATIONAL TO DISPOSITIONAL SOURCES OF POWER DIFFERENTIALS

The discussion so far has centered on situations in which there are clear cut (and often assigned) power differentials: the experimenter assigns one person to be the perceiver and one person to be the target, by function of social roles the teacher and the job supervisor have more power than the student and the employee, the person with the ability to give a reward has a fairly unambiguous power over the person who does not have such a reward. Each of these power differences, though, are really more based on features of situations than on features of persons.

Many actual interactions do not feature such clear cut situation-based power differences. Neither are most interactions so neatly planned that only one person has an expectation about the other. What will happen in such situations? Will confirmation simply not occur, even if one person has an expectation about the other? Or will one person naturally step into the role of the high power perceiver whereas another person may more naturally play the part of the lower power target?

Research on dispositional differences in the propensity to power suggests the possibility that the latter possibility may actually occur. Research on the need for power (e.g., Veroff & Veroff, 1972; Winter, 1973) as well as work on Machiavellianism (e.g., Christie & Geis, 1970) suggest that some people are more likely to seek power positions than are others. Along with that, some of the work on the consequences of those dispositions for both cognition and behavior suggests that those people more likely to seek positions of power may also be more likely to adapt getting to know motivations and to behave in ways that elicit confirmation, thus functionally making them perceivers.

In terms of Machiavellianism, those high in the disposition are more likely to become leaders in group settings (Geis, 1968) and are more likely to be seen as leaders by others (Geis, Krupat, & Berger, 1970). It has also been hypothesized that high Machiavellians have a focus on getting the task done and work on stable, predictable views of their partners that will aid them in these goals (Geis, 1968). These stable, predictable views map nicely onto the getting to know motives seen earlier, with the implication that this feature of high Machiavellians may make them particularly likely to be perceivers and, because of the relation to the getting to know motive, may make them likely to be perceivers who elicit behavioral confirmation from their targets.

Research on the need for power also suggests that some individuals may naturally step into high power roles. Bennett (1988) has reported that individuals high in the need for power enjoy gaining positions and recognition for power and are particularly likely to assert their will in various situations. People high in need for power prefer situations in which they have the ability to control others (Winter, 1973; Winter & Stewart, 1978), which may similarly make them likely to be behavioral confirmation eliciting perceivers.

These dispositional differences may lead to circumstances conducive to behavioral confirmation emerging even when these differences are not an inherent feature of the social structure. This analysis suggests that confirmation may be a more ubiquitous effect than at first is evident; it may come to bear on situations that are not inherently marked by either power differences or particular patterns of motivations.

FROM INTERPERSONAL TO INTERGROUP SOURCES OF POWER DIFFERENTIALS

One of the most insidious effects suggested by the work on power and behavioral confirmation concerns its implications for the strength and negative effects of stereotypes. The groups about whom individuals hold negative stereotypes are often those who are in positions of lesser power in our society. Indeed, differences between groups about whom stereotypes are held have been shown to be perceived as status differences (Kemmelmeier, 2000).

Lower power positions are ones in which expectations about a person are particularly likely to be behaviorally confirmed. As seen above, people low in power may be particularly likely to fall prey to confirmation, since in addition to their inherent low power, they are also frequently outcome-dependent on the very people holding the stereotype. This outcome dependency may lead them to be particularly likely to adopt a getting along agenda, an agenda that has been shown to lead to behavioral confirmation (Snyder & Haugen, 1995). Indeed, in research suggestive of this idea, it has been shown that large confirmation effects are often found in dyads with a male perceiver and a female target (Christansen & Rosenthal, 1982). In further support for this point about stereotyping, work on the "powerful" self-fulfilling prophesy has found that the effects of teacher expectations on student performance are higher when the students are female, African-American, and of low socioeconomic status (Jussim, Eccles, & Madon, 1996; Madon, Jussim, & Eccles, 1997). These positions, of course, are ones that, in our society, are related to social power, thus providing field study evidence for this point and confirmation of the laboratory evidence about power and confirmation (Copeland, 1994).

Interpersonal Confirmation May Become Group Stereotype Confirmation

The above discussion about the nature of stereotypes in behavioral confirmation scenarios suggests that our analysis may have implications for intergroup processes as well. Stereotypes, although used as expectations about individuals, are actually beliefs about a group of people. What happens, then, when an expectation that is based on a stereotype about a social group of which the target is a member is perceptually and behaviorally confirmed? One potential implication is this: To the extent that the target is seen as a member of the group (i.e., perceived at a category rather than an individuating level; Brewer, 1988; Fiske & Neuberg, 1990), the behavioral confirmation that occurs may not only serve to confirm expectations about the individual, but may in fact serve to reinforce the existing social stereotypes about a *group* of people.

Research on the outgroup homogeneity effect has suggested that members of outgroups are seen as "all alike" (e.g., Jones, Wood, & Quattrone, 1981; Linville, Fischer, & Salovey, 1989; Mullen & Hu, 1989; Ostrom & Sedikides, 1992). The implications of this finding for behavioral confirmation are that, to the extent that an individual is seen as just like other members of that individual's group, stereotypes about the group may serve as expectations for interaction with the individual—expectations that can then be behaviorally confirmed.

The reverse implications, of behavioral confirmation for outgroup perception, are equally impactful. To the extent that all members of a group are seen as alike, the confirmed expectations of the individual who is a member of that group may serve, because of outgroup homogeneity, as a confirmation of the stereotype about that entire group. Thus, having met and interacted with one member of an outgroup, and seen that outgroup member confirm one's expectations, one may confidently generalize—in "to know one of them is to know all of them" fashion—from that experience to the conclusion that all members of the outgroup would fit the stereotype.

DOES POWER CORRUPT?

The analysis of possible individual differences leading to behavioral confirmation in mixed-power dyads and the exploration of negative effects of behavioral confirmation at the intergroup level has implications for understanding the negative and corrupting influences of power as well. The analyses presented in this chapter suggest several ways in which the familiar adage that "power corrupts" may, in some circumstances, become true through the process of behavioral confirmation, for the potentially negative effects of confirmation may lead to corruption as a result of power.

Perhaps the most obvious of these implications is the potential role of Machiavellianism as a determinant of perceiver-target relationships. To the extent that being high in Machiavellianism will make a person more likely to be a high power perceiver, thus making confirmation more likely, in addition to its impact on the likelihood of a person engaging in arguably corrupt practices (see Christie & Geis, 1970), it is possible that confirmation may become an instrument for corruption. At a minimum, having a stable sense of others as a result of a getting to know motivation may give the high Machiavellian information needed to successfully manipulate others. At the other extreme, shaping behavior through confirmation processes may itself be a tool of manipulation for the high Machiavellian.

Individual differences in need for power are also potentially implicated in the possible corrupting influence of power. Research on the need for power has suggested that those high in the disposition may be particularly likely to engage in some negative practices related to corruption, such as backing out of or reneging on agreements (e.g., Terhune, 1968) and engaging in emotional and physical abuse of others (e.g., Dutton & Strachan, 1987; Winter & Stewart, 1978). These practices may be particularly characteristic of those high in the need for power who do not score very high on measures of social responsibility (e.g., Winter & Barenbaum, 1985). These findings, coupled with the possibility that need for power may relate to becoming a high power perceiver, suggest that, like Machiavellianism, for people high in need for power, behavioral confirmation may be either a concomitant phenomenon or an actual tool for engaging in manipulative and perhaps corrupt relationships with others.

Finally, the potential for behavioral confirmation at the individual level to influence processes and relationships at the intergroup level suggests a final way in which power, through confirmation, may corrupt. To the extent that behavioral confirmation is used to reinforce existing stereotypes about different social groups, confirmation may play a role in reinforcing and strengthening existing social stereotypes—stereotypes that may have the negative effects of sustaining existing inequitable social structures.

CONCLUDING COMMENTS

As we have seen, power may be prevalent in social interactions. Even in dyadic interactions that don't appear to be marked by role related power differences, features of the situation and the people within often create power differentials. In intergroup settings, status differences often play out in ways that mimic power, creating situations where stereotype-based interactions become power-tinged interactions.

We have argued that this ubiquity of power differences has crucial implications for the dynamics and outcomes of social interaction. Indeed, the very process of getting acquainted with an interaction partner, the first step in any interaction sequence or relationship, provides rich opportunities for the processes of power to come into play. High power individuals elicit perceptual and behavioral confirmation from their interaction partners of lesser power.

The nature of such influences of power differences is due to the differing motivations that high and low power people bring with them to interactions. High power people act in the service of getting to know their interaction partner, whereas low power people act in the service of getting along with their partner. These patterns of motivations, when held on the part of a perceiver and a target, respectively, are the very ones that lead to behavioral confirmation.

In addition to discussing important implications for the impact of power differences on interpersonal interactions, ways in which broadening an understanding of the power dynamics influence our understanding of intergroup processes—specifically the way that stereotypes and outgroup homogeneity effects may influence and be influenced by the dynamics of interpersonal interaction—have been discussed. These intergroup effects suggest that the effects of power may be far more insidious than at first realized. For, as the current analysis has tried to make clear, power is, in a sense, everywhere, coloring and influencing a wide range of social phenomena including that of interpersonal interaction. To seek a full understanding of the nature of social phenomena therefore should involve exploring both the nature and the effects of power in the many and varied domains of social functioning.

REFERENCES

Asch, S. E. (1940). Studies in the principles of judgments and attitudes: II. Determination of judgments by group and by ego standards. *Journal of Social Psychology, 12,* 433–465.

Bannester, E. M. (1969). Sociodynamics: An integrative theorem of power, authority, interfluence, and love. *American Sociological Review, 34,* 374–393.

Bennett, J. B. (1988). Power and influence as distinct personality traits: Development and validation of a psychometric measure. *Journal of Research in Personality, 22,* 361–394.

Brewer, M. B. (1988). A dual process model of impression formation. *Advances in Social Cognition, 1,* 1–36.

Christiansen, D., & Rosenthal, R. (1982). Gender and nonverbal decoding skill as determinants of interpersonal expectancy effects. *Journal of Personality and Social Psychology, 42,* 75–87.

Christie, R., & Geis, F. L. (1970). *Studies in Machiavellianism.* New York: Academic Press.

Copeland, J. T. (1994). Prophecies of power: Motivational implications of social power for behavioral confirmation. *Journal of Personality and Social Psychology, 67,* 264–277.

Copeland, J. T., & Snyder, M. (1995). When counselors confirm: A functional analysis. *Personality and Social Psychology Bulletin, 21,* 1210–1220.

Dutton, D. G., & Strachan, C. E. (1987). Motivational needs for power and spouse-specific assertiveness in assaultive and non-assaultive men. *Violence and Victims, 2,* 145–156.

Fiske, S. T. (1993). Controlling other people: The impact of power on stereotyping. *American Psychologist, 48,* 621–628.

Fiske, S. T., & Depret, E. (1996). Control, interdependence, and power: Understanding social cognition in its social context. *European Review of Social Psychology, 7,* 31–61.

Fiske, S. T., & Neuberg, S. L. (1990). A continuum of impression formation, from category based to individuating processes: Influences of information and motivation on attention and interpretation. *Advances in Experimental Social Psychology, 23,* 1–74.

French, J. R. P. Jr., & Raven, B. (1959). The bases of social power. In D. Cartwright (Ed.), *Studies in social power* (pp. 150–167). Ann Arbor: University of Michigan Press.

Geis, F. L. (1968). Machiavellianism in a semireal world. *Proceedings of the 76th Annual Convention of the American Psychological Association, 3,* 407–408.

Geis, F. L., Krupat, E., & Berger, D. (1970). Taking over in group discussion. In R. Christie & F. L. Geis (Eds.), *Studies in Machiavellianism* (pp. 392). New York: Academic Press.

Gelles, R. J. (1976). Abused wives: Why do they stay? *Journal of Marriage and the Family, 38,* 659–668.

Glazer-Malbin, N. (1975). Psychological well-being in the post-parental stage: Some evidence from national surveys. In N. Glazer-Malbin (Ed.), *Old family/new family* (pp. 27–66). New York: Van Nostrand.

Goffman, E. (1959). *The presentation of self in everyday life.* Garden City, NY: Doubleday Anchor Books.

Harris, M. J., & Rosenthal, R. (1986). Counselor and client personality as determinants of counselor expectancy effects. *Journal of Personality and Social Psychology, 50,* 362–369.

Hays, R. B. (1985). A longitudinal study of friendship development. *Journal of Personality and Social Psychology, 48,* 909–924.

Heider, F. (1958). *The psychology of interpersonal relations.* New York: Wiley.

Hovland, C. I., Janis, I. L., & Kelley, H. H. (1953). *Communication and persuasion.* New Haven, CT: Yale University Press.

Huston, T. L. (1983). Power. In H. H. Kelley, E. Berscheid, A. Christensen, et al. (Eds.), *Close relationships* (pp. 169–219). New York: Freeman.

Jones, E. E. (1990). *Interpersonal perception.* New York: Freeman.

Jones, E. E., & Davis, K. E. (1965). From acts to dispositions: The attribution process in person perception. *Advances in Experimental Social Psychology, 2,* 220–276.

Jones, E. E., & Pittman, T. S. (1982). Toward a general theory of strategic self-presentation. In J. Suls (Ed.), *Psychological perspectives on the self* (Vol. 1, pp. 231–262). Hillsdale, NJ: Erlbaum.

Jones, E. E., & Thibaut, J. W. (1958). Interaction goals as bases of inference in interpersonal perception. In R. Tagiuri & L. Petrullo (Eds.), *Person perception and interpersonal behavior* (pp. 151–178). Stanford, CA: Stanford University Press.

Jones, E. E., Wood, G. C., & Quattrone, G. A. (1981). Perceived variability of personal characteristics in ingroups and outgroups: The role of knowledge and evaluation. *Journal of Personality and Social Psychology, 7,* 523–538.

Jussim, L. (1986). Self-fulfilling prophecies: A

theoretical and integrative review. *Psychological Review, 93,* 429–445.

Jussim, L., Eccles, J., & Madon, S. (1996). Social perceptions, social stereotypes, and teacher expectations: Accuracy and the quest for the powerful self-fulfilling prophecy. *Advances in Experimental Social Psychology, 28,* 281–388.

Kelley, H. H. (1967). Attribution theory in social psychology. In D. Levine (Ed.), *Nebraska symposium on motivation.* Lincoln, NE: University of Nebraska Press.

Kemmelmeier, M. (2000, March). Maintaining the social order: Hierarchy, prejudice, and discrimination. Presentation at the meeting of the European Association of Experimental Social Psychology, Grenoble, France.

Kerckhoff, A. C. (1974). The social context of interpersonal attraction. In T. L. Huston (Ed.), *Foundations of interpersonal attraction* (pp. 61–95). New York: Academic Press.

Kollock, P., Blumstein, P., & Schwartz, P. (1985). Sex and power in interaction: Conversational privileges and duties. *American Sociological Review, 50,* 34–46.

Linville, P. W., Fischer, F. W., & Salovey, P. (1989). Perceived distributions of characteristics of in-group and outgroup members: Empirical evidence and a computer simulation. *Journal of Personality and Social Psychology, 57,* 165–188.

Madon, S., Jussim, L., & Eccles, J. (1997). In search of the powerful self-fulfilling prophecy. *Journal of Personality and Social Psychology, 72,* 791–809.

Merton, R. K. (1948). The self-fulfilling prophecy. *Antioch Review, 8,* 193–210.

Miller, J. B. (1976). *Toward a new psychology of women.* Boston: Beacon Press.

Mobilio, L. J., & Snyder, M. (1996, June). *Knowledge is power: A study of behavioral confirmation.* Poster session presented at the annual meeting of the American Psychological Association, San Francisco, CA.

Mullen, B., & Hu, L. (1989). Perceptions of in-group and outgroup variability: A meta-analysis integration. *Basic and Applied Social Psychology, 10,* 233–252.

Mullen, B., Salas, E., & Driskell, J. E. (1989). Salience, motivation, and artifact as contributions to the relation between participation rate and leadership. *Journal of Experimental Social Psychology, 25,* 545–559.

Murstein, B. I. (1976). The stimulus-value-role theory of marital choice. In H. Grunebaum & J. Christ (Eds.), *Contemporary marriage: Structure, dynamics, and therapy* (pp. 165–168). Boston: Little, Brown.

Neuberg, S. L., & Fiske, S. T. (1987). Motivational influences on impression formation: Outcome dependency, accuracy-driven attention, and individuating processes. *Journal of Personality and Social Psychology, 53,* 431–444.

Nuberg, S. L., Judice, T. N., Virdin, L. M., & Carrillo, M. A. (1993). Perceiver self-presentational goals as moderators of expectancy influences: Ingratiation and the disconfirmation of negative expectancies. *Journal of Personality and Social Psychology, 64,* 409–420.

Ng., S. K., Bell, D., & Brooke, M. (1993). Gaining turns and achieving high influence ranking in small conversational groups. *British Journal of Social Psychology, 32,* 265–275.

Ostrom, T. M., & Sedikides, C. (1992). Outgroup homogeneity effects in natural and minimal groups. *Psychological Bulletin, 112,* 536–552.

Parks, M. R., & Eggert, L. L. (1991). The role of social context in the dynamics of personal relationships. In W. H. Jones & D. Perlman (Eds.), *Advances in personal relationships* (Vol. 2, pp. 1–34). London: Jessica Kingsley.

Peplau, L. A. (1979). Power in dating relationships. In J. Freeman (Ed.), *Women: A feminist perspective* (2nd ed., pp. 106–121). Palo Alto, CA: Mayfield.

Podsakoff, P. M., & Schriesheim, C. A. (1985). Field studies of French and Raven's bases of power: Critique, reanalysis, and suggestions for future research. *Psychological Bulletin, 97,* 387–411.

Raven, B. H. (1992). A power/interaction model of interpersonal influence: French and Raven thirty years later. *Journal of Social Behavior and Personality, 7,* 217–244.

Raven, B. H. (1993). The bases of power: Origins and recent developments. *Journal of Social Issues, 49,* 227–251.

Rosenthal, R. (1994). Interpersonal expectancy effects: A 30-year perspective. *Current Directions in Psychological Science, 3,* 176–179.

Rosenthal, R., & Jacobson, L. (1968). *Pygmalion in the classroom.* New York: Holt, Rinehart, & Winston.

Schlenker, B. R. (1980). *Impression management: The self-concept, social identity, and interpersonal relations.* Monterey, CA: Brooks/Cole.

Sexton, C. S., & Perlman, D. S. (1989). Couples' career orientation, gender role orientation, and perceived equity as determinants of marital power. *Journal of Marriage and the Family, 51,* 933–941.

Smith, D. M., Neuberg, S. L., Judice, T. N., & Biesanz, J. C. (1997). Target complicity in the confirmation and disconfirmation of erroneous perceiver expectations: Immediate and longer term implications. *Journal of Personality and Social Psychology, 73,* 974–991.

Snyder, M. (1984). When belief creates reality. *Advances in Experimental Social Psychology, 18,* 248–305.

Snyder, M. (1987). *Public appearances/private realities: The psychology of self-monitoring.* New York: Freeman.

Snyder, M. (1992). Motivational foundations of behavioral confirmation. *Advances in Experimental Social Psychology, 25,* 67–114.

Snyder, M., & Haugen, J. A. (1994). Why does behavioral confirmation occur? A functional perspective on the role of the perceiver. *Journal of Experimental Social Psychology, 30,* 218–246.

Snyder, M., & Haugen, J. A. (1995). Why does behavioral confirmation occur? A functional perspective on the role of the target. *Personality and Social Psychology Bulletin, 21,* 963–974.

Snyder, M., Tanke, E. D., & Berscheid, E. (1977). Social perception and interpersonal behavior: On the self-fulfilling nature of social stereotypes. *Journal of Personality and Social Psychology, 35,* 656–666.

Strube, M. J. (1988). The decision to leave an abusive relationship: Economic dependence and psychological commitment. *Journal of Marriage and the Family, 45,* 785–794.

Terhune, K. W. (1968). Motives, situation, and interpersonal conflict within prisoners' dilemma. *Journal of Personality and Social Psychology Monograph Supplement, 8,* 2.

Veroff, J., & Veroff, J. P. B. (1972). Reconsideration of a measure of power motivation. *Psychological Bulletin, 78,* 279–291.

Waller, W. W., & Hill, R. (1951). *The family, a dynamic interpretation.* New York: Dryden Press.

Winter, D. G. (1973). *The power motive.* New York: The Free Press.

Winter, D. G., & Barenbaum, N. B. (1985). Responsibility and the power motive in women and men. *Journal of Personality, 53,* 335–355.

Winter, D.G., & Stewart, A.G. (1978). The power motive. In H. London & J. Exner (Eds.), *Dimensions of personality* (pp. 391–447). New York: Wiley.

Word, C. O., Zanna, M. P., & Cooper, J. (1974). The nonverbal mediation of self-fulfilling prophecies in interracial interaction. *Journal of Experimental Social Psychology, 10,* 109–120.

Zimmerman, D. H., & West, C. (1975). Sex roles, interruptions, and silences in conversations. In B. Thorne & N. Henley (Eds.), *Language and sex: Difference and dominance* (pp. 105–129). Rowley, MA: Newbury House.

PART III

POWER AND GROUPS

9

Social Identity, Leadership, and Power

MICHAEL A. HOGG
SCOTT A. REID

Leadership, power, and corruption are terms that are often closely associated in people's minds. Leaders possess power that they wield over others to control, coerce, and dominate. This belief in a tight linkage between leadership, power, and corruption is very common, and has a wide range of consequences, not the least of which is a widespread distrust of politicians. Many leaders are, indeed, corrupt and wield power in self-interested ways that create enormous human suffering. However, other leaders are principled and benevolent visionaries who alleviate human suffering—forces for good that inspire people to great and noble deeds. Contrast, for example, Adolf Hitler and Idi Amin with Mahatma Gandhi and Nelson Mandela.

Irrespective of the leaders' or group's goals, leaders can use their position of power to forcibly coerce people, or they can use their position of power to more gently gain compliance from followers, or they can act as an inspirational focus for the shared goals of a group. These are very different types of leadership. The key questions addressed in this chapter are what group processes underlie these leader-follower relations, and what processes transform one leader-follower relationship into another—in particular, is coercive exercise of power an inevitable consequence of leadership?

This chapter was made possible by research grant funding to Michael Hogg from the Australian Research Council. Some of the ideas in this chapter were presented by Michael Hogg at the June 1998 convention of the Society for the Psychological Study of Social Issues, at the University of Michigan, Ann Arbor.

The approach taken is framed by the assumption that leadership is a group process. Basic group and intergroup processes, hinging on collective self-definition as a group member, generate different leader-follower relations that have implications for how leaders gain and maintain influence over the group. The relationship between leadership and the exercise of power is discussed, and conditions associated with the responsible and the abusive exercise of power are delineated. The model described in this chapter draws on ideas from the social identity theory of leadership (Hogg, 1996, 1999, in press-a; see also Hogg & Terry, 2000), research on power (Mulder, 1977; Reid & Ng, 1999, 2000), and work on idiosyncracy credit (Hollander, 1958, 1985).

LEADERSHIP RESEARCH

Some Major Themes

Leadership has been a popular research focus for social psychology (e.g., Bass, 1990a; Chemers, 2001; Graumann & Moscovici, 1986; Hollander, 1985; Stogdill, 1974). However, in recent years its popularity has waned in proportion to the ascendancy of social cognition, so that leadership research is now more common in disciplines like organizational psychology (e.g., Wilpert, 1995; Yukl & Van Fleet, 1992). Early research into leadership behaviors, and personality and situational determinants of effective leadership, culminated in Fiedler's (e.g., 1965) well known interactionist model: the leadership effectiveness of a particular behavioral style is contingent on the favorability of the situation to that behavioral style. Fiedler's contingency theory is, in general, well supported, despite some continuing controversy (see Peters, Hartke, & Pohlmann, 1985).

Subsequent research has focused on leadership as a dynamic product of transactions between leaders and followers (Bass, 1990b; Hollander, 1985; Nye & Simonetta, 1996). For example, leaders play a significant role in helping followers achieve their goals, while followers bestow power and status on leaders to maintain or restore equity. Leaders may also accumulate idiosyncrasy credit with the group by conforming to group norms. Idiosyncrasy credit then serves as a resource that may be exchanged to allow the leader to depart from group norms and to be innovative (Hollander, 1958, 1985; Hollander & Julian, 1970).

Recent transactional leadership perspectives, mainly in organizational psychology (Wilpert, 1995), focus on transformational leadership. Charismatic leaders are able to motivate followers to work for collective goals that transcend self-interest and transform organizations (Bass, 1990b; Bass & Avolio, 1993; see Mowday & Sutton, 1993, for critical comment). This focus on charisma is particularly evident in new leadership research (e.g., Bass, 1990b, 1998; Bryman, 1992; Conger & Kanungo, 1987) which proposes that effective leaders should be proactive, change-oriented, innovative, motivating, and inspiring, and have a vision or mission with which they infuse the group. They should also be interested in others, and be able to create commitment to the group, and extract extra effort from and empower members of the group.

Finally, social cognition perspectives on leadership have produced leader categorization theory (Lord, 1985; Lord, Foti, & DeVader, 1984; Palich & Hom, 1992; Rush & Russell, 1988; also see Nye & Simonetta, 1996). People have preconceptions about how leaders should behave in general and in specific leadership situations. These preconceptions are cognitive schemas of types of leader (i.e., categories of leader that are represented as person schemas) which operate in the same way as other schemas (see Fiske & Taylor, 1991). When someone is categorized on the basis of their behavior as a leader, the relevant leadership schema comes into play to generate further assumptions about behavior. Leadership schemas vary in situational inclusiveness. Subordinate schemas apply only to specific situations, whereas superordinate schemas apply to a wide range of situations.

Critical Commentary and New Directions

With only a few notable exceptions, the recent study of leadership has been conducted outside of contemporary mainstream social psychology, and so has not benefitted from some of the recent conceptual advances made within social psychology. Although most perspectives now recognize that leadership is a relational property within groups (i.e., leaders exist because of followers, and followers exist because of leaders), there is no analysis of leadership that describes how leadership may emerge through the operation of basic social cognitive processes associated with psychologically belonging to a group.

In contrast, the most recent analytic emphasis is mainly upon 1) individual cognitive processes that categorize individuals as leaders—the social orientation between individuals is not considered, and thus group processes are not incorporated, or 2) whether individuals have the charismatic properties necessary to meet the alleged transformational objectives of leadership—leadership is a matter of situationally attractive individual characteristics rather than group processes. Both these perspectives have recently invited criticism for neglecting the effects of larger social systems within which the individual is embedded (e.g., Hall & Lord, 1995; Lord, Brown, & Harvey, 2001; Pawar & Eastman, 1997). Lord, Brown, and Harvey (2001) explain that leadership cannot be properly understood in terms of a leader's actions or in terms of abstract perceptual categories of types of leader, and that a paradigm shift in how we understand leadership is called for. Their solution is to explore a connectionist, or parallel constraint satisfaction, level model.

The alternative solution, proposed here, is an elaboration of social identity theory. If leadership is indeed a structural feature of ingroups, then leaders and followers are interdependent roles embedded within a social system bounded by common group/category membership. Thus, leadership dynamics may be significantly affected by the social cognitive processes associated with group membership (and group behaviors); specifically the processes of self-categorization and depersonalization now believed to be responsible for social identity processes, group behavior, and intergroup relations. Leaders may emerge, maintain their position, be effective, and so forth, as a consequence of basic social cognitive processes that cause people 1) to conceive of themselves in terms of the defining features of a common and distinctive ingroup (i.e., self-categorization, or identification, in terms of the ingroup prototype), 2) to cognitively and behaviorally assimilate themselves to these features (i.e., cognitive and behavioral depersonalization in terms of the ingroup prototype, producing ingroup stereotypic or normative perceptions, attitudes, feelings, and behaviors), and 3) to perceive others not as unique individuals but through the lens of features that define relevant ingroup or outgroup membership (i.e., perceptual depersonalization of others in terms of the ingroup or outgroup prototype, producing stereotypical homogenization). If leadership is produced by these group processes contingent on psychologically belonging to the group, then having the prototypical or normative characteristics of a psychologically salient ingroup (i.e., being a prototypical ingroup member) may be at least as important for leadership as being charismatic or having schema-consistent characteristics of a particular type or category of leader (i.e. being schematic of a nominal leader category).

THE SOCIAL IDENTITY THEORY OF LEADERSHIP

The Social Identity Perspective

Social identity theory, more accurately characterized as the social identity perspective (e.g., Hogg, 1996, in press; Turner, 1999), contains a number of compatible and interrelated components and emphases; in particular an original emphasis by Tajfel and Turner and their associates on social identity, social comparison, intergroup relations, and self-enhancement motivation (often simply called social identity theory; e.g., Tajfel, 1972; Tajfel & Turner, 1979; Turner, 1982), a later cognitive emphasis by Turner and his associates on the categorization process (called self-categorization theory; e.g., Turner et al., 1987), and a recent exploration of the motivational role of subjective uncertainty reduction (Hogg, in press; Hogg & Mullin, 1999). Social identity theory and self-categorization theory have been extensively reviewed as an integrated whole elsewhere (e.g., Hogg, 1996, 2001, in press; Hogg & Abrams, 1988, 1999; Hogg, Terry, & White, 1995; Turner, 1999).

According to the social identity perspective, people define and evaluate themselves and others in terms of the groups they belong to: group memberships define the collective self-concept and thus people's social identity. Social identity is evaluative, and thus intergroup relations is a struggle in which groups compete for evaluatively positive distinctiveness and thus positive social identity. The specific strategies that groups and their members adopt depend on perceptions of intergroup status differences and the stability and legitimacy of such differences, as well as the permeability of intergroup boundaries and thus the feasibility of psychologically redefining oneself as a member of a higher status group. The struggle for positive social identity is a group level manifestation of an underlying human motivation to maintain a positive sense of self-esteem.

The fundamental process underlying social identification, social categorization, is described in detail by self-categorization theory. Social categorization perceptually segments the social world into ingroups and outgroups that are cognitively represented as prototypes—context-specific fuzzy sets that define and prescribe attitudes, feelings, and behaviors that characterize one group and distinguish it from other groups. Prototypes are often stored in memory to be engaged by social categorization in a particular context in order to guide perception, self-conception, and action. However prototypes are modified to varying degrees, and they can be entirely constructed by specifics of a particular social context. Prototypes are contextually responsive, and the principle governing this contextual sensitivity is metacontrast. New prototypes form, or existing ones are modified, in such a way as to maximize the ratio of perceived intergroup differences to intragroup similarities; prototypes form to accentuate similarities within a category and differences between categories.

Social categorization of other people perceptually assimilates them to the relevant ingroup or outgroup prototype, and thus perceptually accentuates prototypical similarities among people in the same group and prototypical differences among people from different groups. Thus, the depersonalization process perceptually differentiates groups, and renders perceptions, attitudes, feelings, and behaviors stereotypical and group normative. Because people are not viewed as unique and multifaceted individuals but as more or less exact matches to the relevant ingroup or outgroup prototype, prototypicality, not individuality, becomes the focus of attention. Depersonalization simply refers to change in the basis of perception; it does not have the negative connotations of terms such as "deindividuation" or "dehumanization." Social categorization of self, self-categorization, has the same effect but more so. It not only depersonalizes self-perception, but goes much further in actually transforming self-conception and assimilating all aspects of one's attitudes, feelings, and behaviors to the ingroup prototype; it changes what people think, feel, and do.

Social categorization of self and others satisfies an epistemic/self-evaluative motive to reduce subjective uncertainty (the uncertainty–reduction hypothesis—e.g., Hogg, in press). Situational or more enduring subjective uncertainty, particularly relating to self-conceptualization, motivates social identification and group formation, particularly with high entitativity groups (e.g., Campbell, 1958; Hamilton & Sherman, 1996) that are distinctive and have simple, consensual, and prescriptive prototypes. These prototypes best resolve uncertainty about what to do, what others will do, and about who one is. Uncertainty reduction and self-enhancement provide the motivational parameters for the cognitive processes underlying the contextual salience of self-categorization. People, influenced by self-enhancement and uncertainty reduction motives, categorize the social context in terms of categories that are chronically accessible in memory or rendered accessible by the immediate context. The categorization that becomes salient is the one that best accounts for relevant similarities and differences among people in the context (structural/comparative fit), best accords with the social meaning of the context (normative fit), and best satisfies self-enhancement and self-evaluative concerns.

Social Identity and Leadership

The social identity theory of leadership (Hogg, 1996, 1999, in 2001; also see Hogg & Terry, 2000) rests on the premise that as self-categorization as a group member becomes increasingly psychologically salient, leadership endorsement and thus leadership effectiveness becomes increasingly based on how prototypical the leader is, rather than on other bases of leadership. There are three processes that operate in conjunction to make prototypicality an increasingly influential basis of leadership processes as a function of increasing social identity salience: prototypicality, social attraction, and attribution and information processing. These processes are described mainly in terms of emergent leadership in new groups. However, they also apply to situations in which established leadership roles are structurally assigned. ·

Prototypicality. When group membership is psychologically salient, social categorization of self and other ingroup members depersonalizes perception, cognition, affect, and behavior in terms of the contextually relevant ingroup prototype. Group members conform to, and thus are influenced by, the prototype. Those people who are more prototypical to begin with will be less influenced than those who are less prototypical to begin with; the former make fewer changes than the latter in order to approximate the prototype. In salient groups, people are highly sensitive to prototypicality, as it is the basis of perception and evaluation of self and other group members. Thus, they notice and respond to very subtle differences in how prototypical fellow members are; there is a clearly perceived gradient of prototypicality within the group, with some people clearly perceived to be more prototypical than others (e.g., Haslam et al., 1995; Hogg, 1993).Within a salient group, then, people who are perceived to occupy the most prototypical position are perceived to best embody the behaviors to which other, less prototypical, members are conforming. There is a perception of differential influence within the group, with the most prototypical member appearing to exercise influence over less prototypical members. In new groups, this is an "appearance" because the most prototypical person does not actively exercise influence; it is the prototype, which he or she happens to embody, that influences behavior. In established groups the appearance is backed up by actual influence (see below).

Prototypes are contextually sensitive to the intergroup social comparative context (the metacontrast principle). Thus, if the context remains unchanged, the prototype remains unchanged, and the same individual group member will occupy the most prototypical position. It follows that the longer a particular individual occupies the most prototypical position, the stronger and more entrenched will be the appearance that he or she actively exercises influence over others. In new groups this person is perceived to occupy an embryonic leadership role; although leadership has not been exercised. There is an embryonic role differentiation into "leader" and "followers."

As group membership becomes more salient, and members identify more strongly with the group, prototypicality becomes an increasingly influential basis for leadership perceptions. People also, of course, rely on general and more task-specific schemas of leadership behaviors (what Lord and his colleagues call "leader categories"—e.g., Lord, Foti, & DeVader, 1984). However the importance of these schemas is either unaffected by self-categorization, or they become less important as group prototypicality becomes more important. In either case, leadership schemas should become less influential relative to group prototypicality as group membership becomes psychologically more salient.

Social Attraction.   Leadership is more than passively being prototypical; it involves actively influencing other people. One way in which this is made possible is via the social attraction process (e.g., Hogg, 1992, 1993; Hogg & Hains, 1996). Self-categorization depersonalizes the basis of attraction within groups, such that more prototypical members are liked more than less prototypical members. Where there is a consensual prototype this produces consensual liking for prototypical members. Prototypical people may acquire, in new groups, or possess, in established groups, the ability to actively influence because they are socially attractive and thus able to secure compliance with suggestions and recommendations they make (research confirms that liking increases compliance—e.g., Berscheid & Reis, 1998). Thus, the most prototypical person is able to exercise leadership by having his or her ideas accepted more readily and more widely than ideas suggested by others. This empowers the leader, and publicly confirms his or her ability to exercise influence. Consensual depersonalized liking, particularly over time, confirms differential popularity and public endorsement of the leader. It imbues the leader with prestige and status, and begins to reify an intragroup status differential between leader and followers.

Social attraction also may be enhanced by the behavior of highly prototypical members. More prototypical members tend to identify more strongly, and thus display more pronounced group behaviors; they will be more normative, show greater ingroup loyalty and ethnocentrism, and generally behave in a more group serving manner. These behaviors further confirm their prototypicality and thus enhance social attraction. A leader who acts as "one of us," by showing strong ingroup favoritism and intragroup fairness, is not only more socially attractive, but is also provided with legitimacy. According to the group value model of procedural justice, members feel more satisfied and more committed to the group if the leader is procedurally fair (Tyler, 1997; Tyler & Lind, 1992; see Platow, Reid, & Andrew, 1998).

Attribution and Information Processing.   Prototypicality and social attraction work in conjunction with attribution and information processing to translate perceived influence into active leadership. As elsewhere, attribution processes operate within groups to make sense of others' behavior, but such processes are prone to the fundamental attribution error (Ross, 1977) or correspondence bias (e.g., Gilbert & Malone, 1995; Trope & Liberman, 1993), a tendency to attribute behavior to underlying dispositions that reflect invariant properties, or essences, of the individual's personality. This effect is more pronounced for individuals who are perceptually distinctive (e.g., figural against a background) or cognitively salient (e.g., Taylor & Fiske, 1978).

When group membership is salient, people are sensitive to prototypicality and attend to subtle differences in prototypicality of fellow members. Highly prototypical members are obviously most informative about what is prototypical of group membership, and so, not surprisingly, within a group context they attract the most attention. They are subjectively important and are distinctive or figural against the background of other less informative members. Research in social cognition shows that people who are subjectively important and distinctive are considered disproportionately influential and have their behavior dispositionally attributed (e.g., Erber & Fiske, 1984; Taylor & Fiske, 1975). Together, the relative prominence of prototypical members and their apparent influence (they appear to have influence due to their relative prototypicality, and may actively exercise influence and gain compliance as a consequence of consensual social attraction) is likely to encourage an internal attribution to intrinsic leadership ability, or charisma. This attribution will be facilitated if cultural theories of the causes of leadership favor the belief that leadership reflects personality (e.g., in individualist cultures); see Morris & Peng (1994).

In groups, then, the behavior of highly prototypical members is likely to be attributed, particularly in diachronically stable groups, to the person's personality rather than the prototypicality of the position occupied. The consequence is a tendency to construct a charismatic leadership personality for that person that, to some extent, separates that person from the rest of the group and reinforces the perception of status-based structural differentiation within the group into leader and followers. This may make the leader stand out more starkly against the background of less prototypical followers, as well as draw attention to a potential power imbalance; thus further fueling the attributional effect.

Empirical Support for the Social Identity Theory of Leadership

Direct tests have focused on the core prediction that as a group becomes more salient emergent leadership processes and leadership effectiveness perceptions become less dependent on leader schema congruence and more dependent on group prototypicality. There is solid support for this idea from laboratory experiments (e.g., Duck & Fielding, 1999; Hains, Hogg, & Duck, 1997; Hogg, Hains, & Mason, 1998; Platow & van Knippenberg, 1999) and a naturalistic field study (Fielding & Hogg, 1997).

In illustration, two of these studies are described here. Hains, Hogg, and Duck (1997) studied emergent leadership perceptions and evaluations in ad hoc and relatively minimal groups. Three independent variables (group salience, group prototypicality, and leader schema congruence) were manipulated in a 2 × 2 × 2 design. Under conditions of high or low group salience, student participants (N = 184) anticipated joining a small discussion group formed on the basis of attitude congruence. They were informed that a randomly appointed group leader was group prototypical or nonprototypical (group prototypicality) in terms of the attitude dimension, and had a behavioral style (on the basis of a pretest) that was congruent or incongruent with a leader schema (leader schema congruence). Dependent measures were taken ostensibly in anticipation of the upcoming discussion. In addition to checks on each of the three manipulations, we also measured group identification (11-item scale) and perceived leader effectiveness (10-item scale). As predicted, when group membership was salient, people identified more strongly with the group and endorsed the prototypical leader as being much more effective than the nonprototypical leader; low salience participants did not differentiate between prototypical and nonprototypical leaders. Although leader schema congruent leaders were perceived overall to be more effective than schema incongruent leaders, we found that this effect disappeared for high salience participants on one leadership effectiveness item. Although social attraction for the leader was not explicitly tested, the 10-item leadership effectiveness scale contained an item measuring liking for the leader; thus leadership effectiveness was associated with liking.

To complement this laboratory experiment, Fielding and Hogg (1997) conducted a field study of leadership in small interactive 'outward bound' groups where real leaders emerged and actually lead the groups in wilderness and outdoor experiences. This study included 13 mixed-sex, approximately 11-person groups of people mainly in their 20s from around Australia (N = 143). The groups stayed together for three weeks. The laboratory experiment was replicated as closely as possible, but in a measurement-based regression format. Leadership schemas, group membership variables, and leadership effectiveness perceptions were measured a week to 10 days apart. In this study we were also able to measure social attraction. As predicted, 1) group identification, perceived leadership effectiveness, and social attraction for the leader increased over time as the group became a more cohesive entity, and 2) perceived leadership effectiveness was a positive function of social attraction for, and group prototypicality of, the leader; this was amplified among high identifying participants. Perceived leader schema congruence of the leader was a predictor of perceived leadership effectiveness, but was uninfluenced by identification.

In addition to direct support from explicit tests of the social identity model, there is also indirect support from a range of studies of leadership that are in the general social identity tradition (de Cremer & van Vugt, in press; Foddy & Hogg, 1999; Haslam et al., 1998; Platow, Reid, & Andrew, 1998; van Vugt & de Cremer, 1999). There is also support for the idea that prototype-based depersonalized social attraction may facilitate leadership. There is some direct evidence from the studies by Fielding and Hogg (1997) and de Cremer and van Vugt (in press), whereas in other studies social attraction is a component of the leadership evaluation measure (e.g., Hains, Hogg, & Duck, 1997; Hogg, Hains, & Mason, 1998).

The attribution and associated structural differentiation components of the theory only have indirect support. For example, Fiske (1993; Fiske & Dépret, 1996) shows how followers pay close attention to leaders, and seek dispositional information about leaders because detailed individualized knowledge helps redress the perceived power imbalance between leader and followers. Other research, in organizational settings, shows how charismatic leadership personalities are attributionally constructed for organizational leaders who initiate change (Conger & Kanungo, 1987) or who are distinctive or hold office under crisis conditions (Meindl, Ehrlich, & Dukerich, 1985). Further research is currently under way, but it should be recognized that the empirical status of the leadership theory rests on good evidence for social identity theory as a whole.

LEADERSHIP, POWER, AND THE ABUSE OF POWER

Despite the popular view that leadership, power, and the abuse of power are closely linked, scientific definitions of leadership usually distinguish leadership from power (e.g., Chemers, 2001; Lord, Brown, & Harvey, 2001). Leadership is a process of influence that enlists and mobilizes others in the attainment of collective goals—it imbues people with the groups attitudes and goals, and inspires them to work towards achieving them. Leadership is not a process that requires people to exercise power over others in order to gain compliance or, more extremely, in order to coerce or force people. The social identity theory of leadership is consistent with this type of definition.

Prototypical leaders do not need to exercise power (i.e., persuade, gain compliance, coerce, or resort to force) in order to have influence; they are influential by virtue of their position and the depersonalization process that assimilates members' behavior to the prototype. They and their suggestions are intrinsically persuasive because they embody the norms of the group; they have referent power (Raven, 1965) or position power, and therefore do not need to exercise personal power (Yukl & Falbe, 1991). Indeed, the influence process associated with being a highly prototypical leader is the influence process associated with social identification with a group—the process of referent informational influence that produces normative behavior in salient groups (e.g., Hogg & Turner, 1987; Turner, 1982). Followers pay close attention to the prototype and to those who are prototypical, and engage in systematic, deliberative, and central route processing of information about the leader and the leader's message. This produces internalized cognitive change—true attitude change—in members (e.g., Mackie, 1987; Mackie & Queller, 2000).

In addition to not needing to exercise power, it is possible that prototypical leaders may be unable to exercise power coercively. High prototypicality is associated with strong ingroup identification; self and group are tightly fused prototypically and thus any form of negative behavior directed against fellow members is effectively directed against self. There may exist an empathic bond between leader and followers that protects against any desire to exercise coercive power over others, let alone destructive use of power or the abuse of power.

Nevertheless, leaders often do exercise power in harmful ways, and abuse of power can be aided by being a leader. To explain how this might happen and how it might be constrained, consider a model that integrates the social identity theory of leadership with 1) the idea that prototypicality is a resource for power (Reid & Ng, 1999, 2000), 2) Hollander's ideas on idiosyncracy credit (Hollander, 1985; Hollander & Julian, 1970), and 3) the concept of power distance (Mulder, 1977).

Leadership is a diachronic process. It requires responsiveness to the dynamics of social life, it depends upon interdependent relations with followers, the vicissitudes of social change, and the fortunes associated with being effective and successful. To capture this diachronic process a stage model describing the relationship between leadership and abuse of power is proposed. Although later stages emerge from earlier ones, stage transitions are not inevitable—they can be inhibited by a number of intervening mechanisms.

Stage 1: Leader (Re)Emergence

From a social identity perspective, people who are perceived to be highly prototypical emerge as group leaders if the group is salient (for example due to intergroup threat, high uncertainty, strong need for positive social identity), and the group prototype is consensual and distinct. This is the leadership described above—it depends on influence through shared internalized goals, not on compliance or coercion processes.

People can emerge as leaders due merely to their prototypicality (the leadership position is contextually accessible); but people can also be motivated to become a leader (i.e., being a leader is psychologically accessible) and can actively engage in prototypical behavior, or in prototype defining behavior, in order to increase their chances of emerging as a leader. For example, by communicating a clear message that at once defines and delineates the ingroup position from that of the outgroup (a message that communicates the prototypical content of the ingroup norm), the leader enhances his or her chances of receiving support from ingroup members, and makes it possible to mobilize the group (Ng & Reid, 1999). Should this occur, the individual stands a strong chance of emerging as leader.

There is support for the idea that prototypicality acts as a resource for emergent leaders. Reid and Ng (2000) analyzed intergroup discussions between pro- and anticapital punishment adherents, to discover that leader emergence was tied to the ability to gain speaking turns with prototypical content. The reason that only prototypical utterances correlated with emergent leadership, is that such utterances are focused on by both ingroup and outgroup members. Speakers who attempt to interrupt using prototypical utterances are more likely to be successful in gaining the floor, whereas the reverse is true for speakers using nonprototypical utterances. Thus, leadership emergence relies on the effective communication of prototypical ingroup norms, which is constrained by ingroup members' preference for receiving prototypical information.

Stage 2: Stabilization and Legitimization of the Leadership Position

Passage of time, coupled with a stable intergroup context, ensures a steady prototype and allows an individual to remain in the leadership position. The longer an individual remains in a leadership position the more they will be socially liked and the more consensual social attraction and the more entrenched the fundamental attribution effect will be. In this way an established leader can become more prototypically influential.

One consequence of becoming an established prototypical leader is the accumulation of idiosyncrasy credits (e.g., Hollander, 1985; Hollander & Julian, 1970). The credits can be spent to allow the leader increasingly to adopt more active aspects of being a leader, including normative innovation and the ability to strategically maintain his or her leadership position. Indeed, Platow and van Kippenberg (1999) show that prototypical leaders receive strong endorsement regardless of whether they make equal, ingroup favoring or outgroup favoring resource allocations. When a leader is nonprototypical, in contrast, strong endorsement is received only if the leader allocates resources using an ingroup favoring strategy. Clearly, being prototypical allows a leader to do more than simply confirm the group identity, it enables the leader to form and alter the normative consensus, and define (or even redefine) the role or position of the group in relation to other groups. That is, a leader in a prototypical position has the capacity to redefine the group prototype, and as such can decide to exercise power over others in order to gain compliance with his or her agenda.

Being prototypical provides the leader with the ability to accumulate further power. Engaging in prototypical behavior serves as a form of idiosyncrasy credit that allows the leader to steer the group in new directions. The more the leader exercises his or her compliance focused power, the more idiosyncrasy credit that is gained, and the more entrenched becomes the prototypical position. There is thus a feedback loop; prototypicality enables the leader to exercise power, which leads to the accumulation of more power, which enables the leader to further control the prototypical ingroup position. Most notably, by exercising power, the leader increases legitimate power (the leader creates and acts on a mandate), expert power (the leader is imbued with leader-like characteristics), and referent power (social identity processes lead to social attraction).

Although an established leader has the power base to maintain his or her position, it is often advantageous if the group continues to view them as highly prototypical. However, as we have seen, social contextual changes impact prototypicality. Thus, over time and across contexts, the leader may decline in prototypicality while other members become more prototypical; opening the door, particularly under high salience conditions, to a redistribution of influence within the group. An established leader is well placed in terms of resources to combat this by redefining the prototype in a self-serving manner to proto-typically marginalize contenders and prototypically centralize self. This can be done by accentuating the existing ingroup prototype, by pillorying ingroup de-viants, or by demonizing an appropriate outgroup. Generally all three tactics are used, and the very act of engaging in these tactics is often viewed as further evidence of effective leadership. National leaders often engage in these tactics. During the 1982 Falklands War between Britain and Argentina, Margaret Thatcher, the British Prime Minister, accentuated her nationalistic prototype of Britain, pilloried deviant groups within Britain who did not represent her pro-totype, and demonized the Argentinian outgroup. Her leadership ratings rose significantly.

Leadership endurance also benefits from consensual prototypicality, be-cause of the latter's effect on social attraction phenomena. In groups with less consensual prototypes, there is greater dissensus of perceptions of and feelings for the leader and thus the leader may have less power and may occupy a less stable position. It is in the leader's interest to maintain a consensual prototype. Simple and more clearly focused prototypes are less open to ambiguity and alternative interpretations and are thus better suited to consensuality. In addi-tion, ingroup deviants serve an important function; by creating and rejecting such deviants the leader is well able to clarify the self-serving focus of the pro-totype. Another strategy is to polarize or extremitize the ingroup relative to a specific evil outgroup. These processes operate quite starkly in extremist groups with all-powerful leaders. For example in Cambodia in the 1970s Pol Pot con-structed a very simple and orthodox national prototype, he engaged in a cam-paign of prototypical purification that involved exterminating deviants, and he polarized and demonized the "decadent" West.

Stage 3: Structural Role and Power Differentiation

Over time, the leader's power base increases, and he or she becomes entrenched in the prototypical position, at least as perceived by followers. However, there is another aspect of the prototype based leadership process. The leader increasingly becomes perceptually separated by followers from the rest of the group through structural role differentiation grounded in social attraction and attributional processes. The leader is seen as "other" in relation to the rest of the group. A paradox emerges—the person who embodied the essence of the group by being most prototypical has now become effectively an outgroup member within the group—and an embryonic intergroup relationship begins to emerge between leader and followers. However, the leader is perceived to be charismatic and thus can still have influence without resorting to the coercive exercise of power; instead the leader may try to influence the social comparative context in order to accentuate or redefine self as ingroup prototypical. In addition, although the empathic bond that protects against abuse of power is actually severed, the leader probably still feels strongly enough identified with the group that suffi-cient residual empathic bonding persists to protect against abuse of power.

However, at the same time as the embryonic intergroup relationship between leader(s) and followers is emerging, this relationship is also becoming marked by power differentiation into a superior-subordinate relationship. The emergence of power differentiation can be understood in terms of Mulder's (1977) power distance theory, in which power, rather than being viewed in terms of dichotomous categories, is conceptualized as a continuum of power distance. Power is defined as the relative power distance of A from B. When a leader's power base becomes large enough, a wide power distance gulf opens up between leader and followers. This sets up conditions for the leader to recategorize the leader-follower relationship into a power- and status-based intergroup superior-subordinate relationship. There exists the potential for self-categorization in which the leader recognizes and subscribes to his or her legitimate power and status in relation to followers.

The potential to exercise power over, rather than on behalf of, others now exists. The embryonic power-based intergroup differentiation into leaders and followers enables intergroup behaviors. Research shows that the possession of reward power over another group is a strong basis for discrimination against an outgroup (e.g., Ng, 1980, 1982, 1996), that as the power of one group over another increases, so does the degree of discrimination (e.g., Sachdev & Bourhis, 1985), and that intergroup discrimination is mediated by social identification (e.g., Hogg & Abrams, 1988).

The emergence of intergroup relations is strengthened by stereotyping processes. Leaders often stereotype followers by default, because they feel less dependent on them, and their numerosity produces cognitive overload that inhibits processing of individuating information. According to Goodwin (Goodwin & Fiske, 1996; Goodwin et al., 2000), leaders also stereotype followers by design, because they believe that followers are socially judgeable (e.g., Leyens, Yzerbyt, & Schadron, 1992; Yzerbyt et al., 1994). In this case they believe that leadership involves making judgments about other people. Leaders also stereotype followers because they are motivated to remain in power, and stereotypes serve to differentiate groups, and to reify and accentuate status differentials (e.g., Tajfel, 1981). Leaders and followers grow further apart and leaders can increasingly exercise power to have influence that contributes further to the separation, and so on.

Stage 4: Abuse of Power

Stage 3 describes how power- and status-based intergroup relations between leaders and followers may evolve within a group, and how such relations create the potential for the exercise of coercive power over others. The potential may not be realized, particularly if the existence of promotively interdependent goals allows leadership through influence or the exercise of power on behalf of the group or through gaining compliance.

However, there are circumstances that translate the potential to abuse power into the actual abuse of power. A relatively inevitable consequence of role differentiation is that the leader gradually realizes that he or she is effectively treated by followers as an outgroup member—a positive high status deviant, but none the less a deviant who cannot readily share in the life of the group. The leader may at this point try to veer away from the abyss by engaging in behaviors aimed at confirming his or her ingroup prototypicality. If this is unsuccessful, a sense of rejection by, and distance and isolation from, the group may occur (possibly also a recognition of reduced influence among followers) that may embitter the leader and, since the empathic bond is severed, allow the leader to gain compliance through the exercise of power over others. This may involve coercive behavior and abuse of power, because the interests of the leader and the group have diverged—the leader is effectively exercising his or her will over others. The influence process is one that involves coercion rather than attitude change.

This effect is much stronger in hierarchical extremist groups where the leader-follower role and power differentiation are more tangible and stark. The potential for abuse of power is much more accentuated in these types of groups. The effect will also be stronger in groups where there is a leadership clique rather than a single leader, because a typical intergroup relationship has effectively emerged and thus the relationship between leaders and followers is an intergroup relationship where one group (the leaders) has disproportionate legitimate power over the other group (the followers). Such a relationship will be competitive and potentially exploitative—far removed from prototype based leadership.

Leaders generally react negatively to perceived threats to their leadership position. In Stage 2, where a leader is prototypically influential and no intergroup differentiation has yet emerged, threats to leadership largely come from prototype slippage—social contextual factors may reconfigure the group prototype and thus reduce the leaders prototypicality. Leaders then strive to redefine the prototype to better fit themselves. They can accentuate the existing ingroup prototype, pillory ingroup deviants, or demonize an appropriate outgroup. At Stage 2 these tactics generally do not involve the abusive use of power over followers.

However, at Stage 4 perceived threats to leadership are automatically perceived in intergroup terms as collective challenge or revolt on the part of the followers. This makes salient the latent intergroup orientation between leaders and followers, and engenders competitive intergroup relations between leaders and followers—competitive relations in which one group has consensually legitimate and overwhelming power over the other. Under these circumstances leadership becomes coercion, based on the relatively limitless and abusive exercise of power over others. The dynamic is similar to the way in which a power elite reacts to a perceived challenge to its privileged position (e.g., Wright, 1997), but because it occurs within the power-legitimizing framework of a common group membership the reaction is potentially all the more extreme.

THE TAMING OF POWER

The problem of abuse of power and how to tame power is an ancient and complex one that overlaps social psychology, moral philosophy, politics, economics, and history. For instance, the Greeks contended with systems of democracy, oligarchy, and tyranny, only to find that democracy was continually undermined by the transient popularity of some demagogue; at the same time, Taoists concluded that the problem of containing power is insoluble (Russell, 1938).

The analysis developed in this chapter examines the relationship between group leadership and the exercise and abuse of power. Building primarily on the social identity theory of leadership, we show how highly prototypical leaders of salient groups, particularly newly-emerged leaders, provide leadership through influence. They do not need to exercise power over followers, and indeed may not actually be able to exercise the more coercive forms of power in this way (Stage 1). Enduring tenure renders leaders more influential and facilitates normative innovation. Leaders still do not need to exercise power over followers because they now have the capacity to ensure that they remain prototypical and thus influential (Stage 2). Further tenure differentiates the leader from the followers (Stage 3). It creates an intergroup differentiation based on widening, reified, and consensually legitimized role and power differences. The potential to use and abuse power is now all too real, however it may not occur. The conditions that translate the potential into reality are ones that render salient the latent power-based intergroup relationship between leaders and followers—for example, a sense of threat to one's leadership position, a feeling of remoteness and alienation from the group, or a sense of becoming less influential in the life of the group (Stage 4).

The abuse of power resides in the psychological reality (based on self-categorization and social identity processes) of a sharp role, status, and power discontinuity between leaders and followers that reconfigures cooperative intragroup relations as competitive intergroup relations. Such intergroup relations within a group provide ideal conditions for unilaterally exploitative intergroup behavior. This is because the overarching common group identity and the diachronic process of leadership emergence strongly legitimizes the status quo. There exists what social identity theory refers to as a social change belief structure without cognitive alternatives (Tajfel & Turner, 1979; also see Hogg & Abrams, 1988). Because power and leadership are attractive to some people, this belief system can be coupled with a belief in intergroup permeability that encourages followers to try to gain admittance to the leadership clique. This, of course, marshals support for the leader and prevents the followers from forming a united front.

This is, paradoxically, a relatively optimistic analysis of power. Although power can become concentrated in leadership, and conditions can strongly support abuse of power by leaders, power can certainly be tamed or at least contained. The challenge is that it is the group, not the leader, that has to take the initiative in arranging conditions that contain power, and yet the group is relatively powerless in the face of a leader who is wielding power in oppressive ways. Nevertheless, anything that inhibits the attribution of charisma and the process of structural differentiation, and which regrounds leadership in prototypicality will inhibit the exercise of power. This may include quite contrasting conditions—on the one hand, reduced group cohesion, reduced prototype consensuality, and increased diversity, and on the other hand, any external group threat that refocuses attention on common group identity. Although the natural course of intergroup relations creates these conditions, overly powerful leaders can protect themselves to some extent against them. The processes may be quite complicated. For example, if a group becomes less cohesive, more diverse, and less consensual about its prototype, it is less likely that followers will agree on and endorse the same person as the leader. The leader's power base is fragmented, and numerous new contenders emerge. Although this limits the leader's ability to abuse power, it is a threatening state of affairs, particularly for a leader who has been accustomed to exercising power—powerful incumbent leaders are very likely to react in draconian ways.

External threat can make the group so cohesive and consensual that leader and group become re-fused and the empathic bond reestablished. The leader no longer needs, or indeed is able, to exercise power, particularly in destructive ways. External threat may also focus the group on promotively interdependent goals, with the consequence that followers do not grant status to leaders unless leaders earn such status through appropriate contribution to group goal achievement (e.g., Ridgeway, 2001; Ridgeway & Diekema, 1989). Leaders who exercise power in order to misappropriate a share of rewards will face a resistant coalition of followers. Power abuse becomes a less effective or viable form of leadership. Leaders need to reposition themselves to act as prototypical group members who, through being prototypical, contribute more to the group's goals than do less prototypical followers.

CLOSING COMMENT

In this chapter the social identity theory of leadership (Hogg, 1996, 1999) is extended to provide an analysis of the relationship between leadership and the abuse of power. Leaders do not need to exercise power, certainly not exploitative power over others, in order to be influential—automatic processes associated with self-categorization and depersonalization render prototypical group members influential in salient groups. However, over time these same processes, in conjunction with power-distance processes, create a latent and steeply hierarchical intergroup orientation between leaders and followers that provides the potential for unilateral and coercive exercise of power by the powerful over the powerless. This potential can readily be realized by factors, such as the leader's perception of alienation, lack of influence, or leadership threat, that make the intergroup orientation the salient basis for self-categorization. Power can be tamed by factors that prevent the development or reduce the salience of the hierarchical, power-based, intergroup relationship between leaders and followers.

While there is good support for some core aspects of the social identity theory of leadership, other aspects, notably the attribution dimension and the role differentiation aspect, are currently being investigated. The four-stage model of leadership and power described in this chapter still needs full investigation, although most of the components are well grounded in established theoretical concepts.

REFERENCES

Bass, B. M. (1990a). *Bass and Stogdill's handbook of leadership: Theory, research and managerial applications*. New York: Free Press.

Bass, B. M. (1990b). From transactional to transformational leadership: Learning to share the vision. *Organizational Dynamics, 18*, 19–31.

Bass, B. M. (1998). *Transformational leadership: Industrial, military, and educational impact*. Mahwah, NJ: Erlbaum.

Bass, B. M., & Avolio, B. J. (1993). Transformational leadership: A response to critiques. In M. M. Chemers, & R. A. Ayman (Eds.), *Leadership theory and research: Perspectives and directions* (pp. 49–80). London: Academic.

Berscheid, E., & Reis, H. T. (1998). Attraction and close relationships. In D. T. Gilbert, S. T. Fiske, & G. Lindzey (Eds.), *The handbook of social psychology* (4th ed., Vol. 2, pp. 193–281). New York: McGraw-Hill.

Bryman, A. (1992). *Charisma and leadership in organizations*. London: Sage.

Campbell, D. T. (1958). Common fate, similarity, and other indices of the status of aggregates of persons as social entities. *Behavioral Science, 3*, 14–25.

Chemers, M. M. (2001). Leadership effectiveness: An integrative review. In M. A. Hogg & R. S. Tindale (Eds.), *Blackwell handbook of social psychology: Group processes*. Oxford, UK: Blackwell.

Conger, J. A., & Kanungo, R. N. (1987). Towards a behavioral theory of charismatic leadership in organizational settings. *Academy of Management Review, 12*, 637–647.

de Cremer, D., & van Vugt, M. (in press). Why do people cooperate with leaders in managing social dilemmas? Instrumental and relational aspects of structural cooperation. *Journal of Experimental Social Psychology*.

Duck, J. M., & Fielding, K. S. (1999). Leaders and sub-groups: One of us or one of them? *Group Processes and Intergroup Relations, 2*, 203–230.

Erber, R., & Fiske, S. T. (1984). Outcome dependency and attention to inconsistent information. *Journal of Personality and Social Psychology, 47*, 709–726.

Fiedler, F. E. (1965). A contingency model of leadership effectiveness. In L. Berkowitz (Ed.), *Advances in experimental social psychology* (Vol. 1, pp. 149–190). New York: Academic.

Fielding, K. S., & Hogg, M. A. (1997). Social identity, self-categorization, and leadership: A field study of small interactive groups. *Group Dynamics: Theory, Research, and Practice, 1*, 39–51.

Fiske, S. T. (1993). Controlling other people: The impact of power on stereotyping. *American Psychologist, 48*, 621–628.

Fiske, S. T., & Dépret, E. (1996). Control, interdependence and power: Understanding social cognition in its social context. *European Review of Social Psychology, 7*, 31–61.

Fiske, S. T., & Taylor, S. E. (1991). *Social cognition* (2nd ed.). New York: McGraw-Hill.

Foddy, M., & Hogg M. A. (1999). Impact of leaders on resource consumption in social dilemmas: The intergroup context. In M. Foddy, M. Smithson, S. Schneider, & M. A. Hogg (Eds.). *Resolving social dilemmas: Dynamic, structural, and intergroup aspects* (pp. 309–330). Philadelphia: Psychology Press.

Gilbert, D. T., & Malone, P. S. (1995). The correspondence bias. *Psychological Bulletin, 117*, 21–38.

Goodwin, S. A., & Fiske, S. T. (1996). Judge not, lest . . . : The ethics of power holders' decision making and standards for social judgment. In D. M. Messick & A. E. Tenbrunsel (Eds.), *Codes of conduct: Behavioral research into business ethics* (pp. 117–142). New York: Russell Sage Foundation.

Goodwin, S. A., Gubin, A., Fiske, S. T., & Yzerbyt, V. Y. (2000). Power can bias impression processes: Stereotyping subordinates by default and by design. *Group Processes and Intergroup Relations, 3,* 227–256.

Graumann, C. F., & Moscovici, S. (Eds.). (1986). *Changing conceptions of leadership.* New York: Springer-Verlag.

Hains, S. C., Hogg, M. A., & Duck, J. M. (1997). Self-categorization and leadership: Effects of group prototypicality and leader stereotypicality. *Personality and Social Psychology Bulletin, 23,* 1087–1100.

Hall, R. J., & Lord, R. G. (1995). Multi-level information processing explanations of followers' leadership perceptions. *Leadership Quarterly, 6,* 265–287.

Hamilton, D. L., & Sherman, S. J. (1996). Perceiving persons and groups. *Psychological Review, 103,* 336–355.

Haslam, S. A., McGarty, C., Brown, P. M., Eggins, R. A., Morrison, B. E., & Reynolds, K. J. (1998). Inspecting the emperor's clothes: Evidence that random selection of leaders can enhance group performance. *Group Dynamics: Theory, Research. and Practice, 2,* 168–184.

Haslam, S. A., Oakes, P. J., McGarty, C., Turner, J. C., & Onorato, S. (1995). Contextual changes in the prototypicality of extreme and moderate outgroup members. *European Journal of Social Psychology, 25,* 509–530.

Hogg, M. A. (1992). *The social psychology of group cohesiveness: From attraction to social identity.* New York: New York University Press.

Hogg, M. A. (1993). Group cohesiveness: A critical review and some new directions. *European Review of Social Psychology, 4,* 85–111.

Hogg, M. A. (1996). Intragroup processes, group structure and social identity. In W. P. Robinson (Ed.), *Social groups and identities: Developing the legacy of Henri Tajfel* (pp. 65–93). Oxford, UK: Butterworth-Heinemann.

Hogg, M. A. (1999). *A social identity theory of leadership.* Manuscript submitted for publication, University of Queensland.

Hogg, M. A. (2001). Social Categorization, depersonalization, and group behavior. In M. A. Hogg & R. S Tindale (Eds.), *Blackwell handbook of social psychology: Group processes.* Oxford, UK: Blackwell.

Hogg, M. A. (in press). Subjective uncertainty reduction through self-categorization: A motivational theory of social identity processes. *European Review of Social Psychology.*

Hogg, M. A., & Abrams, D. (1988). *Social identifications: A social psychology of intergroup relations and group processes.* London: Routledge.

Hogg, M. A., & Abrams, D. (1999). Social identity and social cognition: Historical background and current trends. In D. Abrams & M. A. Hogg (Eds.), *Social identity and social cognition* (pp. 1–25). Oxford, UK: Blackwell.

Hogg, M. A., & Hains, S. C. (1996). Intergroup relations and group solidarity: Effects of group identification and social beliefs on depersonalized attraction. *Journal of Personality and Social Psychology, 70,* 295–309.

Hogg, M. A., Hains, S. C., & Mason, I. (1998). Identification and leadership in small groups: Salience, frame of reference, and leader stereotypicality effects on leader evaluations. *Journal of Personality and Social Psychology, 75,* 1248–1263.

Hogg, M. A., & Mullin, B.-A. (1999). Joining groups to reduce uncertainty: Subjective uncertainty reduction and group identification. In D. Abrams & M. A. Hogg (Eds.), *Social identity and social cognition* (pp. 249–279). Oxford, UK: Blackwell.

Hogg, M. A., & Terry, D. J. (2000). Social identity and self-categorization processes in organizational contexts. *Academy of Management Review, 25,* 121–140.

Hogg, M. A., Terry, D. J., & White, K. M. (1995). A tale of two theories: A critical comparison of identity theory with social identity theory. *Social Psychology Quarterly, 58,* 255–269.

Hogg, M. A., & Turner, J. C. (1987). Social identity and conformity: A theory of referent informational influence. In W. Doise & S. Moscovici (Eds.), *Current issues in European social psychology* (Vol. 2, pp. 139–182). Cambridge, UK: Cambridge University Press.

Hollander, E. P. (1958). Conformity, status, and idiosyncrasy credit. *Psychological Review*, 65, 117–127.

Hollander, E. P. (1985). Leadership and power. In G. Lindzey & E. Aronson (Eds.), *The handbook of social psychology* (3rd ed., Vol. 2, pp. 485–537). New York: Random House.

Hollander, E. P., & Julian, J. W. (1970). Studies in leader legitimacy, influence, and innovation. In L. Berkowitz (Ed.), *Advances in experimental social psychology* (Vol. 5, pp. 34–69). New York: Academic.

Leyens, J.-P., Yzerbyt, V. Y., & Schadron, G. (1992). Stereotypes and social judgeability. *European Review of Social Psychology*, 3, 91–120.

Lord, R. G. (1985). An information processing approach to social perception, leadership and behavioral measurement in organizations. *Research in Organizational Behavior*, 7, 87–128.

Lord, R. G., Brown, D. J., & Harvey, J. L. (2001). System constraints on leadership perceptions, behavior and influence: An example of connectionist level processes. In M. A. Hogg & R. S. Tindale (Eds.), *Blackwell handbook of social psychology: Group processes*. Oxford, UK: Blackwell.

Lord, R. G., Foti, R. J., & DeVader, C. L. (1984). A test of leadership categorization theory: Internal structure, information processing, and leadership perceptions. *Organizational Behavior and Human Performance*, 34, 343–378.

Mackie, D. (1987). Systematic and nonsystematic processing of majority and minority persuasive communications. *Journal of Personality and Social Psychology*, 53, 41–52.

Mackie, D. M., & Queller, S. (2000). The impact of group membership on persuasion: Revisiting "who says what to whom with what effect." In D. J. Terry & M. A. Hogg (Eds.), *Attitudes, behavior, and social context: The role of norms and group membership* (pp. 135–155). Mahwah, NJ: Erlbaum.

Meindl, J. R., Ehrlich, S. B., & Dukerich, J. M. (1985). The romance of leadership. *Administrative Science Quarterly*, 30, 78–102.

Morris, M. W., & Peng, K. (1994). Culture and cause: American and Chinese attributions for social and physical events. *Journal of Personality and Social Psychology*, 67, 949–971.

Mowday, R. T., & Sutton, R. I. (1993). Organizational behavior: Linking individuals and groups to organizational contexts. *Annual Review of Psychology*, 44, 195–229.

Mulder, M. (1977). *The daily power game.* Leiden, The Netherlands: Martinus Nijhoff Social Sciences Division.

Ng, S. H. (1980). *The social psychology of power.* London: Academic.

Ng, S. H. (1982). Power and intergroup discrimination. In H. Tajfel (Ed.), *Social identity and intergroup relations* (pp. 179–206). Cambridge, UK: Cambridge University Press.

Ng, S. H. (1996). Power: An essay in honour of Henri Tajfel. In W. P. Robinson (Ed.), *Social groups and identities: Developing the legacy of Henri Tajfel* (pp. 191–214). Oxford, UK: Butterworth-Heinemann.

Ng, S. H., & Reid, S. A. (in press). Power. In W. P. Robinson & H. Giles (Eds.), *Handbook of language and social psychology* (2nd ed.). Chichester, UK: Wiley.

Nye, J. L., & Simonetta, L. G. (1996). Followers' perceptions of group leaders: The impact of recognition-based and inference-based processes. In J. L. Nye, & A. M. Bower (Eds.), *What's social about social cognition: Research on socially shared cognition in small groups* (pp. 124–153). Thousand Oaks, CA: Sage.

Palich, L. E., & Hom, P. W. (1992). The impact of leader power and behavior on leadership perceptions: A LISREL test of an expanded categorization theory of leadership model. *Group and Organization Management*, 17, 279–296.

Pawar, B. S., & Eastman, K. (1997). The nature and implications of contextual influences on transformational leadership. *Academy of Management Review*, 22, 80–109.

Peters, L. H., Hartke, D. D., & Pohlmann, J. T. (1985). Fielder's contingency theory of leadership: An application of the meta-analytic procedure of Schmidt and Hunter. *Psychological Bulletin*, 97, 287–300.

Platow, M. J., Reid, S., & Andrew, S. (1998). Leadership endorsement: The role of distributive and procedural behavior in interpersonal and intergroup contexts. *Group Processes and Intergroup Relations*, 1, 35–47.

Platow, M. J., & van Knippenberg, D. (1999, July). *The impact of leaders' ingroup prototypicality and normative fairness on leadership endorsements in an intergroup context.* Paper given at the XII General Meeting of the European Association of Experimental Social Psychology, Oxford, UK.

Raven, B. H. (1965). Social influence and power. In I. D. Steiner & M. Fishbein (Eds.), *Current studies in social psychology* (pp. 371–382). New York: Holt, Rinehart & Winston.

Reid, S. A., & Ng, S. H. (1999). Language, power, and intergroup relations. *Journal of Social Issues, 55,* 119–139.

Reid, S. A., & Ng, S. H. (2000). Conversation as a resource for influence: Evidence for prototypical arguments and social identification processes. *European Journal of Social Psychology, 30,* 83–100.

Ridgeway, C. L. (2001). Social status and group structure. In M. A. Hogg & R. S. Tindale (Eds.), *Blackwell handbook of social psychology: Group processes.* Oxford, UK: Blackwell.

Ridgeway, C. L., & Diekema, D. (1989). Dominance and collective hierarchy formation in male and female task groups. *American Sociological Review, 54,* 79–93.

Ross, L. (1977). The intuitive psychologist and his shortcomings. In L. Berkowitz (Ed.), *Advances in experimental social psychology* (Vol. 10, pp. 174–220). New York: Academic.

Rush, M. C., & Russell, J. E. A. (1988). Leader prototypes and prototype-contingent consensus in leader behavior descriptions. *Journal of Experimental Social Psychology, 24,* 88–104.

Russell, B. (1938). *Power: A new social analysis.* London: George Allen & Unwin.

Sachdev, I., & Bourhis, R. Y. (1985). Social categorization and power differentials in group relations. *European Journal of Social Psychology, 15,* 415–434.

Stogdill, R. (1974). *Handbook of leadership.* New York: Free Press.

Tajfel, H. (1972). Social categorization. English manuscript of 'La catégorisation sociale'. In S. Moscovici (Ed.), *Introduction à la Psychologie Sociale* (Vol. 1, pp. 272–302). Paris: Larousse.

Tajfel, H. (1981). Social stereotypes and social groups. In J. C. Turner & H. Giles (Eds.), *Intergroup behaviour* (pp. 144–167). Oxford, UK: Blackwell.

Tajfel, H., & Turner, J. C. (1979). An integra-

tive theory of intergroup conflict. In W. G. Austin & S. Worchel (Eds.), *The social psychology of intergroup relations* (pp. 33–47). Monterey, CA: Brooks/Cole.

Taylor, S. E., & Fiske, S. T. (1975). Point-of-view and perceptions of causality. *Journal of Personality and Social Psychology, 32,* 439–445.

Taylor, S. E., & Fiske, S. T. (1978). Salience, attention, and attribution: Top of the head phenomena. In L. Berkowitz (Ed.), *Advances in experimental social psychology* (Vol. 11, pp. 249–288). New York: Academic.

Trope, Y., & Liberman, A. (1993). The use of trait conceptions to identify other people's behavior and to draw inferences about their personalities. *Personality and Social Psychology Bulletin, 19,* 553–562.

Turner, J. C. (1982). Towards a cognitive redefinition of the social group. In H. Tajfel (Ed.), *Social identity and intergroup relations* (pp. 15–40). Cambridge, UK: Cambridge University Press.

Turner, J. C. (1999). Some current issues in research on social identity and self-categorization theories. In N. Ellemers, R. Spears, & B. Doosje (Eds.), *Social identity* (pp. 6–34). Oxford, UK: Blackwell.

Turner, J. C., Hogg, M. A., Oakes, P. J., Reicher, S. D., & Wetherell, M. S. (1987). *Rediscovering the social group: A self-categorization theory.* Oxford, UK: Blackwell.

Tyler, T. R. (1997). The psychology of legitimacy: A relational perspective on voluntary deference to authorities. *Personality and Social Psychology Review, 1,* 323–345.

Tyler, T. R., & Lind, E. A. (1992). A relational model of authority in groups. In M. P. Zanna (Ed.), *Advances in experimental social psychology* (Vol. 25, pp. 115–191). New York: Academic.

van Vugt, M., & de Cremer, D. (1999). Leadership in social dilemmas: The effects of group identification on collective actions to provide public goods. *Journal of Personality and Social Psychology, 76,* 587–599.

Wilpert, B. (1995). Organizational behavior. *Annual Review of Psychology, 46,* 59–90.

Wright, S. C. (1997). Ambiguity, social influence, and collective action: Generating collective protest in response to tokenism. *Personality and Social Psychology Bulletin, 23,* 1277–1290.

Yukl, G. A., & Falbe, C. M. (1991). Importance

of different power sources in downward and lateral relations. *Journal of Applied Psychology*, 76, 416–423.

Yukl, G., & Van Fleet, D. D. (1992). Theory and research on leadership in organizations. In M. D. Dunnette & L. M. Hough (Eds.), *Handbook of organizational psychology* (2nd ed., Vol. 3, pp. 147–197). Palo Alto, CA: Consulting Psychologists Press.

Yzerbyt, V. Y., Schadron, G., Leyens, J.-P., & Rocher, S. (1994). Social judgeability: The impact of meta-informational cues on the use of stereotyping. *Journal of Personality and Social Psychology*, 66, 48–55.

10

Effects of Power on Bias

Power Explains and Maintains Individual, Group, and Societal Disparities

SUSAN T. FISKE

*I*n a hypothetical investment firm with offices nationwide, individual male investment advisors routinely refer to female colleagues using derogatory sexual epithets, openly discuss their alleged sex lives, question their need to work, subject them to crude sexual jokes and, ironically, accuse them of being hysterical. Male managers frequently deny support, training, mentoring, promotion, referrals, credit, salaries, bonuses, and awards to female investment advisors, and do not respond to women's complaints about treatment by male peers. At the group level, male investment advisors gang up to play sexual pranks on groups of women in the office, exclude them from outings, and conspire to raid their accounts. At the level of company culture, the incentive programs typically award cufflinks, men's custom-made dress shirts, extra-large t–shirts, fighter planes, and "Top Gun" baseball hats. Moreover, the pattern of hiring, salaries, promotion, and attrition favors men over women.

In a hypothetical university, individual college students of color report that White peers demean their academic accomplishments and exclude them from social events, while advisors routinely underestimate their abilities, refer them to remedial programs without checking their records, and counsel them out of challenging courses. Campus police pull them over for no apparent reason, and campus store clerks follow their every move. At a group level, Black, Latino, Asian, and White students report minimal social mixing, they track themselves into particular majors and dorms. At the level of university culture, ethnic studies and cultural events most often occur separately from mainstream White courses and events.

These examples may ring familiar to most readers; they are the common stuff of contemporary intergroup life, at the individual, group, and societal level. In each case, some people control resources (money, training, recognition, inclusion) desired by other people. In each case, the people in control assign resources to a great extent based on group membership. In each case, stereotypes of subordinates are used to maintain and explain their lack of resources. And in each case, subordinates stereotype powerholders only when they give up on prediction and control over resources.

Over the last several years, a research program has tackled the role of power in stereotyping, prejudice, and discrimination. This approach defines power as control over resources. At the individual, group, and societal levels, it has examined the role of power in stereotyping, with forays into prejudice and discrimination. The bottom line is that stereotyping down differs from stereotyping up, at every level, but that stereotypes justify the system of inequality. This chapter will unabashedly focus on this author's own collaborations, rather then attempting a comprehensive literature review. The current perspective presented here on power in the broader literature is available in other venues (Dépret & Fiske, 1993; Fiske, 1993b, 1998). The chapter starts with theoretical perspectives and evidence concerning individual power, then moves to group power, and finishes with societal power dynamics.

THEORETICAL CONTEXT: INDIVIDUAL STEREOTYPING

The Continuum Model and Interdependence

People can form impressions of each other in more or less effortful ways, according to the Continuum Model (Fiske, Lin, & Neuberg, 1999; Fiske & Neuberg, 1990; Fiske & Pavelchak, 1986). The less effortful way relies on ready-to-mind categories, conveniently linked to stereotypic content. The more effortful way relies on more detailed assessment of the individual. In this view, effort typically depends on appropriate information and motivation. Much of the current stereotyping literature fits this general model of relatively automatic, convenient category-based processes, potentially supplemented by more individuating processes, depending on information and motivation. Indeed, the most impressive progress across the stereotyping area over the last two decades documents the automaticity of category-based processes (Fiske, 1998).

Some interesting and socially significant mechanisms for overriding the default category-based processes are motivations occasioned by social interdependence, at the individual, group, and societal levels. As reviewed elsewhere (Fiske, 2000), being outcome dependent entails needing another individual to obtain resources that matter, that is, being in a power relation. The current author's collaborations have typically operationalized outcome dependency by asking two people to work first individually and then together on a task, for which they can win a prize depending on their joint performance; in the control condition, the person is eligible for the prize based on individual performance, but still expects to work with the other person. When one person needs the other to win the prize, the outcome dependency motivates individuating impression formation processes, in the service of perceived accuracy.

Specifically, the documented process operates as follows: Outcome dependency undermines a sense of control and motivates close attention to the powerholder's attributes, particularly those that disconfirm stereotypic expectations. Thus, outcome dependency sets the attentional stage, but does not guarantee going beyond stereotypes. However, outcome dependency also motivates dispositional (trait) inferences to those same counter-stereotypic attributes, painting an individualized personality portrait of the powerholder, rather than the default category-based one. Finally, outcome dependency motivates impression ratings based on the evaluative implications of the individual's attributes, rather than just the person's social category. This pattern reliably occurs across a variety of studies employing varied operationalizations of both independent and dependent variables. Task outcome dependency consistently produces the individuated, accuracy-oriented effect, whereas evaluative outcome dependency produces a positivity bias (Stevens & Fiske, 2000). Thus, merely being judged by another person does not constitute outcome dependency in the same sense as coordinating joint performance for a tangible reward. Resource control determines symmetrical power relations.

Power as Lack of Dependency and Stereotyping by Default

The consistency of these findings underlies a way of thinking about people with power. At a minimum, those who singlehandedly control resources lack the motivation of being outcome dependent, compared to those who are dependent for resources. The theory of power-as-control (Fiske, 1993a) posited that powerful people are vulnerable to stereotyping their subordinates, for three reasons: First, they need not individuate down the hierarchy as much as those below them need to individuate up, in order to control resources. Second, sometimes they cannot expend the mental effort to individuate because greater numbers of people inhabit the lower hierarchy, compared to the upper hierarchy, and these greater numbers at the bottom discourage individuation. Third, people who self-select for positions of power may have personal dispositions that encourage stereotyping, so perhaps they want not to individuate. The first of these hypotheses, "need not," has focused a research program on power-as-control, or lack of dependency. Essentially, this hypothesis suggests that powerful people stereotype by default, for lack of being motivated to attend to individuating information about their subordinates.

Power as Self-Entitlement, Stereotyping by Design. Power is not simply carelessness. An additional line of theory posits that powerholders stereotype to uphold their positions. This theory, at the individual level, argues for stereotyping by design, specifically that powerholders seek to maintain their own personal power by actively seeking stereotypic information about subordinates that justifies their relative status. Based on social judgeability theory this hypothesis (Goodwin & Fiske, 1996; Goodwin, Operario, & Fiske, 1998) argues that people with power feel entitled to their positions and entitled to judge others (Yzerbyt et al., 1994). Because they feel entitled to judge, they use readily available social categories, but bolster the categories with stereotype-consistent information, to justify their stereotypes and their own position.

EVIDENCE:
INDIVIDUAL POWER AFFECTS STEREOTYPING

Taken together, these hypotheses view power as instigating a duet of motives. The powerful person's independence from others (lack of dependency) supports passive neglect of individuating information, the situational "need not," stereotyping by default. On a more effortful front, the powerful person's defense of the power position encourages active thinking in support of self-entitlement. This section addresses evidence for each in turn.

Lack of Dependency: Stereotyping by Default

Power bestows independence from others, a lack of dependency for resources. For example, one study (Goodwin et al., 2000, Study 3) brought participants into the laboratory allegedly to investigate task allocation in working groups. Participants expected to meet at the end of the experiment to play three roles in round-robin fashion: powerful task allocator to some of the other participants, powerless task receiver to others of the participants, and neutral observer to still other participants. Thus, as in most organizations, people had both superiors and subordinates in the same setting. A prize of movie passes was contingent on performance of the tasks allocated, with some tasks entailing better odds than others.

This study separated two aspects of power: the effect of outcome contingency, which results from being dependent for one's outcomes, and the effect of entitlement, which results from controlling the outcomes of others. This section focuses on powerful people's lack of outcome dependency; the next section focuses on the latter results. When in the roles of both task allocators and neutral observers, participants had outcomes independent of their partners, but when they were in the role of task receivers, they were dependent on their partner. We measured their attention to information about group members with whom they had the various task relationships, predicting that outcome dependency would increase attention to counter-stereotypic terms. The stereotypes in this case were gender, and the relevant information included pretested trait terms such as, for females, conscientious, tender, jealous, and demanding, and for males, self-confident, ambitious, authoritarian, and too rational.

The powerful perceivers resembled the irrelevant perceivers in their inattention to counter-stereotypic information, as predicted by the power-as-control hypothesis that the powerful need not bother to individuate their subordinates because they are not dependent on them. These processes fit the idea of stereotyping by default.

Study 4 in the same paper (Goodwin et al., 2000) addressed people's evaluations of the subordinates, whom they had presumably ignored. In another workgroup context, participants were either bosses or assistants; the bosses received a fixed payment in lottery tickets, but the assistants' pay depended on joint performance with the bosses. Control participants worked independently. All participants rated potential work-group members, based on college major (the stereotypic category in this case) and four mixed personality traits, stereotype-consistent and -inconsistent. Correlations of overall impression ratings with each participant's own prior separate ratings of college major and the personality traits then indexed the extent to which impressions were category-based (majors) or individuating (traits).

The bosses, who were not dependent on the assistants, hardly used individuating trait information ($r = .28$, $p < .10$), comparable to the independent controls ($r = .24$, $p < .10$), and considerably less than the outcome-dependent assistants ($r = .65$, $p < .01$), a pattern consistent with the attentional patterns in the task-allocation study, and consistent with the by-default account of power as lack of contingency.

Self-Entitlement: Stereotyping by Design

The same set of studies (Goodwin et al., 2000) tested the more active form of stereotyping—by design—the effortful use of stereotype-confirming information. In the task allocation study, powerful allocators were both independent—not dependent, as already noted, by virtue of not needing the powerless receivers to win the prize—and simultaneously in control, by virtue of determining the tasks, which had better and worse odds for winning the prize, for the powerless receivers. Stereotyping by design was duly revealed in allocators' exaggerated attention to stereotype-confirming attributes, relative to the powerless receivers and neutral observers. Being in control thus motivated self-justifying attention.

In the boss-assistant study, similarly to the task allocation study, the bosses were both independent, as already noted, by virtue of not needing the powerless assistants to win the lottery tickets, and simultaneously in control, by virtue of determining partner selection and therefore the powerless receivers' chances. In keeping with the active form of stereotyping, the bosses made the greatest use of category-based (college major) information ($r = .37, p < .01$), compared to the assistants ($r = .13$, n.s.) and the independent controls ($r = .17$, n.s.). This pattern fits the attention data from the allocator-receiver study, as well the theory of being in control as causing stereotyping by design.

Additional evidence for stereotyping by design comes from the first two studies in the same paper, both of which held dependency constant, and varied degrees of control over the target. In one study (Goodwin et al., 2000, Study 1), decision makers reviewed job applications, with the expectation that they had no or 30% actual control over the applicants' likelihood of obtaining a summer internship. Higher degrees of control elevated attention to stereotype-consistent information, in keeping with the previous effects of control.

In a dispositional analog to degrees of situational control, levels of trait dominance produced parallel results. Dominance orientation entails a preference for controlling interactions, assuming one is in charge, and entitled to be, but it is silent on issues of one's own dependence on others. As predicted, high dominance decision makers exaggerated their attention to stereotype-consistent information, relative to low dominance decision makers, in a study (2) that used the decision maker/applicant design (Goodwin et al., 2000, Study 1).

Another pair of studies (Operario & Fiske, in press-a) also examined individual differences in powerholder dominance. High and low dominance interviewers judged subordinates who were contingent for a lottery and an available research assistant (RA) job. Although no stereotypes were provided, high dominance interviewers felt free to use irrelevant and superficial cues to sociability, but did not use competence information in their hiring decision. In contrast, low dominance interviewers ignored sociability information but used the highly relevant competence information to determine hiring. Although using sociability information is not equivalent to stereotyping, both entail more superficial forms of impression formation brought on by dominance.

Finally, in a similar vein, raters told that they were expert judges of personality, and therefore entitled to judge, in effect assuming a position of power, felt free to use irrelevant evaluative primes in forming impressions (Croizet & Fiske, 2000). All participants used applicable primes, but only those labeled as experts entitled to judge, used conceptually nonapplicable but evaluatively loaded primes in evaluating a target.

Individual Processes: Conclusion

Power entails both absence of dependency and presence of entitlement, as noted leading respectively to processes of stereotyping by default and by design. We have argued that lack of dependency leads to neglect and that control over someone else's resources leads to entitlement and self-justification. These power-based processes matter because bias on the part of peers, while problematic, pales in comparison to bias from above. Some definitions of racism, for example, limit it to prejudice combined with power (Jones, 1997; Operario & Fiske, 1998).

THEORY AND EVIDENCE:
GROUP POWER AFFECTS STEREOTYPING

The intergroup level of analysis differs famously from the interpersonal level (for a collection of perspectives, see Sedikides, Schopler, & Insko, 1998). With regard to power at the intergroup level, the current author's collaborations have investigated only half the equation, namely how relatively powerless people regard those on top, whether a powerful group or powerful individuals. The next program of research will investigate biases of the powerful in groups, but this is a promissory note. It is, nevertheless important, if subordinates responding to powerful groups are to be believed. A variety of evidence indicates that subordinates perceive more discrimination when they respond to power at a group level, whether responding to real or artificial groups.

Power in Laboratory Groups

Individuals dependent on other individuals individuate the powerholders, as reviewed earlier, by attention to stereotype-disconfirming cues, personalized dispositional attributions, and attribute-based impression ratings. These processes all presumably function to increase perceived accuracy and felt control in dealing with powerful individuals. Our group-level theory predicts that when the powerful become a group, all individuation ceases, and the powerless abandon accuracy, as if they do not expect the possibility of control. A powerful group is seen as impervious to outside influence and intent on its own interests (Dépret & Fiske, 1993; Fiske & Dépret, 1996).

Indeed, the data bear out the theoretical analysis. Outcome dependency by itself increases individuation, as long as the powerholding group can be viewed as individuals. For example, when individuals depended on an outgroup of potentially differentiated individuals, they perceived more outgroup variability when dependent than not (Guinote & Fiske, 2000). The smaller the dependent ingroup, the more they perceived group variability, an effect mediated by perceived loss of control (Guinote, Brown, & Fiske, 2000). Potentially differentiated powerholders merit individuation, in an effort to restore prediction and possibly control.

Similarly, people whose outcomes are controlled by a loose aggregate of individuals from various college majors individuated them, as outcome dependency would suggest. But other individuals in the same situation, when confronted with a high power group of people sharing a single college major—and therefore a homogeneous entity—stereotyped them. The specific situation entailed trying to concentrate, while several outgroup distractors attempted to interfere; the outgroup also would evaluate whether the participant had succeeded or failed, with consequences for a prize (Dépret & Fiske, 1999). Powerless participants confronting a homogeneous group stopped attending to stereotype-inconsistent information and making dispositional inferences. More to the intergroup point, they felt more unhappy and proceeded to invoke some group cohesion processes: greater ingroup liking and preference. Perceiving the outgroup as powerful and homogeneous and therefore having the potential to discriminate increases ingroup formation and identification, which of course furthers the intergroup distinctions and mutual stereotyping, to the especial detriment of the less powerful group. But ingroup identity buffers against potential discrimination.

Power in Real Groups

Several studies from the current author's lab show that real ingroup identification correlates with perceived discrimination by real and powerful outgroups. For example, greater ethnic identification increased sensitivity to ambiguous prejudice by an interaction partner (Operario & Fiske, in press-b). In an interpersonal interaction paradigm, minority participants expected to converse with another participant, but the White conversation partner made no eye contact, sat far away, resisted small talk, soon excused herself from the room, and never returned. In the ambiguous prejudice condition, she had previously stated on an information sheet that she enjoyed meeting different types of people; in the unambiguous conditions, she stated that she was uncomfortable meeting people who differed from her. High identifiers reported discrimination regardless of ambiguity, whereas low identifiers reported only the unambiguous discrimination. Moreover, survey evidence indicated correlations between high ethnic identification and perceived personal discrimination. Gender identification also affected perceived discrimination, in a similarly paired experiment and survey (Operario, Fiske, & Mody, 2000).

Theoretically, the identity-discrimination link is mediated by the accessibility of race (or other identity category) a link supported by mediational analyses of survey data. Moreover, manipulating the salience of race changed the accessibility of ethnic identity, which in turn changed perceived discrimination (Zemore, Morewedge, & Fiske, 2000).

Group Processes: Conclusion

At the individual level, being powerful can promote stereotyping, and at the intergroup level, the powerless apparently feel that group power promotes stereotyping. The point is that, from the powerless perspective, group-based power is particularly fraught with the negative consequences of bias, compared to a more individualized power, but ingroup identification buffers this process.

THEORY AND EVIDENCE:
SOCIETAL POWER AFFECTS STEREOTYPING

At the societal level, group power is recognized as control over resources, in the dual forms of status (e.g., prestigious jobs and economic success) and competition (resource and power trade-offs). Stereotyping and prejudice at the societal level follow directly from these principles, which echo the individual and group reactions to disparities in resource control.

Two theories argue that, at the societal level, people seek to maintain the general social hierarchy by defending the relative positions of groups in society. System justification (Fiske, 1998; Glick & Fiske, 1996, 1998, in press; see Jost & Major, in press, for a collection of perspectives) explains and maintains the respective outcomes of various groups. System justification, like individual self-entitlement, implies relatively active processes associated with holding power (in contrast to relatively passive processes associated with power as a lack of outcome dependency and therefore a lack of individuating motives).

A Theory of Stereotype Content

Our specific form of system justification theory holds that the (stereotypic) traits of different outgroups explain and maintain their positions vis à vis the ingroup. Our stereotype content theory differentiates four kinds of groups. Two kinds of groups form the classic cases of prejudice: 1) the ingroup, viewed as both warm and competent, positive on the two basic dimensions of person perception and group dynamics and 2) the disdained outgroups, seen as both low status and draining resources from the ingroup (in the U.S., people on welfare, poor Whites, poor Blacks, homeless people). The other two cases comprise ambivalent perceptions: 3) the envied outgroups, seen as high status but competing with the ingroup, who are viewed as competent but not warm (Asians, Jews, rich people, business women, Black professionals), and 4) the pitied outgroups, seen as low status but not competing with the ingroup, who are viewed as incompetent but warm (elderly, mentally or physically handicapped, housewives).

Perceived status correlates with perceived competence, and perceived competition correlates with perceived lack of warmth. In this rationale, groups get what they deserve: They get the status they deserve by virtue of competence, and they get the relationship to the ingroup they deserve by virtue of warmth. Every outgroup carries some negative quality, but with nods to positive qualities that explain and maintain the status quo. Thus, successful, threatening outgroups are respected for their undeniable status, but disliked as sacrificing human qualities. Unsuccessful, unthreatening outgroups are disrespected for their low status, but liked for their human qualities that allow caretaking. Unsuccessful but threatening outgroups who drain resources are neither respected nor liked. Surveys of respondents across the U.S. and ages 18–80 affirm these societal stereotypes. Experiments with hypothetical outgroups further show that status and competition can respectively predict perceived competence and warmth (Fiske et al., 1999; Fiske et al., 2000).

The societal status and competition dynamics boil down to intergroup power dynamics. High status groups are seen as possessing resources (which they deserve, so they are respected), and competing groups are seen as taking away the ingroup's resources (which they do not deserve, so they are disliked). Power as resource control permeates intergroup stereotypes.

A Case Study in System Justification: Ambivalent Sexism

As a relatively subordinate group in society at large, women constitute a useful case of societal system justification, especially in light of the variety of subtypes for women. Across North American and European samples, subtypes of women include traditional housewives, business or career women, lesbian/feminist/athletes, and sexy women (Fiske, 1998). Different kinds of prejudice turn against these different types, and the primary marker is hostility toward nontraditional women and paternalistic benevolence toward traditional women (Glick et al., 1997).

Both hostile and benevolent sexism explicitly incorporate power dynamics, according to the Ambivalent Sexism Inventory (ASI, Glick & Fiske, 1996). Hostile sexism entails dominating power relations, competition across gender roles, and tension over heterosexual control—in each of these domains, nontraditional women challenging men's societal and cultural power. Benevolent sexism entails paternalistic power relations, cooperation around complementary gender roles, and idealized heterosexual intimacy. Moreover, hostile sexism predicts the ascription of negative traits, and benevolent sexism predicts the ascription of positive traits to women. Sexism directed toward men is highly correlated with sexism directed toward women (Glick & Fiske, 1999a), suggesting that both represent ideological stances regarding the societal roles of men and women as reflected in the structure of interpersonal relationships.

The power dynamics resulting from the essentially universal structural features of ambivalent sexism are evident in its cross-cultural reliability (Glick et al., in press). Across 19 nations—in the Americas, Europe, Australia, Asia, and Africa—among 15,000 students and older adults, the theoretically derived factor structure of ambivalent sexism holds up, supporting its structural power dynamics across cultures. Each of thee countries shows the predicted dimensions of correlated but separate hostile and benevolent sexism, with the latter divided into the three specified dimensions of power, gender roles, and heterosexuality. And its predictive validity (hostile and benevolent sexism ascribing respectively negative and positive traits to women) holds up as well.

Even more relevant to issues of power and stereotyping, ASI national averages (even from these non-representative samples) predict gender inequality across nations. Across nations, men's hostile sexism scores correlate with United Nations indices of gender empowerment (women in high-status jobs and in government, $r = -.53$, $p < .05$) and gender development (women's education, longevity, and standard of living, relative to men in the same country, $r = -.47$, $p < .05$). Men's benevolent sexism scores correlate substantially but marginally, given the small sample of countries (respectively, $r = -.40, -.43, p < .10$). Women's ASI scores correlate marginally or not at all, again supporting the idea that powerholders (at the level of society, men) determine the distribution of resources and the prevalent, system-justifying ideology.

Societal Processes: Conclusion

Cultural stereotypes about outgroups in general and women in particular ride on resource control, that is, power dynamics. At the societal level, stereotypes and prejudice maintain and explain the status quo, justifying the system of power relations.

OVERALL CONCLUSION

Power affects bias at various levels of analysis. Individual outcome dependency (being lower in power) encourages individuation, but its lack in powerholders allows stereotyping by default. What's more, powerholders' entitlement to individual control over other people's outcomes encourages stereotyping by design. Outcome dependency on an aggregate of individuals encourages individuation, but outcome dependency on a homogeneous outgroup encourages stereotyping and ingroup favoritism. Powerful groups that lack outcome dependency and are entitled to control the resources of others may be especially pernicious sources of bias. At the societal level, all groups stereotype each other, and indeed the groups on whom no one depends and whose resources society controls receive the worst stereotypes (incompetent and not warm). Other outgroups that involve a mixture of dependency and control receive ambivalent stereotypes of incompetence or lack of warmth, but not both. These themes of dependency and resource control are echoed in the specific case of ambivalent sexism, across cultures. Power dynamics cut across bias in individuals, groups, and societies.

The hypothetical company and the hypothetical university introduced in the beginning of this chapter can improve their records of bias by emphasizing mutual outcome dependency, as well as equitable structures of control. Undermining power dynamics will collapse the stereotyping that explains and maintains inequalities.

REFERENCES

Croizet, J. C., & Fiske, S. T. (2000). Moderation of priming by goals: Feeling entitled to judge increases the judged usability of evaluative primes. *Journal of Experimental Social Psychology, 36,* 155–181.

Dépret, E. F., & Fiske, S. T. (1993). Social cognition and power: Some cognitive consequences of social structure as a source of control deprivation. In G. Weary, F. Gleicher, & K. Marsh (Eds.), *Control motivation and social cognition* (pp. 176–202). New York: Springer-Verlag.

Dépret, E. F., & Fiske, S. T. (1999). Perceiving the powerful: Intriguing individuals versus threatening groups. *Journal of Experimental Social Psychology, 35,* 461–480.

Fiske, S. T. (1993a). Controlling other people: The impact of power on stereotyping. *American Psychologist, 48,* 621–628.

Fiske, S. T. (1993b). Social cognition and social perception. In M. R. Rosenzweig & L. W. Porter (Eds.), *Annual review of psychology* (Vol. 44, pp. 155–194). Palo Alto, CA: Annual Reviews.

Fiske, S. T. (1998). Stereotyping, prejudice, and discrimination. In D. T. Gilbert, S. T. Fiske, & G. Lindzey, (Eds.) *The handbook of social psychology* (4th ed., 357-411). New York: McGraw-Hill.

Fiske, S. T. (in press). Interdependence reduces prejudice and stereotyping. In S. Oskamp (Ed.), *Reducing prejudice and discrimination*. Mahwah, NJ: Erlbaum.

Fiske, S. T., & Dépret, E. (1996). Control, interdependence, and power: Understanding social cognition in its social context. In W. Stroebe & M. Hewstone (Eds.), *European review of social psychology*. (Vol. 7, pp. 31–61). New York: Wiley.

Fiske, S. T., Cuddy, A., Glick, P., & Xu, J. (2000). *Ambivalent stereotypes, predicted by social structure: Status and competition predict competence and warmth*. Manuscript submitted for publication.

Fiske, S. T., Lin, M. H., & Neuberg, S. L. (1999). The Continuum Model: Ten years later. In S. Chaiken & Y. Trope (Eds.), *Dual process theories in social psychology* (pp. 231–254). New York: Guilford Press.

Fiske, S. T., & Neuberg, S. L. (1990). A continuum model of impression formation, from category-based to individuating processes: Influence of information and motivation on attention and interpretation. In M. P. Zanna (Ed.), *Advances in experimental social psychology* (Vol. 23, pp. 1–74). New York: Academic.

Fiske, S. T., & Pavelchak, M. A. (1986). Category-based versus piecemeal-based affective responses: Developments in schema-triggered affect. In R. M. Sorrentino & E. T. Higgins (Eds.), *Handbook of motivation and cognition: Foundations of social behavior* (pp. 167–203). New York: Guilford Press.

Fiske, S. T., Xu, J., Cuddy, A. J. C., & Glick, P. S. (1999). (Dis)respect versus (dis)liking: Status and interdependence predict ambivalent stereotypes of competence and warmth. *Journal of Social Issues, 55*, 473–491.

Glick, P., Diebold, J., Bailey-Werner, B., & Zhu, L. (1997). The two faces of Adam: Ambivalent sexism and polarized attitudes toward women. *Personality and Social Psychology Bulletin, 23*, 1323–1334.

Glick, P., & Fiske, S. T. (1996). The Ambivalent Sexism Inventory: Differentiating hostile and benevolent sexism. *Journal of Personality and Social Psychology, 70*, 491–512.

Glick, P., & Fiske, S. T. (1998). Gender, power dynamics, and social interaction. In J. Lorber, M. M. Ferree, & B. Hess (Eds.), *Revisioning gender* (2nd ed., pp. 365–398). Thousand Oaks, CA: Sage.

Glick, P., & Fiske, S. T. (1999a). The Ambivalence toward Men Inventory: Hostility and benevolence toward men. *Psychology of Women Quarterly, 23*, 519–536.

Glick, P., & Fiske, S. T. (1999b). Sexism and other "isms": Interdependence, status, and the ambivalent content of stereotypes. In W. B. Swann, Jr., J. H. Langlois, & L. A. Gilbert (Eds.), *Sexism and stereotypes in modern society: The gender science of Janet Taylor Spence* (pp. 193–222). Washington: APA.

Glick, P., & Fiske, S. T. (in press). Ambivalent stereotypes as legitimizing ideologies: Differentiating paternalistic and envious prejudice. In J. T. Jost & B. Major (Eds.), *The psychology of legitimacy: Ideology, justice, and intergroup relations*. Cambridge University Press.

Glick, P., Fiske, S. T., Mladinic, A., Saiz, J. L., Abrams, D., Masser, B., Adetoun, B., Osagie, J. E., Akande, A., Alao, A., Brunner, A., Willemsen, T. M., Chipeta, K., Dardenne, B., Dijksterhuis, A., Wigboldus, D., Eckes, T., Six-Materna, I., Expósito, F., Moya, M., Foddy, M., Kim, H-J., Lameiras, M., Sotelo, M. J., Mucchi-Faina, A., Romani, M., Sakalli, N., Udegbe, B., Yamamoto, M., Ui, M., & Ferreira, M. C. (in press). Beyond prejudice as simple antipathy: Hostile and benevolent sexism across cultures. *Journal of Personality and Social Psychology*.

Goodwin, S. A., & Fiske, S. T. (1996). Judge not, unless . . . Standards for social judgment and ethical decision-making. In D. M. Messick & A. Tenbrunsel (Eds.), *Codes of conduct: Behavioral research and business ethics* (pp. 117–142). New York: Russell Sage.

Goodwin, S. A., Gubin, A., Fiske, S. T., & Yzerbyt, V. (2000). Power can bias impression formation: Stereotyping subordinates by default and by design. *Group Processes and Intergroup Relations, 3*, 227–256.

Goodwin, S. A., Operario, D., & Fiske, S. T. (1998). Situational power and interpersonal dominance facilitate bias and inequity. *Journal of Social Issues, 54*, 677–699.

Guinote, A., Brown, M., & Fiske, S. T. (2000).

Perceived control, integration of information and perceived group variability as a function of group size. Unpublished manuscript, University of Massachusetts at Amherst.

Guinote, A., & Fiske, S. T. (2000). *The effect of outcome dependency on perceived group variability: Evidence for outgroup differentiation.* Unpublished manuscript, University of Massachusetts at Amherst.

Jones, J. (1997). *Prejudice and racism.* New York: McGraw-Hill.

Jost, J. T., & Major, B. (Eds.). (in press). *The psychology of legitimacy: Ideology, justice, and intergroup relations.* Cambridge University Press.

Operario, D., & Fiske, S. T. (1998). Racism equals power plus prejudice: A social psychological equation for racial oppression. In J. L. Eberhardt & S. T. Fiske (Eds.), *Confronting racism: The problem and the response* (pp. 33–53). Thousand Oaks, CA: Sage.

Operario, D., & Fiske, S. T. (in press-a). Effects of trait dominance on powerholders' judgments of subordinates. *Social Cognition.*

Operario, D., & Fiske, S. T. (in press-b). Eth-nic identity moderates perceptions of prejudice: Judgments of personal versus group discrimination and subtle versus blatant bias. *Personality and Social Psychology Bulletin.*

Operario, D., Fiske, S. T., & Mody, M. (2000). *Gender identity and perceived discrimination.* Manuscript submitted for publication.

Sedikides, C., Schopler, J., & Insko, C. A. (Eds.). (1998). *Intergroup cognition and intergroup behavior.* Mahwah, NJ: Erlbaum.

Stevens, L. E., & Fiske, S. T. (2000). Motivated impressions of a powerholder: Accuracy under task dependency and misperception under evaluative dependency. *Personality and Social Psychology Bulletin, 26,* 907–922.

Yzerbyt, V. Y., Schadron, G., Leyens, J-Ph., & Rocher, S. (1994). Social judgeability: The impact of meta-informational cues on the use of stereotypes. *Journal of Personality & Social Psychology, 66,* 48–55.

Zemore, S., Morewedge, C., & Fiske, S. T. (2000). *Racial identity and perceived discrimination, as mediated by accessibility of race.* Unpublished manuscript, University of Massachusetts at Amherst.

11

The Power Interaction Model
Theory, Methodology, and Empirical Applications

MENI KOSLOWSKY
JOSEPH SCHWARZWALD

*C*onflict between parties is a fact of life and is to be expected in most social settings. In some situations, the conflict may manifest itself only as a mild disagreement, whereas, in others, mortal combat is not out of the question. Handled properly conflict can lead to positive change and growth, yet if mishandled it can hinder relations and even lead to destruction. The process of gaining compliance in conflict situations is a central issue in the theoretical and empirical literature of social and organizational psychology. This literature focuses on understanding three main issues: 1) the means used by one party to influence the attitudes or behaviors of another party, 2) the effectiveness of the influence attempts in gaining compliance, and 3) and the various consequences, both positive and negative, associated with these attempts. The present chapter focuses on conflicts in dyadic relationships and presents Raven's (1992, 1993) Interpersonal Power Interaction Model (IPIM) for understanding the process by which one party chooses tactics for changing behavior or attitudes in the other party.

The quality of a relationship between parties is determined to a large extent by the means used for coping with conflicts (Raven & Kruglanski, 1970). Theoretically and practically, the implications are broad and involve international, intergroup, and personal relations. This chapter deals with social power at the personal level. Under what circumstances, at the interpersonal level, does one party try to gain compliance from another? Examples are all around us: a supervisor in an organization trying to convince a reluctant subordinate, a teacher

195

imparting information to a recalcitrant student, and a wife trying to convince a husband about a major family decision. The choice of power tactic or means for influence may determine the degree of compliance and the quality of relationship. If the choice is appropriate, then compliance and outcome are conducive to furthering the goals of the parties. Inappropriate choice can lead to resistance, or compliance, with little resulting gain. A teacher who uses reasoning to convince a reluctant student to join a specific group for presenting a team project may enhance the student's achievement and instill confidence in future undertakings. In contrast, a supervisor who in a given situation exercises inappropriate tactics such as threat may indeed change subordinate behavior but, at the same time, be responsible for negative consequences such as low productivity and dissatisfaction. Furthermore, the decision to use an inappropriate tactic may stem from the influencing agent's personal needs. In such a situation, negative consequences may result as the target's feelings or the goal of the influencing attempt may be compromised.

The Raven (1992, 1993) model focuses on situations involving a conflict between two parties and provides guidelines for examining relevant personal, situational, and cultural variables underlying the process. Investigators (Scholl, 1992, 1999) have distinguished between *promotive* control which refers to cases where the interests of the influencing agent concur with those of the target and *restrictive* control where the influencing agent pushes an idea that is against the interest of the target. Scholl (1999) illustrates the difference between both concepts by citing an example of a lawyer who can give good advice to a friend so that he or she wins a dispute with another neighbor (promotive control). By contrast a lawyer can use his or her legal knowledge in a dispute with a neighbor by threatening to sue if the neighbor does not comply. This chapter focuses on the latter case where the influencing agent attempts to gain compliance when the target disagrees.

Social power and influence have frequently been used interchangeably, yet the two terms describe distinct phenomena. The former refers to the potential sources available to an individual for influencing another person to comply and do what he or she would not have done otherwise. In contrast, the latter describes the specific tactics explicitly exercised by the influencing agent in attempting to gain compliance. An elaboration of the distinction is instructive. Assume that a supervisor is interested in changing a subordinate's behavior. Although the subordinate is reluctant to comply, he or she may, nevertheless, follow instructions because of the actual application of a specific tactic such as reward or because he or she believes that the supervisor has the potential to reward. The actual exercise of power tactics is considered "influence" whereas the potential to exercise power refers to "power." Empirically, compliance would appear to be a function not just of the former tactics but also of the latter.

The field has been rife with investigations using different assumptions and different instruments (Cody, McLaughlin, & Schneider, 1981; Falbo & Peplau, 1980; Kipnis, Schmidt, & Wilkinson, 1980). Based on an extensive survey, Podsakoff & Schriesheim (1985) concluded that the most prevalent approach for classifying power tactics was devised by French and Raven (1959) who identified five distinct tactics: 1) Coercive power: threat of punishment; 2) Reward power: promise of monetary and/or non-monetary compensation; 3) Legitimate power: drawing on one's right to influence; 4) Expert power: relying on one's superior knowledge; and 5) Referent power: based on target's identification with influencing agent. In a later elaboration, Informational power was also considered, in its potential, as a source of power (Raven, 1965, 1983). Previously included with expert power, informational power, based on presentation of persuasive material or logic, was now conceived as distinct from expert power. The importance of such a distinction is emphasized by Petty and Cacioppo (1986) who point out that attitude and behavior change can follow a central route (as with informational power) or a peripheral route (as with expert power). Others have used different terms for informational power, for example, rational persuasion (Yukl & Tracy, 1992) or persuasiveness (Yukl & Falbe, 1991).

The French and Raven (1959) typology of social power is thought to be "the most comprehensive and insightful theory of social influence in functional terms or more generally" (House, 1993, p. 222). Indeed, it has been used in a variety of fields for studying interpersonal power and influence. These include familial relations (McDonald, 1979, 1980; Raven, Centers, & Rodrigues, 1975; Rollins & Thomas, 1975), education (Erchul & Raven, 1997; Jamieson & Thomas, 1974), marketing and consumer psychology (Gaski, 1986; Mackenzie & Zaichkowsky, 1980), and health and medicine (Raven, 1988; Rodin & Janis, 1982).

Despite the broad acceptance of this typology of power in survey texts of social and organizational psychology, Podsakoff and Schriesheim (1985), in their careful and thorough review, identified several substantive and methodological problems. Echoing and elaborating on limitations suggested by others (Kipnis & Schmidt, 1983; Kipnis, Schmidt, & Wilkinson, 1980), concerns were raised with regard to conceptual overlaps between categories, inconsistent operational definitions, and at times, low agreement between observations and prediction. For example, allusions to expertise may involve elements of referent and informational power. Moreover, the problem is heightened by the fact that differing power tactics are often used in combinations (e.g., expert power and informational power). In other words, influencing agents tend to reveal profiles of powers that is, constellations of tactics rather than simple clear preferences for individual ones (Bui, Raven, & Schwarzwald, 1994; Hinkin & Schriesheim, 1989; Kipnis, 1990; Schriesheim & Hinkin, 1990). In addition, several investigators using different conceptualizations have argued that the five (or six) tactics defined in the original typology are not exhaustive (Kipnis & Schmidt, 1983). In examining the issue of commonality, Yukl and Tracy (1992) identified a nine-factor taxonomy (rational persuasion, inspirational appeal, consultation, negotiation, exchange, personal appeal, collision, legitimating, and pressure) of power tactics.

Methodological criticism has been lodged at the use of single measurement items for each power tactic along with ranking techniques that produce forced and artificial correlations (Podsakoff & Schriesheim, 1985; Schriesheim, Hinkin, & Podsakoff, 1991). Particularly pressing has been the absence of uniform measures for assessing power profiles across situations. The use of disparate instruments also has contributed to the reported inconsistencies and the resulting ambiguities have made interpretations and comparisons difficult.

THE INTERPERSONAL POWER INTERACTION MODEL

In response to some of these criticisms, Raven (1992, 1993) proposed the Interpersonal Power Interaction Model (IPIM). The new model expands on the original typology and provides a conceptualization of tactics available to an influencing agent and the choice process. The new approach takes the perspectives of both the influencing agent and the target.

Conceptualizing the IPIM Power Tactics

While still maintaining the basic conception of six power tactics, evidence was cited from research that required further differentiation among some of these tactics. Coercion and reward were divided into four categories: *impersonal coercion*—threat of punishment; *personal coercion*—threat of disapproval or dislike; *impersonal reward*—promise of monetary or nonmonetary compensation; and *personal reward*—promise to like or approve.

Legitimate power was divided into four categories: *legitimate reciprocity*—the request is based on the agent having done something positive for the target; *legitimate equity*—the request is based on compensating for either hard work or sufferance by the agent, or harm inflicted by the target; *legitimate dependence*—the request is based on social responsibility to assist another who is in need; and *legitimate position*—the request is attributed to the right one has for power because of status or position.

Adopting Kelman's (1956, 1961) and Raven's (1974) theoretical framework for understanding social influence processes, the current authors applied and elaborated on their conceptualization as it relates to the IPIM. In Table 11.1, one can see that agents' resources are associated with specific tactics and target motivation. The left column of the table lists the agent's four underlying resources: control, attractiveness, credibility, and normative. These resources empower the influencing agent with the potential to exercise power. In the next column, the 11 tactics of the IPIM associated with each resource are listed and assumed as either available (power) or actually expressed (influence). The right most column presents the target's motivation for compliance.

From Table 11.1 it is apparent that the ability to control can be exercised with different forms of reward and coercion. If compliance ensues, it can be attributed to utilitarian motives that is, a desire to gain reward or avoid punishment. If control loses relevance such as may occur when a supervisor is re-

TABLE 11.1. Theoretical Framework for the IPIM Taxonomy
of Power Tactics

Agent'sPower Resources	Power Tactics	Target's Motivation for Complying
Control	Personal reward Personal coercion Impersonal reward Impersonal coercion	Utilitarian
Credibility	Information Expertise	Reality testing (Rational)
Attractiveness	Reference	Unit maintenance or formation
Normative	Legitimate position Legitimate reciprocity Legitimate dependence Legitimate equity	Obligation

placed, target compliance is no longer expected. Agent attractiveness is manifested via reference. Here, target compliance is motivated by a desire to maintain or establish a relationship with the agent (unit formation). Continued expression of the change is expected as long as the referent is still viewed as such by the target. The credibility resource is expressed as expertise and information and the target's motivation are logic and reality testing. Contrary information is likely to make the target question the original reason for compliance. The last resource, normative, stems from external norms or standards and can be applied by using the four different legitimacy tactics (dependence, equity, dependence, and position). Here, the target's motivation is obligation. The target feels that by heeding the request of the supervisor the order of the system is maintained. Compliance is expected to terminate when the target no longer feels obligated to heed the agent or the organizational norm has lost its meaning (e.g., a prisoner does not have to comply to prison rules when freed).

Compliance, as defined in the model, refers to the target's change in attitude or behavior. However, this change may not necessarily be accompanied by private acceptance of the influencing agent's views. In situations where control, attractiveness, or normative resources are either available or applied, targets comply for utilitarian, personal, or obligatory reasons that are independent of the content of the request. By contrast, in situations where credibility resources are available or exercised, targets comply because they agree with the content of the request. This can be attributed to the fact that information or expert opinion was the vehicle used for convincing the target. It should be noted that the distinctions presented here resembles Katz's (1960, 1968) psychological functions of attitudes (utilitarian, knowledge, ego-defense, and value expression) in which he argues that people develop and change attitudes to satisfy various psychological needs.

Conceptualizing the IPIM power preference process

As mentioned above, the IPIM is more than just a mere taxonomy of power tactics. It considers power choice from two perspectives: the influencing agent and the target. In either case, the model views the involved parties as acting rationally by taking into consideration cost-benefits associated with their choice of power tactic (influencing agent) or their decision to comply (target). The process is an iterative one, subsuming preparations for influence attempts, preliminary analysis of potential impact, and feedback regarding eventual effects. These effects or outcomes may include intepersonal or job satisfaction, organzitional commitment, performance, and productivity.

Though the agent and target are viewed as acting rationally, the model delineates exogenous and mediating variables that impact the process by directing the choice of power tactics or the decision to comply. The following discussion of the theory focuses on the determinants relevant to the influencing agent's choice process.

Exogenous Variables

The IPIM delineates personal, motivational, and situational factors that are expected to direct the choice of power tactics acting through mediating perceptions. In the presentation here, the personal and motivational factors have been combined. It seemed that such a scheme is more parsimonious as it does not require making subtle distinctions between variables that often overlap.

Personal and motivational factors allude to personality and source of motivation. Biographical variables such as gender, ethnicity, and age are considered here as normative and included in the next section on situational factors.[1] Personality factors have been shown to impact power preference (Fodor & Farrow, 1979; Stewart & Rubin, 1976; Winter & Green, 1971). For example, high need for achievement individuals tend to have tight control over targets (Raven, Freeman, & Haley, 1982) and authoritarian workers are inclined to prefer legitimate

---

1. Categorization is a useful tool for organizing a set of postulates that are derived from a theory. Nevertheless, one must be aware that taxonomies are not perfect and elements between categories may overlap. Whether the impetus to behave is derived from the individual or from his or her surroundings cannot always be clearly determined. This type of ambiguity is apparent when trying to distinguish between individualism and competitiveness; one may consider these two as personal variables or as reflecting cultural or social norms. In the current chapter, this overlap exists at different levels of the presentation. At the power tactic level, a target may comply to personal reward or personal coercion because of the attractiveness of an agent rather than because of control (see Table 1). In a similar vein, legitimacy of position may evince features common to personal and organizational dimensions. Gender can be perceived as a personal, demographic indicator yet we have categorized it as situational. The reader who is interested in the subject of categories and some of the problems associated with their definition is referred to Smith and Medin (1981).

and coercive tactics to accomplish their goals (Adornoet al., 1950; Altemeyer, 1988).

Moreover, the impetus to change another individual may be externally motivated (directive from above) or internally motivated (self-esteem, need for power, security, etc.) and not purely a desire on the part of the influencing agent to change target attitude or behavior. A low self-esteem subject who has a need for elevating self-image may resort to unacceptable behaviors such as dishonesty (Aronson & Mettee, 1968), affiliation with marginal groups (Kaplan, 1980), or expression of prejudicial attitudes (Ehrlich, 1973). By exercising harsh power tactics where soft ones are just as effective and available, low self-esteem individuals are actually trying to elevate their feelings of superiority by demonstrating to themselves and others that *they* were the cause of the change. Such behavior abuses social power as it may be exercised at the expense of the target's feelings (Raven & Kruglanski, 1970). At the same time, the abuse of power appears to start a vicious circle of degradation and devaluation of the target (Kipnis, 1976) that, in turn, makes the influencing agent want to control the target more closely by repeating the application of negative influence tactics.

Situational factors include social norms, work setting (e.g., school, home, and job), organizational culture, and position (high vs. low status). Thus, in a school setting, teachers and students could be expected to choose different power tactics (Koslowsky & Schwarzwald, 1993). Etzioni (1964) argued that organizations can be classified by the type of power used: 1) coercive, as seen in prisons and correctional institutons, 2) uilitarian, as found in business and industry, and 3) normative, as seen in religious and political organizations. In his discussion of Etzioni's typology, Schein (1965) argues that different power tactics would be expected from each organzitional type. Thus, prison guards would more frequently resort to coercive means for attaining obediance (Koslowsky & Schwarzwald, 1993) whereas managers, in high tech firms, can be expected to use expertise for an influence strategy (Newstrom & Davis, 1989).

Organizational status was found to be related to the type of power tactic chosen by workers (Yukl & Falbe, 1991). Managers had more position power over subordinates than over peers, a tendency that was most apparent for legitmate power. Coercive power was greater for middle mangers than for lower level ones. When the data for peers were analyzed, legitimacy, expertise, and perusiveness were the most important reason cited for compliance.

Gender, although often considered a demographic indicator, is viewed here as normative in nature. The findings regarding the relationsip between gender and power are mixed. Some researchers (e.g., Aguinis & Adams, 1998; Cowan, Drinkard, & MacGavin, 1984) have found that gender alone has little, if any relationship, with power strategies whereas others argue that women and men differ in their preferences (e.g., Bonn, 1995; Bui, Raven & Schwarzwald, 1994; Falbo & Peplau, 1980; Horowitz & Frankel, 1990; Johnson, 1976; Jordan, Cowan, & Roberts, 1995). Studies reporting gender distinctions interpret harsh tactics as more legitimate for men than for women, as would be dictated by gender-role expectations (Burgoon, Dillard & Doran, 1983; Eagly, 1983, 1987, 1995;

Eagly & Johnson, 1990; Gruber & White, 1986). In a recent study among adolescents, gender explained a significant proportion of the variance in power usage (Schwarzwald & Koslowsky, 1999). The authors attributed the gender effect to sociocultural role development. Further discussion on why power tactics differ by men and women can be found in Pratto and Walker (this volume).

Mediating Variables

The theory assumes that four perceptions of power tactics mediate between the exogenous variables and the measured outcome: 1) relative availability of varying power tactics, 2) their efficacy in terms of speed, quantity, and quality of behavior change and compliance, 3) their cost in terms of time, effort, prestige, and other commodities, and 4) their social acceptability vis-a-vis social norms, role expectations, and stereotypes. The individual is assumed to assess each of the power tactics included in the IPIM and choose those which are most available, effective, inexpensive, and acceptable.

Raven (1992) conceptualizes the role of these mediators as links between exogenous variables and the choice of power tactics. Sometimes, defining the exact role of the mediator variables is difficult. According to investigators (e.g., Hollander, 1992) who report that women (an exogenous variable in the model) are less likely to use strong tactics, it is not clear to what degree this preference is a function of women's differential perceptions of these tactics in terms of relative availability or social acceptability (mediating variables in the model) when used by them. In similar fashion, those lacking in self-esteem (e.g., Bugental, this volume; Kipnis, 1976; Raven, Freeman, & Haley, 1982), tend to use stronger tactics. Here too, questions arise as to the potentially differential perceptions of efficacy or costs attributed to tactics by the less confident.

The Interpersonal Power Inventory (IPI)

Raven, Schwarzwald, and Koslowsky (1998) developed the Interpersonal Power Inventory (IPI) for assessing compliance to the power tactics delineated in the IPIM. The scale applies to conflict situations or, in Scholl's (1999) terminology, situations involving restrictive control. The construction of the scale took into consideration past criticisms of instruments used in power research and operationalized the new framework described in the model. The authors tested whether the items included within each tactic represent homogeneous and independent factors. In addition, the empirical structure was examined for the purpose of determining whether the 11 power tactics could be subsumed under a smaller number of higher order dimensions.

The scale consists of 33 items, three for each of the 11 power tactics. Using a critical incident type technique, subjects are told:

> Often supervisors ask subordinates to do their job somewhat differently.
> Sometimes subordinates resist doing so or do not follow the supervisor's

directions exactly. Other times, they will do exactly as their supervisor requests. We are interested in those situations that lead subordinates to follow the requests of their supervisor.

Think about a time when you were being supervised in doing some task. Suppose your supervisor asked you to do your job somewhat differently and, though you were initially reluctant, you did exactly as you were told.

After reading each statement carefully, subjects are asked to indicate how likely it is that their compliance could be attributed to each of the 33 reasons in the scale (the choices ranged from 1 "definitely not a reason" to 7 "definitely a reason"). The scale comes in two forms, one for subordinates and another for supervisors. With both forms, respondents are required to focus on the subordinates' compliance behavior.

Scale Features. The psychometric features of the IPI including reliability and validity of the scale were analyzed. Considering the fact that each tactic is composed of three items, the internal consistency measures (coefficient alphas ranging between .67–.86) were quite satisfactory. A cross-cultural validation using data from a group of Israeli participants revealed internal consistency findings similar to those obtained originally from American participants.

In a more recent investigation, Koslowsky, Schwarzwald, and Ashuri (in press) tested the convergent and discriminant validity of the IPI using Campbell and Fiske's (1959) multitrait, multimethod approach. For this purpose, five power tactics (reward, coercion, referent, expertise, and legitimacy of position) which appear in the Schriesheim, Hinkin, and Podsakoff (1991) scale were compared with their equivalent scales in the IPI. The findings provided support for both types of validity for the IPI.

Analyses for determining the independence of the tactics were also conducted. Using principal components analysis, two underlying structures or factors, soft and harsh, were identified. Soft refers to tactics that rely on the influencing agent's personal assets and harsh refers to tactics that are available to the individual by the nature of his or her status. The soft factor included expertise, reference, information, and legitimacy of dependence whereas the harsh factor included personal and impersonal coercion, personal and impersonal reward, legitimacy of position, equity, and reciprocity. A mapping procedure (smallest space analysis) yielded a similar pattern in that two distinctive areas appeared. It is interesting to note that in each of these analyses, legitimacy of position was shown to have common elements with the two factors in the principal components analysis and the two areas in the smallest space analysis. This commonality may be attributed to the fact that a position or status in an organization is also perceived as a personal achievement thus imbuing this tactic with harsh and soft features.

Consistent with earlier literature (e.g., Bass, 1981; Yukl & Falbe, 1991), the tactics available to an influencing agent can be said to originate from either personal or positional/organizational factors. Personal tactics emanate from the influencing agent's traits and achievements such as education, experience, and popularity. The positional tactics are granted to the agent by the institution or defined by the cultural/social milieu or organizational setting. In our research, we have preferred the terms soft and harsh tactics as labels for emphasizing the quality of the relationship between influencing agent and target rather than focusing on the source of the tactics (Barry & Shapiro, 1992; Falbe & Yukl, 1992).

In reference to the framework delineated in Table 1, harsh tactics reflect the control and normative power resources granted to the agent by organizations or social milieu. Soft tactics, on the other hand, are internally derived and include credibility and attractiveness as power resources available to the influencing agent. Others also have found underlying power structures of the tactics and applied similar terms for distinguishing between them (Bass, 1981; Brass & Burkhardt, 1993; Scholl, 1999; Yukl and Falbe, 1991). For example, Yukl and Falbe (1991) suggested that power bases in an organization are derived from either position, that is, granted by the organization, or personal characteristics, that is, those that emanate from the individual him- or herself. The latter distinction is parallel to the harsh-soft distinction mentioned above.

The reader may wonder whether individual tactics or global measures are preferable when assessing how agents influence targets. It seems that the answer to this quandary depends on the researcher's goals. As fine distinctions do exist, descriptive analysis often requires identifying specific tactics applied in a given situation. For example, a particular use of the tactics involves the development of power tactic profiles associated with personal characteristics or situational contingencies.

Global measures of powers have advantages, as well. In particular, the global distinctions provided by the factors yield a more reliable measure for many types of inferential analysis such as determining relationships between power and antecedents or consequences. Furthermore, as the situation frequently dictates which tactics are permissible, a global measure derived from several tactics provides a more accurate means for comparing profiles among situations.

In interpreting findings from the scale, one must keep in mind the fact that the questionnaire deals with a critical incidents procedure in which compliance took place and then requests respondents to decide how reasonable it is to attribute their compliance to each of the tactics described in the scale. The questionnaire thus ask for an attribution response regarding the extent to which power tactics were the cause of compliance.

The attributional approach here concurs with the perspective of social power as described in the psychological definitions proposed by Cartwright (1959), French and Raven (1959), Heider (1958), and other investigators. There may very well be more objective definitions: supervisors have expert power if they have had a wealth of experience or training in the area in which influence is attempted, or reward power is said to be present if supervisors can promote their subordinate or give them raises. Alternatively, one could take a more subjective approach by requiring subordinates to assess whether supervisors have such resources. With the first method we may indeed obtain good, reliable measures but would they be measuring social power? If interviewed, some respondents might say that the supervisor does not use a particular tactic though an objective analysis indicates it is available. Also, questions regarding usage do not reveal the reason for compliance. It is for this reason that we have preferred the attributional approach which seems to provide a link between a particular power tactic and compliance as reported by the respondent. In two studies using the IPI (Koslowsky, Schwarzwald, & Ashuri, in press; Raven, Schwarzwald, & Koslowsky, 1998), supervisors and subordinates were found to agree in their perceptions of reasons for compliance lending support to the notion that the attributional approach reflects reality. A direct comparison of the different approaches, focusing on the relative utility and biases inherent in each one, awaits future investigation.

EMPIRICAL STUDIES USING THE IPI

With the development of the IPI, the authors examined several issues based on the Interpersonal Power Interaction Model. All of the findings reported below were obtained from field studies in different organizational settings. This section reviews findings in three distinct areas: 1) personal characteristics of supervisors, specifically leadership style and professional distance between supervisor and subordinate, 2) organizational type as indicated by task complexity, and 3) organizational outcomes including job satisfaction and commitment.

Supervisor Characteristics

The IPIM posits that the choice made by an influencing agent and the degree of compliance are related to personal characteristics of the agent. Findings regarding leadership style and distance between agent and target that were thought to be relevant to compliance to harsh and soft tactics are presented.

Leadership Style. Schwarzwald, Koslowsky, and Agassi (1998) examined personal characteristics as a potential correlate of manager's preference for certain power sources and the degree of subordinate compliance. Furthermore, as the ability to influence is a major component of supervisor effectiveness, leadership style was deemed as relevant for understanding social power. The authors focused on the distinction between transformational and transactional leaders who have been found to differ in their influencing capacity and their effect on organizational outcomes including performance level, job satisfaction, organizational commitment, and citizenship behavior (e.g., Avolio and Bass, 1988, 1995; Hater & Bass, 1988; Kon, Steers, & Terborg, 1995).

The transactional style reflects the more common and traditional arrangement of relationships between supervisors and subordinates where work is exchanged for pay. An explicit or implicit agreement exists between supervisors and subordinates that defines goals to be reached by the subordinate for gaining desired rewards. The transformational style, by contrast, creates an environment in which the use of reward systems as the primary mechanism for motivation is less central and, instead, subordinates' compliance is seen as a function of their leader's charisma, intellectual stimulation, individualized consideration, and inspirational motivation. In practice, such leaders arouse a willingness to obey by employing referent power and vision for motivating subordinates to work for goals of self-actualization rather than for safety and security. These two styles are not assumed to be opposites on a single continuum but are conceived as representing different qualitative categories of leadership. Based on these distinctions, subordinates in conflict situations were expected to comply more willingly with transformational leaders than to transactional ones.

The leadership study was conducted in a police district in central Israel and involved captains ($N = 40$) and their subordinate police officers ($N = 240$). Using the IPI as the measure of compliance in a conflict situation between captains and their officers, a greater willingness to comply was observed for high as compared to low transformational captains. This tendency was salient for both harsh and soft sources, providing some important insight into the effectiveness of influence tactics by captains in the police department.

In interpreting these findings, we argued that in situations requiring immediate action the advantage of the transformational leader manifests itself even when the more appropriate mode for attaining compliance dictates the use of harsh sources. For situations requiring action without delay as often occurs among security personnel (police, firemen, military), harsh sources may be more appropriate and, therefore, more effective in inducing immediate change. By contrast, in situations that are less urgent or may allow for a relatively long time period before the desired attitudinal and behavioral change occurs, soft sources like information or explanation that are internalized gradually are more conducive for achieving the desired effect. The advantage of the transformational leader is observed across the board substantiating the notion that subordinates are willing to comply to such leaders even when the power sources are considered atypical (i.e., harsh) to the leadership style.

Our data attest to the fact that subordinates comply with requests made by transformational leaders regardless of the specific power sources being applied. This advantage over the transactional leader can be understood by contemplating leadership as a process which develops over time rather than through a single encounter (Hollander, 1992; Avolio & Bass, 1995). In the course of their interactions with leaders, subordinates develop expectancies about leaders' behaviors. Transactional leaders demonstrate a predominant concern for getting the task accomplished and are not particularly interested in followers' needs. Transformational leaders, however, continuously show concern for subordinate needs, treat them with respect, and employ a flexible orientation towards them. This does not imply that the transformational leader never resorts to harsh tactics or punishment. Yet, when these behaviors are used, they are perceived as atypical and situationally contingent. As such, harsh sources that are often less relevant to the task itself and may be perceived as arbitrary are probably interpreted as typical behavior for the transactional leader and utilitarian or necessary for the transformational leader.

Professional Distance. A second leadership characteristic thought to be a correlate for compliance is the professional distance between supervisors and subordinates. Koslowsky, Schwarzwald, and Ashuri (in press) argued that in a conflict situation a subordinate who perceives the supervisor as similar on professional distance (e.g., education, experience, seniority) will find it more difficult to comply. The rationale for this expectation can be understood from two perspectives. First, the reluctance to go along with supervisor requests reflects the lack of a clear advantage for him or her. Namely, in a conflict situation where both parties have similar knowledge or experience, it would be difficult for the subordinate to accept the supervisor's opinion since subordinates perceive themselves to be similar to their supervisor. Moreover, supervisors with qualifications resembling those of their subordinates may arouse feelings of discomfort or inequity among subordinates who feel that their supervisors are receiving greater rewards (position, salary) for similar investments (e.g., education, experience). In such a situation, the subordinate may respond by refusing to comply in order to restrict supervisor control and, thereby, restore equity. This contention is in line with findings by Schwarzwald and Goldenberg (1979) who reported that promotion to a leadership position from within a group consisting of individuals with approximately similar qualifications arouses feelings of inequity among non-promoted candidates. In such cases, these unsuccessful candidates tended to restrict their supervisors to a narrower range of authority.

In the study on professional distance conducted by Koslowsky, et al. (in press) nurses (N = 232) and their supervisors (N = 32) from two municipal hospitals completed the IPI scale and a six-item measure for determining subjective professional distance. Among the items were "I rely on my supervisor's professional judgment" and "My supervisor has the knowledge to help me solve professional problems." An objective index consisting of the difference in education and experience between subordinate and supervisor was also determined.

The analysis revealed an interaction between professional distance (for both professional distance indices) and supervisor seniority. Nurses who were similar to their supervisors on professional criteria reported a lower level of compliance than their counterparts who worked for supervisors with superior professional criteria. This tendency was seen for both harsh and soft sources. However, the above pattern of results was observed only for recently promoted supervisors. For the more senior ones, professional distance was not related to degree of compliance. Apparently, in conflict situations, newly promoted supervisors with little advantage over nurses arouse resistance to comply.

Organizational Types

A major assumption of the IPIM is that situational antecedents explain power tactics preference. Using this premise as a guideline, Schwarzwald, Koslowsky, and Ochana-Levin (2000) examined power usage and compliance in two organizational settings: routine consisting of routine or repetitive tasks performed by workers and complex, consisting of complex or creative tasks performed by workers. Three major characteristics can be said to distinguish these types of organizations: level of control, delegation of authority, and recruitment of workers. In organizations with routine tasks, supervisors maintain close control, restrict the subordinates' freedom of action, and selection or replacement of new employees is relatively easy. For example, in a supermarket, cashiers must ask their supervisor for authorization on many types of transactions. Even a simple task such as correcting entries made into the cash register often requires approval. As the training process is relatively short, it is relatively easy to hire workers. With complex tasks, a different picture can be observed. Workers here are less restricted and have more independence, supervision is much less extensive and the hiring procedure is more involved. For example, a programmer works at his or her own pace, is expected to work on more difficult problems, and only experienced and educated programmers are hired.

In the IPIM, Raven (1992) argues that harsh tactics like reward and coercion typify close control and supervision. On this basis, it was hypothesized that, for routine tasks, harsh tactics will be more prevalent than for complex tasks. In contrast, for soft power tactics will be more prevalent. Additionally, we also thought that workers would report greater compliance to harsh tactics in organizations involving simple tasks as compared to those characterized by complex activities.

The participants in the study were supervisors ($N = 97$) and workers ($N = 291$) from four organizations (two of whose workers did routine work—supermarket and assembly line—and two whose workers did complex work—hospital and hi-tech). Supervisors and workers completed the IPI whose format required participants to report usage prevalence for each power tactic described in the scale. Workers also completed the usual compliance format of the IPI described above.

The study supported the expectations with regard to the prevalence of harsh power tactics usage. In organizations involving routine tasks, as compared to those involving complex tasks, the usage of harsh power tactics was more prevalent and compliance to these tactics was greater. It was also observed that across both organizations, supervisors, as compared to subordinates, reported greater usage of soft tactics and resorted less frequently to harsh tactics. Further research is needed for detecting whether this inconsistency is a function of supervisor's impression management or workers' defensiveness, or, perhaps, different views of reality in assessing prevalence of power tactics usage.

Organizational Outcomes

The third aspect of the model's application focuses on the relationship between reported compliance to power sources and organizational outcomes. In particular, job satisfaction and organizational commitment, two of the more commonly used criteria measures, were examined. It was expected that reported compliance to harsh power tactics, as compared to soft ones, would be associated with lower levels of job satisfaction and organizational commitment. This expectation was derived from the assumption that compliance associated with fear of punishment, promise of reward, or the desire to fulfill contractual obligations (i.e., harsh tactics) emphasizes subordination rather than voluntary acceptance (Avolio & Bass, 1988). From a slightly different perspective, Hunt (1984), in referring to French and Raven's (1959) conceptualization, argued that positive affective reactions are likely responses to soft power tactics whereas harsh tactics are more likely to arouse negative affect. These relationships were tested in two studies.

In the first study (Raven, Schwarzwald, & Koslowsky, 1998), a group of Israeli hospital workers (technicians, clerks, laboratory assistants, $N = 101$) filled out the IPI and the short version of the Minnesota Job Satisfaction Questionnaire (MSQ; Arvey et al., 1989). The soft tactics were found to correlate and distinguish between high and low job satisfaction. As expected, the findings revealed that greater compliance to soft tactics was positively associated with higher degrees of job satisfaction. However, the degree of compliance to harsh tactics did not relate to job satisfaction.

The second study (Koslowsky, et al., in press), which was described previously, involved nurses who filled out the IPI, the MSQ, and the nine-item version of the Organizational Commitment Scale (OCS; Cook et al., 1981; Porter et al., 1974). Regarding job satisfaction, stepwise discriminant analysis supported our expectations for both types of tactics: The degree of reported compliance with soft tactics was associated with high satisfaction whereas the parallel relationship for harsh sources was lower and sometimes even reversed. The pattern obtained for the association between organizational commitment and compliance revealed that organizational commitment was positively related to degree of compliance regardless of type of tactic (soft or harsh).

The different patterns of responses observed between the two types of attitude measures and compliance to harsh and soft tactics may reflect the nature or focus within each measure. The fact that a worker is more satisfied when complying to soft rather than harsh tactics is to be expected as the former are more personal or work related. By contrast, compliance, per se, regardless of the content of the tactic, indicates a devotion, loyalty, or attachment to the organization. This would imply that resistance to harsh tactics could be expected to be associated with low commitment. Such a study requires a change in the responses available to the subject so as to include compliance and resistance as alternatives (see Falbe & Yukl, 1992). It is suggested here as a future research direction in applying the IPI.

In conclusion, the IPIM can serve as an overarching theory in the field of power and the IPI can provide greater methodological unity and coordination. The highly idiosyncratic nature of the research employed in the field has made it hard to compare and contrast results in a rigorous fashion. Using the IPIM theory along with the IPI scale may perhaps limit the wholesale generalization of findings while offering a more integrated, standardized approach. In the meantime, some satisfaction can be gotten from the fact that considerable consistency in the data presented here was obtained. Considerable strides have been made and further exploration of other personal and situational characteristics, as well as outcome measures, would add to the present state of knowledge of social power.

FUTURE RESEARCH

Although the IPIM was introduced only about a decade ago, it has already spawned several empirical investigations. Nevertheless, there are still many questions relating to the use of power that remain unanswered. At present, our research group is currently examining whether power tactics are used as a means to express advantage of the ingroup over the outgroup (Brewer & Kramer, 1985; Brown, 1988; Mackie & Ahn, 1998). The literature has already indicated that for gaining such an advantage individuals are biased in allocating resources, in evaluating, and in attributing success and failure. The differentiation between harsh and soft tactics will help provide a structured approach for analyzing the effect of ingroup–outgroup biases.

Another area that has not been adequately explored in the literature is whether supervisors, in trying to gain compliance, relate similarly to all subordinates (Podsakoff & Schrieheim, 1985). It is conceivable that they would not. Rather, soft tactics would be exercised more often with the more competent subordinates whereas harsh tactics with the less competent ones. If this is the case, it could explain why inconsistent relationships between power usage and organizational outcomes have been reported over the years. Generally, such studies have looked at subordinates as a group rather than as individuals and as such a study design that differentiates between competent and incompetent subordinates may yield more consistent relationships.

In this chapter, it has been demonstrated that compliance varies by leadership style with transformational leaders, regardless of tactics used, more likely to attain compliance than transactional ones. In this context, one may speculate whether Fiedler's (1967, 1993) LPC (least-preferred co-worker) contingency theory, would provide a frame of reference for examining social power. His theory posits that leadership effectiveness depends on whether leaders are task or relationship oriented and the degree to which situational control exists. It would be interesting to examine if task and relationship oriented leaders choose different power tactics for influencing subordinates. In addition, as the theory assumes that both style and situational control determine leaders' effectiveness, would the distinction between harsh and soft tactics help explain the dynamics involved here?

These are just a few examples of areas that need further study. Researchers armed with the IPI have a tool that will allow them to test and compare findings with an agreed upon standard. Identifying critical antecedents and correlates of social power as well as testing hypotheses derived from the IPIM such as the role of organizational climate (situational), the need of power (personal), and cross-cultural applications (normative factors) await further investigation.

REFERENCES

Adorno, T. W., Frenkel-Brunswick, E., Levinson, D. L., & Sanford, R. N. (1950). *The authoritarian personality*. New York: Harper and Row.

Aguinis, H., & Adams, S. K. R. (1998). Social-role versus structural models of gender and influence used in organizations: A strong inference approach. *Group and Organization Management, 23,* 414–446.

Altemeyer, B. (1988). *Enemies of freedom*. San Francisco: Jossey-Bass.

Aronson, E., & Mettee, D. R. (1968). Dishonest behavior as a function of differential levels of induced self-esteem *Journal of Personality and Social psychology, 9,* 121–127.

Arvey, R. D., Bouchard, T. J. Jr., Siegal, N. L., & Abraham, L. M. (1989). Job satisfaction: Environmental and genetic components. *Journal of Applied Psychology, 74,* 187–192.

Avolio, B. J., & Bass, B. M. (1988). Transformational leadership, charisma, and beyond. In J. G. Hunt, B. R. Baliga, H. P. Dachler, & C. H. Schriesheim (Eds.), *Emerging leadership vistas* (pp. 29–50). Lexington, MA: Lexington Books.

Avolio, B. J., & Bass, B. M. (1995). Individual consideration viewed at multiple levels of analysis: A multi-level framework for examining the diffusion of transformational leadership. *Leadership Quarterly, 6,* 199–218.

Barry, B., & Shapiro, D. L. (1992). Influence tactics in combination: The interactive effects of soft versus hard tactics and rational exchange. *Journal of Applied Social Psychology, 22*(18), 1429–1441.

Bass, B. M. (1981). Stodgill's handbook of leadership (Rev. ed.). New York: Free Press.

Bonn, M. (1995). Power strategies used in conflict resolution by popular and rejected black South African children. *Early Child Development and Care, 114,* 39–54.

Brass, D. J., & Burkhardt, M. E. (1993). Potential power and power use: An investigation of structure and behavior. *Academy of Management Journal, 36,* 441-470.

Brewer, M. B., & Kramer, R. (1985). The psychology of intergroup attitudes and behavior. *Annual Review of Psychology, 36,* 219–243.

Brown, R. (1988). *Group processes*. Oxford, UK: Blackwell.

Bui, K. V., Raven, B. H., & Schwarzwald, J. (1994). Interpersonal satisfaction and influence tactics in close heterosexual relationships. *Journal of Social behavior and Personality, 9,* 429–442.

Burgoon, M., Dillard, J. P., & Doran, N. E. (1983). Friendly and unfriendly persuasion: The effects of violations of expectations by males and females. *Human Communication Research, 10,* 283–294.

Campbell, D. T., & Fiske, D. W. (1959). Convergent and discriminant validation by the multitrait-multimethod matrix. *Psychological Bulletin, 56,* 81–105.

Cartwright, D. (1959). Power: A neglected variable in social psychology. In D. Cartwright (Ed.), *Studies in social power* (pp. 1–14). Ann Arbor, MI: Institute for Social research.

Cody, M. J., McLaughlin, M. L., & Schneider, M. J. (1981). The impact of relational consequences and intimacy on the selection of interpersonal persuasion tactics: A reanalysis. *Communication Quarterly, 29,* 91–106.

Cook, J. D., Hepworth, S. J., Wall, T. D., & Warr, T. B. (1981). *The experience of work*. New York: Academic Press.

Cowan, G., Drinkard, J., & MacGavin, L. (1984). The effects of target, age, and gender on use of power strategies. *Journal of Personality and Social Psychology, 47,* 1391–1398.

Eagly, A. H. (1983). Gender and social influence: A social psychological analysis. *American Psychologist, 38,* 971-981.

Eagly, A. H. (1987). *Sex differences in social behavior: A sex-role interpretation*. Hillsdale, NJ: Erlbaum.

Eagly, A. H. (1995). The science and politics of comparing women and men. *American Psychologist, 50,* 145–158.

Eagly, A. H., & Johnson, B. T. (1990). Gender and leadership style: A meta-analysis. *Psychological Bulletin, 108,* 233–256.

Ehrlich, H. K. (1973). *The social psychology of prejudice.* New York: Wiley.

Erchul, E. P., & Raven, B. H. (1997) Social power in school consultation: A contemporary view of French and Raven's bases of power model. *Journal of School Psychology, 35,* 437–471.

Etzioni, A. (1964). *Modern organizations.* New York: McGraw-Hill.

Falbe, C. M., & Yukl, G. (1992). Consequences for managers of using single influence tactics and combinations of tactics. *Academy of Management Journal, 35,* 638–652.

Falbo, T., & Peplau, L. A. (1980). Power strategies in intimate relationships. *Journal of Personality and Social Psychology, 38,* 618–628.

Fiedler, F. E. (1967). *A theory of leadership effectiveness.* New York: McGraw-Hill.

Fiedler, F. E. (1993). The leadership situation and the black box in contingency theories. In M. M. Chelmers & R. Ayman (Eds.), *Leadership theory and research:* Perspectives and directions (pp. 1–28). San Diego, CA: Academic Press.

Fodor, E. M., & Farrow, D. L. (1979). The power motive as an influence on use of power. *Journal of Personality and Social Psychology, 37,* 2091-2097.

French, J. R. P. Jr., & Raven, B. H. (1959). The bases of social power. In D. Cartwright (Ed.), *Studies in social power* (pp. 150–167). Ann Arbor, MI: Institute for Social Research.

Gaski, J. F. (1986). Interrelations among channel entity's power sources: impact of the exercise of the reward and coercion on expert, referent, and legitimate power sources. *Journal of Marketing Research, 23,* 62–77.

Gruber, K. J., & White, J. W. (1986). Gender differences in the perceptions of self's and other's use of power strategies. *Sex Roles, 15,* 109–118.

Hater, J., & Bass, B. M. (1988). Supervisors' evaluations and subordinates' perception of transformational and transactional leadership. *Journal of Applied Psychology, 73,* 695–702.

Heider, F. (1958). *The psychology of interpersonal relations.* New York: Wiley.

Hinkin, T. R., & Schriesheim, C. A. (1989). Development and application of new scales to measure the French and Raven (1959) bases of social power. *Journal of Applied Psychology, 74,* 561–567.

Hollander, E. P. (1992). The essential interdependence of leadership and followership. *Current Directions in Psychological Science, 1,* 71–75.

Horowitz, T., & Frankel, E. (1990). *Patterns of violence among use in Israel.* Jerusalem: The Henrietta Szold Institute.

House, J. (1993). John R. P. French, Jr.: A Lewinian's Lewinian. *Journal of Social Issues, 49,* 221–226.

Hunt, J. G. (1984). Leadership and managerial behavior. In J. E. Rosenzweig & F. E. Caste (Eds.), *Modules in management.* Chicago: Science Research Associates.

Jamieson, D. W., & Thomas, K. W. (1974). Power and conflict in the student-teacher relationship. *Journal of Applied Behavioral Sciences, 10,* 321–336.

Johnson, P. (1976). Women and power: Toward a theory of effectiveness. *Journal of Social Issues, 32,* 99–110.

Jordan, E., Cowan, A., & Roberts, J. (1995). Knowing the rules: Discursive strategies in young children's power struggles. *Early Childhood Research Quarterly, 10,* 339-358.

Kaplan, H. B. (1980). *Deviant behavior in defense of self.* New York: Academic Press.

Katz, D. (1960). The functional approach to the study of attitudes. *Public Opinion Quarterly, 24,* 163–204.

Katz, D. (1968). Consistency for what? The functional approach. In R. P. Abelson, E. Aronson, W. J. McQuire, T. M. Newco, M. J. Rosenberg, & P. H. Tannenbaum (Eds.), *Theories of cognitive consistency: A sourcebook.* (pp. 179–191). Chicago: Rand-McNally.

Kelman, W. C. (1956). Three processes of acceptance of social influence: Compliance, identification, and internalization. *American Psychologist, 11,* 361.

Kelman, W. C. (1961). Processes of opinion change. *Public Opinion Quarterly, 25,* 57–78.

Kipnis, D. (1976). *The powerholders.* Chicago: University of Chicago Press.

Kipnis, D. (1990). *Technology and power.* New York: Springer-Verlag.

Kipnis, D., & Schmidt, S. M. (1983). An influence perspective on bargaining within organizations. In M. H. Bazerman & R. J.

Lewicki (Eds.), *Negotiating in organizations* (pp. 303–319). Beverly Hills: Sage.

Kipnis, D., Schmidt, S. M., & Wilkinson, I. (1980). Intraorganizational influence tactics: Explorations in getting one's way. *Journal of Applied Psychology, 65,* 440–452.

Kon, W. L., Steers, R. M., & Terborg, J. R. (1995). The effects of transformational leadership on teacher attitudes and students performance in Singapore. *Journal of Organizational Behavior, 16,* 319–333.

Koslowsky, M., & Schwarzwald, J. (1993). The use of power tactics to gain compliance: Testing aspects of Raven's (1988) theory in conflictual situations. *Social Behavior and Personality, 21,* 135–144.

Koslowsky, M., Schwarzwald, J., & Ashuri, S. (in press). On the relationship between subordinates' compliance to power sources and organizational attitudes. *Applied Psychology: An International Review.*

Mackenzie, S. B., & Zaichkowsky, J. L. (1980). An analysis of alcohol advertising using French and Raven's theory of social influence. In K. B. Monroe (Ed.), *Advances in consumer psychology* (Vol. XIII, pp. 708–712). Provo, UT: Association for Consumer Research.

Mackie, D. M., & Ahn, M. N. (1998). Ingroup and outgroup inferences: When ingroup bias overwhelms outcome bias. *European Journal of Social Psychology, 28,* 343–360.

McDonald, G. W. (1979). Determinants of maternal and paternal power in the family. *Journal of Marriage and the Family, 41,* 775–790.

McDonald, G. W. (1980). Parental power and adolescents' parental identification: A re-examination. *Journal of Marriage and the Family, 42,* 289–296.

Newstrom, J. W., & Davis, K. (1989). *Organizational behavior.* New York: McGraw-Hill.

Petty, R. E., & Cacioppo, J. T. (1986). *Communication and persuasion: Central and peripheral routes to attitude change.* New York: Springer-Verlag.

Podsakoff, P. M., & Schriesheim, C. A. (1985). Field studies of French and Raven's bases of power: Critique, reanalysis, and suggestions for future research. *Psychological Bulletin, 97,* 387–411.

Porter, L. W., Steers, R. M., Mowday, R. T., & Boulian, P. V. (1974). Organizational commitment, job satisfaction, and turnover among psychiatric technicians. *Journal of Applied Psychology, 59,* 603–609.

Raven, B. H. (1965). Social influence and power. In D. Steiner & M. Fishbein (Eds.), *Current studies in social psychology* (pp. 371–382). New York: Holt, Rinehart, Winston.

Raven, B. H. (1974). The comparative analysis of power and power influence. In J. T. Tedeschi (Ed.), *Perspectives on social power* (pp. 172–200). Chicago: Aldine.

Raven, B. H. (1983). Interpersonal influence and social power. In B. H. Raven & J. Z. Rubin (Eds.), *Social psychology* (pp. 399–444). New York: Wiley.

Raven, B. H. (1988). Power and compliance in health care. In S. Maes, C. C. Spielberger, P. B. Defares, & I. G. Sarason (Eds.), *Topics in health psychology* (pp. 119–244). London/New York: Wiley.

Raven, B. H. (1992). A power/interaction model of interpersonal influence: French and Raven thirty years later. *Journal of Social Behavior and Personality, 7,* 217–244.

Raven, B. H. (1993). The bases of power: Origins and recent developments. *Journal of Social Issues, 49*(4): 227–251.

Raven, E. H., Centers, R., & Rodrigues, A. (1975). The bases of conjugal power. In R. S. Cromwell & D. H. Olson (Eds.), *Power in families* (pp. 217–234) . New York: Halstead.

Raven, B. H., Freeman H. E., & Haley, R. W. (1982). Social science perspectives in hospital infection control. In A. W. Johnson, O. Grusky, & B. H. Raven (Eds.), *Contemporary health services: Social science perspectives* (pp. 139–176). Boston: Auburn House.

Raven, B. F., & Kruglanski, A. W. (1970). Conflict and power. In P. G. Swingle (Ed.), *The structure of conflict* (pp. 69–109). New York: Academic Press.

Raven, B. H., Schwarzwald, J., & Koslowsky, M. (1998). Conceptualizing and measuring a power/interaction model of interpersonal influence. *Journal of Applied Social Psychology, 28,* 307–322.

Rodin, J., & Janis, I. L. (1982). The social influence of physicians and other health care practitioners as agents of change. In H. S. Friedman & R. M. DiMatteo (Eds.), *Interpersonal issues in health care* (pp. 33–50). New York: Academic Press.

Rollins, B. C., & Thomas D. W. (1975). A theory of parental power and compliance.

In R. E. Cronwell & D. H. Olson (Eds.), *Power in families* (pp. 38–60). New York: Sage.

Schein, E. H. (1965). *Organizational psychology*. Englewood Cliffs, NJ: Prentice-Hall.

Scholl, W. (1992). The social production of knowledge. In M. von Cranach, W. Doise, & G. Murphy (Eds.), *Social representations and the social bases of knowledge* (pp. 37–42). Berne, Switzerland: Huber.

Scholl, W. (1999). Restrictive control and information pathologies in organizations. *Journal of Social Issues, 55*, 101–118.

Schriesheim, C. A., & Hinkin, T. R. (1990). Influence bases used by subordinates: A theoretical and empirical analysis and refinement of the Kipnis, Schmidt, and Wilkinson subscales. *Journal of Applied Psychology, 75*, 246–257.

Schriesheim, C. A., Hinkin, T. R., & Podsakoff, P. M. (1991). Can ipsative and single-item measures produce erroneous results in field studies of French and Raven's (1959) five bases power ? An empirical investigation. *Journal of Applied Psychology*, 76, 106–114.

Schwarzwald, J., & Goldenberg, J. (1979). Compliance and assistance to an authority figure in perceived equitable or non-equitable situations. *Human Relations*, 32, 877–888.

Schwarzwald, J., & Koslowsky, M. (1999). Gender, self-esteem, and focus of interest in the use of power strategies by adolescents in conflict situations. *Journal of Social Issues, 55*, 15–32.

Schwarzwald, J., Koslowsky, M., & Agassi, V. (August 1998). Captain's Leadership Type and Police Officers' Compliance to Power Bases. Paper presented at the American Psychological Association 1997 Convention, San Francisco, CA.

Schwarzwald, J., Koslowsky, M., & Ochana-Levin, T. (June, 2000). Usage of and compliance to power strategies as a function of organizational type. *International Conference on Psychology*. Haifa, Israel.

Smith, E. E., & Medin, D. L. (1981). *Categories and concepts*. Cambridge, MA: Harvard University Press.

Stewart, A. J., & Rubin, Z. (1976). The power motive in the dating couple. *Journal of Personality and Social Psychology, 34*, 305–309.

Winter, D. G., & Green, D. L. (1971). Motives, involvements, and leadership among black college students. *Journal of Personality, 39*, 319–332.

Yukl, G., & Falbe, C. M. (1991). Importance of different power sources in downward and lateral relations. *Journal of Applied Psychology, 76*, 416–423.

Yukl, G., & Tracy, J. B. (1992). Consequences of influence bases used with subordinates, peers, and the boss. *Journal of Applied Psychology, 77*, 525–535.

PART IV

POWER IN SOCIETY

12

Power/Interaction and Interpersonal Influence

Experimental Investigations and Case Studies

BERTRAM H. RAVEN

Quite a few years have now passed by since John R. P. French first presented our articles (French & Raven, 1959) on the bases of social power that had defined social influence as a change in the belief, attitude or behavior of a person—the target of influence, which results from the action, or presence, of another person or group of persons—the influencing agents. Social power was defined as the potential for such influence (Cartwright, 1965; French & Raven, 1959). It was posited that most forms of social influence, and, in their potential, most bases of power, could be considered as stemming from five different bases of power—reward, coercion, legitimate, expert, and referent power—or six, if we include information or persuasion (Raven, 1965). The formulation was developed inductively, as French and I sat and asked each other questions about various forms of social influence, as related to the manner in which change is induced. We drew on our knowledge of the sociological and psychological literature of that time, especially the experimental social psychology literature, as well as our knowledge and experiences of critical incidents in

This chapter draws on a number of articles that have been published previously, particularly Raven (1990, 1992, 1993, 1999), Gold and Raven (1992), and Raven, Schwarzwald, and Koslowski (1998).

The author is grateful to Jacqueline Goodchilds and Gregg Gold who reviewed the draft of this manuscript.

which social influence had been attempted and exerted. Though there have been some criticisms and suggestions for improvement (e.g., Podsakoff & Schriesheim, 1985; Yukl, 1989), the resulting typology has been characterized as the most frequently utilized model of dyadic power in the social psychological and industrial/organizational literature (House, 1993; Mintzberg, 1983; Podsakoff & Schriesheim, 1985).

THE SIX BASES OF POWER

The French and Raven (1959) model proposed six bases of power, resources that an influencing agent can utilize in changing the beliefs, attitudes, or behaviors of a target. For those who may not be familiar with the original system, consider the bases of power that a supervisor might use to correct the way in which a subordinate does his or her job: Reward (offer a promotion or salary increase for compliance); Coercion (threaten some punishment such as a loss in pay for noncompliance); Legitimacy (emphasize that the supervisor has the right to prescribe such behavior and a subordinate has an obligation to comply); Expertise (the supervisor knows what is best in this case); Reference (appeal to a sense of mutual identification such the subordinate would model his or her behavior after the supervisor); and Information (carefully explain to the subordinate why the changed behavior is ultimately preferable). (Information was described in the original paper as a form of influence, but later also included as a basis of power.) Information (or persuasion) is the basis of power that leads the target of influence to fully accept the recommended change, without further reference to the influencing agent. Reward and Coercion lead to change such that the target continues to relate his or her changed behavior to the influencing agent, but with such continued change dependent on the target's belief that the agent will be able to observe or otherwise determine that the target has complied. Legitimacy, Expertise, and Referent power result in change which is socially dependent, but where surveillance by the influencing agent is unimportant. The six bases of power and their social dependence are presented in Table 12.1. Much of the earlier research stemming from French and Raven's (1959) power typology, and, indeed many studies even today, utilize only the five or six original bases of power. Over the years, many researchers following this approach, have responded to criticisms and suggestions, and incorporated findings from basic research in social psychology, to develop what is called the Power/Interaction Model of Interpersonal Influence (Raven, 1992, 1993; Raven, Schwarzwald, & Koslowski, 1998).

FURTHER DIFFERENTIATING THE BASES OF POWER

Though we still believe that most social influence can be understood in terms of the six bases of power, some of these bases have been elaborated and further differentiated. The six bases with their elaborations are presented in Table 12.2.

TABLE 12.1. The Six Bases of Power

Basis of Power	Social Dependence of Change	Importance of Surveillance
Coercion	Socially Dependent	Important
Reward	Socially Dependent	Important
Legitimacy	Socially Dependent	Unimportant
Expert	Socially Dependent	Unimportant
Reference	Socially Dependent	Unimportant
Informational	Socially Independent	Unimportant

Coercive Power and Reward Power: Personal versus Impersonal Forms

In our original statement, we considered coercive and reward power in terms of tangible rewards and real physical threats—threats of being fired or fined, promises of monetary rewards, and bonuses or promotion within an organization. However, it should be clear that personal approval from someone whom one likes can result in quite powerful reward power; and a threat of rejection or disapproval from someone whom one values highly can serve as a source for powerful coercive power. Considering personal, as well as impersonal, forms of reward and coercion helped us to understand certain forms of influence that had previously been inappropriately categorized as referent power (which also depends upon the target evaluating the influencing agent positively).

TABLE 12.2. Further Differentiating the Bases
of Social Power

Basis of Power	Further Differentiation
Coercion	Impersonal Coercion
	Personal Coercion
Reward	Impersonal Reward
	Personal Reward
Legitimacy	Formal Legitimacy (Position power)
	Legitimacy of Reciprocity
	Legitimacy of Equity
	Legitimacy of Dependence
Expert	Positive Expert
	Negative Expert
Reference	Positive Referent
	Negative Referent
Informational	Direct Information
	Indirect Information

Legitimate Power: Position, Reciprocity, Equity, Responsibility

This source of influence is based on a structural relationship between the influencing agent and the target. Implicitly, or explicitly, the agent says, "I have a right to ask you to do this and you have an obligation to comply."

Legitimate Position Power. Usually, legitimate power is defined as based on position: The supervisor, being supervisor, has the right to influence a subordinate, and the subordinate is obliged to comply. Thus terms such as "obliged" or "obligated," "should," "ought to," and "required to," may signal the use of legitimate power. In the expansion of the model, and based on theory and research in social psychology, three additional forms of legitimate power, which are based on other social norms, were included.

Legitimate Power of Reciprocity. This is based on an often powerful social norm that says that when someone does something for us, we should feel obligated to do something for them in return (Gouldner, 1960). "I am glad that you appreciate my changing your working hours for you. Now would you be so good as to do what I ask . . . " Robert Cialdini (1993) refers to this power strategy as "the old give and take" (p. 19).

Legitimate Power of Equity. The equity norm requires that we should do something to compensate someone who has suffered or worked hard, or someone whom we have harmed in some way. (Walster, Walster, & Berscheid, 1978) "Your mistake on the job really made my project much more difficult, so you might at least make up for it by doing what I ask." (This might also be referred to as the "compensatory norm.")

Legitimate Power of Responsibility or Dependence. According to this norm, we have some obligation to help others who cannot help themselves, or others who are dependent upon us (Berkowitz & Daniels, 1963). This form of legitimate power has sometimes been referred to as the "power of the powerless". The supervisor who appeals to the subordinate, saying, "I really can't get my job done unless you help me by doing as I ask," is using this form of legitimate power.

Informational Power: Direct and Indirect Forms

Informational power, or persuasion, is based on the information, or logical argument, that the influencing agent can present to the target in order to implement change. However, information can sometimes be more effective if it is presented indirectly. The early research on the effectiveness of overheard communications, as compared to direct communications would seem to bear this out. (Walster & Festinger, 1962). A direct influence attempt is sometimes threatening to a target's sense of independence and autonomy, and also may raise suspicions that he or she is being manipulated. A person in a lower power position (e.g., a nurse) who attempts to influence a person of higher status (e.g., a doctor) may employ such a technique, saying something like, "I understand that such-and-such medication was helpful to a patient down the hall who had a similar problem."

THE POWER/INTERACTION MODEL OF INTERPERSONAL INFLUENCE

The basic experimental paradigm for our early research on the bases of social power was quite simple: An influencing agent employs one or more of the bases of power to attempt to change the behavior of a target. The degree and manner of compliance would be measured, with additional variables added, such as whether the agent could observe the change or not, the extent to which any changed behavior was continued, the characteristics of the agent (position, gender, age, etc.) and the characteristics of the target. Also measured were the attitudes of the target toward the agent before and after the influence attempt. From this simple paradigm, there has gradually evolved an overarching theoretical model, which is called the Power/Interaction Model of Interpersonal Influence. This model is examined from the perspective of the influencing agent and the target of influence. Figure 12.1 summarizes the model from the perspective of the agent. The model from the perspective of the target is presented elsewhere (Raven, 1992, 1993).

The Motivation to Influence

This model assumes a rational agent, who is attempting to determine what basis of power or method of influence he or she wishes to utilize in implementing change to reach his orher outcome objectives. But various other motivations might affect the choice of influence strategies. These motivations, as shown in the upper left corner of Figure 12.1, lead the agent to an assessment of the various bases of power and other forms of influence that might be available. These motivations might include a need for power, a need to demonstrate independence, a need to satisfy role requirements, a need to enhance one's self-esteem and self-efficacy, a desire to harm or benefit the target, and a desire for status in the eyes of third parties. Such motivations would affect the choice of power strategies, sometimes reducing the agent's effectiveness in influencing the target.

Assessment of Available Power Bases

In the top middle box of Figure 12.1, the various bases of power that might be available are shown. The influencing agent reviews those that might be available and then must assess these alternative courses of action in terms of whether

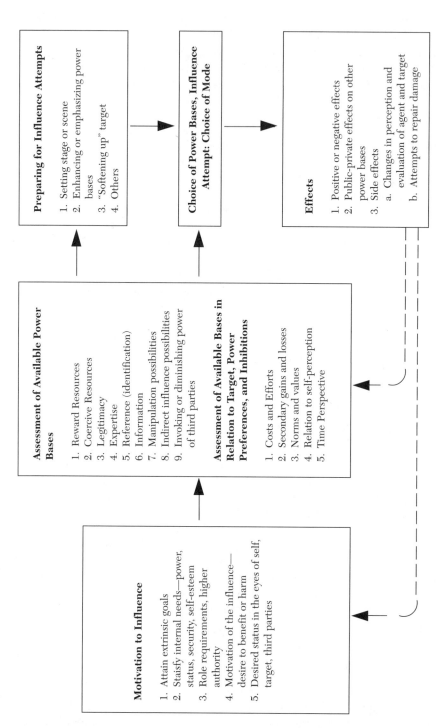

Motivation to Influence

1. Attain extrinsic goals
2. Staisfy internal needs—power, status, security, self-esteem
3. Role requirements, higher authority
4. Motivation of the influence—desire to benefit or harm
5. Desired status in the eyes of self, target, third parties

Assessment of Available Power Bases

1. Reward Resources
2. Coercive Resources
3. Legitimacy
4. Expertise
5. Reference (identification)
6. Information
7. Manipulation possibilities
8. Indirect influence possibilities
9. Invoking or diminishing power of third parties

Assessment of Available Bases in Relation to Target, Power Preferences, and Inhibitions

1. Costs and Efforts
2. Secondary gains and losses
3. Norms and values
4. Relation to self-perception
5. Time Perspective

Preparing for Influence Attempts

1. Setting stage or scene
2. Enhancing or emphasizing power bases
3. "Softening up" target
4. Others

Choice of Power Bases, Influence Attempt: Choice of Mode

Effects

1. Positive or negative effects
2. Public-private effects on other power bases
3. Side effects
   a. Changes in perception and evaluation of agent and target
   b. Attempts to repair damage

Figure 12.1. Power/Interaction Model of Interpersonal Influence from Perspective of Influencing Agent.

they would be effective in implementing change—what would be the likelihood that he or she would be successful or unsuccessful?

Assessment of the Costs of Differing Influence Strategies

The agent might also go through a cost-benefit analysis of the influence strategy. Informational influence or persuasion would ordinarily be highly desirable, but may require more time and effort than is available. Coercion, as indicated earlier, may result in more rapid compliance, but carries with it the costs of having to maintain surveillance, the hostility of an unhappy subordinate, and sometimes the violation of one's personal value system or generally accepted social norms. The legitimacy of dependence ("I need your help") may lead to loss of respect and perhaps may imply an obligation to return the favor.

Selecting the Power Strategy

The agent then will be guided by an assessment of the available power resources, and would include an assessment of the target of influence in terms of what the agent feels would work for the target and at what costs. These include expectancies (Barry, this volume; Jones, 1990; Kelley, 1971) of the behavior of the target, including how the target would respond to various power strategies—expectancies based, in part, on the agent's prior experience in similar situations in interacting with this or similar other targets. In addition, such factors as status, prejudices, and stereotypes will affect how the agent feels that a target will respond to various power strategies, as well as how the target anticipates power strategies from the agent. (Gold, 2000) Rind and Kipnis (1999) found that informational power would be selected by influencing agents who felt that the target was more intelligent; authority techniques (legitimate position power) and indirect manipulative strategies were selected if the target was seen as less intelligent. These factors, combined with the agent's personality and motivation, as described above, then determines which power strategy will be selected. For further analyses of this process of power strategy selection, see the chapter by Koslowsky and Schwarzwald in this volume.

Preparing the Stage for Influence Attempts

Though the influencing agent may often have immediate access to his or her bases of power, it is often the case that some preparation or stage-setting is necessary. (See upper right box of Figure 12.1.) Jones and Pittman (1982) describe a number of these self-presentational strategies as does Schlenker (1980) in his discussion of impression management—devices to set the stage for the use of a particular power strategy. To use coercion, it is sometimes necessary to first make the target realize (through intimidation) that the agent has both the means and the will to follow through on the threat. To use expert power, it may first be necessary to demonstrate one's expertise (self-promotion), as well as convincing the target that the agent is trustworthy and credible. (Nesler, Aguinis, Quigley, & Tedeschi, 1993) Ingratiation would enhance personal reward and personal coercive power. Authorization is a device whereby one attempts to establish one's formal legitimate power. The agent may enhance legitimate power of reciprocity by offering unsolicited favors, or use guilt induction to pave the way for the legitimate power of equity. Furthermore, various techniques might be utilized to convince the target that the agent will be watching and aware, which is important for effective use of coercion or reward.

Invoking the Power of Third Parties

When the influencing agent does not feel confident that his or her available power resources are not sufficient to accomplish the change, the agent may decide to invoke the power of third parties. This may be done quite directly: A supervisor who feels that his expertise is not sufficient may bring in a respected expert to tell the subordinate what to do. Or it may be done less directly, as a mother might remind the recalcitrant child that the father will be home soon and will use his coercive power to bring about compliance. Or the referent power of a dear departed grandparent might be invoked. Hafez al-Asad, after several unsuccessful attempts to influence his brother, Rifat, in his coup attempt, invoked the great referent and legitimate power of their mother, whom he brought in from their small rural village (Bilgé, 1992). Whether by direct or subtle invocation, the power of third parties can be very potent indeed.

Implementing the Power Strategy and Its Aftermath

Once the influencing agent has implemented the power strategy, he or she must deal with the aftermath. Was it successful? Did the target change as desired? If so, then the agent's estimation of him- or herself will be affected. There might be a review of how the agent attributes the successful influence. Did the target change because the target chose to do so, or because the target felt compelled to do so? The answer would depend in part, of course, on what bases of power were utilized, as well as prior perceptions of the target (Rodrigues, 1995; Rodrigues & Lloyd, 1998). Barry, in this volume, also offers some useful insights into this process in his discussion of expectancy violations (he could also have added "expectancy confirmations"). If a supervisor uses legitimate position power and the expected compliance does not occur, then the supervisor will reevaluate their mutual role expectancy. He might now assume that only coercive power will work. Similarly, if the target, under threat of coercive power, does not comply and the threatened punishment does not materialize, then the coercive power of the agent will be reduced. Conversely, if the target complies in response to reward power and then does not receive the reward, there will not only be a reduction in the reward power of the influencing agent, but also a likely reduction in other bases of power as well, such as referent power, personal reward power, and, perhaps, legitimate position power.

The agent will, in any event, reevaluate his or her bases of power after the encounter and respond accordingly. To restore lost coercive power, more harsh intimidation may be called for. Lost legitimate power may be restored by invoking the legitimate and coercive power of third parties (e.g., higher levels of management). Does the target, having been influenced, feel resentful toward the agent? Then certain ameliorative strategies might be called for. Does the agent feel more powerful now? Hold the target in higher or lower esteem? The complex ways in which the agent is affected by the influence, successful or unsuccessful, and the way the agent now perceives the target is spelled out in the insightful analyses of the metamorphic effects of power described by Kipnis (1976, this volume). That model made more meaningful the observation by Lord Acton (1887), that "Power corrupts and absolute power corrupts absolutely"—and also helps us to appreciate when that statement is more or less likely to be true.

CASE STUDIES OF SOCIAL POWER IN ONGOING INTERACTION

Over the years, research on the bases of power model and influence strategies was carried out mainly within the tradition of experimental social psychology. Our first experiments on legitimate and coercive power were conducted in a laboratory setting (Raven & French, 1958), as were many of the experiments that followed. (e.g., DeBono & Harnish, 1988; Johnson, 1978; Kruglanski, 1970; Molm, 1994; Price & Garland, 1981) Typically, such an experiment would introduce two or more bases of power as independent variables and measure various behaviors and questionnaire responses as dependent variables. More recently, research examining this model has utilized simulations and questionnaires, often introducing vignettes in which various power strategies were utilized and then measuring responses (e.g., Aguinis et al., 1994; Brown & Raven, 1994; Bui, Raven, & Schwarzwald, 1994; Humphrey et al., 1988; Litman-Adizes, Fontaine, & Raven, 1978; Raven, Schwarzwald, & Koslowski, 1998; Rodrigues & Lloyd, 1998; Schwarzwald & Koslowski, 1999; Zaleski, Janson, & Swietlicka, 1997). While experimental and quantitative research has contributed greatly to the development and acceptance of social psychology generally, as well as research on social power, it is important that we recognize its limitations. Experiments usually involve one or two influence attempts in a very restricted and contrived situation, necessarily limited by the attempts at experimental control. Questionnaire simulations and vignette studies may allow for examination of multiple influence attempts (though they often don't), but they depend on the perceptions, memories, or imaginings of the respondents, which may be very questionable. The very nature of much of this research has led us to gather our data from the most readily available participants, namely college sophomores, and for some of our findings there might be serious questions as to whether these would apply to more general populations (Sears, 1986) There is also concern that an overemphasis on experimental control and quantification had lead researchers to ignore richer data that could be obtained from ongoing observations in the real world, from historical, biographical, political analyses that do not lend themselves readily to quantification (Gergen, 1982; Hansen & Kahnweiler, 1993; Ring, 1967; Sampson, 1991; Smith, 1983).

Perhaps most important, the quantifiable, experimentally controlled study cannot possibly grasp the complexity of many situations in which social power and interpersonal influence are involved. A typical situation includes a process in which the influencing agent and the target enter the situation each with their prior experience, predilections, motivations, and perceptions of one another. They will each typically survey the situation, examine what their resources are for influence or resistance to influence, and go through preparatory stages and stage-setting devices in anticipation of influenced attempts. The agent may make an initial attempt to test the waters, the target responds, they reassess their relationship, and the agent may again go through further preparations and attempt a specific power strategy, which may or may not be successful. The target responds in kind, there is a reassessment of their perception of one another, or their respective resources, and so forth. The richness, the complexity, of this interaction can only be fully understood through careful and complete observation of an extended interaction. Through attempts to apply theoretical models to case studies, researchers can feel more confident regarding the external validity of quantitative research. Established theories may be questioned if our case history data do not seem consistent with them. Modifications in the theory may be called for, with further quantitative tests (Eckstein, 1975).

Below are three historical case study analyses whereby the application of the Power/Interaction Model is examined to ongoing situations:

The Hitler-Von Schuschnigg Confrontation

The 1938 confrontation of Adolf Hitler with Austrian Prime Minister Kurt von Schuschnigg at Hitler's mountain retreat in Obersalzberg paved the way for German annexation of Austria (Raven, 1990). Hitler was determined to convince von Schuschnigg to relax its military presence on the German border and to give free reign to the Austrian National Socialists. In my analysis, I relied primarily on von Schuschnigg's (1947) detailed stenographic notes that he prepared immediately after the confrontation and that were translated and cited by Payne (1975). In my analysis, I found evidence of Hitler's dual motivations, not only to accomplish his political goals but also to satisfy his needs to humiliate and destroy the Prime Minister, whom he hated. This appeared to have affected his choice of power strategy such that he chose to use bald coercive power even though he might have accomplished his ends with informational power or legitimate power of reciprocity. In his description, we can observe the stage-setting and preparatory devices: the very nature of the room in which they met, the seating of the Prime Minister in a smaller chair facing the imposing throne of Hitler, the emphasis on mutual background in the huge portrait of Frederick the Great behind Hitler. Guilt induction, in order to enhance legitimate power of equity, was accomplished through confronting the Prime Minister with secret documents suggesting inappropriate behavior. Before King Frederick's heroic portrait, he then accused von Schuschnigg of committing treason against the German race, by actions such as secretly fortifying the Austrian border. Austria was entitled to fortify its own borders, but Hitler presented this as a treacherous act, and, apparently even managed to induce a sense of guilt (establishing the power of legitimate equity). Such devices also helped to establish Hitler's ability to maintain complete surveillance, necessary for the exercise of coercive power. The threat of coercive power was made manifest in various devices, including the demonstration of Germany's military might, and Hitler's bald threat to crush Austria militarily. As in his public presentations, including his confrontation with English Prime Minister Neville Chamberlain, Hitler used his unique dramatic ability, portraying an overwhelming sense of God-given mission. Sometimes he portrayed uncontrollable madness, even loudly calling forth his adjutant, General Keitel, indicating that he might violate all rules of diplomatic propriety and place the visiting statesman under arrest. Such devices, also used by terrorists and hijackers, has the effect of making the most extreme threats seem credible. Hitler's influence strategies proved to very effective in accomplishing his goals. von Schuschnigg capitulated completely, and signed a statement complying with all of Hitler's demands, and soon thereafter German troops marched in to annex Austria. A more complete discussion of this power confrontation is presented in Raven (1990).

The Truman-MacArthur Confrontation

The 1950 confrontation between President Harry Truman and Douglas MacArthur, then Commander of the United Nations Forces in South Korea (Raven, 1990) occurred when MacArthur was flush with victory in driving the North Koreans out of South Korea. He now was determined to finish the job by invading North Korea and destroying the Communist government there. To help implement this strategy, he would accept the offer of military assistance from the Chinese Nationalists from Taiwan. Truman had good reason to believe that such a move would bring the People's Republic of China into the fray, with disastrous international consequences. To carry out an analysis of the Power/Interaction Model, this author (Raven, 1990) drew on memoirs and reports by Truman and MacArthur, both immediately after the event and many years later, as well as reports by those who were close to them (Lovitt, 1967; MacArthur, 1951; MacArthur, 1964; Truman, 1956; Whitney, 1956). Analysis again examined manifest and latent motivations to influence or to avoid influence.

For MacArthur, a need for power seems to have played a prominent role, sometimes leading him to reject influence even if it had a clear informational base. There was also his dislike and disrespect for Truman, which would render many of Truman's strategies, of expertise, referent power, legitimate position power, and personal reward power, quite ineffective.

Both Truman and MacArthur arrived at Wake Island by air at about the same time. The stage-setting devices here included an almost humorous sparring in landing scheduling. By eventually getting MacArthur to land first, Truman, in effect, forced MacArthur to put out the red carpet as he welcomed Truman, showing appropriate obeisance and deference. Legitimate position power was somewhat blurred—Truman was Commander-in-Chief of the U.S. Armed Forces in which MacArthur was a general, but MacArthur was also Commander of the United Nations Forces in the Far East. MacArthur greeted Truman with relatively informal dress. Truman admonished him for not recognizing the respect and authority due a Commander-in-Chief. Truman, realizing his own power limitations with respect to MacArthur, attempted to invoke the legitimate power and expert power of authorities whom MacArthur would respect, including the former general and current Secretary of Defense, George Marshall.

Failing in the use of other bases of power, Truman drew on his ultimate coercive power, subtly indicating the possibility that MacArthur might be removed from office. He left Wake Island with the expectation that his power strategies had been effective. MacArthur, however, did not consider Truman's threat sufficiently credible. The general knew that he had many strong supporters in Congress and in the U.S. generally, while Truman's popularity was not so great. Following through on the threat to remove MacArthur from office would be extremely risky for Truman. Soon thereafter, MacArthur ordered the UN troops across the 38th parallel into North Korea, and accepted the assistance of the Chinese Nationalists. The United Nations forces essentially destroyed the North Korean armed forces, but Truman's fears were realized as the overwhelming forces of the People's Republic of China entered the fray. After several months of severe losses, and MacArthur further flaunting orders from Truman, Truman did indeed relieve MacArthur of his command, but still at considerable costs. (A more complete discussion of this power/interaction is presented in Raven, 1990.)

The Churchill-Roosevelt Interaction

The third case study examined the strategies used by British Prime Minister Winston Churchill early in World War II to induce President Franklin Roosevelt to give Britain 50 aging destroyers and commit the U.S. to more active alignment with Britain (Gold & Raven, 1992). The data consisted of a large volume of correspondence exchanged between Churchill and Roosevelt beginning with formal declarations of war between Britain, France, and their allies against Germany and Italy, and continuing until what was called the Lend-Lease agreement (Churchill, 1941, 1948, 1949; Roosevelt, 1941a, 1941b, 1950).

The United States was clearly favorable toward the Allies, and supported their war efforts, though often surreptitiously. Churchill felt that a stronger commitment and greater support was called for. Roosevelt, though sympathetic, had political considerations since many Americans were strongly opposed to the U.S. becoming involved with what they saw as a yet another European war. In his 1940 election campaign, Roosevelt had promised firmly to keep the U.S.

out of war. The voluminous communications that we reviewed were then examined through the lens of our Power/Interaction model.

The power relationship between Churchill and Roosevelt was sharply different from that which characterized Hitler/von Schuschnigg and Truman/ MacArthur, first because Churchill and Roosevelt were really coequals, whereas Hitler had many more power resources than did von Schuschnigg, and Truman, ultimately was MacArthur's Commander-in-Chief. Furthermore Churchill and Roosevelt always felt that they were really working toward the same ultimate goals, and had great and growing respect and admiration for one another. Thus, Churchill could draw more readily on his referent power, which he tried to enhance by emphasizing their common background with their navies, their common culture and heritage (Churchill also had roots in America). Churchill frequently focused on their common threat from the Axis powers. He could also feel more comfortable in using the legitimate power of dependence and reciprocity. The analysis gives many examples of such strategies. The power/interaction here becomes particularly interesting since both men were experts on power strategy and counter-strategy and sensitive to the power resources and resistance that the other might utilize. Churchill also frequently used a form of legitimate power of reciprocity, the "rejection then retreat" strategy (Cialdini, 1993; Cialdini et al., 1975), making a very great request and then, when this was rejected, as expected, requesting a smaller concession. (A more detailed analysis of the Roosevelt-Churchill interaction is presented in Gold & Raven [1992].)

EXAMINING COMPLEX STRATEGIES AND THE USE OF FRAMING

In my discussion so far, I have been demonstrating that how a theoretical model can help us to understand real life power situations and in this way help also to validate our theory. I also believe that the examination of the complex real life situation may also help us to elaborate on our theory in ways which would be more difficult through controlled experiments or analyes of questionnaire data. Here are a few examples:

The Strategy of Interpretative Commitment Made Public

In the difficulty days of June 1940, with France in very great peril from the attacks of Germany and with Britain, increasingly alone and in danger, Churchill pulled out all stops, using all of his strategies to try to get a more firm commitment and actual military support from the United States, invoking the power of third parties, appealing to the legitimacy of equity and reciprocity, and using informational power with fear appeal. He was therefore heartened to receive a message from Roosevelt, delivered with full secrecy (Kimball, 1984), and read it with keen anticipation. What he read was a masterful message of exhortation but with few very vague and nonspecific commitments. Rather than express his understandable frustration, chagrin, and anger, Churchill converted this into a strategy called "interpretative commitment." (Gold & Raven, 1992)

Churchill, it would seem, realized what social psychologists would later demonstrate—that we can bring about changes in people's behavior by first getting them to commit themselves to that behavior and encourage them to act on that commitment. This influence can be further enhanced if we can manipulate them into making their commitment public. (Festinger, 1957; Pallak & Cummings, 1976) But Roosevelt did not by any means commit himself to decisive action in support of Britain and the allies. No matter. Churchill took advantage of the diplomatic vagueness of the message, reinterpreted in accordance with his wishes, and sent messages of triumph to French Premier Reynaud and Canadian Prime Minister MacKenzie King, referring to Roosevelt's message as "a magnificent document . . . (with) the United States . . . committed beyond recall to . . . becoming a belligerent" (Languor & Gleason, 1952, pp. 531–532). Next, he attempted to get Roosevelt to make this secret communication public.

When this author has described this event in class, students are often able to cite personal incidents that were similar. For example, a female student, wishing to convert a long-term relationship with a male student into marriage, reinterprets his comment that "Yeah, well, maybe that wouldn't be such a bad idea," into a firm commitment "Wonderful. I knew you were finally ready. We can do this right after June graduation . . . I can't wait to tell my parents and friends." Of course, this strategy would not work if the man had no real intentions for marriage. It only works if he was tending toward marriage, but was somewhat conflicted—"interpretative commitment made public" might do the trick. Apparently, it can be a very clever and effective strategy. It so happens that, sadly for Churchill, he was dealing with a master of power strategies. Roosevelt responded that his message was "in no sense intended to commit this government to the slightest military activity," and given that it was subject to misinterpretation, it should "not be published under any circumstances" (Langer & Gleason, 1952, p. 531).

Framing the Social Power Strategy

In selecting the bases of power, an influencing agent will need to assess both the positive and the negative effects of that strategy. Coercive power may be effective in the short time and might bring rapid change, but that change may not continue once the possibility of surveillance is reduced, and the target may harbor hostile feelings toward the influencing agent as a result. Reward power, offering some positive incentive for compliance, may sometimes carry the negative after effect of being seen as a bribe and may therefore lead to resentment. A clever influence strategist will sometimes find it advisable to reframe an influence attempt so as to minimize such negative effects. Here are some examples:

Reframing Coercive Power into Informational Power with Fear Appeal

As German bombing of Britain in 1939 became more intense, there was serious speculation in some quarters that Britain might be bombed into defeat. If Britain were to sign a peace agreement with Germany, what would happen to the British fleet? There was further speculation that would be what Germany would demand as part of a settlement, and in the United States some began to have serious concerns. These concerns were, strengthened in a comment by Churchill to U.S. ambassador Joseph Kennedy, saying that "If they got the British fleet . . . then your troubles would begin." (Langer & Gleason, 1952, p. 491) (Note also that sometimes indirect informational power is more effective than direct informational power.) After he had failed in a number of attempts to get Roosevelt to increase U.S. commitment to Britain and the Allies, and to gain additional armaments, Churchill in his frustration might quite reasonably have reacted in frustration and with threats: "If you won't help us now in our time of greatest need, and we are defeated, we may be inclined to offer Germany our fleet as part of the settlement." Such coercive power would very likely have led to serious resentment on the part of Roosevelt and the United States. Instead, Churchill chose a different tack, in essence saying something like, " Unless the United States gives Britain the weapons and support we are asking for, in the face of severe Germany bombing, we might be forced to seek a peace settlement, there might even be a new British government that would be inclined to agree to turning over the British fleet to Germany." The effective implications of these messages are similar. The difference is that the first is coercive power, the second is informational power with strong negative implications. It was the latter course that Churchill followed, thus, very likely, having a strong impact on U.S. policy, without the severe negative side effects (Gold & Raven, 1992).

Reframing Reward Power into Legitimate Power of Reciprocity

There is evidence that Churchill did, indeed, consult with his advisors about strategies that he might use in getting Roosevelt to commit himself more fully to the Allied war effort. When we offer someone a reward in exchange for their doing something for us, we must deal with some negative side effects. The reward may be perceived as a bribe and may lead to some degree of resentment, even if it is accepted. There are sometimes advantages therefore if the commodity that we offer can instead be used to build our legitimate power of reciprocity.

In October 1939, Churchill wrote in a memo: "I think I ought to send something to our American friend in order to keep him interested in our affairs." (Leutz, 1977, p. 105) What then should he offer? Churchill knew that the U.S. was increasingly concerned about the danger of submarine attacks on American ships. Britain had developed a very important highly prized new weapon, a sonar device for detecting enemy submarines. To add to his legitimate power of reciprocity, Churchill elected to offer the device to Roosevelt with no strings attached. Only later would he request a favor, when the unsolicited gift was still salient. Roosevelt, however, was sensitive to a preparatory device for legitimate reciprocity. He expressed his gratitude for the gift, but politely refused it. British Ambassador Lothian then offered to exchange the sonar device for the American developed Nordan bomb sight. Again, Roosevelt declined. Given that this offer followed the British initiative in offering the sonar, perhaps there was still an element of legitimate obligation.

But Churchill did not give up easily. Soon thereafter, he furnished valuable military intelligence and secret summaries of war developments, this time without asking first. This was followed by a British decision to purchase American tobacco even though similar products could be purchased more cheaply from other countries, and Britain sorely needed the cash reserve. Each of these were presented as gifts, without formal obligation. But the cumulative effect was to build a sense of obligation and to increase Britain's legitimate power of reciprocity—with many advantages over offering each of these with strings attached. Next Churchill sent a telegram to Roosevelt saying that Britain would no longer search for contraband in American ships bound for Europe, a practice that could be justified legally in light of the war conditions—especially since some American shippers were allowing the shipment of contraband—but which was rather distasteful for Americans. Roosevelt expressed his appreciation for this decision (Kimball, 1984). These unilateral actions, it is believed, helped, at least to some degree, to set the groundwork for greater American support for Britain.

Reframing Coercive Power into Informational and Referent Power. This example turns to a power confrontation in China, in the year 961, which is famous in Chinese history. The first emperor of the Song Dynasty in China, Kuang-yin Zhao, had reason to fear that his generals were becoming more independent and powerful, to the point that individually or collectively they might attempt to overthrow the dynasty. At this stage, he still had sufficient control of armed forces so that he could have presented them with the most extreme forms of coercive power, which might have been sufficient to get them to cease and desist. Instead, he invited the generals to a magnificent banquet in his palace and after an evening of stage-setting conviviality, he addressed them, saying that he was prepared to share the glory and power with them, but he feared that someone might attempt to abuse their military power, such that the country would revert to internecine war and destruction, with many of them killed in the process. He emphasized the mutual threat, their mutual identification with the dynasty, and their collective interests. Thus rather than using his resources to exert his coercive power which, even though successful, would carry with it anger, resentment, distrust, and the continual need for surveillance, Kuang-yin Zhao reframed the influence into referent power plus information with fear appeal. The generals then gave up their individual power, joined forces with the emperor, and a long period of peace reigned. (For a description of this incident of reframing, I am indebted to Yuen Yu Kit and Professor Ying-yi Hong, of the Hong Kong University of Science and Technology.)

RELIGIONS AS MECHANISMS OF SOCIAL CONTROL

In his 1975 presidential address to the American Psychological Association, Donald Campbell (1975) examined religion as a social psychological force. While one can point to many harmful acts which were performed in the name of religion, religion has also made tremendous positive contributions as well, as a source of inspiration, in bringing forth great literary and artistic works, in providing solace for those in despair, in providing a sense of control and understanding, and so forth. In addition, religion has served as a mechanism of social control, influencing believers to restrain from many harmful acts and encouraging acts of kindness and charity. All too frequently, people are frustrated, hostile, and angered toward others, and may resort to violence or even murder. Who knows how many lives were saved by the commandment "Thou shalt not kill" and the terrible consequences which would visited upon any violator.

In the earlier discussion, I had referred to an important social influence mechanism, the invocation of the power of third parties, wherein an influencing agent, feeling that he or she did not have sufficient resources to influence a target, would refer to or bring in the power of someone with greater power resources. A particularly powerful third party is the deity. Nunn (1964) interviewed 367 parents and found that two-thirds of them told their children that God would punish them if they were bad. Nunn (1964) concluded that this device was particularly likely to be used by parents who felt relatively powerless and who thus needed a powerful ally in order to assure compliance. Sakai (personal communication,1998) found that a substantial number of Japanese students, 44%, reported that their parents invoked the power of "gods."

In reading a number of holy works, including sections of the Old Testament, the New Testament, and the Koran, many instances in which the power of the Deity appeared to be a major force in inducing social control are noted (Raven, 1999). A perhaps overly simple and naive scenario, to illustrate how authority figures might have developed a reliance on such a powerful agent, is presented here.

We go back to "a time when murder, theft, rape, and mayhem were rampant and when people were relatively unrestrained in action on their impulses or in acquiring whatever they needed or desired. Imagine a prebiblical sage and chieftain (most likely a male, otherwise religions might have developed differently) attempts to restrain a shepherd who is ready to murder a neighbor who had just stolen one of the shepherd's sheep" (Raven, 1999, p. 170). The chieftan tries informational power, explaining why this is not good for the community at large, and the influence attempt is rejected. The shepherd similarly rejects the chieftain's expert power, his legitimate power, and even his coercive power or reward power (since the murderous act could be accomplished without the chieftain seeing it happen). The sage then develops the concept of a deity, who is omnipotent (he can determine for the shepherd life or death, heaven or hell), omnipresent (he is everywhere and can exert his power anywhere), and omniscient (he knows everything, so that surveillance is always possible). Surely an influencing agent with such qualities could utilize all of the bases of power. But in order to effectively invoke the power of God, the sage must first go through some very elaborate preparatory devices: He must first convince the shepherd that such a being exists. He must demonstrate that the Deity has supernatural ability to accomplish miraculous things. He must offer convincing proof that He is omniscient, all-seeing, all-knowing . He must demonstrate that the Lord not only has ultimate means of reward (even to life after death in heaven), and coercion (to everlasting hell), and is ready to following through on these extreme threats and promises. There must be a case for expert power (extreme wisdom), and legitimate position power. Legitimate power of reciprocity is established by convincing the shepherd that the Lord has given the shepherd and his family, including his ancestors, wonderful things, including life itself. Legitimate power of equity is established through making the shepherd feel guilty because of the shepherd's past misdeeds or violations of the Lord's precepts—the concept of original sin essentially establishes the guilt of a person from the very moment of birth.

Of course, it is too much to expect that this one ancient sage would be able to accomplish all of these things—and that is why this example seems especially naive. But rather, these devices have been perfected over many hundreds of years by thousands of sages, in oral history and oral laws, later converted into written laws, with these rewritten and improved upon by thousands of religious authorities, serving to develop the strategies and act as rewrite editors for those who preceded them. A magnificent work growing out of such collectively inspired (some might say "Divinely inspired") creativity is the Bible, which can be looked at as a convincing preparatory of stage-setting device collectively designed to demonstrate and establish God's power. His omniscience, omnipotence, and omnipresence is demonstrated time after time.

The story of Adam and Eve offers the first instance of God's legitimate power of equity and reciprocity, as well as coercive power and reward power. Adam and Eve owe something to the Lord for their very existence, and for providing them with a beautiful Garden of Eden—and by extension, we all should have that sense of obligation. But instead of showing their gratitude, they disobey the Lord, eating fruit that was specifically forbidden. The power of equity stems from a target's obligation to obey an influencing agent in order to atone for something inappropriate or harmful that the target had committed. The preparatory emotion for equity is guilt. Not only are Adam and Eve guilty for their misdeed, but so are all of their descendants. In banishing them from the Garden of Eden, the Lord gives the first indication of His coercive power, His readiness and ability to inflict punishment on those who disobey. Such coercive power is demonstrated throughout the Bible in even more violent form. The legitimate power of reciprocity also is emphasized throughout, emphasizing what the Lord has done for us, and our obligation to obey in return. The Ten Commandments are introduced with "I am the Lord your God, which has brought thee out of the land of Egypt and out of the house of bondage" (Exodus 20:2) (legitimate reciprocity) and reinforced by a threat (coercion) to "visit the iniquity of the fathers upon the children (even) unto the third and fourth generation . . . " (Exodus 31:14). A good logical case could have been made for the value of many of the commandments: murder violates some of our basic values and leads to wars and destruction for everyone; theft encourages countertheft and destroys social relationships; and adultery undermines mutual trust and may be harmful for both children and adults. But such informational power is in no way suggested in the presentation of the Ten Commandments.

The socalled Binding Story is presented to emphasize the Lord's legitimate position power and the requirement of unquestioned obedience even to the most difficult and unreasonable request.

Abraham and Sarah, previously distraught at their not having any children Sarah is beyond childbearing age, are overjoyed at the birth of Isaac due to the intervention of the Lord. Abraham should sense the legitimate power of reciprocity, but aside from that, obedience to the Lord is an overwhelming obligation even without reciprocity. When the Lord then asks Abraham to take Isaac to the mountain, kill him, and sacrifice him by fire, Abraham shows no hesitation. He binds the trusting Isaac and is about to plunge his knife into him when the angel of the Lord tells him to stop, since Abraham has now passed the test; he has demonstrated his loyalty and readiness to obey the Lord without question. Religious services draw on this story to stress the virtue of unquestioning obedience and readiness to sacrifice at the Lord's command. Added to the story is further emphasis on reward power—Abraham and his descendants are eternally blessed for Abraham's obedience.

Religions differ in the bases of power that are utilized by clergy and other religious authorities and which are ascribed to God, and such emphases are evident even in the language they use. The bases of power utilized by religious authorities, in turn, reflect, at least in part, the views that such authorities have of people whom they wish to influence—to what extent do people have the ability to determine for themselves what is right or wrong, to what extent do they respect the expertise or legitimate power of their religious leaders? When good, religious people are described as "God-fearing" there is a clear implication of the predominance of coercive power. Traditional and fundamentalist religions emphasize coercive power, and also legitimate power (position power, reciprocity, equity), plus ultimate expert power, as opposed to informational power. Adherence and unquestioned acceptance of the literal word of the Lord are absolute necessities. Suppose we were to congratulate an ultraorthodox Jew on the wisdom of his or her ancestors of biblical times. They, after all, proscribed the eating of pork products and shellfish, which in a hot climate, we only recently realized, can lead to serious illness (e.g., trichinosis) and death. Rather than hearing an expression of gratitude for the congratulations, we would more likely hear annoyance and indignation: "That is *not* why we avoid pork or shellfish. It is because it is stated in the Bible that such food is forbidden—no further reason is necessary." It then is not a matter or logic or taste, as the rabbinical commentary in *Siphrei* states "Let not a man state 'I do not like the flesh of swine;' on the contrary he should say, 'I like it, but what can I do, seeing that the *Torah* has forbidden it to me.'" In informational power, traditional fundamentalists see a threat to the very core of their religion, for if one depends on informational power with reason, then he or she might also question other proscriptions and requirements. If the reason for the dietary laws is to protect followers from illness and death, then why should we continue to practice them when refrigeration is readily available as well as medication for any resulting illness. This, in turn, would lead to questioning of other religious principles and proscriptions. The result is what some fundamentalist religious authorities have disparagingly called a cafeteria-type religion in which one accepts the parts that one likes and rejects the others, a most undesirable state of affairs if you do not trust people to make their own decisions about what is proper behavior. Of course, a similar choice of religious power strategies operates in most religions.

Just as a rational influencing agent would assess the power strategies that are available, their practicality, the extent to which the target will respond to a particular strategy, and what the after-effects are likely to be, religious authorities may, at various levels of consciousness, go through a similar process. If the authority questions the basic values of coreligionists, distrusts their judgment, is concerned that informational power might either be ineffective or lead to other transgressions as side effects, then some of the harsher bases of power would more likely be utilized, with greater preparatory strategies, stressing the omniscience of the Lord, making salient the possibilities of eternity in heaven or hell, emphasizing the legitimate position power or legitimate reciprocity of the Lord, and so forth. As clergy view their parishioners as having basic values that are positive and trust their intellectual ability to evaluate their own and other behaviors, then they will choose the more rationally-based power strategies. Here we might draw a parallel to the findings regarding differing power strategies used by transformational, as compared to transactional, leaders. (Koslowsky & Schwarzwald, this volume) We can also draw an analogy to the discussions by Kipnis (this volume) of the ways in which psychotherapists perceive and deal with their clients. Religious authorities who question the intellectual capacity and the basic morality of their parishioners will be more likely to invoke the coercive and reward power of a God who threatens hell or promises heaven. Religious figures who respect the intellectual and moral capacity of people will be more likely to utilize informational power and to encourage active discussion and questionning by their memers. Following Kipnis's reasoning further, the former will be more likely to attribute what they consider moral and appropriate behavior to the coercive and reward power of the Lord; the latter will be more likely to attribute good behavior to the basic moral tendencies of their adherents, even if they might on occasion require a friendly reminder as to what would be the right path.

It would be particularly interesting to examine religions and their religious authorities, using some measure, such as Kohlberg's (1984) measures of moral development, and relate such measures to the comparative use of power strategies. (For some direction in this regard see Miller and Bersoff (1992) and Miller, Bersoff, and Harwood (1990.) Of particular interest would be situations in which the power utilized by religious authorities is not synchronized with the ideologies and moral development of the religious adherents. Karen Armstrong discusses the problems which such conflict might present (Armstrong, 1993).

SUMMARY AND DISCUSSION

This chapter began with a review of the French and Raven (1959) bases of power typology and its expansion into a Power/Interaction Model of Interpersonal Influence. It is satisfying to see the range of research and theory that has developed from this simple typology. Some empirical studies which were stimulated by this model have been reviewed here, and some others are included in this volume (Barry, this volume; Koslowsky & Schwarzwald, this volume). While most studies have been quantitative investigations, using experimental, questionnaire, and interview techniques, much of the original thinking in this area began with thoughtful analyses of examples of actual interactions. A case for additional research using case study and historical methods was then made. Such nonquantitative examinations of ongoing interaction can help to establish external validity of the model and method. By examining longer-term on-going interaction, we can also gain insight into more complex social power strategies that cannot be observed in questionnaires or shortterm experimental laboratory situation. The analysis of confrontations between Hitler and von Schuschnigg, Truman and MacArthur, and Churchill and Roosevelt provided examples of the value of such case study analysis. In particular, such analyses allowed us to see more clearly how framing the social influence strategy can contribute to the process. In addition, we could observe how the give-and-take of influence attempt, resistance, and further influence attempts, over a period of time can affect the outcomes. Clearly some influencing agents are more effective than others in being able to analyze the ways in which a target may respond and adjust his or her power strategies accordingly. Some targets of influence are better able to understand the sequential nature of power strategies and can therefore be more effective in parrying such attempts. Reviews and analyses of other such case studies, using the Power/Interaction Model as a tool, can greatly improve the influence and negotiation process.

An ambitious attempt to understand how religions can function as mechanisms of social control was started here. In this, I must admit, I feel humbled by this project. Given the complexity of this topic, a much broader and intensive knowledge of comparative religion is called for. I thus present this as a very preliminary example of how the Power/Interaction model can be helpful in understanding the power influence of religion, as well as understanding the tensions that may develop between religious authorities and religious adherents. The model has been helpful in understanding some religious documents and religious services. For example, one might wonder why an all-powerful Deity would need to be blessed and given elaborate praise at a religious service. Such practices become more meaningful if we view them as collective preparatory devices designed to establish and maintain the various bases of power of the Lord. Religious rituals often lack any clear rationale per se, but it is that lack of rationale that makes them more effective in establishing the requirement of unquestionned obedience. The very nature of the house of worship reflects the bases of power used in religious services: consider the overwhelming power represented in the Gothic cathedral with the bishop in his pulpit well above the worshippers, as compared to the simple room with chairs in a circle which is characteristic of a Quaker meeting house.

Among the religious case studies that could be examined through the lens of the Power/Interaction Model would be religious cults, and, in particular, some cults where adherents are exploited and led to commit extreme acts, even suicide. The same sort of analysis would be useful in understanding other mechanisms of social control as well, including our legal systems. An awareness of such influence strategies may also help protect innocent people from indoctrination and alienation from society at large. Discussions of law and order, the deterrent value of the death penalty, the value of incarceration under various conditions, and questions about instruction in ethics and morals in the schools, may all benefit from a power/interaction analysis.

REFERENCES

Acton, Lord (John Emerich Dalbert). (1887). Letter to Bishop Mandell Creighton.

Aguinis, H., Nesler, M. S., Quigley, B. M., & Tedeschi, J. T. (1994). Perceptions of power: A cognitive perspective. *Social Behavior and Personality*, 22, 377–384.

Armstrong, K. (1993). *A history of God: The 4,000-year quest of Judaism, Christianity, and Islam.* New York: Random House.

Berkowitz, L., & Daniels, L. R. (1963). Responsibility and dependence. *Journal of Abnormal Psychology*, 66, 429–436.

Bilgé, K. S. (April, 1992). *The learned lion: An analysis of Hafez al-Asad and the 1984 coup attempt via the Raven Power/Interaction Model of Interpersonal Influence.* Paper presented at the Western Psychological Conference for Undergraduate Research, Santa Clara, CA.

Brown, J. H., & Raven, B. H. (1994). Power and compliance in doctor/patient relationships. *Journal of Health Psychology (Revista de Psicología de la Salud)*, 6, 3–21.

Bui, K. T., Raven, B. H., & Schwarzwald, J. (1994). Influence strategies in dating relationships: The effects of relationship satisfaction, gender, and perspective. *Journal of Social Behavior and Personality*, 9, 429–442.

Cartwright, D. (1965). Influence, leadership, and control. In J. G. March (Ed.), *Handbook of organizations* (pp. 1–47). Chicago: Rand McNally.

Churchill, W. S. (1941). *Blood, sweat and tears.* New York: Putnam.

Churchill, W. S. (1948). *The second world war: The gathering storm.* Boston: Houghton Mifflin.

Churchill, W. S. (1949). *The second world war: Their finest hour.* Boston: Houghton Mifflin.

Cialdini, R. B. (1993). *Influence: Science and practice* 3rd ed. (pp. 33–39). New York: HarperCollins.

DeBono, K. G., & Harnish, R. J. (1988). Source expertise, source attractiveness, and the processing of persuasive information: A functional approach. *Journal of Personality and Social Psychology*, 55, 541–546.

Eckstein, H. (1975). Case study in theory in political science. In F. I. Greenstein & N. W. Polsby (Eds.), *Handbook of political science: Strategies of inquiry* (pp. 79–137). Reading, MA: Addison-Wesley.

French, J. R. P. Jr., & Raven, B. H. (1959). The bases of social power. In D. Cartwright (Ed.), *Studies in social power* (pp. 150–167). Ann Arbor, MI: Institute for Social Research.

Gergen, K. (1982). *Toward transformation in social knowledge*. New York: Springer-Verlag.

Gold, G. J. (2000). *Predicting the intentions and behavior of others: Factors affecting accuracy*. Unpublished doctoral dissertation. University of California, Los Angeles.

Gold, G. J., & Raven, B. H. (1992). Interpersonal influence strategies in the Churchill-Roosevelt bases for destroyers exchange. *Journal of Social Behavior and Personality, 7*, 245–272.

Gouldner, A. W. (1960). The norm of reciprocity: A preliminary statement. *American Sociological Review, 35*, 161–178.

Hansen, C. D., & Kahnweiler, W. M. (1993). Storytelling: An instrument for understanding the dynamics of corporate relationships. *Human Relations, 46*, 1391–1409.

House, J. S. (1993). John R. P. French, Jr.: A Lewinian's Lewinian. *Journal of Social Issues, 49*(4), 221–226.

Humphrey, R. H., O'Malley, P. M., Johnston, L. D., & Bachman, J. G. (1988). Bases of power, facilitation effects, and attitudes, and behavior: Direct, indirect, and interactive determinants of drug use. *Social Psychology Quarterly, 51*, 329–345.

Johnson, P. B. (1978). Women and power: Toward a theory of effectiveness. *Journal of Social Issues, 32*(3), 99–110.

Jones, E. E. (1990). *Interpersonal perception*. New York: W. H. Freeman.

Jones, E. E., & Pittman, T. S. (1982). Toward a general theory of strategic interaction. In J. Suls (Ed.), *Psychological perspectives of self* (Vol. 1, pp. 231–263). Hillsdale, NJ: Erlbaum.

Kelley, H. H. (1971). Attribution in social ineraction. In E. E. Jones, D. Kanouse, & H. H. Kelley (Eds.), *Attribution: Perceiving the causes of behavior* (pp. 1-26). Morristown, NJ: General Learning Press.

Kimball, W. P. (1984). *Churchill and Roosevelt: The complete corresondence: I. Alliance merging*. Princeton, NJ: Princeton University Press.

Kipnis, D. (1976). *The powerholders*. Chicago: University of Chicago Press.

Kruglanski, A. W. (1970). Attributing trustworthiness in supervisor-worker relations. *Journal of Experimental Social Psychology, 6*, 214–232.

Leutz, J. R. (1977). *Bargaining for supremacy: Anglo-American naval collaboration*. New York: Norton.

Litman-Adizes, T., Fontaine, G., & Raven, B. H. (1978). Consequences of social power and causal attribution for compliance as seen by powerholder and target. *Personality and Social Psychology Bulletin, 4*, 260–264.

Lovitt, R. (1967). *The Truman-MacArthur controversy*. Chicago: Rand McNally.

MacArthur, D. (1951). Report to the Joint Senate Committee on Armed Services and Foreign Relations. *Military situation in the Far East*. Washington, DC: Government Printing Office.

MacArthur, D. (1964). *Reminiscences*. New York: McGraw-Hill.

Miller, J. G., & Bersoff, D. M. (1992). Culture and moral judgment: How are conflicts between justice and interpersonal responsibilities resolved? *Journal of Personality and Social Psychology, 62*, 541–554.

Miller, J. G., Bersoff, D. M., & Harwood, R. L. (1990). Perceptions of social responsibilities in India and in the United States: Moral imperatives or personal decisions. *Journal of Personality and Social Psychology, 58*, 33-47.

Mintzberg, H. (1983). *Power in and around organizations*. Englewood Cliffs, NJ: Prentice Hall.

Molm, L. D. (1994). Is punishment effective? Coercive strategies in social exchange. *Social Psychology Quarterly, 57*, 75–94.

Nesler, M. S., Aguinis, H., Quigley, B. M., & Tedeschi, J. T. (1993). The effects of credibility on perceived power. *Journal of Applied Social Psychology, 17*, 1407–1425.

Nunn, C. Z. (1964). Child control through a "coalition with God." *Child Development, 35*, 417–432.

Payne, R. (1975). *The life and death of Adolf Hitler*. New York: Praeger

Podsakoff, P. M., & Schriesheim, C. A. (1985). Field studies of French and Raven's bases of social power: Critique, reanalysis and suggestions for future research. *Psychological Bulletin, 97*, 387–411.

Price, K. H., & Garland, H. (1981). Compliance with a leader's suggestions as a function of perceived leader/member competence and potential reciprocity. *Journal of Applied Psychology, 66*, 329–336.

Raven, B. H. (1965). Social influence and power. In I. D. Steiner & M. Fishbein (Eds.),

Current studies in social psychology (pp. 371–382). New York: Holt, Rinehart, Winston.

Raven, B. H. (1990). Political applications of the psychology of interpersonal influence and social power. *Political Psychology, 11,* 493–520.

Raven, B. H. (1992). A power/interaction model of interpersonal influence. *Journal of Social Behavior and Personality, 7,* 217–244.

Raven, B. H. (1993) The bases of power: Origins and recent developments. *Journal of Social Issues, 49*(4), 227–281.

Raven, B. H. (1999). Influence, power, religion, and the mechanisms of social control. Journal *of Social Issues, 55*(1) 161–186.

Raven, B. H., & French, J. R. P., Jr. (1958). Legitimate power, coercive power, and observability in social influence. *Sociometry, 21,* 83–97.

Raven, B. H., Schwarzwald, J., & Koslowski, M. (1998). Conceptualizing and measuring a power/interaction model of interpersonal influence. *Journal of Applied Social Psychology, 28,* 307–332.

Rind, B., & Kipnis, D. (1999). Changes in self-perceptions as a result of successfully persuading others. *Journal of Social Issues, 55*(1), 141–156.

Ring, K. (1967). Experimental social psychology: Some sober questions about frivolous values. *Journal of Experimental Social psychology, 3,* 113–123.

Rodrigues, A. (1995). Attribution and social influence. *Journal of Applied Social Psychology, 25,* 1567–1577.

Rodrigues, A., & Lloyd, K. L. (1998). Re-examining bases of power from an attributional perspective. *Journal of Applied Social Psychology, 28,* 973–997.

Rollins, B. C., & Thomas, D. W. (1975). A theory of parental power and compliance. In R. E. Cromwell & D. H. Olson (Eds.), *Power in families* (pp. 38–60). New York: Sage.

Roosevelt, F. D. (1941a). *The public papers and addresses of Franklin D. Roosevelt: 1939 volume.* New York: MacMillan.

Roosevelt, F. D. (1941b). *The public papers and addresses of Franklin D. Roosevelt: 1940 volume.* New York: MacMillan.

Roosevelt, E. (1950). *F.D.R. his personal papers 1928–1945: volume II.* New York: Duell, Sloan, Pearce.

Sampson, E. E. (1991). *Social worlds/personal lives: An introduction to social psychology.* New York: Harcourt, Brace, Jovanovich.

Schlenker, B. R. (1980). *Impression management: The self-concept, social identity, and interpersonal relations.* Monterey, CA: Brooks-Cole.

Schwarzwald, J., & Koslowski, M. (1999). Gender, self-esteem, and focus of interest in the use of power strategies by adolescents in conflict situations. *Journal of Social Issues, 55*(1), 15–32.

Sears, D. (1986). College sophomores in the laboratory: Influences of a narrow database on social psychology's view of human nature. *Journal of Personality and Social Psychology, 14,* 515–560.

Smith, M. B. (1983). The shaping of American social psychology: A personal perspective from the periphery. *Personality and Social Psychology Bulletin, 9,* 165–180.

Truman, H. S. (1956). *Memoirs: Years of trial and hope.* Garden City, NY: Doubleday.

von Schuschnigg, K. (1947). *Austrian requiem* (pp. 13–24). New York: Putnam.

Walster (Hatfield), E., & Festinger, L. (1962). The effectiveness of "overheard" persuasive communications. *Journal of Abnormal and Social Psychology, 65,* 395–402.

Walster (Hatfield), E., Walster, G. W., & Berscheid, E. (1978). *Equity theory and research.* Boston: Allyn & Bacon.

Whitney, C. (1956). *MacArthur: His rendezvous with history.* New York: Knopf.

Yukl, G. A. (1989). *Leadership in organizations* (2nd ed.). Englewood Cliffs, NJ: Prentice-Hall.

Zaleski, Z., Janson, M., & Swietlicka, D. (1997). Influence strategies used by military and civil supervisors: Empirical research. *Polish Psychological Bulletin, 28,* 325–332.

13

Cloaking Power
Legitimatizing Myths and the Psychology of the Advantaged

EMMELINE S. CHEN
TOM R. TYLER

*M*ention "preferential treatment" in the context of college admissions policies, and most people immediately think of policies that allow or prohibit affirmative action (i.e., preferential treatment based upon gender or ethnicity). This association of terms is a byproduct of the very public, ongoing debate over the justice and wisdom of affirmative action policies. However, there is another category of preferential treatment within college admissions that has deep historical roots, affects many students at elite universities, and is rarely mentioned in the public discourse (see Karabel & Karen, 1990; Lamb, 1993; Larew, 1991 for exceptions). That policy is legacy admissions, and unlike affirmative action policies, its intended beneficiaries are the children of the already advantaged—namely, the wealthy and privileged.

LEGACY PREFERENCES

The use of legacy criteria in college admissions refers to the common practice among colleges and universities of giving legacies—that is, children of alumni—

This chapter was written while the first author was supported by a Chancellor's Opportunity Predoctoral Fellowship from the University of California, Berkeley and by a Henry Mitchel MacCracken Fellowship from the New York University. The authors would like to thank Shelly Chaiken, Ed Chen, and Kimberly L. Duckworth for helpful comments regarding the ideas in this chapter.

241

a preference in the admissions process. This preference is comparable to the affirmative action preference in that both are administered solely on the basis of group membership and beneficiaries of both preferences typically have significantly lower grade-point averages and test scores than other admitted students (Karen, 1991). While many have called for the abolishment of affirmative action practices, critics of legacy admissions are few, and discussions of the appropriateness of such admissions are quickly silenced (Leslie, Wingley, & Chideya, 1991; Muro, 1991).

Why do these two types of preferential treatment evoke such different reactions? In their self-proclaimed fight for a "level playing field," shouldn't affirmative action opponents rally against legacy admissions as another impediment to the meritocratic process?

CLOAKING POWER THROUGH LEGITIMIZING MYTHS

The answers to these questions can be found in the status difference between the two types of beneficiaries. While preferences that benefit the disadvantaged are widely publicized, preferences that benefit the advantaged are often hidden or cloaked—both from the public eye, but more importantly, from the advantaged themselves—through the use of legitimizing myths. (See Table 13.1 for a comparison of preferential treatment policies.)

We define *legitimizing myths* as the views that people hold that enable them to believe that their achievements are based on ability and effort, rather than unfair advantage. In this chapter, we examine the concept of legitimizing myths and the protective, psychological function that such myths serve for the self-esteem of powerful individuals are examined.

We argue that social processes allow people to engage in personal actions that create attributional ambiguity about the causes of events. Attribution theory recognizes that people seek to understand the causes of events, such as their successes or failures in life (Heider, 1958). A key attributional distinction is between causes for an event that lie within the person—for example, effort and intelligence—and causes that lie outside the person's own disposition. People draw fewer conclusions about themselves from successes and failures that are attributed to external events.

Inferences about the causes of events shape how people feel about and react to these events. Attributional ambiguities about why events happen allow people latitude in the way they understand those events. We contend that when

TABLE 13.1. Comparison of Preferential Treatment Policies

Type of policy	Who benefits?	Level of awareness
Affirmative action	The disadvantaged	Widely publicized
Legacy admissions	The advantaged	Often hidden or cloaked

the cause of an advantaged person's success is unclear, that success is interpreted through legitimizing myths. This interpretation process permits the advantaged to cloak the exercise of power. In particular, we posit that privileged individuals make personal inferences of intelligence and effort for successes that may have actually been caused by external forces. For example, in the case of legacy admissions, the "success" of being admitted to a college may have been heavily influenced by an external force—a parent's graduation from that college.

Throughout this chapter, the example of legacy admissions. We will explain public and self-perceptions of this preference—as well as other real-life advantages accorded the powerful—within the framework of legitimizing myths.

WHO ARE THE POWERFUL?

The term "powerful" is used interchangeably here with the terms "advantaged," "wealthy," and "privileged." We equate these terms based on our assumption that people who are advantaged—that is, those who are wealthy and privileged—hold the power in society. We consider this a logical assumption since by definition, advantaged individuals command a disproportionately large share of societal resources—financial and otherwise—in comparison to disadvantaged individuals.

LEGITIMIZING MYTHS

Background

The term "legitimizing myths" is not new. It has been used by social justice researchers to describe widespread ideologies—general systems of beliefs and values—that dictate the justice of existing social inequalities (cf. Jost & Banaji, 1994; Pratto et al., 1994; Sidanius, 1993). For example, Sidanius, Pratto, and their colleagues have broadly defined legitimizing myths as "attitudes, values, beliefs, or ideologies that provide moral and intellectual support to and justification for the group-based hierarchical social structure and the unequal distribution of value in social systems" (Sidanius, 1993, p. 207). More specifically, they describe legitimizing myths as "ideologies that promote or maintain group inequality" and as being "widely accepted within a society, appearing as self-apparent truths" (Pratto et al., 1994, p. 741).

Such definitions have been used to explain why disadvantaged individuals accept the legitimacy of the status quo even though it typically provides them with unfavorable outcomes relative to those received by the advantaged. From this perspective, ideologies are tools used by the privileged to maintain the acceptance of disadvantage among those receiving poor political, legal, or social outcomes in society. In fact, most researchers have assumed that powerful individuals endorse legitimizing myths out of a desire to keep the masses quiet so that the advantaged can freely enjoy the privileges that accompany their high-status positions. In short, legitimizing myths have traditionally been considered conscious misrepresentations used to oppress the disadvantaged.

A New Conceptualization

Self-Esteem Maintenance. This chapter presents a conceptualization of legitimizing myths that differs from the traditional viewpoint in several ways. First, while other researchers focus on how legitimizing myths encourage the disadvantaged to accept social inequality, we assert that legitimizing myths also enable powerful individuals to maintain high levels of self-esteem by believing in merit-based explanations for their success in life. We contend that legitimizing myths shield the advantaged from acknowledging—even to themselves—that they have benefited from preferential opportunities not available to the general public. Privileged individuals can then maintain a high sense of self-esteem and self-worth derived from their mistaken yet self-serving belief that they have wholly earned their advantages in life (see Figure 13.1).

The proposed self-esteem maintenance model proposed here should not be confused with Tesser's (1988) self-evaluation maintenance theory. Tesser's theory posits that individuals maintain high self-esteem by either "basking in the reflected glory" of successful others or withdrawing from those who are overly successful—and thus threatening—in relevant self-concept domains. Like Tesser and other self-esteem researchers, we assume that individuals want to maintain high self-esteem (see Baumeister, 1998). However, our conceptualization of legitimizing myths emphasizes the social processes that enable individuals to interpret their life experiences in self-flattering ways—that is, on people's attributions about the causes of life events, while Tesser's model focuses on the effect of interpersonal relations on self-esteem.

With Legitimizing Myths

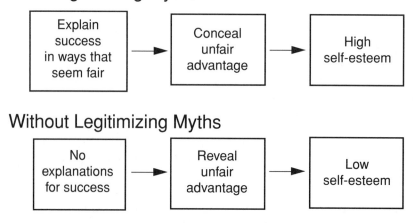

Without Legitimizing Myths

FIGURE 13.1. Proposed self-esteem maintenance model.

Genuine Beliefs. The traditional viewpoint portrays legitimizing myths as propaganda proliferated by powerful people in their campaign of oppression. We do not support this view. Instead, we contend that the advantaged genuinely believe in legitimizing myths. In fact, we insist that powerful individuals must wholeheartedly accept these myths in order to maintain their positive feelings about themselves. Moreover, we posit that this absolute acceptance of legitimizing myths enables privileged individuals to protest against preferences granted to the disadvantaged with a clear conscience, since we suspect that these individuals honestly believe that they have never benefited from unfair preferences.

For example, we argue that those admitted to colleges via legacy programs do not think of themselves as receiving "preferential treatment." Instead, we hypothesize that such individuals are convinced that they earned admission on their own merits. Consequently, they can condemn affirmative action programs for lowering academic standards without any awareness of hypocrisy, since they see themselves as upholding the meritocratic standards that they believe governed their own application process.

Emphasis on Personal Actions and Social Processes. Finally, past definitions of legitimizing myths have highlighted the general ideologies that justify the status quo. We acknowledge that certain ideologies are often used by the advantaged to justify the distribution of privileges in the current status quo and have studied the effects of such justifications on levels of emotional distress (Chen & Tyler, 1998, 1999). However, our conceptualization of legitimizing myths primarily stresses the specific, personal actions and the social processes that enable the advantaged to consider themselves deserving of their success.

That is, we emphasize the things that advantaged people do to facilitate their belief that their wealth and power is deserved. These personal actions allow the advantaged to focus on their own causal role in achieving their successes, while minimizing the influence of distal external forces such as their parents' connections. In this way, the advantaged can distinguish themselves from the disadvantaged, whom they perceive as seeking advancement through unfair "special" treatment—external interventions to shape outcomes that "ought" to be shaped by personal effort and achievement alone.

Our conceptualization of legitimizing myths also highlights the social processes that facilitate this advantageous interpretation of the causes of personal success. The secrecy that envelopes most selection procedures creates a *veil of ambiguity* whenever favorable outcomes are bestowed upon privileged individuals. In the ensuing attributional ambiguity about the true causes of such successes, the highly salient nature of personal actions enables powerful individuals to make convenient, self-serving misattributions that help them maintain high levels of self-esteem. In other words, these attributional ambiguities mask the role of external forces in causing success, thereby allowing people to focus upon the connection between their personal actions and personal success.

WHY CLOAK POWER?

Our hypothesis is that legitimizing myths enable the privileged to cloak the exercise of power. This is necessary since advantaged people do not want to view themselves as having used power and unfair advantage to achieve their success. However, it is not clear why the advantaged should care so much about earning their privileges. Why don't the powerful simply admit that the world is unfair and that they have benefited—and continue to benefit—from this injustice? In other words, why don't the advantaged simply acknowledge that their success is due to external forces and feel favored by their connection to these forces?

We believe that attributing the causality for success to external forces is psychologically distressing because people are motivated to interpret their successful experiences as products of their own abilities and efforts (Smith, 1985). We posit that this individualistic motivation stems from three sources: 1) the need for cognitive consistency, 2) the justice motive, and 3) the desire for respect (see Figure 13.2). We hypothesize that individuals who can meet these needs by viewing their successes as merit-based have higher levels of self-esteem than individuals who see their successes as products of unfair advantage. In short, as stated earlier, we view legitimizing myths as self-esteem maintenance mechanisms. Simply put, legitimizing myths hide blatant exertions of power. This enables advantaged individuals to believe that they are entirely deserving of their privileged positions in life and to maintain positive feelings about themselves.

The Need for Cognitive Consistency

One strong motivation for cloaking power is to protect advantaged individuals from the damaging realization that their success in life has been achieved through unfair advantage, rather than by merit alone. Such a realization—if acknowledged—would cause psychological distress because it is cognitively inconsistent with the cherished beliefs of meritocracy and equal opportunity so prevalent in American society (Kluegel & Smith, 1986). Indeed, the negative consequences of this type of realization have been shown in laboratory experiments. Women who are told that they have been preferentially selected for a leadership position view themselves more negatively than women who believe that their selection is based on merit (Heilman, Simon, & Repper, 1987; Major, Feinstein, & Crocker, 1994).

The Justice Motive

The motivation to cloak power is further strengthened by the universal justice motive. Social justice research has provided overwhelming evidence that people are strongly influenced by their sense of right and wrong (Tyler, in press; Tyler et al., 1997; Tyler & Smith, 1998). All individuals want to believe that they are

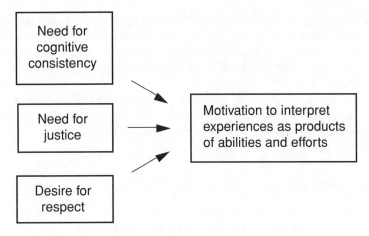

FIGURE 13.2. Motivations to cloak power.

receiving fair outcomes—that is, outcomes consistent with their efforts and abilities. We believe that the advantaged are no different. In fact, researchers have found that both the unfairly disadvantaged and the unfairly advantaged experience distress (Walster, Walster, & Berscheid, 1978). In other words, both those who receive too little and those who receive too much become upset.

Studies of affirmative action beneficiaries demonstrate that the disadvantaged suffer from self-doubt and a loss of self-esteem when told that their opportunities are undeserved, rather than based on merit (Tyler et al., 1997). According to justice theories, the advantaged should experience similar feelings when informed that their wealth and status are the results of unjust advantage, not personal achievement—a hypothesis confirmed by research on the advantaged (Tyler, in press). Consequently, in order to maintain their high self-esteem, privileged individuals need to believe that their wealth and power are justly deserved—that they have earned their advantages in life fairly, through their own hard work.

However, because advantaged individuals benefit from the current status quo, they are also motivated via self-interest to preserve the current state of affairs. Hence, the need for legitimizing myths. That is to say, the advantaged have a strong motivation to find explanations for the status quo in which the outcomes they have received through connections to wealth and power can be interpreted as being the products of their own efforts and talents. Their ability to find such explanations is facilitated by social processes that make personal effort and talents salient while simultaneously cloaking the operation of wealth and power.

Without legitimizing myths, the advantaged would be directly confronted with the injustice of their situation and consequently would experience distress. One way to combat this distress is to eliminate injustice by redistributing resources and opportunities. In other words, if powerful individuals gave away their advantages and actually competed on a level playing field, they could take justified pride in their achievements, which would then completely reflect true merit. However, the privileged must balance their desire to see justice done with the self-interested motivation to keep their advantages (see Taylor & Moghaddam, 1994).

Legitimizing myths provide a solution. By cloaking the connection between power and success, legitimizing myths allow powerful individuals to benefit from privileges without the feelings of guilt and low self-worth that would follow the realization that one is unjustly advantaged.

The Desire for Respect

Finally, powerful individuals, like everyone else, have a desire to be respected by others (Tyler & Blader, 2000; Tyler, Degoey, & Smith, 1996; Tyler & Smith, 1999). We contend that this desire for respect is the third factor that encourages people to both perceive and present themselves as wholly responsible for their success in life.

In market societies like the United States, people signal their wealth by buying and displaying luxury goods such as expensive cars, houses, or clothing. Yet simply being rich or occupying a powerful position in society does not automatically earn respect from others, as evidenced by the contempt that many hold toward dictators who seize power and wealth by force. Equally important, if not more so, is the manner in which individuals are perceived to have accumulated their wealth. If people are thought to have earned money through hard work and the use of their talents, then they are highly respected within American society. In other words, Americans reserve their respect for self-made icons such as Bill Gates or the protagonists in the Horatio Alger stories, people who are perceived as having earned their wealth and power.[1]

In contrast, Americans look down upon those who have achieved wealth and power through inheritance, chance, or disreputable means (see Lancaster, 1996, and Welle, 1999 for examples involving nepotism). Such individuals only gain respect after "proving" themselves worthy of their power in some way, for instance, by demonstrating their superior intelligence through admission to an elite university—a success that most people assume requires intellectual ability since admissions preferences for the powerful are generally cloaked.

In one memorable instance of disrespect, political pundit Jim Hightower insulted former President George Bush with his remark that Bush was "born on third base and thought he hit a triple" (Sklar & Collins, 1997, p. 7). By belittling Bush in this manner, Hightower expressed the traditional meritocratic views that people should not take personal credit for successes that do not reflect

---

1. Whether or not such perceptions are actually true is a different matter. For example, in the Horatio Alger stories, the way protagonists achieve success is through chance encounters with wealthy benefactors (Weiss, 1969).

their own efforts and abilities and people should not derive high self-esteem from bogus achievements. These cultural views were also noted by Michael Davies, the executive producer of the popular television game show "Who Wants to Be a Millionaire," when he observed, "In this country [America], lottery winners are not really respected because they never earned it" (James, 1999, p. E10). In other words, merely possessing the trappings of success does not earn an individual respect. Such trappings must first be attributed to internal causes within the person—motivation, intelligence, daring, or so forth.

Consequently, in order to gain the respect of others, powerful individuals must find ways to present themselves as having worked for their money, power, and influence. Legitimizing myths are helpful in this regard because they enable the privileged to gain the appearance of cultural capital that is merit-based, while simultaneously cloaking—both to onlookers and to the advantaged themselves—the true role played by power in gaining selective outcomes.

THE IMPORTANCE OF PERSONAL ACTIONS

Provide Salient, Alternative Explanations

We emphasize the significance of personal actions because we believe that they furnish internal, causal explanations for success that serve as strong, salient alternatives to explanations that link success to wealth and power. These internal, causal explanations allow the powerful to justify to themselves and to others why they have received certain advantages in life.

For example, Katharine Graham, the former publisher of *The Washington Post*, served as a cub reporter for one year at the *San Francisco News* before being appointed to the editorial staff of the *Post* by its owner—her father (Dye, 1983). We propose that Graham's one-year stint at the *San Francisco News* provided her with journalism experience—albeit very short—that she could then point to as proof that she deserved her editorial position. If Graham had gone directly from college to an editorial post, she would have had difficulty persuading herself that she had earned the more prestigious position on the basis of merit. However, the yearlong reporting job legitimized her attainment of the job in her own eyes and in the eyes of other people. This enabled her to attribute more of her career success to her own abilities, rather than her father's helping hand.

There are many other situations where one clear explanation for success is linked to external forces—such as a parent's connections— rather than an individual's intelligence or motivation. For instance, some students who are admitted to elite universities have parents who are personally acquainted with important university officials (see Gladstone & Frammolino, 1996), while some actors and actresses who land starring roles have famous show business parents who arranged their auditions (see Stein, 1997). In both situations, the children can maintain higher levels of self-esteem if they can convince themselves that they were selected solely on the basis of talent rather than because their parents knew the admissions officers or casting directors. Legitimizing myths are particularly useful in situations like these because they cloak the connections of power and create attributional ambiguity regarding the true cause of success. This enables advantaged individuals to ignore the potential external cause and attribute their success to their own personal actions and effort.

In the social processes of college admissions and casting for a lead role, the personal actions of submitting the application and taking part in the audition are crucial because they provide the powerful with alternative explanations that legitimize each selection process. Both processes let advantaged individuals engage in a behavior, applying for admission or trying out for a part, that they can later point to as the cause of their subsequent success. In addition, the effort involved in either gathering the necessary materials for the application, such as taking the SAT and writing essays, or in preparing for the audition makes these actions—and their corresponding alternative, causal explanations of merit—extremely salient to the applicants.

Both legacy applicants and non-legacy applicants must complete the same application where they detail exactly why they believe that they deserve admission. Consequently, legacy applicants are much more likely to attribute their subsequent selection to their own hard work and ability—a self-serving attribution that also conveniently increases their self-esteem and sense of self-worth, rather than to the less salient, causal influence of their parents' past college attendance. However, as noted, earlier studies suggest that this factor is very important in actual admissions decisions, since legacies have significantly lower levels of achievement than do nonlegacies (see Karen, 1991).

Concealing Special Connections

The salience of personal actions conceals the special connections at work behind the scenes. If an inexperienced actor landed a starring role without engaging in an audition, it would be obvious to everyone, including the actor himself, that he had benefited from some type of preferential treatment. It would also be impossible for the actor to believe that the casting director had chosen him on the basis of ability when the director was never presented with any such evidence. In other words, bypassing the normal selection procedure would force the actor to admit that he had won the role on the basis of privilege—his parents' connections—alone, a potentially self-damaging realization. In contrast, participating in the audition process helps the actor to blend in with other aspiring film stars. This makes it less likely that his success is considered with suspicion—either by onlookers or even himself.

To sum up, personal actions provide attributional ambiguities that enable powerful individuals to make self-serving misattributions legitimizing the positive outcomes that they have attained (see Figure 13.3).

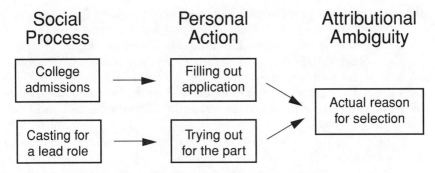

FIGURE 13.3. The creation of attributional ambiguity.

THE VEIL OF AMBIGUITY

Gatekeeping Selection Procedures

Legitimizing myths work by concealing the true causal forces through which powerful individuals have attained their positive outcomes. Such myths typically arise in situations involving semiambiguous gatekeeping selection procedures that lead to coveted positions in society, for example, admissions to elite colleges or hiring for competitive jobs. The guidelines and acceptance criteria for these procedures are generally known and accepted as being merit-based. The public also is aware that these rules are occasionally bent—as in the case of the legacy and affirmative action preferences—so that some individuals are accepted who would not have been chosen without such help. However, the reasons that specific individuals have been accepted or rejected are never revealed because of "privacy" concerns.

Practically speaking, the combination of these factors produces a veil of ambiguity surrounding selected individuals, since no one except the members of the selection committee knows for certain the specific details of why each applicant is chosen or rejected. (See Brutus & Ryan, 1998 for an experiment that attempted to operationalize the attributional ambiguity found in real-life selection procedures.)

Assumption of Superiority

This veil of ambiguity favors the powerful, since the preferences from which they benefit are typically shrouded and hidden from public view. Consequently, when the advantaged are chosen for positions that are scarce and highly desired—such as slots in Harvard University's entering class—it is generally assumed that they were chosen for this honor based on their past achievements. That is to say, advantaged persons are regarded as deserving of positive outcomes, unless explicitly proven otherwise. This "assumption of superiority" is the exact opposite of the "suspicion of inferiority" that envelopes stigmatized individuals who have passed some gatekeeping barrier, such as members of minority groups typically targeted by affirmative action policies (see Major et al., 1994; Steele, 1992). In stark contrast to members of advantaged groups, minority group members often suffer from the suspicion—harbored by both their peers and sometimes even themselves—that they were not actually selected on the basis of merit and are, instead, "affirmative action" hires (see Table 13.2).

The assumption of superiority that is granted to the powerful suggests that a possible explanation for the absence of public outrage over legacy preferences is the presumption that children of elite college alumni are naturally gifted and talented. If people believe that legacies would have earned admission based on merit alone, then they should regard any advantage granted to legacies in the selection process as insignificant and therefore unworthy of protest. In other words, one reason why opponents of affirmative action do not also demonstrate against legacy preferences may be their mistaken belief that the advantage granted to affirmative action beneficiaries is far greater than the advantage granted to legacy students.

In actuality, there is solid evidence documenting that the legacy advantage is quite substantial. Not only does it garner extra reviews of applications, additional considerations, and admissions for legacy applicants who would have been rejected using the normal criteria (see Feldman, 1988; Karabel & Karen, 1990; Karen, 1991; Larew, 1991), but an examination of Harvard University's admissions records found that legacy students were significantly less qualified than other admitted students (Larew, 1991). This is a stark contrast to the public assurances of admissions officers who claim that the legacy preference is a mere "tip," used to choose between two equally qualified applicants. In short, if members of the public—or legacies themselves—believe that legacies have qualified for admission on the basis of merit, they are wrong.

SELF-SERVING MISATTRIBUTIONS

The veil of ambiguity surrounding selection procedures enables powerful individuals to embrace the psychologically satisfying belief that they have achieved

TABLE 13.2. How Attributional Ambiguity Is Resolved

Status of beneficiaries	What's salient	Awareness level of potential preferential treatment	Onlookers' conclusion
Disadvantaged	Disadvantaged status (e.g., race, income, sex)	High	Suspicion of inferiority (Major et al., 1994; Steele, 1992)
Advantaged	Personal actions	Low	Assumption of superiority

success on their own. This is consistent with Sampson's (1986) observation that it is "tempting for those who benefit from a particular arrangement of power and privilege to believe deeply that they deserve their exalted status" (p. 99). In other words, even though the advantaged may be aware that they may have benefited from some type of preferential treatment, such as the legacy preference, the veil of ambiguity makes it impossible for the powerful to know exactly how much of a difference this preference has made in their individual cases. This ambiguity facilitates cognitive distortion to justify advantage (Taylor & Moghaddam, 1994; Walster et al., 1978).

Because the true causes of their success are shrouded by the veil of ambiguity, advantaged individuals are free to attribute their success to personal ability or effort without fear of being proven wrong. Moreover, since the privileged are motivated to perceive themselves as having earned their position in life, they are more likely to resolve the attributional ambiguity about their deservingness by underweighting the influence of powerful connections and overweighting the influence of their own abilities and efforts (see Crocker & Major, 1989; Major & Crocker, 1993).

The Super-Wealthy

The argument made here is not confined to the arena of college admissions. Our belief that the advantaged are capable of misattributing their powerful position in life to their own efforts is confirmed by the research findings of others who have examined the psychology of the advantaged. For instance, Stanley and Danko (1996) surveyed millionaires and their families to understand the processes of wealth accumulation. In their interviews with the adult children of the super-wealthy, Stanley and Danko found evidence that these advantaged individuals are able to ignore the assistance they have received from their family background and fully believe that they have earned their privileges on the basis of merit alone.

> Like many other gift receivers, James views himself as "self-made." In fact, about two out of every three adult children who receive significant cash gifts periodically from their own parents view themselves as members of the "I did it on my own" club. We are amazed when these people tell us in interviews, "We earned every dollar we have" (Stanley & Danko, 1996, p. 156).

EXPERIMENTAL FINDINGS

Laboratory research indicates that privileged individuals may perceive success itself as proof that they have done something to deserve this success. For example, Steil (1983) conducted an experiment in which participants were assigned to use one of two methods to complete a task. One method made it easy for "advantaged" participants to complete the task, while "disadvantaged" participants found that—regardless of their efforts—their assigned method made completing the task impossible. Steil found that although the advantaged participants acknowledged the method as a key factor that assisted their task performance, they also rated the effects of effort, luck, and intelligence on their performance more highly than did the disadvantaged participants. In short, by persisting in believing that effort and intelligence were factors in their success, members of the advantaged group could "also believe that they did better because they deserved to do better" (Steil, 1983, p. 250).

The findings from Steil's (1983) study suggest that even if powerful individuals are aware that they may have been "helped" in achieving success, they are motivated to continue to make salient the importance of their efforts and talents. Consequently, advantaged individuals are more likely to believe that their positive outcomes are entirely merited and deserved.

Just World Theory

These justifying processes are more broadly documented by Lerner (1980) under the general framework of just world theory. Lerner suggests that people have a basic psychological need to believe that justice exists in the world. To support this belief, they interpret events in ways that make sense from a psychological perspective. For example, if people observe an innocent person being victimized, they come to believe that the person deserved his or her fate in some way. This is true even when the actions shown clearly suggest that the person was a random victim of misfortune. The psychological processes of justification encourage the advantaged to feel that they deserve the success they have attained, especially when veils of ambiguity conceal the true causes of successful events.

George W. Bush: Smart or Merely Well-Connected?

For example, it is well known that presidential candidate George W. Bush graduated from Yale University (Nelson, 2000). Since Yale has a reputation of being a highly selective academic institution, Bush's Yale degree immediately certifies him as a man of some intellect. However, after learning that his father, former President George Bush, is also a Yale alumnus, a question presents itself: Was the younger Bush admitted to Yale on the basis of his academic merit alone, or did he benefit from his father's alumnus status and general influence? The fact that the younger Bush's college transcript consists mainly of Cs suggests that legacy preference played a role in his selection as a Yale student (Bruni, 1999). However the power of legitimizing myths is such that we can never be sure. Because of the cloaking power of legitimizing myths, Bush has been granted the assumption of superiority and has had ample time—as well as the benefits of his Yale education—to learn enough to appear as though he might have actually deserved the Yale acceptance letter on his own.

What can never be known in this, or any other such case, is whether the selected individual made as much of the opportunity as someone else might have. There is another person somewhere in the world who would have been admitted instead of every legacy admission, just as there is another person who would have been admitted instead of every affirmative action admission. We can never be sure how these people would have fared if they had been given the opportunity of an elite education. We can imagine a counterfactual situation in which those other people were admitted, but we can never know where this hypothetical alternative would have led. Would those individuals have achieved more? Unfortunately, the achievements of those who did attend Yale and other elite universities are salient and seem to justify their admission, while the potential achievements of others—if they had received the same opportunity to attend an elite college—are only nonsalient speculative possibilities.

WHY NOT SELL ADMISSIONS?

Setting a Price for College Admissions

We will close our discussion of legitimizing myths by focusing on one last example of preferential treatment that favors the powerful, namely, the effect of donor status on admissions at elite colleges. Being a candidate for legacy admission requires that one's parents attended a specific school. But what if one is merely wealthy? How can that advantage be used to secure an individual an opportunity? It is commonly understood, though never explicitly stated, that donating—or indicating one's willingness to donate—a significant amount of money to a university may help one's child gain admission (Rodriguez, 1996; Wallinger, 1998). Applicants admitted on the basis of this admissions preference are known informally as "development" cases at the University of Pennsylvania (Sanoff, 1997), "provost's discretion" at the University of Michigan (Hoover, 1998), "VIP admissions" at the University of California (Frammolino & Gladstone, 1996), and "paying guests" at Harvard University (Feldman, 1988), to name a few.

Interestingly, although colleges defend this practice by saying that the future of their institutions depends on the continued generosity of substantial donors, these universities do not advertise or even openly admit the existence of such preferences (Leslie et al., 1991; "Merit" double standard, 1996). If the purpose of this type of preference is truly to raise money, why doesn't Harvard, for example, simply set the price of a place in its entering class at $1 million dollars? The answer, of course, is that openly selling spots in its entering class would greatly decrease the prestige—though not the quality—of a Harvard education. Harvard's classes would be filled with the richest students in the world, but the Harvard degree would be devalued as a signifier of excellence. Instead of certifying an individual as possessing a high level of talent and intelligence, a degree from Harvard would simply indicate one's willingness and ability to pay for an excellent education.

Furthermore, setting a fixed price on college admissions would lessen the legitimizing value of attending Harvard. The admitted students, as well as everybody else, would know that they were not chosen on the basis of their personal merit. Consequently, the honor of being admitted to Harvard would diminish, as would the lift to a person's feelings of competence and self-esteem. In order for attainment to have value in encouraging a person's feelings of self-worth and self-esteem, as well as in garnering respect from others, the attainment must be perceived as reflecting internal, dispositional characteristics, that is, a person's intelligence, effort, or ability.

It is important to note that this devaluation of the symbolic worth of the Harvard degree would occur irrespective of the actual quality of education provided by the university. As noted, students who attend Harvard—for whatever reason—are well-educated. This demonstrates that the legitimizing value of elite colleges is a product of their allegedly merit-based selection procedure, in addition to the actual learning process that takes place during the college years. Attending elite universities benefits students in two ways. First, being admitted certifies students as possessing a certain degree of merit and motivation. Second, students receive a high-quality college education at these universities.

This fictitious scenario illustrates two necessary characteristics of selection procedures if they are to act as legitimizing myths. First, in order for legitimizing myths to work, there must be some truth to the myths. For instance, the action of filling out a college application can only conceal the influence of hefty donations if other people are submitting applications and gaining admission on the basis of genuine merit. If the application process is a complete sham, then the legitimizing myth has lost its power of simulating authenticity. The legacy and special donor programs operate in the shadow of a general meritocratic admissions process, and they do so for good reason: It is the general meritocratic process that legitimizes special cases.

Second, the actual preference granted to the powerful must be cloaked as much as possible, or at least publicly presented as an extremely rare occurrence. The reputation of a gatekeeping institution such as Harvard can only be sustained if the vast majority of its students appear qualified to be there and if the actual reasons why the powerful have been selected are closely guarded. Just as vanity presses—which publish books in exchange for a fee—are looked down upon, a college that sold admissions would not be respected. Indeed, the prestige of an elite university depends on its image of meritocracy.

In short, legitimizing myths serve multiple functions. Not only do legitimizing myths give the powerful the semblance of having earned their advantages, but they also help to perpetuate the reputation of the selective institutions as having based their decisions on merit, rather than being unduly influenced by power.

Corruption in the Eye of the Beholder

To illustrate this point even further, consider the following real-life scenario, as described by former Stanford University undergraduate admissions dean, Jean Fetter (1995):

> [T]wo formally dressed foreign gentlemen . . . explained that they were visiting Stanford on behalf of their corporate director. . . The director was very eager to have his son attend Stanford. "Would $10,000," they politely asked, "be sufficient?"
>
> It soon became clear that the financial question dealt with the cost of gaining admissions rather than the cost of attending Stanford. The somewhat surprised assistant dean attempted to explain that the selection of the freshman class was not conducted that way, and she patiently described the selection criteria and process. Undaunted, the two businessmen pulled out a checkbook and persisted, "Well, how much does it cost?" (pp. 226–227)

In her comments, Fetter (1995) makes clear that she is shocked by the assumption that money might affect one's chances of being admitted to Stanford. She even states her disbelief at the businessmen's claim that "they had not had this kind of problem [of being rebuffed] at the other colleges they had visited" (p. 227). However, in an earlier chapter entitled "Special Talents, Special Considerations," Fetter states,

> While it is absolutely true that student places are earned and not bought, it would be disingenuous of any dean of admissions to claim that donors to the university are ignored. . . [I]t is important for the dean of undergraduate admissions to be fully informed and aware of the repercussions that admissions decisions might have with major donors. (1995, p. 80)

In other words, although Stanford does not explicitly sell admission to college, Fetter acknowledges that the selection process is indeed influenced by the prospect of significant donations. (To be fair, this practice is certainly not limited to Stanford nor even to other elite private universities.)

Putting the two paragraphs together suggests that the businessmen's mistake was not in assuming that money might influence the admissions process, but rather in their approach. Instead of blatantly addressing the admissions office, the businessmen might have fared better if they had visited the office of development first, and expressed their director's great admiration for Stanford and his desire to make a "substantial" contribution to various campus building projects. If the businessmen had then casually mentioned that their director's son would soon be applying to Stanford, the office of development might have called undergraduate admissions to ensure that the admissions office's selection process would not produce any negative "repercussions" with regards to the potential gift.

While selling Stanford admissions directly would have been clearly labeled corruption (see "Furor over 'selling,'" 1978), taking special note—or simply "being aware"—of the financial consequences of admitting or rejecting a specific applicant is an accepted part of the typical admissions procedure.

This example is mentioned to illustrate that corruption is in the eye of the beholder. What may seem horribly and obviously unethical in one situation can appear perfectly acceptable—and legitimate—when phrased and framed appropriately. The key is knowing which legitimizing myths to invoke and when. When legitimizing myths are used to their full extent, the powerful can benefit from unfair advantage and yet truly believe that they are just like everyone else: hard-working and incredibly successful, with no one to thank except themselves.

APPLYING LEGITIMIZING MYTHS TO DIFFERENT ARENAS

Although this chapter has have focused on the legitimizing myths used by the powerful to justify advantages in the education arena, we wish to emphasize that the concept of legitimizing myths has broad application to other domains as well. For instance, legitimizing myths can also be used to examine psychological reactions to racial inequality. In American society, there is a long history of within-race preferences, and such preferences have typically benefited Whites and hurt minorities. The concept of legitimizing myths helps us understand why White Americans have engaged in efforts to view themselves as egalitarian and antiracist, rather than as privileged and racist. Such efforts preserve White Americans' sense of their own fairness, as well as the general fairness of the social system.

As with theories dealing with economic advantage, justice theories suggest that it would damage the self-esteem of Whites to view themselves as benefiting from unfair social advantages that are derived from their race, rather than "fair" advantages that have been earned through personal achievement. Myrdal (1944) recognized the potential psychological conflicts caused by this contradiction between the reality of privilege and the psychology of justice, and he sought to use these conflicts as the basis for a social-change strategy. His analysis of the history of African-Americans in the United States repeatedly contrasted the reality of race relations to the ideals of American society in an effort to motivate change on the part of White Americans. We argue that facing this contradiction, however, does not necessarily activate the motivation to change. It can also activate a motivation to legitimize or cloak the operation of racism. Such defensive motivations are like those discussed here in the context of college admissions policies, since civil rights programs are typically framed in terms of efforts to lessen the unfair privileges of Whites.

In short, we would like to stress that there are many types of advantage that are maintained through legitimizing myths. The advantages discussed in this chapter are a mere sampling of the wide range of privileges enjoyed by the powerful and concealed by legitimizing myths. In addition to issues of racial inequality, there are issues of gender inequality and inequality linked to age. Our point is that the basic psychological processes that we have outlined in this chapter operate in a wide variety of situations.

Beyond Preferential Treatment

The powerful are often able to circumvent typical procedures that are intended to ensure that only the "deserving" succeed. Yet their violations of "fair" procedure often pass unnoticed because they are framed and cloaked by legitimizing myths.

As stated earlier, we believe that the framework of legitimizing myths can be extended to the study of a wide variety of public policy issues. For instance, while direct vote-buying is frowned upon as being entirely corrupt, lobbying is an acceptable method of "persuading" legislators to agree with a particular point of view, since legislators can easily articulate reasons for being "convinced" by the lobbyists' arguments. In essence, lobbying conceals the actual underlying method of vote-buying and makes it appear legitimate, rather than appearing as a corruption of the political process. Similarly, people are allowed to influence elections by spending money to advertise for a particular candidate, which may help the candidate win the election. Such an effort is considered perfectly reasonable, since it preserves the myth that the more qualified candidate with the "better" message will be elected.

We contend that similar legitimizing myths are prevalent throughout our society and that for the most part, such myths serve the interests of the powerful at the expense of the disadvantaged. It is our hope that the recognition of the importance of these legitimizing myths will reveal the inconsistency of objecting to the injustice of programs that assist the disadvantaged while simultaneously ignoring how the advantaged have been helped by the cloaked use of money and power.

REFERENCES

Baumeister, R. F. (1998). The self. In D. T. Gilbert, S. T. Fiske, & G. Lindzey (Eds.), *The handbook of social psychology* (4th ed., Vol. 1, pp. 680–740). Boston: McGraw-Hill.

Bruni, F. (1999, November 6). The education of George W. Bush, and the voter. *New York Times,* p. A9.

Brutus, S., & Ryan, A. M. (1998). A new perspective on preferential treatment: The role of ambiguity and self-efficacy. *Journal of Business and Psychology, 13,* 157–178.

Chen, E. S., & Tyler, T. R. (1998, August).

Advantage without guilt: World views and attitudes toward the disadvantaged. Poster session presented at the annual meeting of the American Psychological Association, San Francisco.

Chen, E. S., & Tyler, T. R. (1999). *Maintaining advantages without feeling guilt: Using justifications to alleviate emotional distress.* Manuscript in preparation, New York University.

Crocker, J., & Major, B. (1989). Social stigma and self-esteem: The self-protective properties of stigma. *Psychological Review, 96,* 608–630.

Dye, T. R. (1983). *Who's running America?: The Reagan years.* Englewood Cliffs, NJ: Prentice-Hall.

Feldman, P. H. (1988). *Recruiting an elite: Admission to Harvard College.* New York: Garland.

Fetter, J. H. (1995). *Questions and admissions: Reflections on 100,000 admissions decisions at Stanford.* Stanford, CA: Stanford University Press.

Frammolino, R., & Gladstone, M. (1996, May 6). Donations and admissions—Is there a tie at UCLA? *Los Angeles Times,* p. A1.

Furor over "selling" university admissions. (1978, July 3). *U.S. News & World Report, 85,* 55–56.

Gladstone, M., & Frammolino, R. (1996, April 11). UC Berkeley panel handles admission requests by VIPs. *Los Angeles Times,* p. 1.

Heider, F. (1958). *The psychology of interpersonal relations.* Hillsdale, NJ: Erlbaum.

Heilman, M. E., Simon, M. C., & Repper, D. P. (1987). Intentionally favored, unintentionally harmed?: Impact of sex-based preferential selection on self-perceptions and self-evaluations. *Journal of Applied Psychology, 72,* 62–68.

Hoover, R. (1998, June 14). White U-M hopefuls get a break: Some are admitted with "provost's discretion." *Detroit News,* p. B1.

James, C. (1999, November 18). Game shows, greedy and otherwise. *The New York Times,* pp. E1, E10.

Jost, J. T., & Banaji, M. R. (1994). The role of stereotyping in system-justification and the production of false consciousness. *British Journal of Social Psychology, 33,* 1–27.

Karabel, J., & Karen, D. (1990, December 8). Go to Harvard; Give your kid a break. *The New York Times,* p. 25.

Karen, D. (1991). "Achievement" and "ascription" in admission to an elite college: A political-organizational analysis. *Sociological Forum, 6,* 349–380.

Kluegel, J. R., & Smith, E. R. (1986). *Beliefs about inequality: Americans' views of what is and what ought to be.* New York: Aldine de Gruyter.

Lamb, J. D. (1993). The real affirmative action babies: Legacy preferences at Harvard and Yale. *Columbia Journal of Law and Social Problems, 26,* 491–521.

Lancaster, H. (1996, October 15.) Managing your career: Should you join a company where Mom or Dad is boss? *The Wall Street Journal,* p. B1.

Larew, J. (1991, June). Why are droves of unqualified, unprepared kids getting into our top colleges?: Because their dads are alumni. *The Washington Monthly, 23,* 10–14.

Lerner, M. (1980). *The belief in a just world.* New York: Plenum Press.

Leslie, C., Wingley, P., & Chideya, F. (1991, June 24). A rich legacy of preference. *Newsweek, 157,* 59.

Major, B., & Crocker, J. (1993). Social stigma: The consequences of attributional ambiguity. In D. M. Mackie & D. L. Hamilton (Eds.), *Affect, cognition, and stereotyping: Interactive processes in group perception* (pp. 345–370). Orlando, FL: Academic Press.

Major, B., Feinstein, J., & Crocker, J. (1994). Attributional ambiguity of affirmative action. *Basic and Applied Social Psychology, 15,* 113-141.

"Merit" double standard reveals campus hypocrisy. (1996, March 27). *USA Today,* p. A10.

Muro, M. (1991, September 18). Class privilege. *The Boston Globe,* pp. 43, 46.

Myrdal, G. (1944). *An American dilemma.* New York: Harper and Brothers.

Nelson, L. -E. (2000, February 24). Legacy. *The New York Review of Books,* pp. 4–7.

Pratto, F., Sidanius, J., Stallworth, L. M., & Malle, B. F. (1994). Social dominance orientation: A personality variable predicting social and political attitudes. *Journal of Personality and Social Psychology, 67,* 741–763.

Rodriguez, R. (1996, August 8). The dirty little secret of college admissions. *Black Issues in Higher Education, 13,* 12–14.

Sampson, E. E. (1986). Justice ideology and social legitimation: A revised agenda for psychological inquiry. In H. W. Bierhoff, R. L. Cohen, & J. Greenberg (Eds.), *Justice in social relations* (pp. 87–102). New York: Plenum Press.

Sanoff, A. P. (1997, April 14). Did they admit me? *U.S. News & World Report, 122,* 48–58.

Sidanius, J. (1993). The psychology of group conflict and the dynamics of oppression: A social dominance perspective. In S. Iyengar & W. J. McGuire (Eds.), *Explorations in political psychology* (pp. 183–219). Durham, NC: Duke University Press.

Sklar, H., & Collins, C. (1997, Oct. 20). Forbes 400 world series. *The Nation, 265,* 6–7.

Smith, K. B. (1985). I made it because of me: Beliefs about the causes of wealth and poverty. *Sociological Spectrum, 5,* 255–267.

Stanley, T. J., & Danko, W. D. (1996). *The millionaire next door: The surprising secrets of America's wealth.* New York: Pocket Books.

Steele, C. (1992, April). Race and the schooling of black Americans. *Atlantic Monthly, 269,* 68–78.

Steil, J. M. (1983). The response to injustice: Effects of varying levels of social support and position of advantage or disadvantage. *Journal of Experimental Social Psychology, 19,* 239–253.

Stein, R. (1997, Nov. 23). Daddy's girls: When director fathers cast their daughters, it can be a good thing—or a bad thing. *San Francisco Chronicle,* p. 56.

Taylor, D. M., & Moghaddam, F. M. (1994). *Theories of intergroup relations: International social psychological perspectives.* Westport, CT: Praeger.

Tesser, A. (1988). Toward a self-evaluation maintenance model of social behavior. In L. Berkowitz (Ed.), *Advances in experimental social psychology* (Vol. 21, pp. 181–227). New York: Academic Press.

Tyler, T. R. (in press). Social justice. In R. Brown & S. Gaertner (Eds.), *The Blackwell encyclopedia of social psychology* (2nd ed., Vol. 4). London: Blackwell.

Tyler, T. R., & Blader, S. L. (2000). *Cooperation in groups.* Philadelphia: Psychology Press.

Tyler, T. R., Boeckmann, R. J., Smith, H. J., & Huo, Y. J. (1997). *Social justice in a diverse society.* Denver, CO: Westview Press.

Tyler, T. R., Degoey, P., & Smith, H. J. (1996). Understanding why the justice of group procedures matters. *Journal of Personality and Social Psychology, 70,* 913–930.

Tyler, T. R., & Smith, H. J. (1998). Social justice and social movements. In D. T. Gilbert, S. T. Fiske, & G. Lindzey (Eds.), *Handbook of social psychology* (4th ed., Vol. 2, pp. 595–629). Boston: McGraw-Hill.

Tyler, T. R., & Smith, H. J. (1999). Justice, social identity, and group processes. In T. R. Tyler, R. Kramer, & O. P. John (Eds.), *The psychology of the social self* (pp. 223–264). Mahwah, NJ: Erlbaum.

Wallinger, L. M. (1998, December). What principals and students should know about college admissions. *NASSP Bulletin, 82,* 67–76.

Walster, E., Walster, G. W., & Berscheid, E. (1978). *Equity: Theory and research.* Boston: Allyn and Bacon.

Weiss, R. (1969). *The American myth of success: From Horatio Alger to Norman Vincent Peale.* New York: Basic Books.

Welle, B. (1999, August). *Perceptions of the beneficiaries of nepotism policies.* Poster session presented at the annual meeting of the Academy of Management, Chicago.

14

Confucius, "Jen," and the Benevolent Use of Power

The Interdependent Self as a Psychological Contract Preventing Exploitation

WENDI L. GARDNER
ELIZABETH A. SEELEY

> Adept Kung asked about governing, and the Master said: "Plenty of food, plenty of weapons and the trust of the people."
>
> "If you couldn't have all three," asked Kung, "which would you give up first?"
>
> "I would give up weapons," replied the Master.
>
> "And if you couldn't have both of the others. . .?"
>
> "I would give up food," replied the Master, "There has always been hunger. But without trust, the people are lost,"
>
> —Confucius (tr. Hinton, 1998, p. 129)

At the dawn of this new millennium, trust in American government has reached dismaying lows. In a recent survey, Americans identified "corrupt political leadership" as the single largest barrier to effective government. Additionally, a Gallup poll that asked thousands of Americans to rate the trustworthiness of 26 occupations found that those in government received close to the lowest ratings; Senators were ranked 21st, Congressman 22nd, and state officeholders 23rd (Gallup, 1999). Indeed, only insurance salesmen, television advertisers, and used car salesmen received lower ratings.

Although heralded as a reflection of modern American cynicism, mistrust of those in power has long been a property of Western belief. We owe our system of distributed government, in part, to the mistrust of those in power;

distribution of political power prevented the presumed corruption that would result from the concentration of powers in any single body. Indeed, Madison's contributions to the Federalist papers (1788) repeatedly reassured New Yorkers that ratifying the proposed Constitution and its outline for government would prevent "abuses which must be incident to every power . . . It may be a reflection on human nature, that such devices should be necessary to control the abuses of government . . . ambition must be made to counteract ambition" (Federalist 41 and 51, 1788). A century later, the most famous expression of this belief was realized in Lord Acton's assertion that "power tends to corrupt . . . and absolute power corrupts absolutely" (letter to Mandell Creighton, 1887). This maxim immediately was incorporated into political doctrine, taking on what Rogow and Laswell (1963) termed "the quality of law or a fundamental axiom of mathematics . . . a mandatory article of faith in the public declarations of men of democratic action" (p. 1).

The widespread belief in the corrupting influence of power is almost equally pervasive in psychological doctrine. Personality and social psychologists alike regard power to result in negative consequences. Yet, throughout history, the possession of power appears to have corrupted some, but ennobled others. In this chapter, this conundrum is addressed by first briefly reviewing the literature supporting the Actonian doctrine. It is then argued that both political philosophy and psychological data may be used to support a benevolent view of power, and one factor that may predispose some to wield power for the collective good is explored.

Specifically, this chapter calls upon some of the earliest (c. 500 B.C.) discussions of factors leading to benevolent power. The Confucian concept of "jen" is be introduced, and translated into its modern social psychological analogue, the interdependent self-construal. Next, the mechanisms through which interdependence may influence power are outlined. It is argued that thinking of the self in an interdependent rather than an independent fashion encourages the benevolent use of power through altering the goals of the powerful individual, encouraging perspective taking, and instituting a bond of reciprocal trust with others. Combined, these act as a perceived psychological contract to work for the common good. Current research bearing on each of these points are reviewed.

POWER AND EXPLOITATION

Ample evidence supports the thesis that power can be corrupting. For example, holding power as a chronic motive has been consistently linked to exploitation. Much research has focused upon the values and actions of individuals high in the need for power (abbreviated as nPower, e.g., Veroff, 1957); these individuals are defined as being motivated primarily by the potential of having impact upon others or for pursuing acclaim and advantage (Frieze & Boneva, chapter 5; McClelland, 1975). nPower is commonly revealed through the use of recurrent themes of power and dominance in the interpretation of an image or scenario (Winter, 1973) and appears to have relatively high predictive validity. For example, high nPower has been associated with seeking office in social organizations (McClelland, 1975; Winter, 1988), choosing careers that are characterized by holding a supervisory role (Stewart & Winter, 1974), acquiring and displaying high prestige material goods (Winter, 1973), and attempting to exert influence over others in small group settings (Fodor, 1984; Fodor & Smith, 1982).

Consistent with the widespread belief that power and corruption are intertwined, individuals high in nPower are also more likely to exploit others. For example, men high in nPower have been found to oppress and control female romantic partners to a greater degree than men lower in this motivation (Mason & Blankenship, 1987; Winter, Stewart, & McClelland, 1977), as well as to score higher on measures of rape acceptance and sexual exploitation (Anderson, Cooper, & Okamura, 1997). When placed in supervisory roles, individuals high in nPower have been more likely to utilize their power capriciously; Fodor and Farrow (1979) found that high nPower managers were vulnerable to ingratiation—exploiting their position of power to reward those who complimented them. They also have been more likely to overestimate their own influence and devalue the contributions of others (Fodor & Farrow, 1979), possibly resulting from a lack of perspective taking (Sheldon & Johnson, 1993). Finally, when high nPower individuals lead a group discussion, they have been shown to actually suppress the contributions of subordinates, leading to poorer group decisions (Fodor & Smith, 1982). On a larger level, Winter (1993) has argued that the level of nPower possessed by global leaders is related to the likelihood of attacking a weaker nation.

In addition to the aforementioned studies that focused upon individuals dominated by a need for power, numerous studies have examined the consequences of power as a situational variable. These investigations thus test the "power corrupts" hypothesis more directly by placing power in the hands of research participants and then observing their behavior. One of the most famous, the Stanford Prison experiment (Haney, Banks, & Zimbardo, 1973), randomly assigned young men to the role of prison guard or prisoner, and found that several of the guards abused their power to a shocking extent. A classic study by Kipnis (1972) investigated the corrupting influence of power in a more controlled environment by manipulating the power held by student managers and then investigating their impressions of subordinates. High power managers could deduct pay and fire workers; low power managers could only contact and encourage workers. As Kipnis had predicted, those managers in the high power condition devalued the worth of their subordinates. They not only evaluated the quality of their employees' work as significantly poorer, but also preferred to maintain greater social distance from them.

Similarly, Lindskold and Aronoff (1980) found that in a prisoner's dilemma game, participants given greater power were significantly more deceitful, often competing after promising to cooperate. They also were substantially more exploitive, continuing to compete with partners who consistently cooperated than were those with equal or lower power. Thus, once again, power appeared to have exerted a corrupting influence.

Finally, Bargh, Pryor and colleagues (Bargh & Raymond, 1995; Bargh et al., 1995; Pryor, 1987; Pryor, LaVite, & Stoller, 1993; Pryor & Stoller, 1994) investigated the role that situational power may play in the harassment of women. Pryor (1987) found that men who scored high on a likelihood to sexually harass scale indeed took advantage of being placed in situations of power over a female confederate by behaving in sexually inappropriate ways. Further, men who scored high on this scale were more likely to overestimate the frequency with which words related to sex and words related to power were paired (Pryor & Stoller, 1994); Bargh et al. (1995) similarly found that scores on a likelihood to sexually aggress scale were significantly correlated with an automatic association between power and sex. Indeed after being subliminally primed with power, men scoring high on this scale reported finding a female confederate more attractive. Thus, once again, power and exploitive behavior appear to be strongly linked.

POWER DOES NOT INEVITABLY LEAD TO EXPLOITATION

The results of the above studies, as well as numerous others (e.g., Copeland, 1994; Schopler et al., 1991; Tjosvold & Sagaria, 1978) seem to favor the widespread belief in the corrupting influence of power. But is this influence inevitable? We challenge the Actonian dogma that power inevitably corrupts those who possess it. Indeed, even in the examples given above, a portion of the participants refused to derogate their underlings or exploit their own power. For example, only 4 of the 11 guards in the Stanford Prison Experiment abused their power to any great extent (Haney, Banks, & Zimbardo, 1973). In the Kipnis (1972) study, all participants were arguably placed into positions of power (all were supervisors, were paid more than subordinates, and were instructed that their role was to maintain efficiency among the workers), but it was only individuals who were encouraged to take destructive action (those told that they could fire or transfer employees) that derogated their subordinates. Furthermore, even in the destructive power group, roughly 30% showed little derogation or social distance from subordinates.

Likewise, Lindskold and Aronoff (1980) discarded the data from 21 of their 96 participants because these 21 individuals cooperated across all trials of the game. This is particularly compelling, because all participants in the study were told that their objective was to "get as many points for themselves as possible," yet over one fifth of participants refused to maximize personal gain at another's expense.

Finally the program of research concerning sexual harassment by Bargh and colleagues (e.g., Bargh et al., 1995) showed that the vast majority of men do not have an automatic linkage with sex and power, and thus do not exploit power over a female subordinate. Additionally, in their focus upon the causal role of the goals that are activated in power situations, they explicitly foreshadowed the possibility that power may sometimes be wielded for benevolent ends (see Lee-Chai, Chen, & Chartrand, this volume).

CONFUCIUS, 'JEN', AND THE BENEVOLENT USE OF POWER

Treat others as if their hearts were your own
—Confucius (tr. Hinton, 1998, p. 176).

It is probable that humans have wrestled with the issues of power and corruption from the earliest days of social organization. Some of the first recorded considerations of these issues are found in the teachings of Confucius.[1] Confucius lived and taught in the years after the Chou overthrow of the Shang dynasty. The Shang emperors had ruled by virtue of their lineage, claiming ancestry back to Shang-Ti (the Celestial Lord). In contrast, the Chou emperors argued the right to rule depended fundamentally upon actions rather than lineage, thus imbuing power with an ethical imperative. With the new social order came new challenges: How should society be reinvented? So many intellectuals attempted to answer this question that the period became known as the golden age of Chinese philosophy, and Confucius emerged as a dominant influence.

Two centuries before Plato discussed how to craft a just society, Confucius proposed that a society must work for the benefit of all members rather than for the benefit of its rulers. Five centuries before the Sermon on the Mount, Confucius advised his students to treat others as the self. Importantly, Confucius saw himself as neither moral philosopher nor religious leader but was instead driven by a political mission.[2] Thus, the teachings of Confucius were largely pragmatic, educating future civil servants in the conduct of proper government through the teaching of appropriate social behavior. As such, his writings traverse banal issues of fashion (e.g., length of "gentlemanly" nightgowns) and etiquette (e.g., how much one should eat at a funeral), as well as more difficult topics such as how to rule in such a way that citizens would internalize the norms of society.

At the heart of Confucian teachings was the concept of "jen," the quality that was absolutely necessary for the benevolent use of power. Jen has been translated in different texts variously as "goodness," "compassion," "love for humanity," "empathy," and even "virtue"[3] but importantly, jen does not strongly pertain to individual morality; it is a characteristic that can not be possessed in isolation. Instead, to understand the concept of jen one must understand Confucius' central tenet, that "society is a weave of human relationships" (Hinton, 1998, p. xxi). Jen characterizes a type of selfless caring within these relationships. Indeed, the Chinese character for jen is made up of two elements, that for "human" and that for "two," or, in other words, "humanity in relation." Thus, it is a characteristic that can only be present in one's dealings with others.

It is jen that is expressed in the Confucian sentiment that one should treat others as the self, and this, combined with "te," or living virtuously, would lead to a better society. He argued that the cultivation of jen would naturally lead to an inability to exploit or abuse others, because jen instantiates a reciprocal bond, similar to a psychological contract between individuals to act in the common good.

Confucius was not a radical in terms of the structure of government, indeed he remained a staunch supporter of the existing governmental system with a ruling class. Instead, he was a revolutionary in terms of the attitudes of government, believing that the ruling class should consist of those educated to cultivate the characteristics of jen and te rather than the well-born or wealthy. Because of this belief, he opened his school for members of all classes—rich and poor alike—and placed many well-trained students into positions of power. His texts were used to educate civil servants and administrators for over two thousand years. In fact, it wasn't until he came to be reviled during the Cultural Revolution that his teachings ceased to form the basis for the Chinese educational system. In the past 50 years of the Chinese government, his notions concerning the cultivation of the self in order to ensure the benevolent use of power have fallen out of favor.

However, might Confucian ideas concerning power and benevolence be worthy of continued exploration? Is it possible that power tempered by jen may indeed resist corruption? This question is obviously difficult to determine empirically, given the ambiguities of translating such a concept into operational terms. However, the closest approximation of jen in modern psychological thought can be explored, by drawing parallels with the construct of an interdependent self-construal.

PARALLELS BETWEEN JEN AND INTERDEPENDENCE

The notion of interdependence has received considerable attention in recent years, primarily as a descriptor of the self-construals of members of Asian, Indian, and Latin American cultures (Markus & Kitayama, 1991; Triandis, 1989). Markus and Kitayama (1991) proposed that one important way in which self-definition varies across cultures was the extent to which individuals construe the self as fundamentally separated from or embedded within a larger social whole. Independent self-construals, typical of members of European and North American cultures, define the self in terms of attributes, preferences, and traits that in combination describe a unique and autonomous individual. In contrast, interdependent self-construals focus upon the relationships and roles the individual plays in society. Thus, interdependent self-construal represents the self-in-relation rather than a unique and bounded inner self.

Additionally, Markus and Kitayama (1991) proposed that the distinction between an independent and interdependent self-construal has consequences considerably beyond self-description; that these differences in self-construal reflect and promote an entire system of self-regulation. The fundamental motives of the independent self are proposed to be vastly different from those of the interdependent self. For example, an independent sense of self was thought to encourage the pursuit of one's own goals and the expression of one's unique identity. An interdependent self, in contrast, was thought to encourage the promotion of others' goals, and lead self-expression to take a backseat to belonging. Thus, both the notion of the interdependent self as self-in relation, and the alteration of social thought and behavior to focus outward rather than inward seem to capture important elements of jen or humanity in relation. Indeed, Markus and Kitayama (1991) note that in research concerning the interdependent self and its mandates for social behavior "one can see the clear imprint of the Confucian emphasis on both interrelatedness and kindness" (p. 228).

The influence of independent versus interdependent self-construals upon social thought and behavior has been studied primarily through cross-cultural comparison, and this paradigm has been a fruitful one in describing the important role these self-views play in cultural differences in social behavior (see Fiske et al., 1998, for review). Reliable individual differences have also been found which characterize the dominant self-views of individuals within cultures (Singelis, 1994; Triandis et al., 1985). Additionally, it appears that thinking of the self-in relation may be a characteristic of certain intimate relationships (Aron et al., 1991) or important group memberships (Smith & Henry, 1996).

Gardner, Gabriel, and Lee (1999) argued that because of the universality of the basic needs for both autonomy and belonging, independent and interdependent self-construals should coexist in every individual regardless of culture, to be used adaptively in different social situations. In other words, thinking of the self as interdependent is prevalent in Western as well as Eastern culture. Indeed, the self has been shown to expand rather fluidly to incorporate close others and group memberships in response to interdependence cues (Brewer & Gardner, 1996; Gardner, Brewer, & Pickett, 2000; Trafimow, Triandis, & Goto, 1991; Trafimow et al., 1997). Further, interdependence priming appears to alter basic self-regulation processes (Lee, Aaker, & Gardner, 2000), values (Gardner et al., 1999), and social judgment and decision making (Gardner & Gabriel, 2000; Ybarra & Trafimow, 1998). This chapter now investigates these differing self-views upon the use and abuse of power.

INTERDEPENDENT SELF-CONSTRUAL AND POWER

Across these different methods, either as a chronically activated construct due to cultural or individual differences, or as a temporarily activated construct due to situation or prime, the influence of thinking of the self as interdependent upon the use of power emerges. For example, not all individuals high in nPower appear equally prone to the destructive aspects of power motivation. Indeed, one relatively robust finding in the literature is that the level of nPower predicts positive aspects of power (e.g., leadership roles, career aspirations) equally well for both sexes, but is only a significant predictor of the use of power for exploitation in men (Stewart & Chester, 1982; Stewart & Winter, 1974; Winter, 1988). It has been shown that women in Western culture are socialized to develop a more interdependent self-construal, particularly one that emphasizes bonds with close others (Gabriel & Gardner, 1999). Could this type of interdependence buffer women from the more exploitive aspects of nPower? Answers may be found in cross-cultural data concerning the development of the power motive (Whiting & Whiting, 1975). Two distinct types of power motives emerge: egoistic power associated with aggression and dominance, and nurturant power associated with helping others. More importantly, the types of power were highly associated with socialization practices—individuals encouraged to emphasize individuality and achievement displayed greater egoistic power, whereas those encouraged to develop a more interdependent sense of family relationships displayed greater nurturant power. Importantly, it is precisely these socialization differences in Western culture that have been proposed to underlie gender differences in relational interdependence (Cross & Madson, 1997; Gabriel & Gardner, 1999).

Winter (1988) pursued socialization differences to explain the gender differences in the prediction of nPower and positive (e.g., leadership) versus negative expressions of power (e.g., aggression, exploitation of others). He reanalyzed three sets of data concerning nPower, using socialization that might encourage the development of an interdependent sense of self (e.g., repeated responsibility for close, less powerful others such as one's own children or younger siblings) as a moderator variable. The results overwhelmingly supported the role of socialization; for both sexes the presence of these types of interdependence focused experiences led to a stronger relationship between nPower and positive aspects of the power motive, whereas the absence of these types of experiences led to a stronger relationship between nPower and negative aspects of the power motive (Winter, 1988). His results thus suggest that even those highly motivated by power may be prevented from exploiting their power through encouraging greater responsibility for others.

More direct evidence emerges from manipulations of interdependence in the laboratory. Gardner, Gabriel, and Lee (1999) primed participants with independent or interdependent self-primes (e.g., the word "I" vs. "we") and then measured self-construals, values, and judgments of social obligations. Results revealed that those primed with interdependence defined themselves in a more socially embedded fashion by referring to relationships and groups more often in their self-construals than those primed with independence (who referred more often to traits and preferences). Participants primed with interdependence also endorsed more collective values (e.g., belongingness, family, safety) whereas those primed with independence endorsed more individualist values (e.g., freedom, independence). Finally, participants were more likely to express the belief that helping others was a social obligation after interdependence priming. This pattern of data suggests that priming with interdependence encourages greater inclusion of others into the self, and increases concern for others, but is insufficient to argue that it may invite more benevolent uses of power. However, included among the values inventory (but not previously analyzed) were two values that seem to closely correspond to Winter's (1988) negative and positive expressions of power. Thus, the data was re-examined by the current authors to investigate whether priming the interdependent self might alter the endorsements given to these two values which were labeled "social power (control over others)" and "social justice (care for the weak)." A 2 × 2 (Prime × Value) ANOVA revealed a main effect of value, $F(1,87) = 55.90, p < .01$, showing that, in general, participants placed greater emphasis on social justice ($M = 5.03$) than social power ($M = 3.04$). Additionally, an interaction consistent with the current thesis also emerged, $F(1,87) = 6.74, p < .05$ (Figure 14.1).

Thus, there is evidence in both naturalistic investigations (Winter, 1988) and laboratory experiments (Gardner, Gabriel, & Lee, 1999) that thinking of the self in an interdependent fashion may shift the use of power to prosocial ends. To the extent that construing the self in this way may be seen as a proxy for jen, Confucian assumptions about the influence of jen upon the benevolent use of power appear supported. The possible cognitive mediators of these effects are now explored. Why would defining the self as fundamentally related to others alter the use and abuse of power?

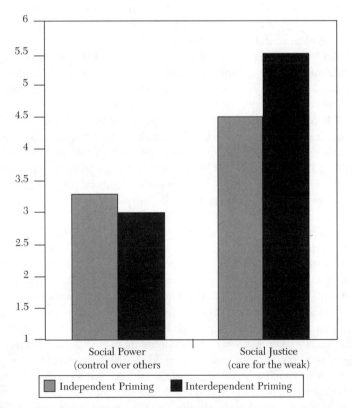

FIGURE 14.1. Values related to negative/exploitive versus positive/nurturant power as a function of independent and interdependent self-primes.

INTERDEPENDENCE, GOALS, AND SELF-EVALUATION

> *Serve first and let rewards follow as they will . . . If you*
> *want to reach a goal, help others reach their goals . . . this*
> *is the method of jen.*
> —Confucius (tr. Hinton, 1998, p. 62)

One mandate of jen is that the desires of the individual become less important than the needs of others in society. Indeed, when one considers the historical figures that are renowned for using power for benevolent ends (e.g., Augustus, Gandhi, Lincoln), one commonality that emerges is that they viewed power as an opportunity for service, utilizing their power as individuals to pursue the betterment of others. Recent work by Chen, Lee-Chai, and Bargh (1999) directly examined the function of self-interest versus social responsibility goals and power related behavior. Building upon the prior work of Bargh et al. (1995) they argued that whenever power is activated, associated goals are activated as well. It is the nature of these goals that will then determine whether power will have a corrupting or ennobling influence.

Chen and her colleagues (Chen, Lee-Chai, & Bargh, 1999) hypothesized that the types of goals that are activated in a power-holding situation will differ as a function of the chronic goals and concerns of the individuals involved. They argued that being placed in a position of power could activate social responsibility goals, or alternatively could activate self-interest goals, depending on the relationship orientation of the powerful individual. Relationship orientation refers to internalized rules for the giving and receiving of benefits in relationships (Mills & Clark, 1994). Individuals high in communal orientation benefit others as a function of their needs, whereas those high in exchange orientation benefit others as a function of expected reciprocity. Chen and her colleagues (Chen et al., 1999) hypothesized that being placed in a position of power should enhance these tendencies through the activation of social responsibility goals in communal oriented participants and self-interest goals in exchange oriented counterparts. As expected, they found that high communals who were subtly primed with power and then given the opportunity to abuse that power (e.g., by distributing time consuming tasks to the self and a partner) were more fair than their low communal (high exchange) counterparts, and indeed more fair than high communals placed in a low power situation. Similarly, Lee-Chai and Bargh (1999) found that communals and exchange individuals diverged even more with increased time in power. They examined individuals placed in a supervisory position across a ten week period, and found that whereas exchange participants' scores upon a Power Abuse Index increased across the ten weeks, communal participants' scores decreased. Thus, there appears to be ample evidence that individuals who differ in relationship orientation differ strongly in the goals that are associated with power. Moreover, the activation of these goals in a power-holding situation clearly alters the behavioral responses to power; in both of these studies, the subsequent behaviors of powerful exchange-oriented participants displayed greater self-interest than their more communally oriented counterparts.

It is likely that holding a relatively interdependent self-construal may be similar to communal relationship orientation in the goals that may become activated in a power-holding situation. For example, Fiske (1992) has shown that cultures that strongly encourage interdependence endorse communal sharing (benefits given according to need) as the dominant means of social interaction. In contrast, cultures stressing independence endorse market pricing (benefits given in exchange for other benefits). Thus, interdependence and the goal of social responsibility encouraged by communal orientations may go hand in hand. Indeed, Markus and Kitayama (1991) argued that a fundamental difference between then independent and interdependent self was the extent to which one's goals were oriented towards individual or group benefit. Finally, within American culture, the extent to which a close other is included in the self (one aspect of interdependence) has been shown to be strongly related to communal orientation and related goals within that relationship (Aron, Aron, & Smollan, 1992).

There is also recent direct evidence that holding an interdependent self-construal leads to a heightened pursuit of the goals of others. For example, Gardner and Gabriel (1999) subtly primed participants with independence or interdependence and then asked them to rate situations in which their own goals were pitted against the goals of close others or a collective. Participants primed with interdependence reported higher behavioral intentions to pursue the goals of both the close others and the collective at the expense of their own goals, whereas the reverse was true for participants primed with independence. Similarly, Trafimow and Finlay (1996) reported that individuals with a stronger interdependent self were more likely to engage in a wide variety of behaviors as a function of what they believed others wanted. For individuals with an independent sense of self, however, behaviors were driven by internal desires.

To the extent that the goals of the interdependent individual become attuned toward communal purposes, standards for self-evaluation and satisfaction should also be focused outward. In other words, such individuals should gain satisfaction through the promotion of others' welfare as much as through the promotion of their own. Gardner, Gabriel, and Hochschild (in press) found that this was indeed the case. Capitalizing on the robust "frog-pond" effect in which individuals have been shown to prefer outshining others in the group (Marsh, 1987), they used a paradigm that pit the achievements of an individual against the achievements of the student body. As expected, they found that participants primed with independence responded negatively to group achievement if they themselves were not doing well. Moreover, their affect was correlated with their own sense of individual achievement on the task. In contrast, participants primed with interdependence responded positively to group achievement, even when they did poorly as individuals. The correlation between individual achievement and affect in this group was nonsignificant, presumably because their affective responses were based as much on the group's performance as their own.

In combination, the results of the above studies strongly support the Confucian hypothesis that jen requires a transformation of motives. When thinking of the self as interdependent, self-interest may take a backseat to service. And, as Chen, Lee-Chai, and Bargh (1999) demonstrated (see also Lee-Chai, Chen, & Chartrand, this volume), under the influence of power, the goal of social responsibility can become even more potent.

INTERDEPENDENCE AND PERSPECTIVE TAKING

> *When the ruler takes interest in the welfare of his subjects,*
> *he will inspire respect . . . sharing and sympathizing with*
> *their opinions—this is how the ruler inspires harmony*
> —Confucius (tr. Yutang, 1938, pp. 120–121)

A major problem with power that has been repeatedly identified in the literature is the disinclination of the powerful to take the perspective of subordinates (Brewer, 1982; Copeland, 1994; Fiske, 1993; Kipnis, 1972; Sheldon & Johnson, 1993; Tjosveold & Sagaria, 1978). For example, Brewer (1982) persuasively argued that the perspective of the powerful is naturally different from that of the subordinate, as the powerful person is less conscious of the constraints on behavior faced by the less powerful. These differences in perspective can lead, in turn, to divergent perceptions of social interactions as well as potentially to problematic behaviors such as sexual attention that the powerful individual does not perceive as undesired.

Perhaps more troublesome, research has shown that powerful individuals often appear relatively unmotivated to correct for these biases. Sheldon and Johnson (1993) demonstrated that individuals with higher levels of power strivings report taking the perspective of another significantly less in their everyday lives. Similarly, Tjosvold and Sagaria (1978) assigned participants to one of five levels of power and found that as power increased, interest in the perspective of the other decreased.

Susan Fiske (1993, see also Fiske, this volume) has persuasively argued that one way power disrupts perspective taking is through biasing processing toward more top-down and stereotype consistent strategies. This bias in social perception can obviously have important consequences for the relatively powerless targets. In an ingenious study by Copeland (1994), participants were given a false expectancy about the relative extroversion of an interaction partner before being placed in a high or low power position. His results revealed that not only did the more powerful member of a dyad report more expectancy confirming impressions, but that these expectancies were confirmed behaviorally in the interaction by the less powerful partner. Thus, the biased processing in the powerful member of the dyad actually altered the behavior of the less powerful.

Not everyone falls prey to these effects, however, and once again, interdependence appears to play a key role. Markus and Kitayama (1991) argued that one major task of the interdependent self was to take the role of the other as a means of maintaining connection.

And indeed, individuals who display stronger nurturance or intimacy strivings report greater perspective taking in their daily lives (Sheldon & Johnson, 1993). Additionally, cross-cultural investigations of perspective taking have revealed that in cultures that encourage interdependent self-construals, more monitoring of others' thoughts and behaviors takes place (e.g., Gudykunst, Gao & Franklyn-Stokes, 1996; Lee, Aaker, & Gardner, in press).

The causal role of interdependent self-construals in perspective taking was examined in a recent study by Gardner and Le (2000). Gardner and Le (2000) first presented participants with persuasive messages concerning two proposed solutions to parking problems on campus. One message was written such that two-thirds of the arguments were pretested as weak and therefore easy to counterargue (e.g., a reserved parking space would become a source of pride, causing students to keep the surrounding area free of litter), and one-third were strong (e.g., Reserved spaces would eliminate missed classes due to parking difficulties). The other message consisted of two-thirds strong and one-third weak argument. Participants read the messages and endorsed a proposal. They were then primed with independence or interdependence as part of a test of "verbal ability," before being told that they would discuss the parking issue with another participant who had selected the opposing proposal. Participants were given five minutes to prepare for the discussion, and were told to list all of their thoughts during this time. Perspective taking was measured in two ways. First, all participants were asked to estimate how much time they intended to spend listening to their partner versus how much time they intended to spend arguing. Second, the thought listings were coded to examine what the participants were doing to prepare for the discussion. Both measures supported hypotheses. Participants primed with interdependence reported significantly higher behavioral intentions to listen to their partner, and more compellingly, listed a larger number of thoughts considering the other's position (e.g., listing strong arguments from the opposing proposal, and weak arguments from their own).

In summary, the damaging effects of power on perspective taking may be ameliorated by maintaining a more interdependent view of the self. The results of the above studies imply that thinking of the self as fundamentally connected does indeed encourage sympathizing with the opinions of others.

INTERDEPENDENCE AND RECIPROCAL TRUST

> *The world once was a common state, but now . . . each man*
> *acquires his own goods and labors for his benefit alone*
> —Confucius (tr. Yutang, 1938, p. 227)

This chapter began with a discussion of the high level of mistrust in modern American society. Although the polls we cited concerned mistrust in government, there is ample evidence that mistrust also characterizes perceptions and dealings with employers and corporations, local institutions (e.g., churches, schools) and even fellow citizens and neighbors (Bellah et al., 1991). As a result of these misgivings, few invest in larger society. Proposals of universal health care, of environmental preservation, even of the strengthening of the public school system are often met with vigorous objection. This reluctance to sacrifice for the greater good has been traced to mistrust; individuals look out for themselves, because they believe that no one else will (Bellah et al., 1991).

The tendency for individuals to protect their singular interests in the face of collective need has been called the Tragedy of the Commons (Hardin, 1968). Although this issue has not often been framed in terms of power, at its heart is the notion of individuals acting as if they each have the privilege to exploit access to collective resources. Indeed, higher nPower predicts greater exploitation in mixed motive games (Winter, 1973), as does higher situational power (Lindskold & Aronoff, 1980; Schopler et al., 1991).

To the extent that one cannot trust the actions of others in a social dilemma, self-protection and exploitation may appear rational at the individual level. Of course, if trust can be maintained, better outcomes result for all involved (see Pruitt, 1998 for review). One way trust has been built in the laboratory is through encouraging communication about the upcoming dilemma, in this way, explicit promises increase confidence that others will behave toward the common good (e.g., Kerr & Kaufman-Gililand, 1994). Additionally, allowing group members to establish a social contract to behave well (e.g., through the establishment of group rules for behavior; Braver, 1995) has also been shown to be highly effective in increasing both trust and collective behavior.

Both of these strategies may be more difficult to implement in real world dilemmas, in which neither promises nor even communication can be expected among all members of a large group. However, it is possible that reciprocal trust and concern may also be instituted as a result of an interdependent self-view. One of the most robust findings in the social dilemma literature is the role of group identity in improving group outcomes (e.g., Brewer & Kramer, 1986; Karau & Williams, 1993). David DeCramer and his colleagues (DeCramer & Van Vugt 1999; Gardner et al., 2000; Van Vugt, & DeCramer, 1999) have argued that this effect is mediated through a transformation of motives toward the collective, in which collective goals take precedent over personal goals. Specifically, they argue that this transformation of motives rests upon a self-view that is fundamentally entwined with the larger whole. Indeed, the effects upon perceived trust and goals as well as upon collective behavior have been replicated with self-primes and individual differences in interdependence, as well as with explicit group identity manipulations (see also Earley, 1993 for a cultural analysis of social dilemmas).

FINAL THOUGHTS

*It is only he who has recognized his absolute self that can
adjust the relations of human society . . . devote yourself to
strange doctrines and principles, and there is sure to be
suffering for all.*

—Confucius (tr. Yutang, 1938, p. 131)

Does power lead to corruption? The purpose of this chapter was not to show that it doesn't *ever*, but rather to suggest that it doesn't *always*. Lord Acton's statement about the inherent evil of power does not have to be accepted as a law, but as a choice. For some, power permits selfish gain; for others, power encourages nobler pursuits. One factor that may determine the directional influence of power is the way in which the powerful construe their place in the broader social context. Possessing an interdependent self-construal appears capable of buffering the less desirable consequences of power, indeed even capable of biasing power towards benevolent ends. Confucius argued that jen would act as a natural deterrent to the abuse of power, through encouraging a psychological contract with others in the social sphere, a type of internal understanding to treat others as one would treat the self. Importantly, he also firmly believed that jen was a way of being that could be cultivated through education.

Interestingly, modern research may now be providing support for Confucian notions. The work reviewed here and elsewhere in this volume demonstrates that the goals and values of powerful individuals may sometimes be attuned toward the benefit of others, and that these motives are shaped through early experiences with responsibility as well as through cultural norms. Moreover, construing the self as interdependent is as possible now as it was two thousand years ago; society may still be understood as Confucius portrayed it—as a complex weave of human relationships. Regardless of how the norms of current American society encourage us to emphasize our own independence and autonomy, the truth is that we are all inextricably bound to countless others; we are embedded within families, neighborhoods, communities, and nations. It was Confucius' fervent belief that the recognition and internalization of these bonds would lead to a better society through encouraging the use of power for collective ends.

REFERENCES

Anderson, K. B., Cooper, H., & Okamura, L. (1997). Individual differences and attitudes toward rape: A meta-analytic review. *Personality and Social Psychology Bulletin, 23,* 295–315

Aron, A., Aron, E. A., & Smollan, D. (1992). Inclusion of Other in the Self Scale and the structure of interpersonal closeness. *Journal of Personality & Social Psychology, 63,* 596–612.

Aron, A., Aron, E. A., Tudor, M., & Nelson, G. (1991). Close relationships as including other in the self. *Journal of Personality & Social Psychology, 60,* 241–253.

Aron, A., Aron, E. A., & Smollan, D. (1992). Inclusion of Other in the Self Scale and the structure of interpersonal closeness. *Journal of Personality & Social Psychology, 63,* 596–612.

Bargh, J. A. & Raymond, P. (1995). The naïve misuse of power: Nonconscious sources of sexual harassment. *Journal of Social Issues, 51,* 85–96.

Bargh, J. A., Raymond, P., Pryor, J., & Strack, F. (1995). Attractiveness of the underling: An automatic power–sex association and its consequences for sexual harassment and aggression. *Journal of Personality and Social Psychology, 68,* 768–781.

Bellah, R. N., Madsen, R., Sullivan, W. M., Swidler, A., & Tipton, S. M. (1991). *The Good Society.* New York, NY: Vintage.

Black, T. E., & Higbee, K. L. (1973). Effects of power, threat, and sex on exploitation. *Journal of Personality and Social Psychology, 27,* 382–388.

Braver, S. (1995). Social contracts and the provision of public goods. In D. Schroeder (Ed.) *Social dilemmas: Perspectives on individuals and groups.* (pp. 69–86). Westport, CT: Prager.

Brewer, M. B. (1982). Further beyond nine-to-five: An integration and future directions. *Journal of Social Issues, 38,* 149–157.

Brewer, M. B., & Gardner, W. L. (1996). Who is this 'we'? Levels of collective identity and self representations. *Journal of Personality and Social Psychology, 71,* 83–93.

Brewer, M. B., & Kramer, R. M. (1986). Choice behavior in social dilemmas: Effects of social identity, group size, and decision framing. *Journal of Personality and Social Psychology, 50,* 543–547.

Chen, S., Lee-Chai, A. Y., & Bargh, J. A. (1999). *Does power always corrupt? Relationship orientation as a moderator of the effects of social power.* Manuscript submitted for publication.

Confucius, (1998). *The analects,* trans. D. Hinton. Washington, DC: Counterpoint.

Confucius. (1938). *The wisdom of Confucius,* trans. L. Yutang. New York: Modern Library.

Copeland, J. T. (1994). Prophecies of power: Motivational implications of social power for behavioral confirmation. *Journal of Personality and Social Psychology, 67,* 264–277.

Cross, S. E., & Madson, L. (1997). Models of the self: Self-construals and gender. *Psychological Bulletin, 122,* 5–37.

DeCramer, D., & Van Vugt, M. (1999). Social identification effects in social dilemmas: A transformation of motives. *European Journal of Social Psychology, 29,* 871–893.

Earley, P. C. (1993). East meets West meets Mideast: Further explorations of individualistic and collectivistic workgroups. *Academy of Management Journal, 36,* 319–348.

The federalist papers. (1788). Available at http://lcweb2.loc.gov/const/fed/abt_fedpapers.html.

Fiske, A. P. (1992). The four elementary forms of sociality: Framework for a unified theory of social relations. *Psychological Review, 99,* 689–723.

Fiske, A. P., Kitayama, S., Markus, H. R., & Nisbett, R. E. (1998). The cultural matrix of social psychology. In D.Gilbert, S.Fiske, & G. Lindzey (Eds.), *The Handbook of Social Psychology, Volume 2,* 915–981.

Fiske, S. T. (1993). Controlling other people: The impact of power on stereotyping. *American Psychologist, 48,* 621–628

Fiske, A. P., Kitayama, S., Markus, H. R., & Nisbett, R. E. (1998). The cultural matrix of social psychology. In D. Gilbert, S. Fiske, & G. Lindzey (Eds.), *The handbook of social psychology* (Vol. 2, pp. 915–981). New York: Oxford University Press.

Fodor, E. M. (1984). The power motive and reactivity to power stressors. *Journal of Personality and Social Psychology, 42,* 853–859.

Fodor, E. M., & Farrow, D. L. (1979). The power motive as an influence on the use of power. *Journal of Personality and Social Psychology, 37,* 2091–2097.

Fodor, E. M., & Smith, T. (1982). The power motive as influence on group decision making. *Journal of Personality and Social Psychology, 42,* 178–185.

Gabriel, S., & Gardner, W.L. (1999). Are there 'his' and 'her' aspects of interdependence? Gender differences in collective versus relational interdependence. *Journal of Personality and Social Psychology, 77,* 642–655.

The Gallop Poll. (1999). Honesty & ethics poll. Available at http://www.pollingreport.com/institut.htm

Gardner, W. L., Brewer, M. B., & Pickett, C. A. (2000). Social exclusion and selective memory: How the "need to belong" influences memory for social events. *Personality and Social Psychology Bulletin, 26,* 486–496.

Gardner, W. L., DeCramer, D., Gabriel, S., & Kelly, M. (2000). *One for all: Interdependent self-construals motivate collective behavior.* Manuscript submitted for publication.

Gardner, W. L., & Gabriel, S. (1999). *The individual as "melting pot": The flexibility of self-construal and worldview among Asian and European Americans.* Manuscript submitted for publication.

Gardner, W. L., Gabriel, S., & Hochschild, L. (in press). When you and I are "we," you are no longer threatening: The role of self-expansion in social comparison processes. *Journal of Personality and Social Psychology.*

Gardner, W. L., Gabriel, S., & Lee, A. Y. (1999). 'I' value freedom, but 'we' value relationships: Self-construal priming mimics cultural differences in judgment. *Psychological Science, 4,* 321–326.

Gardner, W. L., & Le, J. (2000). *The role of interdependence in active versus reactive control strategies.* Manuscript in preparation.

Haney, C., Banks, C., & Zimbardo, P. (1973). Interpersonal dynamics in a simulated prison. *International Journal of Criminology and Penology, 1,* 69–97.

Karau, S. J., & Williams, K. D. (1993). Social loafing: A meta-analytic review and theoretical integration. *Journal of Personality and Social Psychology, 65,* 681–706.

Kerr, N., & Kaufman-Gilliland, C. (1994). Communication, commitment, and cooperation in social dilemmas. *Journal of Personality and Social Psychology, 66,* 513–529.

Kipnis, D. (1972). Does power corrupt? *Journal of Personality and Social Psychology, 24,* 33–41.

Lee, A. Y., Aaker, J., & Gardner, W. L. (2000). The pleasures and pains of distinct self-construals: The role of interdependence in regulatory focus. *Journal of Personality and Social Psychology.*

Lee-Chai, A. Y., & Bargh, J.,A. (1999). *Letting power go to your head: Long-term behavioral effects of social power depend on interpersonal orientation.* Manuscript submitted for publication.

Lindskold, S., & Aronoff, J.,R. (1980). Conciliatory strategies and relative power. *Journal*

of Experimental Social Psychology, 16, 187–198.

Madison, J. (1788). *Federalist no. 41: General view of the powers conferred by the constitution.* Available at http://lcweb2.loc.gov/const/fed/fed_41.html.

Madison, J. (1788). *Federalist no. 51: The structure of the government must furnish the proper checks and balances between the different departments.* Available at http://lcweb2.loc.gov/const/fed/fed_51.html.

Markus, H. R., & Kitayama, S. (1991). Culture and the self: Implications for cognition, emotion, and motivation. *Psychological Review, 98,* 224–253.

Markus, H. R., Kitayama, S., & Heiman, R. J. (1997). Culture and "basic" psychological principles. In E. T. Higgins & A. W. Kruglanski (Eds.), *Social psychology: Handbook of basic principles* (pp. 857–914.) New York: Guilford.

Marsh, H. W. (1987). The big frog little pond effect on academic self-concept. *Journal of Educational Psychology, 79,* 280–295.

Mason, A., & Blankenship, V. (1987). Power and affiliation motivation, stress, and abuse in intimate relationships. *Journal of Personality and Social Psychology, 52,* 203–210.

McClelland, D. (1975). *Power: The inner experience.* New York: Irvington.

Mills, J., & Clark, M. S. (1994). Communal and exchange relationships: Controversies and research. In R. Erber & R. Gilmour (Eds.), *Theoretical frameworks for personal relationships* (pp. 29–42). Hillsdale, NJ: Erlbaum.

Pruitt, D. G. (1998). Social conflict. In D. Gilbert, S. Fiske, & G. Lindzey (Eds.), *The Handbook of Social Psychology, Volume 2,* 470–503.

Pryor, J. B. (1987). Sexual harassment proclivities in men. *Sex Roles, 17,* 269–290.

Pryor, J. B., Giedd, J. L., & Williams, K. B. (1995). A social psychological model for predicting sexual harassment. *Journal of Social Issues, 51,* 69–84.

Pryor, J. B., LaVite, C. M., & Stoller, L. M. (1993). A social psychological analysis of sexual harrassment: The person/situation interaction. *Journal of Vocational Behavior, 42,* 68–83.

Pryor, J. B., & Stoller, L. M. (1994). Sexual cognition processes in men high in the likelihood to sexually harass. *Personality and Social Psychology Bulletin, 20,* 163–169.

Schopler, J., Insko, C. A., Graetz, K. A., Drigotas, S. M., & Smith, V. A. (1991). The generality of the individual-group discontinuity effect: Variations in positivity-negativity of outcomes, players relative power, and magnitude of outcomes. *Personality and Social Psychology Bulletin, 17,* 612–624.

Sheldon, K. M., & Johnson, J. T. (1993). Forms of social awareness: Their frequency and correlates. *Personality and Social Psychology Bulletin, 19,* 320–330.

Singelis, T. M. (1994). The measurement of independent and interdependent self-construals. *Personality and Social Psychology Bulletin, 20,* 580–591.

Smith, E. R., & Henry, S. (1996). An in-group becomes part of the self: Response time evidence. *Personality & Social Psychology Bulletin, 22,* 635–642.

Stewart, A. J., & Chester, N. L. (1982). The exploration of sex differences in human social motives: Achievement, affiliation, and power. In A. J. Stewart (Ed.), *Motivation and society* (pp. 172–218). San Francisco: Jossey-Bass.

Stewart, A. J., & Winter, D. G. (1974). Self-definition and social definition in women. *Journal of Personality, 42,* 238–259.

Tjosvold, D., & Sagaria, S. D. (1978). Effects of power on cognitive perspective taking. *Personality and Social Psychology Bulletin, 4,* 257–259.

Trafimow, D., & Finlay, K. A. (1996). The importance of subjective norms for a minority of people: Between-subjects and within-subjects analysis. *Personality and Social Psychology Bulletin, 22* 820–828.

Trafimow, D., Silverman, E. S., Fan, R. M. T., & Law, J. S. F. (1997). The effects of language and priming on the relative accessibility of the private self and the collective self. *Journal of Cross-Cultural Psychology,* 107–123.

Trafimow, D., Triandis, H. C., & Goto, S. G. (1991). Some tests of the distinction between the private self and the collective self. *Journal of Personality & Social Psychology, 60,* 649–655.

Triandis, H. C. (1989). The self and social behavior in differing cultural contexts. *Psychological Review, 96,* 506–520.

Triandis, H. C., Leung, K., Villareal, M., & Clack, F. L. (1985). Allocentric vs. idiocentric tendencies: Convergent and discriminant validation. *Journal of Research in Personality, 19,* 395–415.

Van Vugt, M., & DeCramer, D. (1999). Leadership in social dilemmas: The efects of group identification in collective action to provide public goods. *Journal of Personality and Social Psychology, 76,* 587–599.

Veroff, J. (1957). Development and validation of a projective measure of power motivation. *Journal of Abnormal and Social Psychology, 54,* 1–8.

Whiting, B. B., & Whiting, J. W. M. (1975). *Children of six cultures: A psycho-cultural analysis.* Cambridge, MA: Harvard University Press.

Winter, D.G., Stewart, A. J., & McClelland, D. C. (1977). Husband's motives and wife's career level. *Journal of Personality and Social Psychology, 35,* 159–166.

Winter, D. G., & Stewart, A. J. (1978). The power motive. In H. London & J. Exner (Eds.), *Dimensions of personality* (pp. 532–545). New York: Wiley.

Winter, D. G. (1973). *The power motive.* New York: The Free Press.

Winter, D. G. (1988). The power motive in women and men. *Journal of Personality and Social Psychology, 54,* 510–519.

Winter, D. G. (1993). Power, affiliation, and war: Three tests of a motivational model. *Journal of Personality and Social Psychology, 65,* 532–545.

Ybarra, O., & Trafimow, D. (1998). How priming the private self or collectiveself affects the relative weights of attitudes and subjective norms. *Personality and Social Psychology Bulletin, 24,* 362–370.

15

Transparency International
Combating Corruption Through Institutional Reform

NIHAL JAYAWICKRAMA

THE PHENOMENON OF CORRUPTION

*C*orruption is a pervasive cancer which infests both the private and public sectors of society. For the purposes of this chapter, however, corruption will be regarded as "the misuse of public power for private profit."[1] In that sense, the focus is essentially on the behavior of officials in the public sector, whether politicians or civil servants, policy makers or administrators. These officials may improperly and unlawfully enrich themselves, or those close to them, by the misuse of the public power entrusted to them. The reasons why they resort to corruption are many and varied. Some may be driven to it by poverty or the inability to match their expenses to their legitimate incomes. For others, the compelling factor is obviously avarice. But whether caused by human need or human greed, corruption has a devastating effect on the governance of a country.

In one form or another, corruption exists within every state. It is a global phenomenon; not one peculiar to developing countries or societies in transition. The dismissal of six members of the International Olympic Committee for accepting bribes and the resignation of the Commissioners of the European Union following findings of corruption against some of them, confirm a long-held belief that this phenomenon has penetrated into international, intergovernmental, and perhaps even nongovernmental institutions and organizations. But not everyone is willing to recognize its existence. A revolution or a violent change of government is sometimes required before a country is prepared to acknowledge that endemic corruption had corroded its institutions to the core.

Other countries are quick to deal with the problem of corruption. For example, among those recently convicted of corruption were the Auditor-General of New Zealand, a French minister who received bribes from a construction and water company, and a Canadian minister who filed false expense claims. In each of these countries, the corrupt act was detected and investigated, and the corrupt official was dealt with according to law. In other words, the institutional mechanisms to combat corruption not only existed in these countries, they actually functioned. It is, therefore, not entirely a coincidence that in the annual Corruption Perception Indices that Transparency International has published since 1995, New Zealand and Canada have achieved consistently high scores for integrity, remaining among the ten least corrupt countries in the world (www.transparency.org).

Corruption involving public officials fall broadly into two categories. Conventional bribery or petty corruption occurs when an official demands or expects speed money or grease payments for doing an act that he or she is ordinarily required by law to do (such as processing an application for a licence, issuing an official document, clearing goods through customs, or providing a utility service), or when a bribe is paid to obtain a service that the official is prohibited from providing (such as tax evasion or avoidance of prosecution, or preferential access to state employment, housing, medical care, or education). A recent national household survey on corruption in Bangladesh revealed that nearly 47% of households had either made a donation or a direct payment for the admission of children into schools. Thirty-six percent had made payments to or through hospital staff or other "influential persons" to secure admission into hospitals. Sixty-five percent had bribed land registrars for recording a false lower sale price of a land transaction. Fifty-four percent had bribed either employees or other "influential persons" to secure bank loans. Thirty-three percent had paid money to obtain electricity connections, while 32% had paid less for water "by arrangement with the meter reader." Forty-seven percent had been able to reduce the holding tax assessment on house and property "by arrangement with municipal staff on payment of money." Sixty-five percent had found it impossible to obtain trade licences without money or influence. Sixty-three percent of those involved in litigation had paid bribes to either court officials or the opponents' lawyers, while 89% of those surveyed were convinced that judges were corrupt; 97% thought the police service was corrupt.[2]

"Grand corruption"[3] occurs when a person in a high position who formulates government policy or is able to influence government decision-making, seeks, as a quid quo pro, payment, usually off-shore and in foreign currency, for exercising the extensive discretionary powers vested in him or her. Grand corruption plays a significant role in four main categories of supply to government: the purchase of aircraft, ships, and military supplies, including telecommunications; the purchase of capital goods required for major industrial and agroindustrial projects; major civil engineering contracts, such as dams, bridges, highways, airports, and hospitals; and the ongoing purchase of bulk supplies, such as oil, fertilizers, and cement, where distribution is through a parastatal company, or where there is a need for standardization, such as repeat orders for pharmaceuticals and school textbooks.[4]

There are several reasons for bribing an official. First, a firm may pay to be included in the list of prequalified bidders and to restrict the size of the list. Second, the firm may pay for inside information. Third, a bribe may induce the official to structure the bidding specifications so that the corrupt firm is the only qualified supplier. Fourth, a firm may pay to be selected as the winning contractor. Fifth, once a firm has been selected as the contractor, it may pay to set inflated prices or to skimp on quality.[5] While the amounts involved in these transactions may range from $100,000 to $100 million, a leading commentator with experience of developing countries dismisses the possibility of a 5% commission being paid to a senior official, a permanent secretary, a minister, or a head of state, as a "laughably low rate."[6] According to the Bribe Payers Index published by Transparency International in 1999,[7] companies in China, South Korea, Taiwan, Italy, Malaysia, Japan, France, Spain, Singapore, the United States of America, Germany, and Belgium (in that order) are the most likely to pay bribes to win or retain business in the emerging markets of the world.

Governments in many of the major exporting countries actually encourage companies to bribe foreign government officials in the pursuit of business. Such encouragement is given not only by their refusal to criminalize the bribing of foreign officials unless it takes place on the soil of the country, but also by the continuing practice of many industrialized countries to permit the deduction for tax purposes of bribes paid abroad (or "commissions" as they are euphemistically labeled) as being "necessary business expenditure." A former British cabinet minister and now chairman of Cable and Wireless, Lord Young, speaking on BBC in April 1994, defended this policy.[8] "The moral problem to me," he said, "is simply jobs. If you want to be in business, you have to do it." He saw nothing immoral or corrupt in paying bribes since, in his view, the giving of gifts was part of the culture of the South. Olusegun Obasanjo, the distinguished Nigerian chief, who is now the popularly elected president of his country, was quick to respond:

> I shudder at how an integral aspect of our culture could be taken as the basis for rationalizing an otherwise despicable behaviour. In the African concept of appreciation and hospitality, the gift is usually a token. It is not demanded. The value is in the spirit rather than in the material world. It is usually done in the open and never in secret. When it is excessive, it becomes an embarrassment and it is returned. If anything, corruption has perverted and destroyed this aspect of our culture.[9]

The falsity of the assumption that corruption is part of the culture of the South has been demonstrated by the popular revolutions against corrupt administrations, whether through street uprisings or the ballot box, in Bangladesh, India, Indonesia, the Philippines, the Republic of Korea, and Sri Lanka. Syed

Hussein Alatas has explained that in Asia, traditional gifts differed from corruption because the scale was specified; because they were not secret, they did not violate the rights of the public; because they were not an embezzlement of government funds for private use; and because they provided revenue for the government.[10] Historical records suggest that even in 17th century Sri Lanka, the Dutch colonizers of its maritime provinces misconstrued the gifts that the native kings who ruled over Kandy, the central hill country, expected of them. For the Dutch, the custom of sending an ambassador with presents did not materially differ from that of a trading firm sending an agent with the cash for which privileges were purchased. The gifts were payment in lieu of cash. In the Kandyan court, however, there was no ambiguity. They were "panduru paddakam," tributes from subordinate kings, which were publicly presented at a "dakum," a "kind of durbar, theatrical in its purpose and effect, at which the ruler appeared to see his subjects and be seen by them and receive their gifts."[11]

The actual scale of corruption and the extent to which it exists in a particular country are difficult to quantify or measure in precise terms. Except for petty corruption, which many individuals may experience in the course of their daily lives, most other forms of corruption are not immediately visible. According to an official of the Asian Development Bank,[12] over the last 20 years, one East Asian country is estimated to have lost $48 billion due to corruption, surpassing its entire foreign debt of $40.6 billion; an internal report of another Asian government revealed that over the past decade, state assets had fallen by more than $50 billion, primarily due to deliberate undervaluing by corrupt officials responsible for a privatization program. In one South Asian country, recent government reports indicated that $50 million was misappropriated daily due to mismanagement and corruption, and studies of corruption in government procurement in several Asian countries had revealed that 20–100% more had been paid for goods and services. A typical example occurred in Indonesia under President Suharto. When the city of Jakarta decided to privatize its water authority, the President directed his Minister for Public Works to divide the city into two geographical units, and to award two concessions to two of the many foreign companies interested in the project. One was French, the Lyonnaise des Eaux, and the other was British, Thames Water International. The local partner of the former was a longtime Suharto business associate, and the local partner of the latter was Suhatro's eldest son. The concessions which were arbitrarily awarded were for 25 years, and of a total value in excess of $1.4 billion.

Any decision motivated by excessive greed is likely to be both irrational and short-sighted. Apart from its direct costs in terms of lost revenue[13] or the diversion of funds from their intended public use into private bank accounts,[14] the indirect costs of corruption are equally disastrous. Few suppliers will be willing to absorb the costs of corruption by reducing their own margins of profit. Instead, the price is increased or the quality of the goods or services reduced to accommodate the commission demanded.[15] On the one hand, the ordinary citizen has to contend with substandard and over-priced goods and services, inefficiency, and waste in the provision of public services, and a substantial loss in productive effort if he or she attempts to resist the demands of corrupt public officials. On the other hand, the distortion of the decision-making process results in wrong suppliers or contractors being chosen, and wholly unnecessary or inappropriate purchases being made or projects undertaken. Against a background littered with white elephants, in an environment of uncertainty, unpredictability, and declining moral values, respect for constituted authority and, therefore, the legitimacy of government, is steadily but surely eroded.[16]

TRANSPARENCY INTERNATIONAL

Transparency International (TI) is a not for profit organization incorporated under German law. Its origins lie in Africa where, in the spring of 1990, representatives of the World Bank stationed on that continent had met, in Swaziland, to discuss an urgent request articulated by African leaders in their long-term perspective study: *Support Better Governance*. The World Bank representative in Kenya, Dr. Peter Eigen, spoke of corruption as a powerful enemy of good governance. He described its enormous reach and its crippling effect on social, economic, and political development. He then proposed a plan of action that had evolved from discussions with colleagues and friends in Nairobi. Clearly, most people were against corruption. Why not, then, channel that opposition into the construction of an effective coalition promoting transparency? The initial reaction of the participants was enthusiastic. It was agreed that the World Bank should develop an anticorruption agenda for itself and for its partners, since the absence of corruption was clearly an important element of an environment conducive to development.[17]

Before long, however, doubts began to emerge about the World Bank's readiness to take the initiative. Senior officials of the Bank argued that it would constitute a violation of the political abstinence prescribed in the Bank's charter. Undeterred, Eigen and his colleagues proceeded with the venture independently of the Bank. They received an overwhelmingly positive response from a cross-section of African society, including academia, the business sector, the media, and the donor community. Corruption had become so widespread that many people had come to accept it as an unavoidable fact of life. Yet underneath that outer resignation, they found considerable hope that corruption could be contained, if not eliminated. After meetings in Eschborn (sponsored by the German Society for Technical Co-operation, the Global Coalition for Africa, and the UN Centre on Transnational Corporations), Kampala, London, and Washington D.C., and with supporters from other continents joining in the deliberations, Transparency International was conceived, and Eigen took early retirement to preside over its birth. The inaugural meeting at Villa Borsig in Berlin in May 1993 was sponsored by the German Foundation for International Development. It was attended by 70 representatives of government and government agencies, foundations, financial institutions, the private sector, academia, and the media. Participants included a head of government, a vice president, a foreign minister, an attorney-general, and a former head of state.[18]

The principal focus of the new organization was described in its first aide-memoire as 'corrupt practices which have the effect of distorting official decision-making and which impact seriously—and negatively—on the developmental processes in developing countries'.[19] Four primary objectives were also identified:

1. to erode the proverbial taboo around corruption by conducting serious, professional discussions of the subject by credible people;
2. to help articulate a consensus about the problems of corruption by defining its reality and impact, and by expressing concern about existing national and international remedies;
3. to help build a coalition against corruption by bringing together concerned partners and mobilizing resources for creating a new mechanism exclusively focusing on this problem; and
4. to stimulate media attention to the crisis of corruption, and to the damage caused by corruption, particularly in developing countries, by adding human misery to the world's poorest people.

Over the years, the organization's mission statement broadened to encompass corruption in all its forms. Its strategies were also refined. Today, the purpose of TI is "to curb corruption by mobilizing a global coalition to promote and strengthen international and national integrity systems" (Transparency International Report, 1997 [April 1997], p. 7).

COMBATING CORRUPTION

The founders of TI based their approach to combating corruption on six principles. These were to determine both the organizational structure of the new nongovernmental organization as well as the strategies which were sought to be employed both at international and national levels.

TI believes that the first principle of combatting corruption effectively, systematically, and sustainably is to adopt a holistic approach to the problem. In that respect, TI rejects conventional wisdom that dictates that corruption can best be combated through the application of the criminal law after the event. A law that criminalizes the offering and soliciting, and the giving and accepting, of a bribe, drawing no distinction between active and passive bribery, is, of course, an essential requirement. Unfortunately, in many countries, notwithstanding laws that prescribe criminal sanctions, corruption continues to flourish. While such legislation is necessary, and may eventually help to establish a value system that could contribute to the creation of an anticorruption culture in the country, containing corruption is not simply a matter of enacting laws. When laws do exist, they are not applied at all or, when they are, they tend to be directed at small fish rather than big fish, or selectively at political opponents no longer holding public office. Therefore, the mere criminalization of bribery is, in itself, inadequate and ineffective. Unlike many other forms of criminal activity, the benefits of corruption flow to those on both sides of the equation, the payer and the receiver. TI has, from the outset, argued that corruption can be contained only by limiting the situations in which it can occur and by reducing the benefits to both recipient and payer (i.e., by rendering both more vulnerable to detection and sanction). Therefore, since corruption takes place where there is a meeting of opportunity and inclination, a strategy to contain corruption must address both these elements.

Opportunity can be minimized through systemic reform using the following methods:

1. Narrowly defining the discretionary element in decision-making. Discretionary power is a powerful source of potential corruption. The wider the discretion, the greater the opportunity for corruption. While it is unrealistic to envisage, and indeed undesirable to create, a situation where the discretionary element is altogether eliminated, it is nevertheless possible to limit the scope for abuse by providing clear, public guidelines containing objective criteria for the exercise of discretion, and by instituting a swift and appropriate appeal mechanism.

2. Redesigning, if not discontinuing, the mass of rules, regulations, procedures, and formalities. This is the raw material on which corrupt officials thrive. There is a direct connection between the complexity of the organization of government and the levels of corruption within it. The more steps there are to be taken and the more approvals needed before a business can be commenced or a building constructed, the greater the number of people involved and the greater the number of gatekeepers who are able to exact a toll. Many rules and regulations serve no broad public purpose, and many procedures and formalities are unnecessarily complex and cumbersome. As Susan Rose-Ackerman observes, "If the state does not have the authority to restrict exports or licence businesses, no one will pay bribes in those areas. If a subsidy is eliminated, the bribes that accompanied it will disappear as well. If price controls are lifted, market prices will reflect scarcity values, not bribes." [20]

3. Applying of the common law principles of administrative law. These require that a public official, when exercising a discretionary power, should:

   pursue only the purposes for which the power has been conferred;
   be without bias, and observe objectivity and impartiality, taking into account only factors relevant to a particular case;
   observe the principle of equality before the law by avoiding unfair discrimination;

maintain a proper balance between any adverse effects which its decision may have on the rights, liabilities, and interests of persons and the purpose which it pursues;

take decisions within a time which is reasonable having regard to the matters at stake; and

apply any general administrative guidelines in a consistent manner while at the same time taking account of the particular circumstances of each case.[23]

The application of these principles will ensure that public officials do not exercise discretionary power vested in them by law for improper purposes, on irrelevant considerations, or unreasonably.

4. Establishing improved, readily accessible and transparent public procurement procedures. The opening of bids should be public, and all decisions should be fully recorded. Indeed, records should be maintained to explain and justify all decisions and actions, thereby ensuring accountability.

5. Creating administrative reforms that minimize the opportunities for corrupt practices. For example, by providing rival sources of supply (what Rose-Ackerman describes as "overlapping and competitive bureaucratic jurisdictions"),[20] such as establishing several offices for the issue of driving licences, the monopoly power of bureaucrats could be reduced. Similarly, the problem of disappearing records in a court registry may be solved by ensuring that authenticated records are supplied to the litigants as well.

6. Demystifying government. This is achieved by rendering the decision-making processes transparent by, for example, publishing tax collectors' handbooks, and placing the onus on a civil servant to make out a case for withholding access to a document. This process can be facilitated by the enactment of a law that enables citizens to obtain information in the possession of the state, that is, an access to information law.

7. Protecting whistleblowers. Whistleblowing is the act of reporting to an authority an illegal conduct, a violation of a code of professional ethics, or an act that endangers public health or safety. Whistleblowers serve the interests of society by encouraging lawful behavior and public accountability and, therefore, need to be protected from victimization.

8. Encouraging a meritocratic civil service. A civil service recruited on the basis of merit, adequately remunerated, and assured of career advancement solely on the basis of merit, is, of course, a sine qua non for minimizing the opportunities for corruption.

To reduce the inclination to engage in a corrupt transaction, it is necessary to strengthen the processes by which corruption is intended to be curbed. These processes constitute the integrity system of a country. It is the national integrity system that delivers the checks and balances and the accountability factor that are critical to any efforts to contain corruption. The integrity system rests on several pillars. These pillars are interdependent. If one pillar weakens, an increased load is placed on the others. If several weaken, their load will tilt and the integrity system may collapse altogether. These pillars include:

1. An independent commission charged with the implementation of anti-corruption legislation. To operate successfully, the commission must possess the following:

   committed political support at the highest levels of government;
   political and operational independence sustained by continuing public pressure;
   adequate powers of access to documentation and to question witnesses;
   leadership that is publicly perceived as being of the highest integrity and personnel of the highest professional ability; and
   accountability, preferably to the legislature.

2. An independent prosecuting agency. Such agency must have the authority to decide whether to institute criminal proceedings, and must not be subject to direction from any external agency, whether political or otherwise. The rule of law requires that prosecutions on behalf of the state be conducted fairly and reasonably. The decision whether to prosecute, or to terminate a prosecution, ought not to be motivated by improper, and particularly political, considerations. The criteria upon which discretion is exercised in such matters should be available both to the legal profession and the public.

3. An independent, impartial, and informed judiciary. The judges must be chosen on merit (i.e., they must possess integrity, ability, and appropriate training or qualifications in the field of law) and not on political affiliation or on the basis of political patronage. They must be adequately remunerated, such remuneration being fixed by law and not reducible; they must enjoy security of tenure, and be irremovable except for just cause and by due process; and they must enjoy personal immunity from civil liability in respect of the bona fide exercise of their judicial functions.[22]

4. An Auditor-General with responsibility for auditing government income and expenditure. The responsibilities of the Auditor-General include ensuring that the executive complies with the will of the legislature, as expressed through parliamentary appropriations; promoting efficiency and cost effectiveness; and preventing corruption through the development of financial and auditing procedures designed to effectively reduce the incidence of corruption and increase the likelihood of its detection. The nature of his or her duties require that the independence and the tenure of office of the Auditor-General be constitutionally protected.

5. An ombudsman who receives and investigates allegations of maladministration. The complaints may range from neglect, inattention, delay, incompetence, inefficiency, and ineptitude in the administration or discharge of duties and responsibilities, to bribery, favoritism, nepotism, and administrative excesses. The ombudsman is not usually vested with power to make binding orders. Based upon his or her findings, he or she makes recommendations in the expectation that, if maladministration or corruption has been identified, the relevant public officials will undertake remedial action. The ombudsman is an independent officer to whom citizens have direct access and whose independence and security of tenure are constitutionally protected.

6. An elected legislature. A legislature that is elected periodically through genuine elections held under conditions that guarantee the free expression of the will of the electors lies at the heart of the integrity system of a country. One of the principal functions of the freely elected representatives of the people is to hold the Executive accountable on a continuous basis. The public scrutiny to which it subjects the Executive, through debate and question time, and through its standing committees—notably, the Public Accounts Committee—promotes both transparency and accountability. Prerequisites for a successful legislature include the existence of political parties sensitive to contemporary aspirations; the nomination of individuals of integrity as candidates; and transparency in regard to the funding of both political parties and candidates.

7. A free media. Since corruption thrives on secrecy, a diligent and professional media, operating within a legal framework that enables it to convey information freely, fairly, and responsibly, has an important role to play both in exposing corruption and in building support for efforts to combat it. The degree to which the media is independent is the degree to which it can serve as an effective public watchdog on the conduct of public officials. Just as the legislature is expected to keep the Executive under day-to-day scrutiny, the media has a responsibility to keep both the legislature and the Executive, along with all other actors whose offices impinge on the public domain, carefully monitored against corruption. While prior censorship, whether direct or indirect, is unacceptable, any other restriction imposed on the media must cumulatively meet two conditions: it must be provided by law, and it must be necessary (i.e., meet a pressing social need) to achieve either respect for the rights or reputations of others, or the protection of national security, public order, public health, or public morals. The media, in turn, ought to disclose from whence it derives its finances so that bias is recognized and any monopoly of power made evident.[23]

The second principle of combatting corruption is to mobilize civil society so that anticorruption strategies can succeed. If corruption has become both widespread and invasive, it is because governments and international financial institutions have condoned the practice, the private sector and its advisers—both financial and legal—have colluded in it, and civil society has become accustomed to it and has begun to live with it. It is not uncommon, particularly before a general election, for political leaders to promise that, if elected to office, they will immediately eliminate corruption in all its forms. It is an issue that touches many peoples' lives and, therefore, evokes an immediate and favorable response. But, in office, anticorruption rhetoric becomes less strident. Over time, the well-intentioned leaders are usually overwhelmed by the enormity of the problem, while the others continue to posture for a while, and eventually succumb to the same temptations that destroyed their predecessors. This has been a recurring pattern across the political map of the world.

When genuine attempts to combat corruption have been unsuccessful, there has generally been one missing ingredient—the involvement of civil society.[24] More often, the political leadership has little or no incentive to combat corruption. If ordinary people expect to pay bribes and are accustomed to dealing with the state through payoffs, a radical change in attitudes will be necessary before any anticorruption strategy can get off the ground. As the section of society that bears the brunt of corruption on a daily basis, civil society is best placed to reverse the public apathy and tolerance of corruption. Therefore, the involvement of civil society—"the sum total of those organizations and networks which lie outside the formal state apparatus"[25]—is vital in reshaping attitudes, reconstructing expectations and, because of its proximity to, and familiarity with, the issues, in monitoring the performance of public officials. Accordingly, TI seeks to promote the emergence of national chapters made up of those elements in the community that constitute civil society: business leaders, journalists, religious figures, academics, nongovernmental activists, and members of professional bodies. Today, 78 such national chapters are in existence or in formation.

The third principle to combat corruption is to recognize that civil society alone cannot change systems; the active participation of governments and parliaments is essential. Indeed, experience suggests that a creative coalition embracing the state, civil society, and the private sector is required. A triangular relationship exists between these groups. Corruption can take root in all three parties to the relationship. It is thus both impossible for one of the parties to address the issue of corruption in isolation from the other two, and arguably impossible to tackle the issue effectively without the participation of all three. Therefore, while choosing not to mold itself in the image of a nongovernmental organization in the traditional sense—activist, grass-root based, confrontational—a national chapter should be nonpartisan in a political sense, possess the capacity to interact profitably with the government, and to help it to design and implement a program of reform. Even a relatively corrupt government may be persuaded to initiate and support a reform program that would eventually strengthen the national integrity system if such program is not perceived as being a threat to its own survival until the next general election. In order not to be diverted from the principal objective of securing institutional reform, national chapters are discouraged from naming names or engaging in investigations.

The fourth principle to combat corruption is to recognize that the involvement of the private sector is essential.[26] The most compelling reason for the private sector to be involved in an anticorruption campaign is self-interest: when there is bribery the best companies usually lose the most, since those who pay bribes do so in order to secure the sale of goods or services that would not otherwise have been bought from them. Neither customer confidence nor good reputations prevail against a rival who has bribed the decision-maker. If, in order to remain competitive, they too are compelled to indulge in unethical practices such as off-the-books accounts, and employ shadowy middlemen, they will no longer be skirting the fringes of criminal conduct but placing themselves increasingly at risk of criminal prosecution. More positively, by its active participation in securing the ultimate success of a government's anticorruption strategy, the private sector will benefit from increased competition, a level playing field, greater legal protection of contracts and property rights, less bureaucratic red tape, enhanced predictability, and increased efficiency in dealing with the public sector.[27]

The fifth principle of combatting corruption is for effective reform to be driven by local needs and considerations. Those who best understand the problems of corruption in a country are those who live and work there, and who have deep insights into their own society and the power structures within it. The reform program will, of course, be informed by events and experiences from abroad, but it has to be completely and competently locally-owned and locally-driven.

The sixth and last principle of combatting corruption is to form creative partnerships with intergovernmental organizations that have ready access to governments, and with other international nongovernmental organizations. Accordingly, both the TI international secretariat and several of its national chapters, especially in Africa, Eastern Europe, parts of Asia, and in the Pacific, have forged mutually productive relationships with the United Nations Development Programme, other components of the UN system, the World Bank, the Asian and African Development Banks, the Organization for Economic Co-operation and Development, and the European Union.

DESIGNING THE TOOLS

Transparency International has so far developed six tools to measure, as well as to secure, transparency and accountability in government.

The first tool is the *TI Source Book* which brings together a wide variety of experience in building national integrity systems to curb corruption. It is available both in print and through the TI website (www.transparency.org). Since it was first published in 1995, it has been adapted and translated into more than 12 languages. It is now widely distributed in the 78 countries in which TI has established national chapters, and its reputation as a leading-edge tool in the furtherance of good governance and transparency is now well-established. A companion volume, available only on the website, is a best practice compilation. It seeks to assemble a wide variety of instruments used to monitor assets, set standards of conduct, enforce effective laws, provide greater access to information, protect whistleblowers, and help establish institutions such as the ombudsman and public accounts committees in legislatures. The best practices guide attracts many hundreds of visitors daily to the website from around the world, including policy makers, reformers, and researchers.

The second tool is a Service Delivery Survey (SDS) to measure the effectiveness and integrity with which public services are provided by the state. It usually provides a relatively accurate picture of the current state of affairs in key service delivery areas. It also provides benchmarks against which reform can be subsequently measured by a follow-up survey. The SDS demonstrates not only the extent of public satisfaction or dissatisfaction, but also whether or not the public is obliged to make extra payments to obtain essential services. The results of these surveys, if published without delay, promote discussion and are evidence of the administration's commitment to transparency and accountability.

The third tool of accoutability is a National Integrity Workshop (NIW) to identify the strengths and weaknesses of the existing integrity system, and to develop an action plan to remedy any defects and strengthen the system as a whole. This mechanism emerged as groups in Uganda and Tanzania began to address their domestic problems, and was the product of the interaction within and between both these countries. It requires the participation of stakeholders from within the government (as identified from the integrity pillars): nongovernmental organizations, including the private sector and business professions, the media, and political parties from across the political spectrum.

The fourth tool is the Corruption Perception Index (CPI) which is not an assessment of the corruption level within a country, but an attempt to assess the level at which corruption is perceived to impact on commercial life, in the view of several thousand businessmen, risk analysts, and business journalists. In an area as complex and controversial as corruption, no single source or polling method has yet been developed that would combine a perfect sampling frame, large enough country coverage, and a fully convincing methodology. TI therefore chose the option of a composite index. The CPI is a poll of polls. The 1999 index (the fifth in the series) is based on 17 credible surveys conducted by reputable organizations using different sampling frames and varying methodologies. It ranks 99 countries in terms of the degree to which corruption is perceived to exist among public officials and politicians. The strength of the CPI is that a combination of sources in a single index increases the reliability of each individual figure. The probability of misrepresenting a country has been lowered by including only those countries that have been the subject of at least three surveys, the premise being that malperformance of one can be balanced by at least two others. The perceptions reflected in the CPI may not be a fair assessment of the actual extent of corruption within a country, but they are a reality. If those in a unique position to observe the behavior of public officials and politicians wrongly believe that the leaders are corrupt, the reasons for that mistaken belief need to be identified and remedied. There is evidence that the CPI has been a catalyst for change in some of the countries listed at the bottom end.

The fifth tool is the Bribe Payers Index (BPI) which reflects perceptions of bribe-paying by companies from the 19 leading exporting countries of the world. First published in 1999, it is based on in-depth interviews conducted by Gallup International Association with private sector leaders in 14 emerging market economies that combine to account for over 60% of imports of all emerging market economies. Those questioned included senior executives of major foreign and national companies, chartered accountants, members of national chambers of commerce, commercial bankers, and commercial lawyers. It was a pioneering effort to measure the supply side of bribery.

The sixth and final tool is the Integrity Pact. It is intended to accomplish two objectives: 1) to enable companies to abstain from bribing by providing assurances to them that their competitors will also refrain from bribing, and that government agencies will work to prevent corruption, including extortion, by their officials and to follow transparent procedures; and 2) to enable governments to reduce the high cost and the distortionary impact of corruption on public procurement. The mechanism envisages the designation of one or several Islands of Integrity, in the form of selected projects, all projects in a sector, or the territorial limits of a particular local authority, in respect to which or within which, corrupt practices would be eliminated by agreement among the government and those companies interested in bidding for services, the supply of goods, or the acquisition of assets.[28] Bidders who violate their commitment not to bribe will be subject to significant sanctions, such as loss of contract, liability for damages, forfeiture of the bid security, and being debarred from all government business for an appropriate period of time. Confidence in this mechanism is enhanced by empowering unsuccessful bidders, who have evidence of corruption by their competitors or the principal, to enforce sanctions themselves, through the courts or by international arbitration. This tool has been utilized, with success, most recently in Panama in connection with the privatization of its telecommunication sector, and in Argentina, in the province of Mendoza, in bidding for public works.

AN ASSESSMENT

Nearly two years ago, *Time* observed that "Transparency International had been instrumental in putting corruption on the world's agenda." As the only network of its kind, TIs international secretariat has been the center of the worldwide campaign against corruption. It was successful in persuading the World Bank and other international financial institutions of their role in tackling corruption. It played a significant role, together with national chapters in countries belonging to the Organization for Economic Co-operation and Development (OECD) and others including the International Chamber of Commerce, in making the

OECD Convention on Combating Bribery of Foreign Public Officials in International Business Transactions a reality. Its success in partnership building is evidenced by the financial support it now receives from several governments, foundations, and private companies, and the collaborative work it is engaged in with United Nations agencies and several other organizations, both governmental and nongovernmental, at the international and regional levels. At the national level, however, its achievements are less impressive. Apart from raising awareness, TI's national chapters have not yet succeeded in securing any significant institutional reform that would "make a difference." One challenge that faces TI is, therefore, the revitalization of its national chapters by providing them with the expertise necessary to interact profitably with their respective governments.

A second challenge is the formulation of anticorruption strategies that are consistent with respect for human rights and the principles of the rule of law. Reference to TI's Corruption Perception Index suggests that corruption can be successfully contained only when anticorruption strategies are consistent with the principles of the Rule of Law. Such strategies must command respect and be supported by the community at large; when they are seen as being arbitrary and unfair they fail to win that support. Consequently, the failure to address the Rule of Law aspect has often been fatal to anticorruption efforts. For example, in Vietnam and China, execution often quickly follows summary trial and conviction for corruption. In Ghana, some still regard the execution by firing squad of three former heads of state as having been the most deterrent anticorruption measure undertaken in that country. Notwithstanding these unusually cruel and repressive measures, China is perceived as one of the most corrupt countries today. So are Vietnam and Ghana. In Sri Lanka, several ad hoc commissions not bound by rules of evidence have tried officials of the previous regime, yet widespread suspicion appears to exist about the integrity of officials of the present regime.

In this regard, there is an urgent need to find ways and means of reconciling certain indispensable legal provisions with human rights. Specific methods include: 1) the offense of unexplained wealth[29] (which is established through a special evidentiary provision containing a rebuttable presumption of fact that a public official who possesses money or property in excess of that which he has legitimately earned, or maintains a standard of living above that which is commensurate with his official emoluments, be deemed, in the absence of a satisfactory explanation, to have acquired such money, property, or other wealth through corruption); 2) a law that enables the tracing, seizure, freezing, and forfeiture of the illicit earnings from corruption; and 3) a law that requires the regular declaration of the assets, income, liabilities and life styles of decision-makers and other public officials who hold positions where they transact with the public and are well placed to extract bribes. It is also necessary to revisit the statutory and other legal provisions which impede the successful combating of corruption. These include very short limitation periods on the institution of criminal proceedings; the lack of jurisdiction to review official acts; the wide immunity from criminal prosecution enjoyed by presidents, members of parliament, judges, and even senior officials; and the mandatory requirement of prior permission from the speaker of parliament to investigate the conduct of parliamentarians.

A third challenge is judicial corruption. Surveys which have been conducted by TI national chapters on every continent reveal that the judiciary is perceived to be one of the most corrupt institutions in many states. Judicial corruption is a complex phenomenon encompassing not only the acceptance of bribes by judges, but also the suspicion of corruption that arises from the interaction of the judiciary with the executive branch of government when political patronage secures appointment, preferential terms of service, and a life after retirement. Suspicion may also arise from unregulated interaction with the legal profession or from too deep an involvement with the local community. The emphasis has always been on judicial independence; rarely if at all on judicial accountability.

A fourth and extremely complex challenge is corruption in the electoral process which is undermining not only democracies that are struggling to be born, but also long established democratic states. The principal reason why a person or organization would fund a political party or a candidate is the expectation of benefiting from the patronage which that person or organization would enjoy if that party or candidate were to be elected to office. The entry of such excessive funding—for example, through an advertising blitz or the straight bribing of electors—invariably leads to the subversion of the electoral process. The failure to preserve the integrity of the electoral process has led not only to the infusion of money from criminal elements in the community, but also to such criminal elements themselves seeking election to public office. The broad immunities from prosecution, and even investigation, that legislators enjoy in certain countries must make political office sufficiently attractive to the most apolitical among them. In the final analysis, however, it is the dependence on such political funding that inhibits even the most reform-willing of democratic governments from undertaking institutional reforms that would have the effect of focusing the searchlight on such benefactors. To do so would be to deny themselves the material support which is vital to mount an effective campaign that would secure reelection.

To meet these challenges, Transparency International will need to develop a more productive working relationship with the executive, legislative, and judicial branches of governments. In recent years, the emphasis has been on expanding the reach of the organization in geographical terms by establishing an increasing number of national chapters, rather than on ensuring that each is a creative coalition embracing the state, civil society, and the private sector. Moreover, the belief is now widespread that TI, as a civil society organization, should exclude politicians from national chapters for fear of impairing its nonpolitically partisan stance. But, as the founders of TI recognized in 1993, neither civil society nor the private sector can make a difference without the active participation of the government and parliament. The inclusion of an active, respected, sympathizer from within the cabinet of ministers, and a cross-party group of legislators, could transform a national chapter into a potent force for reform. Unless its national chapters are able to thus profitably interact with governments, their role will remain that of awareness raising, and TI may find itself thwarted in its efforts to secure the institutional reforms that are so urgently needed to successfully combat the cancer that is corruption.

ENDNOTES

1. J. J. Senturia, *Encylopaedia of the Social Sciences.* Vol.IV, 1931, quoted by George Moody-Stuart, *Grand Corruption* (Oxford, Worldview Publishing, 1997), p. 1. The misuse of public power is, of course, provoked, encouraged and sustained by the bribe giver. Without the giver there would be no receiver.
2. See *Survey on Corruption in Bangladesh*, Survey conducted for Transparency International-Bangladesh by the Survey and Research System with assistance from The Asia Foundation, 1997.
3. The expression "grand corruption" was first used by George Moody-Stuart in 1992 in a privately circulated, first draft of his book, *Grand Corruption*. He defined it as "the misuse of public power by heads of state, ministers, and top officials for private pecuniary profit."
4. Moody-Stuart, *Grand Corruption*, pp. 14–15.
5. *Corruption and Good Governance*, Discussion paper 3 (New York, United Nations Development Programme, 1997), p.24.
6. Moody-Stuart, *Grand Corruption*, p.13.
7. This index was prepared following in-depth interviews conducted by Gallup International Association with private sector leaders in 14 emerging market economies which combine to account for over 60% of imports of all emerging market economies. Many of the questions asked relate to perceptions of bribe-paying by companies from the 19 leading exporting countries of the world. The respondents were interviewed by professional, trained interviewers on the basis of strict confidentiality and anonymity. A total of 779 interviews were conducted which included approximately 55 interviews in each country. Those interviewed included senior executives of major foreign and national companies, chartered accountants, members of national chambers of commerce, commercial bankers, and commercial lawyers.
8. BBC programme: *Talking Politics*, excerpts reproduced in Moody-Stuart, *Grand Corruption*, appendix 3, p.93.
9. Ayodele Aderinwale (ed.), *Corruption, Democracy and Human Rights in West Africa*, (Benin, Africa Leadership Forum, 1994), p.27.
10. S. H. Alatas, *The Problem of Corruption*, (Singapore, Times Books International, 1986), pp.42–45.
11. Sarojini Jayawickrama, 'An Historical relation of the Island Ceylon': Knox and the 'Writing that Conquers', (PhD Thesis, The University of Hong Kong, 1997), p.238. See also Jon S.T. Quah, 'Bureaucratic Corruption in the ASEAN countries: A Comparative Analysis of their Anti-Corruption Strategies', (1982) 13 *Journal of Southeast Asian Studies*, pp.153-177 at 154-155 and 162; and Denis Osborne, 'Corruption as Counter-culture: Attitudes to Bribery in Local and Global Society,' in Barry A.K. Rider (ed.), *Corruption: The Enemy Within* (Netherlands, Kluwer Law International, 1997), pp.9-34.

12. Robert P. Beschel Jr., "The Costs and Consequences of Corruption in the Asian and Pacific Region", a paper presented at a seminar on *Corruption and Governance in Asia: the role of the media*, Manila, April 1998.

13. A bribe of $100 accepted by a customs officer may cost the government $1000 or more in lost customs dues.

14. It is estimated that as much as $30 billion has been deposited in foreign bank accounts by political leaders from some African countries alone.

15. Since bribery makes competition ineffective, even the acceptance of a relatively small bribe could lead to price increases of 50–100%.

16. See, for the costs and consequences of corruption in Africa, *Corruption and Development in Africa,* Document GCA/PF/No.2/11/1997, Global Coalition for Africa, Policy Forum 1997.

17. See Peter Eigen, "Combatting Corruption Around the World", *Journal of Democracy*, Vol.7, No.1, January 1996, pp.158-168.

18. Fredrik Galtung (ed.), *Accountability and Transparency in International Economic Development: The Launching of Transparency International*, (Berlin, German Foundation for Economic Development, 1994).

19. Ibid, p. 114.

20. Susan Rose-Ackerman, "Corruption and Development" in J. Stiglitz and B. Pleskovic (ed.) *Annual World Bank Conference on Development Economics, 1997* (Washington D.C., The World Bank, yet unpublished).

21. The Lusaka Statement on Government Under the Law, endorsed by Law Ministers of The Commonwealth, 1993.

22. For the method of monitoring the effectiveness of the judiciary, see Jeremy Pope (ed.) *National Integrity Systems: The TI Source Book* (Berlin, Transparency International, 3rd ed.,1999), p.62.

23. For the principles which determine whether or not a free media exists, see *The Charter for a Free Press*, which was approved by journalists from 34 countries at the Voices of Freedom World Conference on Censorship Problems, convened by the World Press Freedom Publishers, International Press Institute, Inter-American Press Association, North American National Broadcasters' Association, and the International Federation of the Periodical Press, held in London, January 1987.

24. Pope (ed.), *TI Source Book*, p. 21.

25. Ibid, p.35.

26. Some see the private sector as part of civil society. However, it appears to merit separate mention by reason of its economic power, the important role it plays in development, and an ethos sufficiently different from nonprofit organizations.

27. *Corruption and Development in Africa,* p. 18. For the obligations of the private sector in this respect, see Pope (ed.) *TI Source Book,* p. 88.

28. For documents relating to the Islands of Integrity Concept and the TI Integrity Pact, see *Transparency International Report 1997*, Annex III, pp. 123–128.

29. Sometimes referred to as the offence of "illicit enrichment."

Author Index

Subject Index